THEOLOGY OF THE ICON

Volume II

THEOLOGY OF THE ICON

Volume II

by

LEONID OUSPENSKY

translated by

ANTHONY GYTHIEL

ST VLADIMIR'S SEMINARY PRESS
CRESTWOOD, NY 10707–1699
1992

The publication of this book has been underwritten by a generous contribution by Dr. and Mrs. Demetre Nicoloff, Minneapolis, Minnesota.

Library of Congress Cataloging-in-Publication Data

Ouspensky, Léonide

[Essai sur la théologie de l'icone dans l'Eglise orthodoxe. English]

Theology of the icon / by Leonid Ouspensky; translated by Anthony Gythiel with selections translated by Elizabeth Meyendorff.

p. m.

Vol. 1 is a rev. translation of: Essai sur la théologie de l'icône dans l'Eglise orthodoxe; v. 2 is a translation of: La théologie de l'icône; both were translated originally from Russian.

Includes bibliographical references and index.

ISBN 0-88141-122-1 (v. 1). — ISBN 0-88141-123-X (v. 2) — ISBN 0-88141-124-8 (set)

1. Icons—cult. 2. Orthodox Eastern Church—Doctrines. 3. Orthodox Eastern Church and art. 4. Icon painting. I. Ouspensky, Léonide. Théologie de l'icône. English. 1992. II. Title.

BX378.5.09713 1992 92-12323

THEOLOGY OF THE ICON

Volume II

Originally published in French
under the title *La Théologie de l'icone*
by Les Editions du Cerf in 1980.

Vol. II ISBN 0–88141–123–X
Set (Vol. I & II) ISBN 0–88141–124–8

PRINTED IN THE UNITED STATES OF AMERICA

Contents

11

The Post-Iconoclastic Period

It is significant that the struggle for the image occurred at the juncture of two periods in Church history, each of which formulated a different aspect of the dogma of the Incarnation. Between these two periods stands the dogma of the veneration of icons, like a boundary stone looking in both directions at once, yet uniting the teachings of each.

The entire period of the Ecumenical Councils was essentially christological; it articulated Orthodox teaching concerning the Person of Christ, simultaneously God and man. The icon, which during this whole era was incorporated into all of christological theology, witnessed above all to the reality of the Incarnation. The Church asserted the teaching concerning the icon, both through word and image.

The period that followed, extending from the ninth to approximately the sixteenth century, was pneumatological. The central question, around which both heresies and the Church's teaching revolved, then became that of the Holy Spirit and His activity in man, that is, the effect of the Incarnation. During this period the Church gave testimony above all about its conviction that if "God became man," it is in order that "man might become God"; and the icon, in perfect harmony with theology and with the Liturgy, pointed in a more special way to the fruit of the Incarnation, with the deification of man. With increasing precision, the icon showed the world an image of man become God through grace. It was then, above all, that the classical form of sacred art was being elaborated, and the promises of Christian art of the first centuries fulfilled. Church art flourished: it was an extraordinary flowering associated with a significant rise in holiness especially of the monastic type, and with a magnificent development of theology. Church decoration then acquired its forms. Beginning with the eleventh century, it became a precise, exact, dogmatic system.

New populations entered the Church, especially the Slavs. They had a share in the development of this classic language; and each created a well-defined kind of holiness, its specific type of icon. In this manner, church art, in its classic form, acquired great variety and was exceptionally splendid.

The victory over iconoclasm, proclaimed as the Triumph of Orthodoxy at the Council of 843, did not signal the end of heresy, which continued to play an active role. "Convinced iconoclasts, who would prove it by stubbornly maintaining their views after the last iconoclast emperor had died, seemed to have been just as numerous during the entire half-century that followed the official restoration of religious images."[1] During this period, the Church in Constantinople was in a difficult situation, not only because of the strength of the iconoclasts but also because of dissenting views about them among the Orthodox themselves. Patriarch St Methodius was a benevolent, lenient man. But many Orthodox took a more intransigent attitude than he. The patriarch avoided giving important positions to these hardliners so as not to irritate the iconoclasts. He refrained from making "confessors" out of them, thereby aggravating the conflict. For this he was criticized most severely by the extremists, especially the monks of Studion, whose opposition became so strong that the patriarch had no choice but to excommunicate them. The conflict created by this excommunication led to such great problems that after the death of Methodius on June 14, 847, Empress Theodora, on her own authority—in place of the normal election of a new patriarch by a local synod—appointed Nicetas (called Ignatios in the monastic life), a son of Emperor Michael I, as patriarch. During his patriarchate, the extremists soon occupied all the leading positions. The excommunication of the Studites was lifted, and in turn certain moderates were excommunicated. The iconoclasts regained their strength. Succeeding events modified the course of the Church's anti-heretical struggle. Empress Theodora was sent to a convent, and Michael III became emperor. St Ignatius resigned as patriarch. A new patriarch, St Photius, was elected.[2] Both held their see on two different occasions.[3] This change of

1 André Grabar, *L'iconoclasme byzantin* (Paris, 1957), 13.

2 An accurate description of the epoch is found in Francis Dvornik's article, "The Patriarch Photius and Iconoclasm," *Dumbarton Oaks Papers* 5 (Cambridge, MA, 1953), 67-98.

3 The first from 847 to 858, and from 867 to 877; the second, from 858 to 867, and from 877 to 886.

25. *St Photius the Great*
20th century by Monk Gregory Kroug
Photo: Andrew Tregubov.

patriarchs due to internal conflicts in the Church certainly did not contribute to a normal course of events during this period.

At the end of the period of the Ecumenical Councils that had formulated the dogmas about the Incarnation of the Word, St Photius opened a new era in the struggle for true Church doctrine. Henceforth, the struggle would center above all on the truths associated with the mystery of Pentecost: the Holy Spirit, grace, and the nature of the Church. In other words, if during the period of the Ecumenical Councils the economy of the second Person of the Holy Trinity was revealed, the new era witnessed how theological thought and art were oriented primarily toward the revelation of the third divine Hypostasis. This turning point, which in many respects was decisive for the direction the Church and its art were to follow, carried the stamp of the great hierarch and confessor St Photius (Fig. 25).[4] The life of the Church, its thought and art, are marked by the exceptional personality and activity of this patriarch, not only during this period but well beyond it. "He became the central force in the intellectual and literary movement of the second half of the ninth century...His education had been many-sided, and his knowledge was extensive not only in theology but also in grammar, philosophy, natural science, law and medicine."[5] It is to Patriarch Photius, humanist and inspirer of the eleventh century "renaissance,"[6] that the main credit for the ultimate defeat of iconoclasm belongs.

In the struggle against heresy, Photius possessed exceptional assets: he belonged to a family of confessors of Orthodoxy (he himself, his father, and his uncle had been anathematized by the iconoclasts). Combining a solid theoretical education with flexible, impeccable tactics, he clearly saw the road that was to lead to the defeat of heresy. He reorganized the academy in order to fight against the argumentation of the iconoclasts. During the reign of Ignatius, a certain obscurantism had prevailed: the sciences, to which the iconoclasts were so zealously dedicated, were con-

4 For a long time in the West, the personality and the writings of St Photius have been presented in an extremely negative manner. Only in our time has F. Dvornik reëstablished the truth: see especially his book, *The Photian Schism: History and Legend* (Cambridge, 1948).

5 A. A. Vasiliev, *History of the Byzantine Empire: 324-1453* (Madison, 1964), vol. 1, 296; F. Dvornik, *Photian Schism*, 2.

6 A. Grabar, *L'Art religieux et l'Empire byzantin à l'époque des Macédoniens*, Ecole pratique des Hautes Etudes, *Annuaire* 1939-40, 19.

sidered to be less important than piety. By contrast, Patriarch Photius viewed the latter as being insufficient; he saw one of the great means of fighting heresy precisely in the acquisition of knowledge. A close friend of the patriarch, Constantine (Cyril), the future apostle of the Slavs, was put at the head of the academy. Beginning with his first patriarchate, Photius gathered artists and learned men and began the restoration of paintings in the churches. His name is linked to the ninth-century renaissance of art,[7] which experienced an especially brilliant development during his second patriarchate.

St Photius was absolutely intransigent with regard to iconoclasm. Like the Fathers of the Seventh Ecumenical Council, he viewed this heresy as a denial of the central dogma of Christianity. In his letter to Michael, King of Bulgaria, he called the iconoclasts "Christ-fighters, worse than the Jews."[8] Elsewhere he stated, "In your mind, you [iconoclasts], are conducting an ignoble war against Christ, not openly and directly, but by means of the icon."[9] Like the Fathers of the Seventh Ecumenical Council, he saw in the icon an analogy with Holy Scripture, an idea he further clarified and developed. He drew attention to the primacy of seeing over hearing (a primacy emphasized in patristic writings), and he was emphatic about the importance of teaching through the icon. The one who refuses it has already refused instruction by the Holy Scriptures. To venerate icons means to understand Holy Scripture correctly, and vice versa.[10]

Photius' anti-iconoclast thought and activity are reflected, both directly and indirectly, as much in the objectives, decisions, and judgments of the ninth-century synods as in the general orientation of the theological thought of this period. Thus the Synod of 861, known as "first-second," which took place during his patriarchate and with the participation of Roman legates, was convoked for a new, solemn condemnation of the heresy.[11] The acts of this Synod were burned by the council of 869-870, and thus we unfortunately know nothing of what was said there about iconoclasm.

7 F. Dvornik, "Patriarch Photius," 87-91.

8 PG 102: 695D.

9 PG 101: 949D.

10 *Hom.* 73, Greek ed. of Aristarchos (Constantinople, 1901), vol. 2, 304-5.

11 This is clear from the correspondence between Pope Nicolas I and Emperor Michael III (Mansi XV, 161, 261, 243). See also F. Dvornik, "Patriarch Photius," 77; and K. Héfélé, *Histoire des Conciles*, IV, 1 (Paris, 1911), 272.

The anti-Photian council of 869-870, held during the patriarchate of St Ignatius, returned once more to the problem of iconoclasm. The question was posed at the initiative of Emperor Basil I. The heresy was condemned, and its exponents, led by Theodore Crithinus, were anathematized. During the council, a message from Pope Nicolas I was read, the sixth paragraph of which was directed against iconoclasm:

> With regard to the holy and venerable images of our Lord, of His ever-virgin Mother and all the saints, beginning with Abel, it is fitting to keep unchangeably what the holy Church has always accepted everywhere in the world, and what the popes have ordained and prescribed regarding this. We anathematize John, former Patriarch of Constantinople, and his followers who say that icons should be broken and trampled under foot.[12]

This text, as can be seen, is of no theological interest.

The council of 869-870 (during which the Church of Rome confirmed the council of 843, the Triumph of Orthodoxy) is, ever since the Gregorian Reform, called the Eighth Ecumenical Council by Rome. The Orthodox Church does not recognize this council, which condemned Photius. Consequently, its decisions have no official value. Nonetheless, this council was Orthodox in theory, and its third canon, which deals with sacred art, is of great interest to us. We shall focus on it for a moment because it expresses the orientation of theological thought about the image within the general context of the post-iconoclastic period. The following is the text of the canon:

> We ordain that the holy icon of our Lord be venerated in the same way as the book of the Gospels. Indeed, just as all receive salvation through the syllables contained in it, so do all, both learned and ignorant, draw profit from what the colors of the icon possess. For that which words announce through syllables, the colors in painting show. If one does not venerate the icon of Christ the Savior, let him not see His face at the Second Coming. In the same manner, we venerate and bring homage to the icon of His all-pure Mother, to those of the holy angels, painted as they are described in the words of Holy Scripture, and furthermore to those of all the saints. Let those who do not do this be anathema.[13]

Clearly, this canon represents a brief recapitulation of the main principles of the Seventh Ecumenical Council. But two details should be noted. First, the council states that the icon is useful to the learned and the ignorant—that its importance is therefore the same for all members of the Church, regardless

12 Héfélé, *ibid.*, 324.
13 Mansi XVI, 400; 12 Héfélé, 869-70.

of their cultural level. We surmise that this declaration by a council considered so important in the West was directed against the viewing the icon as a "Bible for the unlettered." As is known, Gregory the Great's notion that "What Scripture is for the literate, the image is for the unlettered" became popular in the West. Even the recognition by the Church of Rome of the council of 869-870 as the Eighth Ecumenical Council did not weaken this view; it is partially held until now.[14] Such a concept of the image has never seemed adequate to the Orthodox East. St Theodore the Studite wrote: "Just as everyone, no matter how perfect, is in need of the Gospel tablet, so [does one need] the painting expressed according to it."[15]

Canon 3 is expressed forcefully: "If one does not venerate the icon of Christ the Savior, let him not see His face at the Second Coming." This is an interesting sentence, because it essentially translates the fundamental truth of the veneration of icons expressed in different words by the decision of the Ecumenical Council: "The one who venerates the icon, venerates the hypostasis of the one it represents."[16] But here the truth is expressed in a more concrete, a more imperative form; the general anti-iconoclast tenor of the sentence thus acquires a clearly eschatological dimension. In this, it also corresponds to the decision of the Seventh Council which emphasized the eschatological aspect of the icon, though less emphatically, through the prophecy of Zephaniah (3:14-15). The vision of Christ at His Second Coming presupposes a confession of His first coming and the veneration of the image of His person that points to it. The reverse is also true: the veneration of the image is a pledge, a condition for the vision of Christ in the glory of His Second Coming. In other words, "the cult of icons will therefore be in a certain sense the beginning of the vision of God,"[17] a beginning of the vision face-to-face. Here we recall the second troparion of the fourth ode of the canon of the Icon of the Holy Face: "In former times, Moses, having asked to see God, was able to contemplate God only obscurely, seeing His back; but the new Israel now sees you, our Deliverer, clearly face to face." The icon not only

14 We certainly cannot maintain today that a church decoration by Matisse or a non-figurative painter represents a "Bible for the unlettered." In such cases, the image (if there is one) is not designed for spiritual instruction, but for purely aesthetic appreciation.

15 PG 99: 1537D.

16 Mansi XIII, 377-80.

17 Vladimir Lossky, *The Vision of God*, trans. A. Moorhouse (New York: St Vladimir's Seminary Press, 1983), 168.

teaches us things about God; it makes God himself known to us. In the icon of Christ, we contemplate His divine Person in the glory with which He will return, that is, in His glorified, transfigured face.

On icons, the third canon of the council concludes, we also represent the Mother of God, the angels and all the saints. This is because, in the eyes of the council, the image of a saint and above all of the Mother of God represents, like the image of Christ, a visible prefiguration of the future: of the eschatological Kingdom of God, a manifestation of His glory in man. "I have given to them the glory which you have given me" (Jn 17:22). "But we know that at this revelation we shall be like Him, for we shall see Him as He is" (1 Jn 3:21).

> This vision of the luminous face of God turned toward each man, the vision of Christ transfigured, is given its theological structure in the doctrine of St Gregory Palamas and in the definitions of the nature of grace by the councils of the fourteenth century.[18]

As we shall see, this vision will also be the theological framework for the content of the icon. Thus, in the nineteenth century, Metropolitan Philaret of Moscow would apply the words of St Paul to the icon, "And we all, who with unveiled face, behold as in a mirror the glory of the Lord, are being transformed into the same image, from glory to glory, as from the Lord, the Spirit" (2 Cor 3:18). Philaret says the following:

> Notice that St Paul does not speak of himself but of *all*. Consequently, he is not speaking of the distinctive privilege of a man inspired by God, but of an action, a state that is available to a great number and, to a certain degree, *to all*. He says, *And we all, with unveiled face, behold the glory of the Lord*. That is, we behold not only the face of Jesus Christ, but his *glory*...We do not watch like passive spectators, but we present our soul to the luminous face of Jesus Christ, like a mirror to receive His light. *We are being transformed into the same image*; we steadfastly try to grow in the likeness of the image of Jesus Christ.[19]

The council of 869-870 was not content with deposing Patriarch Photius; obstacles were set up to get in the way of all he had undertaken to restore and disseminate sacred art. Indeed, the men he had gathered around him for that purpose were put out of action and were unable to continue. Indeed, does not the icon have such a significant meaning that

18 *Ibid.*

19 Homily on the consecration of a church dedicated to the Icon of the Holy Face (November 17, 1855). *Sermons*, vol. III (Paris, 1866), 232. In the nineteenth century, Metropolitan Philaret explained, as can be seen, the power of the image upon the believer in the same context as St John of Damascus.

persons who are anathematized (and who are therefore deprived of the right to teach in the Church) may not paint it?[20]

The struggle of St Photius against iconoclasm reached its peak with the recognition of the Second Council of Nicaea as the Seventh Ecumenical Council, at the (Ignatian) council of 879-880. The (Photian) councils of 867 and 869-70 had already recognized it. But the Church of Rome continued to count only six Ecumenical Councils.[21] Nonetheless, in 879-880, at the insistence of Patriarch Photius, the papal legates concurred unreservedly with this recognition and threatened to excommunicate any who refused to recognize this council as the Seventh Ecumenical Council.[22] According to Francis Dvornik, it was precisely Patriarch Photius who brought the Church of Rome back to unity with the Orthodox Church.[23]

The confession of St Photius was particularly important for its opposition to the error of the *filioque*, an addition made to the Creed, introduced, as is well known, in many Western regions during this period. Thus, in recently converted Bulgaria, Latin missionaries insisted upon this insertion. One of the dogmatic questions raised by the council of 879-880 dealt precisely with this insertion (the council summoned by St Photius in 867 had already addressed this issue). The council proclaimed

20 Canon 7 of this council states: "To make holy and precious icons, as well as to teach one's neighbors the precepts of divine and human wisdom, is very useful, and not to be done by the unworthy. The excommunicated are therefore not allowed to paint icons in the holy churches nor, by the same token, teach there unless they abjure their errors. If someone, after we have made this decision, starts painting holy icons in churches, he will be deposed if he is a cleric, and deprived of the divine Mysteries if he is a layman" (Mansi XVI, 402).

21 F. Dvornik, "Patriarch Photius," 96.

22 "I, Paul [Bishop of Ancona, first of the legates], recognize the venerable Photius as the legitimate and canonically elected Patriarch and, in accordance with the letters of the Pope and the terms of the Commonitorium, I declare that I am in communion with him. I repudiate and anathematize the Synod that was summoned against him in Constantinople [the "Eighth Ecumenical"], together with everything that was done against him at the time of Hadrian. Whoever severs himself from him, is severed from the Church. Moreover, I recognize the Second Council of Nicaea as the Seventh Ecumenical Council" (Héfélé, *Histoire*, 601). Let us note that this Seventh Ecumenical Council was in fact recognized only by the hierarchy of the Church of Rome. The situation in the Western Church as a whole was hardly clear. Thus, while referring to the ecumenical councils, some Western bishops enumerated six, others four, still others only two. The Seventh Ecumenical Council was either rejected or simply ignored (F. Dvornik, *The Photian Schism*, 310-2). Thus, as can be seen, ignorance of the conciliar decisions regarding iconoclasm was matched by equal ignorance about the other heresies condemned by the preceding councils.

23 F. Dvornik, "Patriarch Photius," 96.

the immutability of the Creed of Nicaea-Constantinople, without the *filioque*: "If any one should venture so far in his madness as to propose another creed...or dare to make an addition to, or omission from, the creed handed down to us by the Fathers of the holy Ecumenical Council of Nicaea...let him be anathema." The papal legates made no objection to this decision of the council, and they signed it with all the other participants.[24]

In the anti-iconoclastic struggle, the recognition of the Second Council of Nicaea as the Seventh Ecumenical Council was not merely a formal act of great importance: it was a decisive blow to iconoclasm. Henceforth, iconoclasm was condemned as a heresy by the entire Church, and the decision was final, irrevocable. The dogma of the veneration of icons was thereby recognized as one of the basic truths of Christianity; and the image itself was confirmed as a witness to the Incarnation, and as a way of knowing God and of communion with Him.

We have already spoken of the reaction of the West to the Byzantine crisis of iconoclasm. However, it seems necessary to us to complete our presentation somewhat in the light of the attitude taken in our time regarding this question.

As during the iconoclastic period, the Western Church continued to support with its authority the orthodox position of the Eastern Church. However, neither the cult of the icon nor its significance profoundly affected the consciousness of the Western Church. According to a Roman Catholic theologian of our time, it was the doctrinal struggles that led to a deepening, and to a definition of doctrine—the true stages of dogmatic development. Not knowing such struggles, the West paid little attention to them and did not see in this a real dogmatic development but merely a disciplinary action, an approval of the cult of images, without really understanding any dogmatic implication.[25]

This is true. The West did not see what Byzantium saw in the icon; it did not understand its content. While taking part in the discussion, "it never followed the East in the theological argument, nor did it understand all the implications of the Byzantine theology of icons and everything connected with it."[26] And the implications were indeed numerous. In our

24 K. J. Héfélé, *Histoire des Conciles*, 601. The text of the declaration is found on pp. 602-3. See also A. Vasiliev, *History of the Byzantine Empire*, vol. 1, 331.

25 M. J. Le Guillou, *L'Esprit de l'Orthodoxie grecque et russe* (Paris, 1961), 45.

26 G. Florovsky, "Origen, Eusebius and the Iconoclastic Controversy," *Church History* 19, no. 2 (June, 1950), 77.

day, when the Western attitude toward the icon has changed, there is a gradual awareness of the scope of the discussion that took place in Byzantium, and of their consequences. This is clearly illustrated in the words of Daniel-Rops, who states:

> The icon makes Westerners understand what was really at stake in this "quarrel over images" by which the Byzantine East was so bitterly torn apart for so many years. Is it possible that people killed one another in order to know if one had the right to represent God and His saints? In reality, this was not the issue. We are dealing with a debate in which the most profound truths of the faith were at stake. If the unchanging, imperishable icon is some sort of "type" of the ineffable reality, would denying it not be the same as denying this reality?[27]

The struggle against iconoclasm and the defeat of heresy were of capital importance to the art of the Church. "It is precisely this conflict that helped to free painting from all subsidiary, secondary accretions. It led art to express what had essential value—and only that."[28] However, it seems to us that this return to what is essential was not so much the direct result of the conflict itself as it was a deeper awareness of the significance of the image, provoked by the conflict. It would be more correct to say that the conflict goaded Christianity into stating and working out the christological basis of the image, into formulating its theological foundation. It is an awareness of this theological ground that resulted in the purification and accuracy of the artistic language of the Church. Once the christological foundation of the icon had been laid, there appeared a conscious, determined tendency that clearly showed the content and essence of the icon, and that was based on experience, past and present. Thus the center of gravity moved from the christological aspect of the icon, which had been preponderant until then, to its pneumatological and eschatological dimensions, which found their theological expression in the Liturgy of the Triumph of Orthodoxy, particularly in the kontakion of the feast (see above, p. 151). In art history, this process is known as "spiritualization." It reached its peak in the second half of the eleventh

27 Daniel-Rops, "Devant les icônes," *Ecclesia* no. 3-4 (January, 1952), 10. Daniel-Rops reaches a correct conclusion. However, as a Roman Catholic, he adopts an erroneous view of the image. He makes a serious error by attaching no importance to "the right to represent God and the saints." This is precisely one of "the highest data of the faith" and "the ineffable reality" of which he speaks, and which cannot be expressed otherwise but by historical reality.

28 O. Demus, "L'art byzantin dans le cadre européen," Catalog *L'art byzantin* (Athens, 1964), 93-4.

century, leaving its mark on all genres of sacred and even profane art. In other words, the trend which had already become apparent in pre-iconoclastic art, and the principle of which was expressed by canon 82 of the Quinisext Council, continued and became dominant.

Just as the reaction against iconoclasm was equally important for the whole Church, so also the programs and norms elaborated by Church art of this period had a general impact upon the Church. They served as guiding principles for the development of all Orthodox art. Thus the period that immediately followed iconoclasm witnessed the formation of the canon of sacred art. Let us not forget that the general form of the liturgical synthesis also dates back to this period. The definitive form of what is called the "Byzantine rite" was established in Constantinople after the Triumph of Orthodoxy. A harmonious whole, encompassing architecture, poetry, painting, and chant, was being worked out. All this conformed to only one goal: the expression of the very essence of Orthodoxy.

Apparently, after the defeat of iconoclasm, the veneration of icons was not quickly reestablished everywhere, and icons themselves were not disseminated at once. Immediately after the Triumph of Orthodoxy, during the patriarchate of St Methodius or of St Ignatius, the mosaic in the apse of Hagia Sophia in Constantinople, representing the Virgin enthroned (843-845),[29] was probably restored, as well as the icon of Christ above the entrance to the imperial palace. Nonetheless, it seems that even in Hagia Sophia there were not yet any icons in the proper sense of the term. This is made clear in the homily given by Photius in 867 on the occasion of the solemn dedication of an icon.[30]

Numerous provincial trends played a considerable role in reestablishing sacred art after iconoclasm. In general, this ninth-century art is noted for its great variety of styles and techniques.[31] As to the subjects represented, two main trends emerge from this variety. The first shows Orthodox truth on the dogmatic level.[32] It is precisely in this trend that a

29 This mosaic is attributed to St Lazarus, icon-painter and confessor of Orthodoxy during the period of iconoclasm (commemorated on November 17). See A. Grabar, *L'iconoclasme byzantin* (Paris, 1957), 190-1.

30 *Hom.* 73, ed. Aristarchos (Constantinople, 1901), vol. 2, 294-300. A. Grabar dates this homily from 858 to 865, *Iconoclasme*, 191.

31 A. Grabar, *ibid.*, 192.

32 A typical example is provided by the mosaic in the Cathedral of the Dormition restored during the episcopacy of the Confessor St Theophanes the Marked (*graptos*), Confessor (commemo-

tendency toward a more elevated iconographic style can be detected—a trend toward the hieratic, the "spiritualized." Iconographically, the second trend reflects the struggle with the defeated heresy.[33] This trend is especially manifest in the illustrations of the Psalter, which occasionally were carried to the point of caricature.[34]

However, if this polemic appears in illustrations, it is not at all reflected in church art. More precisely, the struggle against heresy is here shown on a different, non-polemical level. Church art has never been, and cannot be, a polemic in the proper sense of the term, for its aim is different. In its worship, the Church deems it sufficient to oppose error simply by presenting its faith in a positive way. This is why the Orthodox Church could react only by proclaiming the true faith. This could be done by clarifying certain details or by a deepening of teaching,[35] but not by introducing a polemic iconography. This is why in such art we find no reaction even to an event as significant as the break with Rome.[36]

Ninth-century secular art is characterized by its closeness to sacred art.[37] Freed from the caesaro-papism of the iconoclast emperors, the Church now put its stamp on secular art. If during iconoclasm, it was the emperors who led heresy and started the persecution of the Orthodox, the Byzantine emperor was now obliged to prove his Orthodoxy to the

rated on October 11). The cross in the apse has been replaced by an image of the Theotokos with the Child. Above her, three rays and a hand extend from a symbolic heaven. A symbolic image of the Trinity has been put in the conch above: a throne with the Gospel book and a dove. Along the edge of the heavens runs the inscription, "Before the morning star, I have begotten you" (Ps 109). As in the Liturgy of Christmas, we see here how the two births of the Savior are collated: the generation from the Father outside of time, unutterable and therefore unrepresentable, and attested only a text; and the representable human birth from the Virgin. In his *History of Byzantine Painting* (in Russian) (Moscow, 1947), vol. 1, 69, V. Lazarev dates this mosaic from the end of the eighth century (shortly after 787). A. Grabar and Frolov date it after 843.

33 Thus the four Orthodox Patriarchs, defenders of icons, are represented together with the apostles in one of the halls adjoining Hagia Sophia.

34 For example, the Psalter of Khludov, on Mount Athos (*Pantocrator*, no 61), and the Psalter of the British Museum. See A. Grabar, *L'iconoclasme* 61, 196, 202; illustr. 141, 143, 144, 146, 152, 155, 157.

35 This can be seen, for example, in the mosaic of Nicaea (see above, n. 32), and later; for instance, in the iconography of the Transfiguration, where in the thirteenth and fourteenth centuries scenes were introduced of Christ ascending and descending the mountain with His disciples—an echo, no doubt, of the symbolic exegesis of this event and especially of the mountain.

36 A. Grabar, *Byzance* (Paris, 1963), 51-2.

37 A. Grabar, *L'empereur dans l'art byzantin* (Paris, 1936), 173.

Church. This is reflected in art. It was indeed during the post-iconoclastic period that the piety of the emperor became one of the leading themes of the official art of the empire. New iconographic subjects appeared: the emperor before Christ, before the Theotokos, before a saint or a cross.[38]

A change in the system of decorating churches was introduced during the patriarchate of St Photius. He was the inspirer of the iconography and its regulations which were now being refined in Constantinople.[39] The choice of subjects according to the historical principle, which had dominated church decoration up to then, gave way to a dogmatic principle.[40] This new system was adapted at a time when the type of cruciform cupola church—the architectural principle of which is a cube with a dome on top—became universal.[41] In architecture, such a building is the perfect expression of the principles of Orthodox liturgical thought.[42] Unlike classical architecture which, starting from the exterior, moves to the interior and gives content to form, Orthodox architecture starts with the content and gives it form, thereby moving from the interior to the exterior.[43] A decorated, cruciform, domed church provides for a clearer, more vivid expression of its symbolic meaning and, within the limits of the possible, of the Orthodox doctrine of the

38 *Ibid.*, 100. Thus in the ninth-century mosaic of the *kenourgion*, Emperor Basil I, with his wife and children, extends his hands towards a cross. Above the ninth-century entrance to Hagia Sophia (where the emperor, before entering the church, listened to the prayer of entrance and prostrated himself three times), the enthroned Christ is represented, with the emperor (Leo VI?) on his knees before him (*ibid.*, 101). The words written in the Gospel which Christ holds in his hands, "Peace be with you" and "I am the light of the world" (Jn 8:12) lead A. Grabar to conclude that the two essential qualities of the emperor—to be a peacemaker and bearer of the light of Rome—are attributed to Christ, since this is how the emperors had been called, beginning with the third and fourth-century panegyrics (*ibid.*, 103-4). Unfortunately, we must disagree with this author. Indeed, the Gospels containing the words of Christ *precede* the panegyrics; and if the latter attribute to the emperor a light reflected, so to speak, from Christ, there is no reason to do the opposite and attribute to Christ a light reflected, so to speak, from the emperor.

39 André Grabar and Monolis Chatzidakis, *La peinture byzantine du haut moyen âge* (Paris, 1965), 22.

40 V. N. Lazarev, *The Mosaics of St Sophia of Kiev* (in Russian) (Moscow, 1960), 36. M. Alpatov, *General History of the Arts* (in Russian), vol. 1, 229; Ch. Diehl, *Manuel d'art byzantin* (Paris, 1926), 486, 496; P. Lemerle, *Le style byzantin* (Paris, 1943), 83.

41 In Byzantium, this type of church had been in existence since the fifth and sixth centuries. A church dating from the fifth century is found in Salonika; and one from the sixth at Edessa. The eighth-century chapel of St Zeno in Rome is also a cube, surmounted by a cupola. See A. Grabar, *Byzance*, 902.

42 K. Onasch, *Ikonen* (Berlin, 1961), 85.

43 P. Michelis, *Esthétique de l'art byzantin* (Paris, 1959), 62.

Church. This style of architecture was adopted as a basis for the entire Orthodox world. It was modified or refined depending on local taste, and received new aesthetic expression. Variations in composition, new construction and decorative methods were developed in various places. These would subsequently be reflected in the architecture of Byzantium itself.[44]

It seems that one of the earliest examples of this change in church decoration appeared in a church in Constantinople built by Emperor Michael III. We know of this decoration from the homily given by Photius at its consecration (around 864).[45] In the dome is the image of Christ:[46]

> He seems to supervise from above the orderly government of the earth. Thus, through forms and colors, the painter has sought to express the Creator's care for us. In the pendentive is a throng of angels, escorting the Lord. In the apse above the altar radiates the Theotokos, her pure hands outstretched toward us in protection. A choir of apostles, martyrs, prophets, and patriarchs fills the entire church with images.[47]

44 R. A. Katznelson, "The Question of the Connection Between East and South-Slavic Architecture" (in Russian), *Vizantiiskii Vremennik* 13 (Moscow: 1957), 242-62. By the same author, a review of N. Mavrodinov, "Byzantine Architecture" (in Russian), *Viz. Vrem.* 14 (1948), 277-83.

45 Which church this was is not precisely known. On p. 35 of *Mosaïques*, V. Lazarev states that it was Our Lady of the Pharos; so do Jenkins and Mango, *Dumbarton Oaks Papers* 9 (1956). A. Grabar, in *L'iconoclasme byzantin*, 183-4, believes that it was the Odigon.

46 Before Iconoclasm, Christ was represented in the apse; for example at Rome in the church of Sts Cosmas and Damian; at Ravenna in St Vitalis. Numerous examples of this type of iconography are offered by the sixth and seventh-century chapels and churches in Egypt and in Armenia. In the West, such usage continued in the Middle Ages, even up to our time; this was undoubtedly also true among the Christians of Asia. In areas under Byzantine domination (for example, Asia Minor, Latmos, near Smyrna, and Cappadocia), they continued to represent Christ in the apse. Various prophetic visions of God, to which some apocalyptic motifs had been added, were also represented. In Asia Minor, such compositions were repeated up to the eleventh century. In Constantinople in the ninth century, in the church of the Mother of God built by Basil I and in Hagia Sophia, as well as in the tenth-century churches, the apse was occupied by the image of the Theotokos, while the image of Christ was transferred to the cupola. In Baouit and in Saccra, however, the icon of the Virgin appeared in the apse from the sixth century on (A. Grabar, "Sur les images des visions théophaniques dans le narthex," *Cahiers archéologiques* [Paris, 1962]). We also know from written sources that in the fifth century in Constantinople, there was an image of the Virgin in the apse of the church of Blachernae. Beginning with the eleventh century, in all the churches of the Byzantine empire as well as in Russia, the Balkans and the Caucasus, the Mother of God was regularly represented in the apse, while Christ figured in the cupola (A. Grabar, "Sur les images des visions théophaniques," *ibid.*, 374-5).

47 PG 102: 293CD.

A similar system of decoration is mentioned in two orations given by Emperor Leo IV (886-912) for the consecration of churches.[48]

The architecture of the domed cruciform churches, combined with the new system of decoration, most fully expresses the Christian concept of a temple, its liturgical meaning. "It is the most brilliant creation of the doctrine of icons," a Western author states.[49] In a church of this form, the architectural center corresponds to its very meaning; and it is around this one (theological and logical) center that the subjects of decoration are organized. Here, everything is subordinated to an overall plan translating the catholicity of the Church: everything is incorporated into a vast unity. The entire heavenly and earthly creation, destined to become a new creation in Christ the God-man, is gathered around Christ in the dome and around Mary in the apse. The angelic powers, mankind, the animals, the birds, the plants and stars—the entire universe unites to form an unmatched temple of God. The entire world is sheltered under the vault of the church; this is an image of unity restored, the unity that was broken by the fall of man. This is the cosmic aspect of the Church, the body of Christ, since the universe belongs to it—this universe which, after the resurrection of Christ, shares in His glorification and is subject to His power. "All power has been given to me in heaven and on earth" (Mt 28:18). The accursed earth (Gen 3:17) becomes the blessed earth, the first-fruits of a new earth under a new heaven. This cosmic aspect of the Church is expressed not only in the architecture and in the decoration of the places of worship, but also in the subjects of certain icons ("All of creation rejoices in you, full of grace"; "Let every breath praise the Lord"). This union of all beings in God—His universe to come, renewed in Christ and transfigured—is in contrast to the hostility and inner strife that wreck creation.[50] The world of animals and of vegetation (for example, the vegetal or geometric ornamentation) represented in mural decoration (as in the icons) is not merely an ornamental addition: it expresses how the created world is part of the Kingdom of God, through man. Thus, painting corresponds to reality itself, since man brings the first-fruits of the created world to the Church, from its consecration to the

48 A. Grabar, *L'iconoclasme byzantin*, 186.

49 H.-J. Schulz, *Die byzantinische Liturgie* (Freiburg im Breisgau, 1964), 22.

50 Eugene N. Trubetskoi, *A Theology in Images* (in Russian), (Paris, 1965), 43. (English trans. by Getrude Vakar, *Icons: Theology in Color* [New York: St Vladimir's Seminary Press, 1973], 32).

eucharistic sacrifice ("Thine own of Thine own, we offer unto Thee on behalf of all and for all"). Indeed, it is in the Liturgy that the significance of a Christian church is fully realized. Its architecture and decoration have acquired all their meaning from the union of the heavenly and the earthly Church in the person of its members united by the spirit of love in living communion with the Body and Blood of Christ.[51] It is in them and through them that the union of all is actualized. Thus the temple acquires the fullness of meaning which the Father-liturgists of the pre-iconoclast period had already detected in it: it is an image of the Church rising towards eschatological fulfillment. In reality, as in image, it is a component of the Kingdom of God to come.[52]

All this is centered on man so as to place him in conditions most favorable to the exaltation of knowing God and of communing with Him. In an Orthodox church, all efforts are aimed not at creating a place that calls for "solitary meditation, a turning inward, a prolonged private conversation with one's own secrets"[53]—but at including man in the catholic unity of the Church so that in its entirety, earthly and heavenly, it may acknowledge and praise God "with one mouth and one heart."

In Catholicism, church architecture and decoration are marked by great variety, and the architectural style is sometimes radically different, depending on the spiritual traditions. The Orthodox world, by contrast, has always been guided by a faithful search for an architectural, artistic expression that best translates the meaning of a temple understood as a symbolic image of the Church and the universe. Unlike in Roman Catholicism, regardless of the richness and diversity of architectural solutions, when a suitable expression was found, it was definitively adopted, at least in its main features. In conformity with a sense of the Church, its program of decoration also remained the same in its principle, regardless of the type of church and its purpose, whether a cathedral, a monastic or parish church, or even a cemetery chapel.[54] This system of decoration reflected not so much the function of a building linked to a practical

51 E. Trubetskoi, *ibid.*

52 On the symbolism of the church and its decoration, see L. Ouspensky, "Symbolik des orthodoxen Kirchengebäudes und der Ikone," *Symbolik der Religionen* (Stuttgart, 1962), 56-68.

53 R. Cognat, "Architecture de la foi," *Le Figaro* (10 Sept. 1964).

54 A. Grabar, *Byzance*, 52.

purpose: its very changelessness corresponded to that of the essential function of every Christian church—to be a place of the Liturgy. Certainly, the mural paintings might deviate from the ideal balance and the decorations might not be entirely finished. But no matter which aspect was emphasized (christological, mariological, sanctoral or another), its basis always remained the same. This does not mean that the subjects of which this basis was composed always remained unchanged themselves: they continued to develop naturally—or rather, to be precise, their various aspects were clarified. Yet the classical system of decoration developed during the post-iconoclastic period remained as the general formula in the Orthodox Church until the end of the seventeenth century.

A renewal of the mission "among the Bulgarians, Khazars, Russians and the Slavs of Moravia as well as among the Christian but schismatic Armenians (to bring them back to Orthodoxy)" occurred during the time of Photius and at his initiative. "In his day also the theologians of his circle attempted Christian propaganda action among the Arabs."[55] Subjects corresponding to this missionary effort appear in the mural paintings of this period, and above all in illustrations. They express the successive apostolic preaching and the actualization of the economy of the Holy Spirit: the sending of the apostles by Christ, the apostolic preaching to various races, the adoration of Christ by different nations. In the iconography of Pentecost groups are introduced representing the various races to whom the preaching of the apostles was addressed (Acts 2:9-11).

Such Byzantine missions are usually explained as an expansion of Byzantine art, culture, and politics tied to a consolidation and expansion of the empire.[56] Since culture and politics were linked to the Church, it is certain that the cultural influence and the interest of the empire were disseminated with the preaching of Orthodoxy, all the more since culture itself was conditioned by the faith. Culture was intimately linked to

55 A. Grabar, *L'iconoclasme byzantin* (Paris, 1957), 223. In 863, the brothers St Constantine and St Methodius went to Moravia. After their death, their disciples, persecuted by the German clergy, fled to Bohemia and to Bulgaria, via Serbia (Pierre L'Huillier, *Les relations bulgaro-byzantines aux IX-X siècles* [Thessalonika, 1966], 222-3). In his Letter to the Eastern Patriarchs (867), St Photius speaks of the conversion of the people of Rus' and of sending a bishop to that nation. In "Etudes sur le IXe siècle," *Byzantion* 7 (1933), 553-8, Grégoire states that the bishop Photius refers to was sent not to the Crimea or the Caucasus, but to Kiev.

56 In the ninth and tenth centuries, Asia Minor was reconquered, as were Syria and southern Italy.

doctrinal suppositions and was influenced by them, and vice versa. The missions also frequently coincided with the interests of the state, which exploited them for its own ends as much as possible.[57] However, the preaching of Orthodoxy remained the center of gravity. It was a mission of the Church, and Patriarch Photius was guided not by the desire to preach the kingdom of Caesar but rather by what was for him the essential character of Orthodoxy: its universality. Sacred art, "exported" in this manner, was definitely a preaching of Orthodoxy, and not a "civilization" understood as an expansion of Christian culture or of the empire. Certainly, together with the dominant art of the Church, culture also brought its own art, a secular one, the form of which was indeed close to sacred art. However, the unity of Orthodox religious art was a result, a manifestation, not of a cultural, artistic or other influence of the Byzantine empire but of the oneness of doctrine and of the spiritual life. Works born of this art have been preserved in many countries, nations which have nothing in common from either the political or the ethnic point of view. And yet, with the exception of certain details, national differences are not reflected in the character of sacred art.[58]

Let us repeat that in the preaching of Orthodoxy, art was a vehicle not of culture but of the faith, of which it was one of the essential, organic elements. The populations that embraced Christianity received its artistic language that had been forged in the very heart of the Christian world. They accepted Christianity as the living expression, couched in artistic forms, of the truth which they embraced. All the peoples entering the Church accepted the Church in its entirety, with its past, present, and future. The heresies of Arius, Nestorius, and of the iconoclasts were not something alien, but dealt with their own faith, a truth that was indeed theirs. This is why the answer of the Church was always adopted as an antidote against any possible resurgence of such heresies, in one form or another. It is for this same reason that every people joining the Church

57 It is hard to take seriously that "the preachers of Christianity habitually pursued political goals outwardly disguised as religious instruction," and that "as a pledge of security, the Church cleverly imposed the feudal system supposedly established by God Himself" (O. I. Dombrovskii, *ibid.*, 6). Categorical statements of this nature are not a matter of historically attested facts but rather of the author's temperament, which leads him to abandon the province not only of learning but sometimes also of propriety (see, for example, *ibid.*, 101).

58 A. Grabar, *Byzance*, 122. Nonetheless, differences in belief are clearly reflected in the arts of nations that are ethnically related and politically united.

brings its specific, national characteristics to it, and matures according to its own genius as much in the sphere of holiness as in its external expression— sacred art. Every group accepted the painted language of the Church in an active, creative manner by introducing local artistic traditions into it. Thus, building upon a common foundation, every nation created its own artistic language, thereby achieving unity in diversity. In Orthodox countries, the originality of art is due especially to the fact that in the Orthodox Church, the unity of faith and sacrament not only did not exclude a variety of forms of worship, art, and other manifestations of Church life conditioned by national and cultural characteristics but, on the contrary, encouraged such variety because it implied a living experience of the tradition, always renewed, original and creative by necessity. Unlike Rome, Orthodoxy always encouraged the national aspect of the Church in every people.[59] Not only did Orthodox missionaries not impose their language, but on the contrary, when necessary, they composed an alphabet and a grammar to translate Holy Scripture and the Liturgy into the local language. The substructure of the artistic language of the Church remains unchanged; and it is upon this foundation that each people created its own artistic language through a direct, living experience of the truth it had embraced.[60] Holiness and the image were recreated on a common ground accepted by all. Holiness and the image were given a national form and stamp because they were the fruit of a living experience. Thus appeared a specific type of Russian, Serbian, and Bulgarian holiness, as well as specific type of icon corresponding to each.

The activity of St Photius in the missionary and artistic spheres resulted, on the one hand, in the conversion of the Slavic peoples and, on the other, in the development of eleventh-century art. It was this art in full bloom that was adopted so widely and spontaneously by the Slavs.

Beginning with the second half of the eleventh century, the role of Constantinople had truly become extraordinary...Its influence had spread in all directions: it is seen in Cappadocia, in Latmos, in the

59 G. Moravscik, "Byzantinische Mission im Kreise der Türkvölker an der Nordküste des Schwarzen Meeres," *Main Papers*, 13th Byzant. Congress (Oxford, 1966), 14. See also, I. Duitsev, "Centers of Byzantine-Slav Contact and Collaboration," (in Russian), *Trudy Otdela drevnerusskoi literatury* 19 (1963), 107-8.

60 In our time the Marxist concept of a socialist culture, one in content and diverse in its national forms, is in fact a variation of this basic idea of the Orthodox Church.

Caucasus, in Russia, Serbia, Bulgaria, on Mount Athos, in Italy. It combined into one homogeneous whole the creative efforts of nearly all the peoples of the Christian East, imprinting a type of common seal upon them.[61]

The eleventh and twelfth centuries were for Byzantium a period of intense life, as much in the political as in the ecclesiastic spheres. But if, in the political domain, the state entered "a phase that contained all the germs of a fatal disease that inevitably led to the catastrophe of 1204,"[62] these two centuries were, by contrast, a thriving age in the cultural and theological domains.

The tenth century witnessed a renaissance of spiritual life, and St Symeon the New Theologian represents its pinnacle. Ascetic and spiritual writings were disseminated. The writings of Isaac the Syrian were translated into Greek; there appeared the works of Philotheus of Sinai on the Jesus prayer and those of Elias Ecdicos (whose life, admittedly, cannot be dated with certainty).[63] The writings of St Symeon the New Theologian, disseminated by his disciples during the life of the author, influenced the religious and literary circles of Constantinople, and especially after his death.[64] Together with Constantinople, Mount Athos, intimately linked to all Orthodox countries, assumed a special importance in the spiritual life. In Russia and in the Balkans an intense activity developed through the translation of spiritual works. Monasteries were founded, linked to Mount Athos and Constantinople. Spiritual life in these countries began to acquire a national character that became greatly visible in holiness. Such great spiritual flowering was the fertile soil on which sacred art could develop.

On the other hand, the tenth century witnessed a terrible catastrophe in the history of the Church which has not yet been overcome: the schism between East and West. The polemic with the West, and with the Bogomil and Cathar heresies, as well as the struggle against errors within the Church itself, contributed nonetheless to a development of theological thought.

61 V. Lazarev, *History of Byzantine Painting* (in Russian), 105.

62 H. Evert-Kappesova, Supplement to the Report of N. Svoronos, *Supplementary Papers*, 13th Byzant. Congress (Oxford, 1966), 121.

63 Symeon the New Theologian, *Catéchèses*, Introduction, Critical Text and Notes by Basil Krivochéine, vol. I (Paris, 1963), 41, n. 1.

64 *Ibid.*, 61. The title of "New Theologian," given to him while he was alive, means "Renewer of the mystical life" (*ibid.*, 53, n. 1).

Until then the East and the West had not always agreed with each other, as we have seen, and quite often their joint action had been marked by serious misunderstandings. Nonetheless, it was a truly common action, that of two members of the same Church. The Patriarchate of Rome was part of the Church; this is why the numerous and profound misunderstandings became somewhat muted and did not compromise the oneness of this patriarchate with the rest of the Church, its participation in the common sacramental life. It was a member of the Body of Christ, drinking from the same chalice, eating the same bread as the other local churches. What was missing in the Church of Rome could always eventually be supplied by the common patrimony. Inversely, the spiritual riches of the West entered the common treasury of the one Church. But in the eleventh century, Rome separated from the rest of the Church. Sacramental communion was interrupted, and the Church of Rome withdrew from the common life of the Church in this pneumatological period. This is why even the amazingly creative impulse of the Romanesque period, when the West used forms borrowed from the East, was but a brief flame that did not endure. Later, beginning with the close of the Romanesque period, spiritual art in the West entered upon path of progressive laicization, betraying its meaning, its destiny, even its very reason for being.

In 1053-1054, discussions with Rome were centered on the question of the *azyma* (unleavened bread). At about the same period, the dispute about the central question, that of the insertion of the *filioque* into the Creed,[65] became more acrimonious.

The controversy over the *filioque* intensified toward the end of the eleventh century. It is mentioned in every Byzantine polemical treatise. In the twelfth century this question became predominant, if not by the number of pages dedicated to it then at least by its importance. The dispute between Greek and Latin theologians at the Synods of Bari in 1098 and of Constantinople in 1112 dealt mainly with the procession of the Holy Spirit.[66]

The council of 1062 condemned John Italos and the Hellenistic philosophic trend he represented. Let us note that one of the reasons for his condemnation was his opposition to the veneration of icons.[67] In the

65 A. Poppe, "Le traité des azymes," *Byzantinion* 35 (1965), 507.

66 *Ibid.*, 508.

67 A. Vasiliev, *History of the Byzantine Empire*, vol. II (Madison, 1964), 473.

twelfth century, discussions were held with the Latinizers about the words of the eucharistic Liturgy: "For thou thyself are he that offers and is offered"; and also about the question to whom the sacrifice is offered, to God the Father or the Holy Trinity.[68] The councils of 1156 and 1157 condemned those who held a heretical view of the Eucharist, as "inventors of new and strange doctrines."[69]

In the eleventh and twelfth centuries the dogmatic struggle dominated the life of the Orthodox Church. The development of its spiritual life and the theological polemic against heresies and error are most visible in sacred art by what is known as its "spiritualization." According to V. Lazarev, perhaps never before or later did this art reach "such a degree of ideological saturation."[70] The prodigious flowering of the twelfth century was only a continuation of that of the eleventh century, the art of which became "the norm, we can even say the canonical style, for the centuries that followed."[71] Such art acquired a form that most fully reflected the spiritual experience of Orthodoxy. During this period, the image reached a height of expression noted for its clarity and distinctness: such art was inseparably tied to the very reality of the spiritual experience. Form was conceived and executed as the most complete and most convincing way to transmit content—a form that led the attention of the believer to the prototype, and made the acquisition of the likeness with it easier. Here we can clearly see the correspondence of such art to the type of spirituality so strikingly exemplified by St Symeon the New Theologian: "For him, the suffering and humiliated Christ is always and especially the risen Christ, transfigured in glory."[72] Art found the means to express, within the limits of the possible, the beauty so characteristic of the spiritual vision of St Symeon and his disciples. This artistic language was at once changing (since its forms are those of an unfolding experience, and could only vary and change with time) and stable, just as the spiritual experience is itself unchanging in its essence.

68 P. A. Cheremukhin, "The Council of Constantinople in 1157 and Nicholas, Bishop of Methona" (in Russian) *Bogoslovskie Trudy* I (Moscow: 1959), 157-8; "The Doctrine of the Economy of Salvation in Byzantine Theology" (in Russian), *Bogosl. Trudy* III (Moscow: 1964), 154-6. See also, Archbishop Basil, "Les textes symboliques dans l'Eglise orthodoxe," *Messager de l'Exarchat du Patriarche russe en Europe Occidentale*, no 48 (1964), 211.

69 P. A. Cheremukhin, *Bogosl. Trudy* I, 96.

70 Oral reply to the report of K. Weitzmann, 13th Byzant. Congress (Oxford, 1966).

71 K. Weitzmann, "Byzantine miniature and icon painting in the eleventh century," *Main Papers* VII, 13th Byzant. Congress (Oxford, 1966), 18.

72 Symeon the New Theologian, *op. cit.*, 247, note.

Toward the end of the twelfth century, external and internal causes led to total disorder in the Byzantine state apparatus. The empire lost its territories in Europe, and the steady progress of feudalism in the East provoked social strife in the interior of the country. The Latin influence so unpopular among the Greeks increased, and the antagonism against the Latins grew after Rome separated from ecumenical Orthodoxy. Under such conditions, the repeated attempts of the Comneni emperors to resolve the question of union of the churches for political reasons merely added fuel to the fire. All this sapped the strength of the empire and led to catastrophe at the beginning of the thirteenth century. On Easter Sunday of the year 1204, the knights of the Fourth Crusade broke into Constantinople. The world capital of art was sacked. "Monuments of classical art and sacred relics from apostolic times perished or were dispersed to the far corners of Europe."[73] "Constantinople never recovered from the ruin caused by the Latins. The impoverished empire no longer had the strength to recover the incomparable thousand-year-old riches accumulated since the fourth and fifth centuries."[74] Morally and materially, its fall was a decisive calamity for the Byzantine empire. The profanation of what was most sacred profoundly marked the soul of the Greek people. The sack of Constantinople marked the end of the magnificent renaissance of art in the twelfth century. Byzantine painters in large numbers went into exile to the Balkans, to the East or to the West.

Nonetheless, Byzantium was not defeated, either spiritually or culturally. Certainly, on the political and national plane its role had ended. But from the cultural perspective and on the religious level, it still had a word to say. This word was spoken at the time of the Paleologi in the thirteenth-fourteenth centuries.

73 Th. I. Ouspensky, *History of the Byzantine Empire* III (in Russian), (Moscow-Leningrad, 1948), 339.

74 *Ibid.*

12

Hesychasm And Humanism: The Paleologan Renaissance

When the Greeks regained Constantinople in 1261, the state was in full disarray. Misery and epidemics were widespread. Civil wars (three in one generation) were raging. In the meantime, Emperor Michael VIII Paleologus pursued negotiations with Rome (the Council of Lyons, 1274). Under these conditions, sacred art enjoyed a new efflorescence—the last one in Byzantium—which is called the "Paleologan Renaissance."[1]

Today this flourishing is often explained as a resurgence of Greek national consciousness during the Empire of Nicaea. Indeed, after the fall of Constantinople, Nicaea became the political and ecclesiastical center of the independent Greeks; the best spiritual and national forces of Byzantium were concentrated here.[2] The clergy who were able to flee Constantinople emigrated to Nicaea, where monk-scholars created a philosophic and theological academy, the guardian of Orthodox learning in the thirteenth century.[3] It is to Nicaea that the revival of Hellenic culture can be traced. Under such conditions, "a return to the ancient traditions,

1 Until recently, the "Paleologan Renaissance" was viewed as an enigma. Scholars wondered under what influence this rebirth, which contrasted so sharply to the economic and political situation, was able to develop. "Some have chosen to explain it through the influence of the Italian trecento: an unlikely hypothesis because, except for a few cases, it was rather Greek art which had an influence on Italian art at this time" (P. Lemerle, *Le style byzantin* [Paris, 1943], 35-6). See also, A. Grabar, *Byzance* (Paris, 1963), 171-2.

2 Of the three independent centers that were formed on the territory of the dismantled Byzantine Empire—the Empire of Trebizond, the Despotate of Epirus in northern Greece, and the Empire of Nicaea—the latter was to play a dominating role. In Nicaea stood the residence of the patriarch, who continued to carry the title of "ecumenical," of "Archbishop of Constantinople, and who was viewed as the only legitimate head of the Greek church. As before, his jurisdiction extended to the territories canonically dependent on it. Thus the Metropolitanate of Kiev, the only one in Russia at this time, subject to the patriarch, continued to receive Greek metropolitans, and maintained relations with Nicaea" (M. Levchenko, *Ocherki po istorii rusko-vizantiiskikh otnoshenii* [Moscow, 1956], 504-6. See also, G. Ostrogorsky, *Histoire de l'Etat byzantin* [Paris, 1956], 542).

3 Th. Ouspensky, *Istoriia Vizantiiskoi Imperii* III (Moscow-Leningrad, 1948), 542.

which was consciously opposed to the hated Latin culture, was not only natural but in a sense inevitable."[4]

The reemergence of national consciousness was certainly to play an important role, especially since it had cultural, political, and religious ramifications. The empire considered itself Orthodox. This is why there was no clearly defined differentiation between cultural and political life on the one hand, and religious life on the other. Now, the source of this religious vitality was "the Orthodox church, the most stable element in Byzantium."[5] Certainly, the Church was able to maintain its monolithic unity at a time that was tragic for the empire. The anti-Latin struggle was not merely national but also cultural; above all, it was perceived as a religious obligation. The efforts at union, in particular, could not fail to inspire within the Church a reaction of Orthodox Byzantium against the Roman Catholic West, and consequently, an even deeper awareness of the spiritual richness of Orthodoxy. [6] If one does not take into account the role of the Church "which bore the brunt of the battle,"[7] or disregards the crucial factors that played a leading role in the life of the Greek people, if the inner life of the Church is overlooked, one can only be surprised that Byzantium, during the reign of the Paleologi and under such painful conditions, could display such great activity in thought and art.[8] Whatever the case, one fact remains obvious, that "in representative art, the 'Paleologan Renaissance' is expressed almost exclusively in religious painting."[9] Clearly the inner life of the Church, which was later to be a subject of controversy, played a seminal role in the art of the time. The future of the Orthodox Church and of its art was decided through the struggle of hesychasm against what is called "humanism." Once more, the task of formulating Orthodox doctrine against deviations fell to the Church of Constantinople.

In the fourteenth century, the discussions that agitated the Byzantine

4 V. N. Lazarev, "Novyi pamiatnik konstantinopolskoi miniatury XIII veka," *Vizantiiskii Vremennik* 5 (1952), 188, and *Istorii Vizantiiskoii zhivopissi*, vol. 1 (Moscow, 1947), 158-9.

5 G. Ostrogorsky, *Histoire de l'Etat byzantin*, 509.

6 It is indeed illustrative that, at the time of negotiations concerning union, the historian Nicetas Acominatos, working in Nicaea, wrote (1204-1210) a dogmatic-polemic treatise consisting of twenty-seven books, entitled *Thesaurus of Orthodoxy* (PG 139: 1093-1102). See P. A. Cheremukhin, "Uchenie o domostroitelstve spaseniia v vizant. bogoslovii," *Bogoslovskii Trudy* III (Moscow, 1964), 159.

7 Th. Ouspensky, *Istoriia Vizant. Imperii* (1948), 622.

8 V. Lazarev, *Istoriia Vizant. zhivopissi* (1947), 209.

9 A. Grabar, *L'empereur dans l'art byzantin* (Paris, 1936), 226.

26. *St Gregory Palamas.* Byzantine icon, 14th century.

Church dealt with the very essence of Christian anthropology—the deification of man as understood, on the one hand, in traditional Orthodoxy as represented by the hesychasts under the direction of St Gregory Palamas (Fig. 26) and, on the other, in philosophic, religious circles nourished by the Hellenistic heritage and represented by the "humanists" led by Barlaam, a monk from Calabria, and Akyndinos. The so-called "hesychast" councils held in Constantinople in 1341, 1347, and 1351, were especially devoted to these discussions. In the preceding period, Byzantium had experienced a time of external crisis, of inner struggle and intellectual development. The end of the thirteenth century had witnessed renewed discussions on the procession of the Holy Spirit. They paved the way for the definitive expression of the doctrine of man's deification.[10]

The term "hesychasm" is generally associated with the theological discussions that took place in Byzantium at the time. These discussions prompted the Church to clarify its teaching about man's deification. Conciliar decisions gave a theological framework to the doctrine of man's illumination by the Holy Spirit, that is, to what has been from the beginning of Christianity the impetus and vitality of its art, the very principle that governed the artistic forms. Indeed, properly speaking, hesychasm was neither a new doctrine nor a new phenomenon: it was a form of the Orthodox spiritual experience dating back to the sources of Christianity.[11] To limit hesychasm strictly to the

10 J. Meyendorff, *Introduction à l'étude de Grégoire Palamas* (Paris, 1959), 30. (English trans. by G. Lawrence, *A Study of Gregory Palamas* [New York: St Vladimir's Seminary Press, 1974], 42ff).

11 *Hesychia*, impassibility, is the state reached by "sobriety" of the spirit, when the intellect controls the heart and the heart controls the intellect: "(It) is the appropriate Christian expression of *apatheia*, where action and contemplation are not conceived as two different orders of life, but on the contrary are merged in the exercise of 'spiritual action'—*praxis noera*" (V. Lossky, *The Vision of God*, trans. A. Moorhouse [New York: St Vladimir's Seminary Press, 1983], 142-3). The term "hesychasts," as applied to Christian ascetics, can be traced back to the fourth century.

On the subject of hesychasm, see the remarkable study of the monk Basil (Krivochéine), "Asketitcheskoe i bogoslovskoe uchenie sviatogo Grigoriia Palamy," *Seminarium Kondakovianum* VIII (Prague, 1936). See also, J. Meyendorff, *Saint Grégoire Palamas et la mystique orthodoxe* (Paris, 1959) (English trans. by Adele Fiske, *St Gregory Palamas and Orthodox Spirituality* [St Vladimir's Seminary Press, 1974]); *Introduction à l'étude de Grégoire Palamas* (Paris, 1959); *S. Grégoire Palamas: Défense des saints hésychastes*, Introduction, Critical Text and Notes by J. Meyendorff (Louvain, 1959) (Partial English translation by N. Gendle, *Gregory Palamas: The Triads* [New York, 1938]); *S. Syméon le Nouveau Théologien, Catéchèses*, three volumes with Introduction, Critical Text and Notes by Basil Krivochéine (Paris,

Byzantium of the Paleologi would therefore be incorrect. Whether the term is used in its proper sense, as a Christian ascetic practice, or in the narrow sense of the fourteenth-century theological discussions, the phenomenon of hesychasm has a pan-Orthodox scope (Fig. 27).[12] Indeed, according to the council of 1347, "the piety of Palamas and of the monks" is "an authentic piety truly common to all Christians."[13] Anchored in the tradition of the Fathers, the hesychast spiritual renewal, which received its dogmatic expression in the writings of St Gregory Palamas and in the fourteenth-century councils, as well as the discussions surrounding them, exer-

1963-1964, 1965); *Traités théologiques et éthiques*, Introduction, Critical Text and Notes by J. Darrouzès (Paris, 1966); *In the Light of Christ* (New York: St Vladimir's Seminary Press, 1986).

12 Thus in Russia, spiritual "praxis" was observed as soon as Christianity had been introduced. At any rate, a recent work (A. Tachiaos, *The Influence of Hesychasm on the Life of the Church in Russia in 1328-1406*, [in Greek] [Thessalonika, 1962]), gives specific data for the twelfth and thirteenth centuries. On the basis of certain texts (the "Teaching" of Vladimir Monomachos, 1115-1125, and the 1220 "Answer" of Theodosius, Archimandrite of the Lavra of the Kievan Caves), Tachiaos concludes that this practice existed in Russia during the period preceding the Mongolian invasion. The fourteenth century witnessed the increasing influence of hesychasm, and we shall see that in the fourteenth, fifteenth, and part of the sixteenth centuries, Russian art as a whole depended upon it. In the Balkans, the fourteenth century represents "the age of a truly hesychast International" (A. Elian, "Byzance et les Roumains," 13th Byzant. Congress [Oxford, 1966], *Supplementary Papers*, 48).

In the thirteenth century, St Sava, hesychast and first leader of the autocephalous Serbian church (d. 1237), drew upon the writings of St Symeon the New Theologian; and through him, hesychasm governed the life of the Serbian church, that of its monasteries and art. Indeed the high artistic flowering in Serbia coincided with the autocephaly of its church and is linked to the name of St Sava. Through his mediation, all of Serbian church life was marked by hesychasm. A long line of successors to St Sava (Arsenius I, Sava II, Daniel I, Joannicus I, and Eustachius I) became "the most vigilant guardians of hesychasm, and its most fervent champions" (M. Vasic, "L'Hésychasme dans l'Eglise et l'art des Serbes au Moyen Age," *Recueil Ouspensky*, vol. I, 1 [Paris, 1930], 114). The influence of St Sava upon the spiritual and cultural life of Serbia continued until the end of the eighteenth century. St Gregory of Sinai (1266-1346) played an important role in the spread of hesychasm in the Balkans. He settled in Thrace, on the border between Byzantium and Bulgaria. In Bulgaria, hesychasm was disseminated especially at the time of St Theodosius of Trnovo; and it played a leading role when Patriarch Euthymius (1375-1393) was placed at the head of the church (see M. Vasic, *ibid.*). In the fourteenth and fifteenth centuries, the Bulgarian monasteries, together with Mount Athos and Constantinople, served as meeting centers between Slavs and Greeks (D. Likhachev, *Kultura Russi* [Moscow-Leningrad, 1962], 39). "In the fourteenth century, Bulgaria was an immense center through which Byzantine influence moved into Serbia and Russia" (D. Likhachev, *ibid.*). The close cooperation between Walachia and Mount Athos assured the spread of hesychasm also in Romania, where it "strengthened the church hierarchy" (A. Elian, *Byzance et la Roumanie, op. cit.*).

13 Archbishop Basil (Krivochéine), "Les textes symboliques dans l'Eglise orthodoxe," *Messager de l'Exarchat du Patriarche russe en Europe occidentale*, no 48 (1964), 214, n. 36.

27. *St Sava.* Serbian fresco, ca. 1225.
Monastery of Milesevo.

cised an enormous influence on the entire Orthodox world, as much in the realm of the spiritual life as in that of sacred art. The cultural renewal of secular learning and literature was closely linked to the flowering of theological thought, which it either followed without reservation or rejected.

"The fourteenth-century theological discussions resulted from a clash between various trends within the Byzantine church itself."[14] Indeed, the intellectual circles of Byzantium had been in a state of inner turmoil for quite some time. Behind a facade of strict fidelity to Orthodoxy, a certain opposition had manifested itself since the ninth century. It came from a strong undercurrent, the source of which lay with the advocates of secular Hellenism, followers of the neo-Platonic tradition in philosophy. Without breaking with Christianity, this religious philosophy lived a life that was parallel to the doctrine of the Church. Classical Greek thought, overcome and outmatched by theology, reappeared among the representatives of this trend, the "humanists," who, "formed by their studies of philosophy, wish[ed] to see the Cappadocians through the eyes of Plato, Dionysius through the eyes of Proclus, Maximus and John Damascene through the eyes of Aristotle."[15] When these hellenizing philosophers went too far by trying to create a synthesis between Hellenism and the Gospel which, in their view, would replace the tradition of the Fathers, the Church condemned them. In the eleventh century already, the philosopher John Italos was condemned for his Platonism, and a new anathema was introduced into the Synodicon of the Triumph of Orthodoxy both against those "who held that Plato's ideas had real existence" and against those "who devote themselves to studies not merely as an intellectual exercise, but actually adopting the futile opinions of the philosophers."[16]

The Byzantine Fathers were trained in Greek philosophy, but they

14 *Ibid.*, 216.

15 V. Lossky, *The Vision of God*, trans. A. Moorhouse (New York: St Vladimir's Seminary Press, 1983) 156.

16 J. Meyendorff, *St Gregory Palamas and Orthodox Spirituality*, trans. A. Fiske (New York: St. Vladimir's Seminary Press, 1974), 98. In his discussion with Gregory Palamas, Barlaam rose against the hesychast tradition that contradicted his Platonism. A disciple of John Italos, John Petritsis (ca. 1050-1130), a Neo-Platonist and one of the most important people in Georgian culture, complained about the representatives of the traditional trend in Orthodox thought: "Had I found love and help among them, I swear that I would have made the Georgian language similar to the Greek, and could have raised philosophic theories to the same height as Aristotle" (Ch. Amiranchvili, *La miniature géorgienne* [Moscow, 1966], 11, 18).

adopted it as a purely intellectual discipline, as a means of training the mind, as an introduction to theology which, in itself, was based on Holy Scripture. The "humanists" endeavored to explain the elements of faith by means of natural reason. To them, faith was a matter of knowledge, *gnosis.* According to Barlaam, knowledge of God was only possible through the mediation of creation, and such knowledge could only be indirect. St Gregory Palamas did not deny this type of knowledge, but claimed that it was insufficient, and that it was impossible to know directly by natural means that which transcends nature.

One of the main issues that set the hesychasts and humanists in opposition to one another was that of the light of Mt Tabor. The discussion arose out of a disagreement concerning the nature of this light, and its place in the spiritual life of man. The opponents of Palamas saw in the Taboric light a natural, created phenomenon:

> The light that shone on the apostles on Mount Tabor and the sanctification and grace similar to it are either a created mirage, visible through the medium of the air, or else a figment of the imagination, lower than thought and harmful to every rational soul in so far as it derives from the sensory imagination. In short, it is a symbol, the nature of which we cannot determine, whether it belongs to things existing in reality or only in thought related to some object. It is a symbol which occasionally appears in a ghostly fashion, but which has never existed because it has absolutely no being.[17]

It merely reveals a divine presence. By contrast, for St Gregory Palamas, the Taboric light "is the unchangeable beauty of the prototype, the glory of God, the glory of the Holy Spirit, a ray of divinity,"[18] that is, the energy of the divine nature which at the same time properly belongs to the three Persons of the Holy Trinity, an external manifestation of God. However, in the eyes of his opponents, whatever was not part of the divine essence is not God. This is why the operations of God, as distinct from His essence, are a result of this essence. Now, according to the teaching of St Gregory, essence and energy are two aspects, two modes of the existence of God, and the very name of God is related as much to the essence as to the energy.[19] The same God remains absolutely inconceivable in His

17 J. Meyendorff, "Une lettre de saint Grégoire Palamas à Acyndinos, envoyée de Thessalonique avant la condamnation conciliaire de Barlaam et d'Acyndinos," *Pravoslavnaya Mysl.*, no 10 (1953). The Greek text is found in *Theologia* (Athens, 1953).

18 Basil Krivochéine, "Asketicheskoe i bogosl. uchenie...," *op. cit.*, 139.

19 Among the anathemas of the Triumph of Orthodoxy, the Council of 1352 included those

essence, but truly communicates Himself entirely by grace. The Taboric light is one of the modes of God's manifestation or revelation in the world; it is a presence of the Uncreated within the created order, a presence that is not allegorical but actually revealed and contemplated by the saints, an ineffable beauty. Unknowable in His nature, God thus communicates Himself to man through His operations, deifying man's entire being and making him God-like.[20] "And when the saints contemplate this divine light within themselves they behold the garment of their deification."[21] This divine grace is not merely an object of faith; it is also an object of concrete, living experience. For Palamas, as for traditional Orthodox theology in general, deification could not be separated from the vision of God or from personal contact with Him, a "face-to-face" contact.

By contrast, the rationalists could not see how God was, on the one hand, unknowable and, on the other, communicable to men. They viewed the very concept of deification as a pious metaphor. To them, God was unknowable and impenetrable. As for autonomous human reason, it could know everything which is not God. This is why Barlaam and his followers could not tolerate any bridge between God and man other than a symbol. Nicephoras Gregoras wrote: "This dogma was made known to the Church and has been handed down to us by our God and Savior Jesus Christ and His disciples that no one can see God, except through symbols and corporeal prefigurations."[22] As for the hesychasts, a symbol was acceptable only insofar as was consistent

who maintained that the name of God only applies to the one divine essence and not to the energies (Basil, *ibid.*, 119).

20 St Gregory Palamas saw in Barlaam's teaching on created grace a direct link with the Latin doctrine of the *filioque*. "Why, [he asks] has this man [Barlaam] made such a strenuous effort to demonstrate that the deifying grace of the Spirit was created?...Indeed, we understand that the Spirit is given by the Son, that He pours Himself upon us through the intermediary of the Son; on the other hand, the great Basil writes, 'God has abundantly poured out the Spirit through the Son; He has sent Him forth but did not create him' [*Contra Eunomium* V, PG 29: 772D]. If, on hearing all this, we are convinced that grace is created, what, in our view, will then be given, awarded, poured out through the mediation of the Son? Certainly the Spirit Himself, the One who acts by grace, since we would then say that He is the only one to be without beginning, whereas all energy which proceeds from Him is created, as this new theologian maintains? And so, do we thereby not directly arrive at the thought of the Latins that led to their being chased from our church: it is not grace but the Holy Spirit Himself who at the same time is sent from the Son and pours Himself out through the Son" (*Défense des saints hésychastes. Triade* III. 1, 3, [Louvain, 1959], 560-2).

21 *Triad* I, 5, trans. N. Gendle, *Gregory Palamas: The Triads* (New York: Paulist Press, 1983), 33.

22 *Liber dogmaticus quartus*, PG 149: 357AB.

with the history of salvation, and its christocentrism was not silenced. The hesychast disposition toward symbols may be illustrated by the words of Nicolas Cabasilas, himself a hesychast and a friend of St Gregory Palamas: "If that (Old Testament) lamb had accomplished everything, what need would there be of the future Lamb? For if types and images have brought the searched-for salvation, truth and reality are useless."[23] As soon as the Taboric light was understood by the "humanists" as a symbol, the Lord's Transfiguration itself assumed an unreal, symbolic character in their eyes. Replying to Akyndinos, St Gregory asked: "What? Neither Elias nor Moses were really there since they too were used as symbols?...and the mountain was no real mountain because it is also symbolic of the ascent to virtue?" On the other hand, he continued, symbolism was not unknown to the Greek philosophers; how then does Christian doctrine differ from their knowledge?[24]

By denying the suprasensory, immaterial nature of the Taboric light, the "humanists" could neither understand nor accept the Orthodox spiritual experience represented by the hesychasts, who claimed that man, through purification of mind and heart, might be sanctified by the divine, uncreated light. What was questioned in the fourteenth century and was to be given dogmatic definition, was the full demonstration of Christianity as man's union with God.

This union, this synergy of man with God, presupposes that the human being remains undivided. What is united to God is the totality of the

23 *The Life in Christ* I, par. 67, trans. C. J. de Catanzaro (New York: St Vladimir's Seminary Press, 1974); P. A. Cheremukhin, "Uchenie o domostroiteltsve spaseniia v vizantiiskom bogoslovii," *Bogoslovskie Trudy* 3 (Moscow, 1964).

24 "Against Akyndinos," in J. Meyendorff, *Introduction à l'étude de Grégoire Palamas* (Paris: Seuil, 1959), 270-2. [Abridged English translation, *A Study of Gregory Palamas* (London: Faith Press, 1962)]. It is precisely at this time that the representations of the Transfiguration became particularly widespread in sacred art, as an expression of the hesychast doctrine on the light of Tabor. Moreover, in response to the symbolic explanation of the mountain and of the Transfiguration itself, a group of apostles led by Christ is introduced into the iconography of the feast: they are represented as ascending and then descending the mountain. The three apostles at the bottom are portrayed as prostrated, overthrown by an invisible force which, like a hurricane, lifts them up from the ground. The reality and force of the light of Tabor are further emphasized by the gestures of the apostles: James and John cover their eyes with their hands, as they are unable to withstand the brilliance of the divine light emanating from Christ. On the other hand, the halo surrounding Christ receives a particular form: it consists of various spheres and rays, three of which can be distinctly seen, thereby indicating — in conformity with the doctrine of St Gregory Palamas — that the light of Tabor is an energy proper to the essence of the three persons of the Holy Trinity.

spiritual-psychic-bodily composite. In the fullness of his nature, man is not divisible; the human being, as a totality, shares in sanctification and transfiguration. For the hesychasts, the integrity of human nature was self-evident. No part of this nature was viewed in isolation as an autonomous means of knowing God; no part was excluded from union with Him. Not only the mind, but also the soul and the body share in His union.

The spiritual joy which comes from the mind into the body is in no way corrupted by the communion with the body, but transforms the body and makes it spiritual. Because it then rejects all the evil appetites of the body, it no longer drags the soul downwards, but rises together with it. Thus it is that the whole man becomes spirit, as it is written, "He who is born of Spirit, is spirit" (Jn 3:6-8).[25]

Orthodox spiritual experience transcends the ancient, enduring dualism of matter and spirit; the one and the other are united because they share together in what surpasses both of them. "It will be neither the reduction of the sensory to the intelligible, nor the materialization of the spiritual, but a communion of the whole man with the uncreated"[26]—a personal communion which is therefore easier to present than to describe. This experience is naturally antinomian and does not easily yield to the norm of philosophic thought. The "humanistic" negation of the Taboric light is indeed a negation of the possibility of a real transfiguration, experienced in the body. It was precisely the human body which was a stumbling block for them. The concept of the body's participation in divine knowledge and transfiguration eluded them. The doctrine of Barlaam and his followers, which typically saw a created (or, in modern terms, "imaginary and psychic") phenomenon in the light of Tabor, led to a docetist view of the body, to a denial of the possible transfiguration, since what was stressed was the separation between the divine energy and human energy, their autonomy, and the impossibility of uniting the two.

The theology of St Gregory Palamas raises man to an extraordinary height. Continuing the theological tradition that goes back to the anthropology of St Gregory the Theologian and of St Gregory of Nyssa, it emphasizes man's central position in the universe. St Gregory Palamas

25 *Gregory Palamas: The Triads*, trans. N. Gendle (New York: Paulist Press, 1983), 51.

26 V. Lossky, *The Vision of God*, trans. A. Moorhouse (New York: St Vladimir's Seminary Press, 1983), 163.

wrote: "All that exists is drawn together in man, this macrocosm enfolded in the microcosm. He is the head of all God's creatures."[27] Such an anthropology provides a solid foundation to authentic Christian humanism, and it embodies the answer of the Church to the general interest in man so apparent during this time.

It is natural, therefore, that this period also witnessed a greater interest in the image of man in art. The representation of feelings and emotions, so typical of the age, gives it a distinct character. Since the thirteenth century, the time of St Sava, Serbian art already contained the elements that would later characterize the so-called "Paleologan Renaissance." It is above all a very expressive representation of the world of emotions, of the "passionate part of the soul."[28] In the fourteenth century, such traits were expressed in art with great intensity, in connection with the discussions about prayer practice. In the person of Gregory Palamas, the Church placed these traits in their true Christian perspective. In his treatise against the hesychasts, Barlaam "recommended 'causing the complete death of the passionate part of the soul' and 'of all activity common to soul and body,' for 'such activity attaches the soul to the body and fills it with darkness'."[29] St Gregory replied that "...impassibility does not consist in mortifying the passionate part of the soul, but in removing it from good to evil..." He continues: "It is thus not the man who has killed the passionate part of the soul who has the preeminence;...but rather, the prize goes to him who has put that part of his soul under subjection, so that...it may ever tend toward God, as is right."[30] In other words, a sharing in the grace of God does not kill the passionate powers of the soul, but transfigures and sanctifies them. Such transfigured emotions, the expression of the soul's most intimate stirrings, represent one of the typical traits of the sacred art of this period.[31]

27 Basil (Krivochéine), "Asketicheskoe i bogoslovskoe uchenie sviatogo Grigoriia Palamy," *Seminarium Kondakovianum* VIII (Prague, 1936), 103.

28 When he was made head of the church, St Sava invited iconographers from Constantinople and ordered icons from the best painters in Thessalonika. See S. Radojcic, "Icônes de Yougoslavie du XIIe à la fin du XVIIe siècles," in *Icônes* (Paris-Grenoble, 1966), p. lx.

29 J. Meyendorff, *A Study of Gregory Palamas*, trans. G. Lawrence (New York, 1974), 139.

30 *Gregory Palamas: The Triads*, trans. N. Gendle (New York: Paulist Press, 1983), 54.

31 This is seen most clearly in the iconographer Theophanes the Greek (see N. Goleizovskii, "Zametki o tvorchestve Feofana Greka," *Vizantiiskii Vremennik* XXIV, 145) and in Manuel Panselinos (See A. Procopiou, *La question macédonienne dans la peinture byzantine* [Athens, 1963], 45).

Neither the hesychasts nor their opponents have left any writings specifically devoted to art, as had been the case during the iconoclastic controversy. The question of the image did not arise and was not a topic of polemics. But the art of the period shows a mixture of the Orthodox tradition and of elements linked to the "humanist" renaissance—one that reflected the struggle between "humanism" and hesychasm, between a return to the ancient Hellenistic tradition and a deepening of the spiritual life. Such intermixing can be detected as much in the very conception of art as in its nature and its subjects.

The number of borrowings from Antiquity greatly increased in the thirteenth and fourteenth centuries, and these motifs did not merely have a secondary, complementary function. They invaded the subject itself and its expression.[32] Thus, one sees a methodical tendency to represent volume by means of a certain depth. A certain mannered style appeared, for example, in representations from the back, or in profile. Foreshortening was used. Subjects taken from the Testament became especially common. Among these were prefigurations of the Theotokos (for example, the Burning Bush, Gideon's fleece), of Christ (for instance, the Sacrifice of Abraham, Melchisedech), as well as certain symbolic representations of Christ (in the form of an angel). Church decoration lost the unity and the monumental laconism so typical of the previous era. It did not renounce dogmatic principle, but its organic link to architecture began to diminish. "Painters and mosaicists are no longer subservient to the inner space of the church...in order to bring out its meaning. They juxtapose innumerable representations..."[33] An essentially spatial art which, up to that time, had conveyed attitudes rather than gestures, a spiritual condition rather than a series of emotions, witnessed the introduction of a temporal element, the representation of what occurs as time flees: recitation, psychological reactions, and so forth. The connection between what is represented and the viewer also changed. Whether the icon represented a single person or a given scene, it was no longer turned outward, toward the believer who prayed before it. Frequently, the representation unfolded like a scene, having a life of its own, independent of the viewer, as if it were closed in upon itself.

32 A. Grabar, *Byzance* (Paris, 1963), 70; V. Lazarev, *Istoriia Vizantiiskoi zhivopisi* (Moscow, 1947), 224.

33 Olivier Clément, *Byzance et le christianisme* (Paris, 1964), 75.

At this time also, representations of subjects on the altar screen were directly related to the pivotal sacrament of the Church, the Eucharist, became more numerous. Two trends emerged when the Eucharist was transposed into images. On the one hand, there was the search for a coherent theological system that would unveil the entire economy of salvation through images. This trend would lead to the elaboration of the iconostasis which was given its classical form in fifteenth-century Russia.[34] On the other hand, there was the tendency, so typical of this period, to explain the meaning of the sacrament by illustrating certain moments of the Liturgy, for example, the Great Entrance. It is in this latter iconographic theme that the line between what can and cannot be represented was frequently overstepped. There is, for example, the scene in which a hierarch immolates the Christ-Child lying on the diskos (in the fourteenth-century church in Mateic, Serbia)—a specific reminder of a ritual murder. Unquestionably, the theme of the Child on the diskos was a reaction to the twelfth-century liturgical discussions or, more precisely, an echo of them in the camp of the Latinizers. At the time of the Paleologi, such discussions must have grown on fertile soil in the abstract, rationalistic thought of the "humanists."[35]

Parallel to the illustrations of certain moments of the Liturgy, we find a series of iconographic subjects apparently intended to reveal the meaning of the sacrament by means of symbolic images, such as Wisdom's Banquet, or Wisdom giving communion to the apostles. Such motifs intended to represent the text of Proverbs 8:1-7 —"Wisdom has built herself a house..."—in the form of an image. The text was represented in two ways. On the one hand, there was Wisdom—an angel—who embod-

34 See our article "L'Iconostase," in *Contacts* no 46, (Paris, 1964), 83-125.

35 In the thirteenth century, the motif of Christ on the diskos in the representation in the Liturgy became widespread, especially in Serbia. It is also found in the paintings of Mistra, in Trebizond, Bulgaria, Russia, and on Mount Athos (see V. Lazarev, *Freski Staroi Ladogi* [Moscow, 1960], 25.) This motif appeared in the twelfth century; its oldest known example is found in the church of St George in Kurbinovo (Serbia), as well as in Nerezi (see Lazarev, *ibid.*, 24). A bread plate from the twelfth or the beginning of the thirteenth century from Xyropotamou (see Lazarev, *ibid.*) shows the dead Christ-Child on the altar, the Gospel book on His chest. On each side of the altar, the adult Christ is portrayed as "the great hierarch." This is a direct illustration of the words, "You are the Offerer and the Offered"—words that were at the core of the discussions at the Council of 1156-1157; the Christ-child is the Offering, and the Christ-Hierarch is the Offerer. At Mistra (Perivlepte), above the prothesis table, God the Father is represented in the place of the Holy Trinity. Is this not an echo of the discussions on the question: To whom is the Sacrifice of Christ offered, to God the Father or to the Trinity?

ied Divine Wisdom according to the type of personifications in Antiquity. On the other, there was Christ-Wisdom under the guise of an Angel of the Great Council.[36] It should be kept in mind that the theme of Wisdom was very current at the time of the conflict between the hesychasts and their opponents; it is unquestionably in this context that the symbolic image of Sophia became especially widespread at the time of the Paleologi. In the development of this type of symbolism one cannot help but see the influence of the "humanist" renaissance. However, in spite of its incompatibility with hesychast concepts, it must be said that this symbolism, as well as borrowings from Antiquity, were not always alien to hesychasm. The symbolic representation of Wisdom can therefore be understood not only as a "humanist" encroachment, but also as an attempt on the part of the hesychasts to contrast the wisdom of the philosophers to the Wisdom of God.[37] This type of symbolism, used consciously or unconsciously by painters, undermined the realist Orthodox doctrine of icons, and occasionally violated canon 82 of the Quinisext Council (*in Trullo*). This rule, one recalls, abolished those symbols that replaced the direct image of the incarnate Word of God: "While we venerate the images and ancient shadows as signs and prefigurations of the Truth...we prefer to them grace and truth, which is the fulfillment of the law." Now, a "disincarnation" of this type, violating the principle of Gospel realism, was particularly problematic in the case of a eucharistic subject. A fruit of abstract reflection, such symbolism certainly did not correspond to traditional Orthodox thought, anymore than did a confusion between what could and could not be represented.

Symbolic representations that replaced the direct human image, expressive artistic images of the emotional life, a tendency toward naturalis-

36 The oldest known representation of the Wisdom-angel is found in a catacomb of Alexandria and dates back to the sixth century. Next to the angel is the inscription: Sophia Jesus Christ. It is not easy to determine whether this image was originally orthodox or heretical. Concerning the representation of Wisdom, see G. Florovsky, "O pochitanii Sofii Premudrosti Bozhiei v Vizantii i na Rusi," *Words of the Fifth Congress of Russian Academics Abroad*, vol. 1 (Sofia, 1932); J. Meyendorff, "L'iconographie de la Sagesse divine dans la tradition byzantine," *Cahiers archéologiques*, vol. X (Paris, 1959).

37 The appearance at this time, in the narthex of Orthodox churches, of representations of ancient philosophers and Sibyls as somehow announcing Christ may be understood as an attempt to sanctify Hellenic wisdom (N. L. Okunev, "Arilje, Pamiatnik serbskogo iskusstva XIII veka," *Seminarium Kondakovianum* VIII [Prague, 1936], 221-58; K. Specieris, *Representations of Greek philosophers in the Churches* [in Greek] [Athens, 1964]).

tic, Hellenistic traits, the great variety of new iconographic subjects, and the proliferation of Old Testament prefigurations: all this was the product of an era guided by a profusion of new ideas, the time of the "humanist" and of the hesychast renaissances. If traditional painters were not always immune from "humanist" influences, painters who favored humanism, in turn, nonetheless held on to the traditional forms of Orthodox art represented by hesychasm. The Paleologan renaissance did not abandon these traditional forms. Nevertheless, when compared to the preceding era, and under the influence of the ideas of the time, elements that diminished the spirituality of the image were introduced into these traditional forms. Occasionally, such elements even changed the very concept of the icon, its meaning, and consequently its function in the Church. Such elements, the result of an abstract view of God based on a natural knowledge of the world, were related to the Orthodox tradition just as the "humanist" view of the world was to the traditional hesychast attitude. This is why the role and importance which the "humanists" attributed to philosophy and secular knowledge in the spiritual life on the one hand, and, on the other, the hesychast attitude toward them, are useful: they give us indirect indications about the views each held about the content and the function of sacred art.

In his controversy with the "humanists," St Gregory Palamas wrote:

> We do not prevent anyone from being initiated into secular learning if he so desires, unless he has embraced the monastic life. But we advise against becoming too deeply involved with it, and we categorically forbid anyone to expect from it precise information about things divine, for one cannot derive any sure teaching about God from it.

A little further we read: "There is indeed something useful in the philosophers, as there is in a mixture of honey and hemlock. But the danger is great that those who want to separate the honey from the hemlock may accidentally consume a deadly residue."[38] St Gregory Palamas reflected at length and in great detail upon the question of the relationship between secular learning and philosophy on the one hand, and knowledge of God on the other. Despite the profoundly negative evaluation just mentioned, he did not merely deny the importance of secular learning but even recognized that it was relatively useful. Like Barlaam, he recognized in it

38 *Gregory Palamas: The Triads*, I, trans. N. Gendle (New York: Paulist Press, 1983), 28.

one of the paths imparting an indirect, relative knowledge of God. But he strenuously denied that religious philosophy and secular learning could possibly serve as a means of communicating with God or of obtaining direct knowledge about Him. Not only is learning unable to give "any precise information about things divine"; it also leads to error when it is applied in a domain that is alien to it. Worse still, it may even prevent the very possibility of communing with God; it can become "deadly." As can be seen, St Gregory merely protected the reality of communicating with God against encroachment by the field of religious philosophy and natural knowledge. Before such hesychast intransigence regarding the mixture of secular learning (including religious philosophy) and the domain of direct knowledge of God, one may suppose that Gregory viewed the content and functions of sacred art from the same perspective.

Even if in the psychosomatic technique used by the hesychasts one could detect a certain detachment from images, their attitude regarding the veneration and the importance of the icon in worship and prayer remained profoundly faithful to Orthodox doctrine. When St Gregory spoke of icons he did not limit himself to expressing the classic Orthodox view. He also added to it a few characteristic precisions about hesychast teaching and the general trend of Orthodox art. He states:

> Out of love for Him, make an icon of the One who became man for our sake. Through it, remember Him; worship Him through it; through it, raise the mind to the adored body of the Savior seated in glory at the right hand of the Father in heaven. Make icons of the saints in the same manner...; venerate them, not as gods, which is forbidden, but as a sign of your loving communion with them and of your veneration. Through their icons, raise your mind toward them.[39]

As can be seen, St Gregory expresses traditional Orthodox doctrine as much in his veneration of the image as in his view of its basis (the Incarnation) and content. But in the context of his theology, this content sounds a note that is typical of the pneumatological era. For Gregory, the Incarnation was, as it were, the starting point looking forward to its fruit: the divine glory manifested in the human body of God the Lord. The deified body of the Lord has received and transmitted the eternal glory of the divinity. It is His glory that is represented on icons; it is worshipped to the degree that it reveals the divinity of Christ.[40] But since God and the

39 *Decalogus Christianae Legis,* PG 150: 1092.

40 J. Meyendorff, *A Study of Gregory Palamas,* trans. G. Lawrence (New York, 1964), 183.

28. *The Entombment of Christ.* 12th century.
Serbian fresco from Nerezi-Skopje.

saints possess the same grace,[41] their representations are made "in the same fashion."[42]

In light of such a view of the image and its content, it is certain that for the hesychasts the only image that could serve as a means of communing with God was one that reflected this communion in conformity with hesychast teaching. By contrast, artistic elements that were based on philosophic thought and on empirical knowledge of the world could not, anymore than abstract learning, give "any precise formation about things divine." Specifically, a symbolic representation of Jesus Christ that replaces the personal image of the Bearer of divine glory meant an attack upon the very foundation of the doctrine of the icon—a witness to the Incarnation. Such an icon could not therefore "raise the mind to the adored body of the Savior seated in glory at the right hand of the Father." Consequently, it is quite understandable that after the victory of hesychasm, the Church put an end to the development of those elements in its sacred art which undermined its doctrine in one way or another. It was due precisely to hesychasm that "the last Byzantines—in contrast to the Italians—made room for the natural, but without developing a naturalism; made use of depth without imprisoning it in the laws of perspective; and explored the human, without isolating it from the divine" (Fig. 28).[43] Art retained its link with revelation and preserved its synergistic character between man and God.

The doctrine of St Gregory Palamas about the essential communion with the divine energies "destroyed that last trace of rationalism and of iconoclastic positivism,"[44] since it was a development of the position already sketched out in the doctrine about the veneration of icons. In this domain, dogmatic work could be pursued as an elucidation of the very content of the spiritual experience, and therefore of the content of sacred

41 See, for example, Maximus the Confessor, *Opuscula theologica et polemica ad Marianus*, PG 91: 12B; *Ambiguorum Liber*, PG 91: 1076BC.

42 Concerning hesychasm, we learn from the works of certain contemporary authors that this doctrine pursued so-called ways of salvation "outside the practice of the Church, and paid no attention to the cult or to Church dogma"; and that such a system had nothing to do with either the cult of the Virgin Mary or that of the saints. "Faith in Christ the Savior and the grace of the sacraments were alien to them." Hesychasm "attempted to achieve deification by pious prayer, that is, a prayer that killed the spirit"; "the hesychasts were opposed to universal dogma," and so forth. What does all this have to do with hesychasm? The answer remains the authors' secret; at any rate, it is presented to the reader as objective scientific fact.

43 Olivier Clément, *Byzance et le christianisme* (Paris, 1964), 76-7.

44 A. V. Kartashev, *Vselenskie Sobory* (Paris, 1963), 709.

art. Through its dogma about the veneration of icons, the Church recognized that it was possible to translate the result of divine action in man by means of forms, color, and lines; and that this result could be shown. Through its doctrine of the Taboric light, the Church recognized that the divine action transfiguring man originates in the uncreated, imperishable light, the energy of the Divinity felt and contemplated in the body. Thus the doctrine of the divine energies joins that of the icons, since what was formulated dogmatically during the discussions about the Taboric light was the deification of man, and hence the basis of the iconic content. It was at this time that the boundaries of sacred art were established—limits beyond which sacred art cannot go if it is to remain Church art.

The victory of Palamas was decisive for the subsequent history of the Church. Had the Church remained passive before the upsurge of "humanism," the tide of new ideas would unquestionably have led to crises analogous to those in Western Christianity: that of Renaissance neo-paganism and of the Reformation, both conforming to new philosophies. This would have resulted in a radical modification of Church art.[45]

And thus, thanks to hesychasm, sacred art did not overstep the boundary beyond which it would have ceased to express Orthodox doctrine. However, beginning with the second half of the fourteenth century, the living, creative tradition which had produced the Paleologan Renaissance began to give way to a certain conservatism. After the fall of Constantinople in 1453 and the invasion of the Balkans by the Turks, the leading role in sacred art was passed on to Russia.[46] The living hesychast impetus and the dogmas that had formulated Orthodox anthropology in the light of Palamism would bear precious fruit in Russian art and spiritual life. There the renaissance of the fourteenth and fifteenth centuries would have a basis different from the one that produced the Byzantine Paleologan Renaissance. As for conservatism, it would show itself by its very nature to be incapable of resisting the external influence coming from the West.

45 Having found a favorable domain in Roman doctrine, "humanism" enriched the most varied spheres of human activity. Its development, however, followed its own path outside, and even against, the Church. This shows that such "humanism" was not the Christian anthropology which the Church had to reveal.

46 This is why the rest of our account is essentially devoted to Russian sacred art. On account of its historic conditions (and also because of heresies in the Russian church), this is where the destiny of Orthodox sacred art was played out.

M. S. Radojcic has reason to state that "Western influences have done more damage to Byzantine painting than the Turks."[47]

The Council of Constantinople (1351) was the most solemn act by which the Church confirmed the doctrine of St Gregory Palamas. The fourteenth century witnessed how the decisions of this council were adopted by the entire Orthodox Church. One year after the council, its definitions were introduced into the ritual of the Triumph of Orthodoxy. In 1368, shortly after his death, St Gregory Palamas was canonized. He is commemorated on November 14. In addition, the second Sunday of Lent is also dedicated to his memory as "the preacher of divine light" (Vespers, third stichera). He is also hailed as "the torch of Orthodoxy, doctor and pillar of the Church" (troparion). Thus, after the Sunday of the Triumph of Orthodoxy, the Church celebrates the doctrine of the deification of man; and the Council of 843 which closed the christological era of the Church is intimately and liturgically linked to the height of its pneumatological period.

47 S. Radojcic, "Les Icônes de Yougoslavie du XIIe à la fin du XVIIe siècle," in *Icônes* (Paris-Grenoble, 1966), lxxi.

13

Hesychasm and the Flowering of Russian Art

The christianization of Russia was a long process that began well before its official baptism and continued for a long time afterwards. If Christianity, despite pagan opposition which was fierce in some places, was able to become the dominant religion, this is because the Christian segment of the population was already numerically and spiritually important. Be that as it may, there were already several Christian churches during the reign of Prince Sviatoslav (d. 972).[1] But if there were churches, there were icons. Were these icons all imported, or had some of them been painted locally? The latter hypothesis cannot be confirmed, nor can it be excluded. Knowing the great respect for icons by the founder of the mission to the Slavs, St Photius the Patriarch, as well as by his closest collaborators and those who continued his work afterwards, one may venture to say that special attention had been given to this aspect of Orthodoxy and to the dissemination of icons among new converts. This hastened the process of acquainting the population with Christian art and encouraged the appearance of local painters. Beginning with the end of the tenth century, and in the eleventh, Russian-Byzantine workshops existed in Kiev.[2] If the first churches built after the official baptism were decorated by Greek artists invited to Russia, historians also note that Russian artists participated. To judge by the homily of Bishop Hilarion of Kiev (11th century), addressed to the deceased Prince Vladimir, the veneration of icons and the awareness of their importance had already deeply affected the minds and hearts of the people. "Behold this radiant, majestic city," Hilarion said, "these flourishing churches, the progress of Christianity.

1 V. Mochin, "The Periodization of Literary Relations Between Russians and Southern Slavs," (in Russian), *Trudy Otdela drevnerussk. Literatury XIX* (Moscow-Leningrad, 1963), 52. While referring to the oath taken at the time of the treaty between Prince Igor and the Greeks, the Chronicler writes: "All of us who received baptism took the oath at the cathedral, swearing by the church of St Elias, because it was the cathedral church, and many Varangians, and Khazars were Christians" (*Chronicle*, ed. Academy of Sciences [Moscow-Leningrad, 1950], 38-9).

2 V. N. Lazarev, *The Mosaics of St Michael's Church* (in Russian) (Moscow, 1966), 9.

Behold this city sanctified by the icons of saints...in which are heard divine praises and canticles."[3] The Paterikon of the Monastery of the Caves in Kiev records that in the thirteenth century a more ancient tradition mentioned a certain monk Erasmus who "had spent all he had on icons."

Along with Christianity, Russia received a sacred image that had attained its classical form, as well as an already formulated doctrine of icons, and a full-grown technique that had been developed over the centuries. This new faith and its artistic language, which had been elaborated in a bitter and often tragic struggle, were accepted by the Russian people in a creative manner, in keeping with their own way of living the faith. Beginning with the period of assimilation (11th-12th centuries), an original artistic language proper to Russia was developed; during the thirteenth century, its forms took on a specific national character. The spiritual life of the people, their holiness and sacred art, received a national stamp, the result of a new, original way of assimilating Christianity. Thus the holiness of Princes Boris and Gleb is marked by its typically Russian character. Due to their widespread veneration, they were the first Russian saints to be canonized, despite the doubts and opposition of the Greeks. The eleventh century witnessed how two monks of the Monastery of the Caves in Kiev, Alipios and Gregory, canonized as iconographers, gave Russian sacred art an inspiration derived from a living, direct knowledge of Revelation. From the very beginning, all of Russian cultic art (architecture, painting, and music) carried an original stamp. Originally, this manifested itself especially in the great variety of painting styles developed in various historic centers of the state during its feudal division, in conformity with local conditions and the particular character of the people in each part of the immense Russian land.

The horrifying Tartar invasion curbed the creative spirit of the Russian people but did not break it. Under the Tartar yoke they continued to build churches and paint icons, even though the enthusiasm is not to be compared to that of the preceding period. In 1325, at the time of the saintly Metropolitan Peter, Moscow became the religious center of Russia, well before becoming its capital. At this time of unceasing civil wars among the princes, of widespread devastation due to the Tartar invasions, it was the Church that assured the internal unity of Russia[4] and served as a pledge of

3 B. L. Grekov, *Kievan Russia* (in Russian) (Moscow, 1953), 497.

4 M. V. Levchenko, *Notes on the History of Russian-Byzantine Relations* (in Russian) (Moscow, 1956), 551.

29. *St Sergius of Radonezh.*
Russian icon, 1940's.

its future political unity.[5] It was the Church that personified the hopes of the Russian people, together with their aspirations for the liberation and unification of their country. In the persons of its best representatives, above all in St Sergius of Radonezh and the hierarchs of Moscow, the Church accomplished the spiritual unification of the vast Russian lands around Moscow before their political unification.[6] The struggle against the Tartar yoke "was not merely a national task but also a religious one."[7] As for the civil wars and the quarrels of the princes who all shared the same faith, they contradicted the very nature of the Church. Certainly, it is significant that St Sergius consecrated his church to the Holy Trinity, "so that contemplation of the Holy Trinity might conquer the fear of this world's detestable discord," as wrote his biographer Epiphanius, called "the most wise." [8]

The fourteenth and fifteenth centuries, the time of St Sergius (1314-1392) and of the immediate successors who continued his work, witnessed a great flowering of Russian holiness, as well as a rebirth not only of monasticism and eremitism but also of art and culture, of which the monasteries were the centers (Fig. 29).[9] The unification of the Russian people was forged around Moscow. This period of spiritual, cultural and national reawakening witnessed a growing interest in the historic past, in the days of Russian independence, in the painting, architecture and

5 In *The Culture of Russia at the Time of Andrei Rublev and Epiphanius the Wise* (in Russian) (Moscow-Leningrad, 1962), 10, D. S. Likhachev correctly observes that "During the terrible years of the Tartar yoke, the unity of the power of the church in Russia was of great political importance. The ecclesiastic power of the metropolitan extended over all of Russia, and permitted one to glimpse the future unification of his political power." Following the metropolitan, the princes, in turn, adopted the title "of all Russia."

6 It is typical that even a prince like Dimitri Donskoi, who according to the *Nikon Chronicle* "Had brought all the Russian princes under his will," was unable to think along pan-Russian lines, despite his victory at Kulikovo. Before his death, following princely ideals, he honestly distributed the territories surrounding Moscow to his sons; this created a classical hotbed of internal warfare (which fortunately did not take place).

7 D. Likhachev, *The Culture of Russia*, 88.

8 V. N. Lazarev, *Andrei Rublev and His School* (in Russian) (Moscow, 1966), 60; Ephiphanius the Wise, *The Life of St Sergius* (in Russian), in *Monuments of Ancient Art and Literature* (in Russian), vol. 56 (S.Pb., 1885). It is typical that most of the monasteries linked to St Sergius in one way or another were dedicated to the Holy Trinity (G. Fedotov, *The Saints of Ancient Russia* [in Russian] [Paris, 1931], 154), the antithesis of "the hateful discord of the world."

9 In the eighty years between 1420-1500, fifty saints died, who were later canonized by the Church. The number of monasteries also increased during this period: Russia counted close to ninety between the twelfth and fourteenth centuries, and the following century (1340-1440) witnessed the appearance of one hundred and fifty more. The disciples of St Sergius founded fifty new monasteries during his lifetime.

literature of the eleventh through the thirteenth centuries in Kiev, Novgorod, and Vladimir. Overwhelmed by the untold catastrophe of the Tartar invasion, Russia finally emerged from this "trial by fire"; it rose little by little and mustered its strength to free itself from the foreign yoke.

In those days, the country experienced the Gospel's glad tidings more vividly than at any other time before or since. In Christ's suffering, Russia felt her own recent calvary, and the Resurrection filled her with the joy of a soul released from hell. At the same time, the generation of saints that lived in Russia and healed her wounds made her constantly feel the active power of Christ's promise, "I am with you always, even unto the end of the world" (Mt 28:20). The feeling that Christ's power was effectively participating in the life of mankind and in the life of the Russian people finds expression in all Russian art of the time.[10]

Russia lived through a time of intense artistic activity. In the rapid development of architecture, literature, and liturgical creation, it was painting that predominantly expressed the spiritual and cultural life of the Russian people. It is precisely at this time that the pictorial language of sacred art attained its highest expression; it is noted for its expressive form, its freedom and spontaneity, its purity of tone, its intense and joyful colors (Figs. 30 and 31).

During this period Russia was well-informed about what went on in Byzantium. The rebirth of Orthodox Christianity, which in Byzantine discussions had received the name of hesychasm, its theological presuppositions and the debate surrounding the ascetic experience—all this evoked a powerful echo in Russia. We have seen that the language of the sacred image had been shaped over the centuries by the spiritual experience of Orthodox asceticism. It was quite natural, therefore, that the flowering of Russian holiness should be accompanied by a rapid development of sacred art. Ever since the pre-Mongolian period, the contacts of Russian monks with Byzantine monasteries and spiritual centers of the Middle-East allow us to conclude that spiritual *praxis* had played a decisive role in the Russian assimilation of Christian art and the shaping of an ecclesial artistic consciousness. Russian fourteenth and fifteenth-century art was directly influenced by hesychasm. However, its flowering was not linked

10 Eugene N. Trubetskoi, *Icons: Theology in Color*, trans. Gertrude Vakar (New York: St Vladimir's Seminary Press, 1973), 83.

30. *St Clement of Rome.* Russian icon, ca. 1400.
Collection Vander Elst-de-Gruyter, Anvers.

31. *The Archangel Gabriel,* Russian icon, 15th c.

to a dogmatic struggle, as was true for Byzantium. It does not represent an answer to an attack: it is the visible manifestation of a rapid development of the spiritual life, of a flowering of holiness. The words concerning Russian saints may equally be applied to it: "The Russian land, O Lord, brings you a choice fruit of your salutary sowing."[11]

The hesychast movement reached Russia by two paths: directly from Byzantium, whose link to Russia had always remained close, and from Mount Athos and the Southern Slavs. A great number of Russian hierarchs (the Metropolitans Theognostos, Alexis, Cyprian, and Photius) were linked directly to this movement.[12] Liturgically, the introduction of the feast of St Gregory Palamas on the second Sunday of Great Lent established the link of the Russian Church with Byzantine hesychasm. Abundant writings were brought to Russia from Byzantium, Mount Athos, and the Slavic countries. These writings, imbued with hesychast *theoria* and *praxis*, influenced Russian monasticism.[13] Spiritual *praxis* reached a wide circle of disciples, friends or correspondents of St Sergius. His monastery of the Holy Trinity became the spiritual center of Russia,

11 The kontakion of the feast of "All the Saints who sanctified the Russian land." From the liturgical service, ed. the Moscow Patriarchate (Moscow, 1946).

12 The decisions of the Council of 1341 in Constantinople, which had approved the teaching of St Gregory Palamas and condemned the heresy of Barlaam, were sent to the Metropolitan of Russia, St Theognostos (commemorated on March 14). His successor, St Alexis (1298-1378; commemorated on February 12), knew the doctrine of Palamas well because he had spent the years 1353-1355 in Constantinople, that is, shortly after the council that had condemned Barlaam and Akyndinos. The saintly Metropolitans Cyprian—commemorated on September 16; during his pontificate Russia adopted the liturgical feast of St Gregory—and Photius (commemorated on July 2) were also ardent followers of the teaching of Palamas. St Sergius of Radonezh (commemorated on September 25), the greatest representative of Russian monasticism, was in contact with Patriarchs Philotheos and Callistus of Constantinople, who were hesychasts. The nephew of St Sergius, St Theodore (later bishop of Rostov; commemorated on November 28; a well known iconographer, tradition attributes to him the first icon of his uncle) visited Constantinople on several occasions. When he founded the monastery of St Simeon near Moscow, he asked and obtained stavropighial status from the Patriarch of Constantinople (see M. V. Levchenko, *Notes on the History of Russian-Byzantine Relations* [in Russian] [Moscow, 1956], 532).

13 "In the second half of the fourteenth century in Constantinople and on Mount Athos, there were entire colonies of Russians who lived in the monasteries and were occupied in copying books, translating, comparing Russian and Greek liturgical books, and so forth" (D. Likhachev, *The Culture of Russia* [Moscow-Leningrad, 1962], 30). In addition to liturgical books and the lives of the saints, Russian translations were made of the works of St Basil the Great, Isaac the Syrian, Abba Dorotheus, Dionysius the Areopagite, Gregory of Sinai, Gregory Palamas, Symeon the New Theologian, John Climacus, John Chrysostom, Patriarch Callistus, Euthymius of Trnovo, Maximus the Confessor, and others (D. Likhachev, *ibid.*, 33-4, 85).

the main locus of hesychast influence. But the link with Byzantium was particularly productive in the domain of sacred art; numerous icons were brought to Russia and many Byzantine painters worked there. Furthermore, during the fourteenth century, Southern Slavs, fleeing from Tartar pressure, took refuge in Moscow. The Russian hesychast movement, however, was not the result of external contacts with Byzantium by means of books, iconographers, or imported icons. What happened was that the dogmatic struggle raging in Byzantium was echoed profoundly in the Russian spiritual life. It can be said that Russian art of the fourteenth and fifteenth centuries, and partly of the sixteenth, is a type of contribution to this dogmatic struggle in which the Russian church did not directly participate. The theology of hesychasm is reflected in the spiritual content and the entire character of this art; it is conveyed by a deep awareness.

The leading artists of this period were hesychasts themselves or were somehow associated with them. Among them, art history singles out three names which are linked with more or less certainty to specific works or certain artistic trends: Theophanes the Greek (14th cent.), Andrei Rublev (1360/70-1430), and the master Dionysius (b. in the 30s or 40s of the 15th cent.; d. in the opening decades of the 16th). According to Epiphanius the Wise, Theophanes the Greek, in his work, "understood the faraway and the spiritual with his mind, for he perceived spiritual beauty through his enlightened bodily eyes."[14] St Joseph of Volokolamsk spoke of Andrei Rublev and his circle as follows:

> These marvelous, famous iconographers, Daniel, Andrei, his disciple, and *many others* who were like them, had such virtuous zeal for fasting and the monastic life that they were able to receive divine grace. They constantly raised their mind and thought to the divine, immaterial light, and their bodily eye toward the images of Christ, of his All-pure Mother and of all the saints painted with material colors.[15]

The work of the master Dionysius was likewise guided by hesychast theology, and above all by the teaching concerning inner prayer.[16] The "many others like them" included Greeks, Southern Slavs, and Russians influenced directly or indirectly by St Sergius—generations of iconogra-

14 V. N. Lazarev, *Theophanes the Greek and His School* (in Russian) (Moscow, 1961), 113.

15 St Joseph of Volokolamsk, "Answer to the Curious and Brief Story of the Holy Fathers Who Lived in the Monasteries of the Russian Lands," *Great Menaion* of Metropolitan Macarius (September 1-15), (St Petersburg, 1868).

16 N. K. Goleizovskii, "The *Message to an Iconographer* and Echoes of Hesychasm in Russian Painting" (in Russian), *Vizantiiskii Vremennik* XXVI (Moscow, 1965), 237.

phers of an extremely high spiritual and artistic standing. The names of some of the successors are known, though no specific works can be attributed to them. Most, however, remain anonymous.

The development and the flowering of holiness in Russia coincided with the growth of heresies, and the flowering of sacred art with the iconoclasm such heresies demonstrated.[17]

The heresy of the "Strigolniki" appeared toward the middle of the fourteenth century in Northwest Russia (according to some, in Pskov; according to others, in Novgorod). This movement, marked by critical rationalism, was the first directed against the Church. The Strigolniki rejected the Church, its dogma, and the sacraments.[18] There is no direct, precise information about their iconoclasm. Nonetheless, the general nature of this heresy leads us to believe that its followers could not have venerated icons.

Iconoclasm appeared in Rostov in the 1480s. Preached by a certain Marcian, an Armenian, it had a fortuitous character and was inconsequential.[19]

17 Let us also note that the renewal of Russian art and holiness was in contrast to a disquieting reality not only in civil but sometimes also in ecclesiastical life, when peace was broken in the church during times of trouble. Thus in the fourteenth-fifteenth centuries, the Russian church was divided on two occasions. First, John Calecas, the pro-Latin patriarch of Constantinople, removed the metropolitanate of Galich from the Russian metropolitanate, and this provoked a schism. In 1347, Patriarch Isidore, a hesychast, restored unity. In 1416, surrendering to pressure by the Lithuanian Prince Vitovt, a synod of bishops called by him during the lifetime of Metropolitan St Photius, "enthroned" in his place a certain Gregory Tsamblak, who had been deposed previously in Constantinople. In the metropolitan see of Moscow, saints alternated with utterly unworthy men such as, for example, Dimitrius (called "Mitiai"), Isidore, and Zosima. On the other hand, we know from accusations formulated by the church authorities that the clergy and monks were not always and everywhere of a particularly high moral caliber, which was conducive to heretical propaganda. In the western regions, bordering on Roman Catholic areas, numerous norms and regulations established by the church were violated, particularly in Pskov: baptism by aspersion was condoned, sometimes even the use of Latin holy chrism.

18 Apart from these negative characteristics, we know neither the positive aspects of the doctrine of the Strigolniki nor the origins of the heresy or the meaning of its name. Some scholars detect in it an echo of a secret Bogomil tradition, since the anti-church views of the Bogomils invaded Russia as early as the eleventh century and gained followers among the leaders of paganism; others attribute the heresy to eastern influence; and still others regard it as a political and social movement.

19 I. N. Shabatin, "Certain Details of the History of the Russian Church" (in Russian), *Messager de l'Exarchat du Patriarche russe en Europe occidentale*, no 51 (1965), 192.

In the fifteenth century, rationalism manifested itself in the heresy of the Judaizers, first in Novgorod, then in Moscow. This heresy affected first the higher clergy, then the upper-class lay people; it lasted until the beginning of the sixteenth century. Like the Strigolniki, the Judaizers rejected the Church, its hierarchy, sacraments and doctrine. They also denied the Holy Trinity and the divinity of Christ. Their return to the Old Testament, to which they owe their name, was apparent in their cult. They observed the Sabbath and other Jewish feasts, and occasionally even practiced circumcision. The Judaizing heresy was not homogeneous; it consisted of various tendencies that occasionally even contradicted each other.[20] Not all of them rejected icons, and "some of these heretics made references to iconographic subjects to strengthen their arguments."[21] But iconoclasm was basically inherent in this heresy. It is this iconoclasm which led to the conciliar decisions made concerning the Judaizers in October, 1490. The council's verdict states that

> Many of you have mocked the images of Christ and of the All-Pure represented on the icons, while others mocked the Cross of Christ. Still others have uttered words of blasphemy against the holy icons. Others, finally, have destroyed holy icons with axes and burned them in the fire...Others among them have thrown icons away. You have reviled the holy image of those who are painted on the icons.[22]

The heresy of the Strigolniki is not directly reflected in sacred art, anymore than is that of the Judaizers: it merely provoked the spread of certain iconographic subjects that confirmed Orthodox doctrine. The main reaction caused by the heresy was a polemic dealing with the creation and theoretical foundation of sacred art—one that holds particular interest for us.

We have seen that Byzantine hesychast theology had given dogmatic precision to the content of the icon by its doctrine concerning the divine energies. However, when Byzantine hesychasts spoke of the icon, they did not link its veneration or creation to spiritual *praxis.* St Gregory Palamas,

20 A. I. Klibanov, *The Reform Movements in Russia in the Fourteenth to the Beginning of the Sixteenth Centuries* (in Russian) (Moscow, 1960), 205.

21 N. K. Goleizovskii, "Message to an Iconographer," *Vizant. Vremen.* XXVI (Moscow, 1965), 220.

22 Texts published by N. A. Kazakova and Ia. S. Lurié, *The Heretical Anti-feudal Movements in Russia in the Fourteenth to the Beginning of the Sixteenth Centuries* (in Russian) (Moscow-Leningrad, 1955), 383.

for example, alluded to icons only within the framework of his profession of faith. This was perhaps due to the fact that the heresy to which the hesychasts reacted did not demand this type of precision. In fifteenth-century Russia the relationship between hesychasm and the icon was made clear in the response of the Church to the Judaizing heresy. It is expressed in a work entitled *Message to an Iconographer*, included in *The Instructor (Prosvetitel)*, a polemical treatise by St Joseph of Volokolamsk against the heresy.[23] This *Message* was to play an important role in explaining the meaning of sacred art. Its influence can be found in the writings of St Maximus the Greek, Metropolitan Macarius, the monk Zenobius of Otnia, and others. This work consists of the *Message* itself, as well as of three treatises on icons and their veneration. It is addressed to the chief iconographer, that is, the one who directs the others. One scholar who has drawn attention to the hesychast nature of this work surmises that the treatises included in the *Message* were garnered by St Joseph of Volokolamsk at the request of Dionysius, the famous iconographer, "by way of instruction for his apprentices and Russian iconographers in general."[24] The same author notes, with good reason, that the intent of the *Message to an Iconographer* was "to shed light on the most important questions raised during the polemics against the heretics, and at the same time to prevent the creation of new compositions"[25] not consistent with Orthodox doctrine. This last observation is due no doubt to the fact that, even aside from heresy, the iconography of the period following that of Rublev witnessed the beginning of a progressive diminution of its spiritual meaning, of its deep structure. Beauty of artistic form began to take precedence over spiritual depth of the image, which decreased somewhat,

23 Joseph himself has been viewed as being the author of the *Message to an Iconographer*. However, Ia. S. Lurié believes that St Nilus of Sora might rather be the author of the *Message* itself and of the treatises that follow, since this text corresponds word for word to his *Message to a Certain Brother*. In addition, the stylistic particularities of the *Message to an Iconographer* are those of the other works of St Nilus (*ibid.*, 321-2). The entire work could probably be the work of two authors, not one. Indeed, not only do the treatises that make up the work differ from one another, but within the treatises certain sections clearly belong to different hands; in them, one even finds inconsistencies concerning certain questions (among others, in the evaluation in the presentation of the representation of the Holy Trinity). But whatever the partial contributions of Sts Nilus and Joseph in the *Message to an Iconographer*, this common work points to their agreement on what is essential, even if they disagree with each other on certain practical questions.

24 N. K. Goleizovskii, "Message to an Iconographer," *ibid.*, 234.

25 *Ibid.*, 221.

causing dismay. The manner in which *Message* addressed its recipient is revealing: a call to vigilance is sounded. "This message is appropriately addressed to you, since you are the chief iconographer."[26] Joseph of Volokolamsk mentioned Andrei Rublev and Daniel "the Black" as a model, or a reproach, to the iconographers of his time, and not without reason. "The former were never preoccupied with earthly things...but always raised their spirit and thought toward the divine, immaterial light."

The account of the theological basis of icons in the *Message to an Iconographer* is marked by a subdued lyricism, and by the author's experience, which is expressed forcefully. "If Nilus expresses little that is his own, distinguishable from generally accepted spiritual tradition, then at least he expresses it independently. He lives in the patristic tradition. That tradition lives and is alive in him." These words of Florovsky about the work of Nilus of Sora[27] characterize the author of the *Message* best of all. Like any truly creative ecclesial work, while providing an answer to heresy, it is not only a defense of the very existence of the icon and its veneration, but also, most importantly, a positive contribution that explains its spiritual content, and the role of the Orthodox spiritual experience in its creation.

The first treatise is polemical, in the proper sense of the term. It is directed against the Judaizing iconoclast argument "which maintains that to venerate what is made by human hands is not proper." The second treatise, "useful to every Christian," presents the theology of the veneration of icons. The third and last treatise, at once polemical and theological, is devoted to a concrete subject, the representation of the Holy Trinity by the heretics. In the brief analysis we give here of these treatises we shall omit the third; we will return to it when we examine the representation of the Trinity.

What characterizes these treatises is that the doctrine of the icon finds its place in the overall context of the entire divine economy; not a separate chapter, it is ontologically incorporated into the whole of Orthodox doctrine, which is set forth precisely through the icon. The meaning and

26 N. Kazakova and Ia. S. Lurié, *The Heretical Anti-feudal Movements*, 323.

27 Georges Florovsky, *Ways of Russian Theology*, trans. R. L. Nichols (Belmont: Nordland Publishing Co., 1973), 23.

the spiritual content of the image are always emphasized; theoretical statements are never used.

The polemical content of the first treatise consists of a systematic rebuttal of the Judaizing argumentation, which was generally the same as that of Byzantine iconoclasm at its outset: the Old Testament interdiction, the confusion between icon and idol, between veneration and adoration, the refusal to venerate the saints and relics and, judging from the refutation, the concept of the Eucharist as an image. A long section defends the holiness of the church building as the place of worship—a subject that was not part of the Byzantine polemic. This topic, as well as the refusal to venerate the Cross, indicates how far beyond the Byzantine heretics the iconoclasm of the Judaizers had moved. To the classical arguments of the iconoclasts, the author gives an equally classical answer, largely drawn from the works of St John of Damascus, St Theodore the Studite, and from texts of the Seventh Ecumenical Council, but without referring to it. As was true with the eighth and ninth-century Orthodox apologists, the defense of the icon starts here with an elucidation of Old Testament representations, of the difference between idol and icon, between worship of God and the veneration of saints and holy objects. The theological effort of the Byzantine apologists is reexamined here and reinterpreted in terms of the specifics of the author's time and of new circumstances. The essential argument is based on the truth of the Incarnation, with references made to the image of Christ "not-made-with-human hands," and to the icons painted by St Luke the Evangelist. After showing that representations did exist in the Old Testament, the author states:

> How much more appropriate is it then, in this new time of grace, to venerate and bow down before the image of our Lord Jesus Christ painted on the icon by human hands...and to adore His deified humanity taken up to heaven. This also holds true for His All-pure Mother. Likewise, to paint images of all the saints on icons, to venerate and bow before them is equally appropriate. By painting images of the saints on icons, we do not venerate an object but, starting from this visible object, our mind and spirit ascend toward the love of God, object of our desire.[28]

This is an almost literal restatement of the thought of St Gregory Palamas concerning the content of the image of Christ. In general, the spiritual attitude of the author of the *Message* is marked by an understanding of the role and importance of the icon, analogous to that of Gregory Palamas.

28 N. Kazakova and Ia. S. Lurié, 334.

Such hesychast tendency is especially clear in the second treatise, where it lies at the very root of every question that is considered. It must be noted, however, that, in contrast to the Byzantine hesychasts, the author says nothing about either the Taboric light or the divine energies. Nonetheless, it is precisely these themes which form the basis for all the author's judgments and train of thought.

In the second treatise, the teaching "addressed to every Christian," begins by stating the need for the image of the Holy Trinity, the heart of Christian life and doctrine. The Trinity must be represented "so that, thanks to an iconographic representation, we may contemplate spiritually that which our bodily eyes cannot possibly see."[29] The divine Trinity cannot be described; and even though many just men and prophets have announced it, the Trinity is only represented because

> it appeared to Abraham in a sensory manner, in human form, as it wished to appear, as it demanded to be represented. Starting from this visible aspect, our mind and spirit ascend toward the love of God, object of all desire. What is venerated is not the object, but the beholding and the beauty of the divine image.[30]

The apparition of the three divine hypostases to Abraham in the form of three angels—a fact unique in history—is contrasted to the variety of visions and prophetic announcements. It is precisely on this sensory apparition that the so-called "Old Testament" icon of the Trinity is based. In it, "the one nature of the Divinity is honored and venerated."[31] For the author, the outer beauty of the image is synonymous with its inner, spiritual beauty; perceiving this beauty induces spiritual contemplation and leads to inner prayer. Starting with the icon of the Trinity, this concept extends to the icon in general, which is viewed as a link between the present life and that of the age to come. The love it provokes toward what is represented is of such a nature that it links life on earth to that "in which the bodies of the saints will be brighter than the sunlight."[32] This thought seems so important to the author that he repeats it, in its entirety at the end of the third treatise of the *Message.* Disclosing Orthodox trinitarian doctrine, he also attaches great importance to the procession of the Holy Spirit, and refutes the doctrine of the *filioque* at length. We surmise that,

29 *Ibid.*, 336.
30 *Ibid.*
31 *Ibid.*
32 *Ibid.*

within the context of the treatise and its exposition of the doctrine of the image, this authentic acknowledgment of the Holy Spirit represents not a theory, but the pledge of an authentic creativity and spiritual life.

According to the author of the *Message*, "what is specific to icons is the divine meaning, to which all that is external in the icon must be subordinated; and this meaning must be immediately obvious."[33] The icons of Christ, of the Theotokos and of the saints are, like the image of the Trinity, always primarily based on historical reality. The historicity in the icons, which is essential for Orthodox theology, acquires here a very special importance. The icon is a personal image: this excludes all confusion. It is precisely because of this "that it is appropriate to venerate the icon" and "to bow before the one it represents as if before the living person...as before [the Theotokos] herself and no one else."[34] Such a systematic, repeated emphasis on the historic basis of the icon was intended to refute, we suppose, the view of the heretics who considered icons to be idols. According to the author's first treatise, what distinguished the one from the other was the difference in prototypes. The icon points to the Incarnation of the Word of God, while an idol is "a demonic invention." This is why "the prototypes of divine icons are holy and worthy of veneration, while the prototypes of idols are most wicked and impure."[35] On the other hand, it is possible that the author, while emphasizing the historical nature of the icon, had in mind the inaccuracy of the concept of the image that had begun to appear. Perhaps he was thinking of the presence of fictitious elements in iconographic subjects, that would later provoke discussions and protests against "personal inventions."

Beginning with this historical basis, the author emphasizes just as strongly the holiness and spirit-bearing character of the iconic prototype, which ordains and conditions the content of the icon, as well as the attitude we adopt toward it. In this context he often returns to the well-known thesis: "the veneration of icons returns to its prototype; in icons and through them, we worship the truth." The author understands the link between the image and its prototype so concretely that, when referring to the persons represented on the icon, he states: "We venerate

33 N. K. Goleizovskii, "Message to an Iconographer," 226.

34 N. Kazakova and Ia. S. Lurié, *The Heretical Anti-feudal Movements*, 337.

35 *Ibid.*, 333.

their images and bow down before them; thus we think of them as being present among us by the forcefulness of our unquenchable love."[36]

God the Word "appeared in the flesh, condescended to live among men, to work out my salvation through his visible flesh."[37] This is the same body in which

> the Divinity cannot be separated from the flesh...After his resurrection, [Christ] appeared to His disciples in his incorruptible and already divine flesh; He ascended to heaven in the flesh, and is seated at the right hand of the Father in His deified body, not in decomposition or corruption like us.[38]

This is why the author, while emphasizing the inexpressible nature of the Divinity, calls the image of Christ not merely "most pure," which is traditional, but also "divine-human," the image of "His deified humanity." It is precisely the historical-spiritual, human-divine fusion of these two realities that constitutes the criterion of the very content of the iconic expression of the God-manhood of Christ. Not since the eighth and ninth-century apologists has the link between the two realities, the created and the uncreated, as the indispensable content of the icon, been expressed so emphatically, forcefully, and significantly.

The doctrinal aspect of the icon "necessary to every Christian," as the title of the second treatise indicates, is conveyed by means of pure hesychast teaching:

> When adoring your Lord and God...let your whole heart, spirit, and mind be lifted toward a contemplation of the holy, consubstantial and life-giving Trinity, in purity of thought and heart...Let your bodily eyes ascend to the divine, all venerable icon of the consubstantial and life-giving Trinity or to the divine-human image of our Lord Jesus Christ or of His Most-pure Mother or of one of the saints...; venerate them spiritually in your soul and visibly with your body. Be completely turned toward the heavens.[39]

It is typical of the *Message* that much attention is given to teaching that is permeated by the spirit of inner prayer, and that it gives advice about asceticism in life and prayer. "Wherever you may be, O beloved, on sea or on land, at home, walking, sitting or lying down—ceaselessly pray with a pure conscience, saying, 'Lord Jesus Christ, Son of God, have mercy on me,' and God will hear you."[40] Also, "Close your eyes to the visible and

36 *Ibid.*, 241.
37 *Ibid.*, 335.
38 *Ibid.*, 348.
39 *Ibid.*, 351-2.
40 *Ibid.*, 356.

look at the future with your inner eye."[41] Within the context of the *Message,* such instructions, addressed to an iconographer, assume a particular significance: they show what the author considers to be the norm and the orientation of the iconographer's creative activity.

The *Message to an Iconographer* presents nothing new about the doctrine of icons. But in the light of hesychasm it discloses an existential attitude toward the icon by recommending the hesychast *praxis* of inner prayer as the source of both its veneration (or, more precisely, of our active reception) and its creation. Since the icon is ontologically linked to the Orthodox doctrine of man's deification by the uncreated, divine light, the attitude toward its creation derives from the Christian practice of "spiritual action." In other words, in the light of hesychasm, the content of the message presupposes a certain spiritual attitude to create it, as well as to perceive it, in a productive manner. What is involved in both cases is man's spiritual rebirth. "The Spirit that renews gives him new eyes, even new ears. Henceforth, as man he no longer perceives the sensory in a sensory fashion; having become more than man, he contemplates sensory realities in a spiritual manner."[42]

This understanding of the content of the icon in the light of hesychast doctrine indicates how high the author sets his standards with regard to artistic creation. The painter must be acutely aware of the responsibility that rests upon him when creating an icon. His work must be informed by the prototype it represents in order for its message to become a living, active force, shaping man's disposition, his view of the world and of life. A true iconographer must commune with the prototype he represents, not merely because he belongs to the body of the Church, but also on account of his own experience of sanctification. He must be a creative painter who perceives and discloses another's holiness through his own spiritual experience. It is upon this experience of communing with the archetype that the operative power of an iconographer's work depends.

As has been noted, the treatises in the *Message to an Iconographer* contain no theoretical statements. At that time, there was no "theory of art" as we understand it. The aesthetic appreciation of a work corre-

41 *Ibid.,* 358.

42 St Symeon the New Theologian, *Catéchèses* II (Paris, 1964); Introduction, Critical Text and Notes by Basil Krivochéine, *Catéchèse* XIV, 213-5.

32. Detail of an icon by Master Dionysius.

sponded to an understanding of its theology. Art was theology expressed through aesthetic categories. An icon's beauty was understood as a reflection of the holiness of its prototype. In other words, the Orthodox doctrine about the deification of man *was* the "theory of art." From this doctrine derives the practice of both spiritual life and art. Therein lies the organic unity of the spiritual life and its artistic expression.

The recipient of the *Message to an Iconographer*, supposedly the master Dionysius, decorated the church of the Nativity of the Virgin in the Monastery of St Therapontus between 1500 and 1502, together with his sons. The frescoes are in visible agreement with the *Message*, as much in their motifs as in the quality of their spirituality. Their leading theme is an affirmation of Orthodox doctrine against the heretical errors enumerated by the council of 1490. The divinity as well as the humanity of Christ are re-affirmed; in them, the coronation of the Virgin assumes a central position, and the role of the ecumenical councils is emphasized. According to a contemporary scholar, the frescoes of the Monastery of Therapontus constitute on the spiritual level the visible illustration of "hesychast psychological theory."[43] The figures drawn by Dionysius are imbued with a beauty that is not of this world (Fig. 32); "this is the result of inner prayer [of spiritual *praxis*]."[44] Dionysius omitted

> details that could have interfered with a perception of the idea. He shows what is essential: spiritual inwardness, the guarding of the spirit, attention, the power of wisdom shining through a piercing yet inward-looking gaze, love of beauty, and humbleness. Like Nilus of Sora and the author of the *Message*, he chose to translate the ideal, embodied in a concrete image, and let the viewer judge himself by comparison.[45]

In its theological content and spiritual temper, the *Message to an Iconographer* is in agreement not only with the art of Dionysius, but more generally with Russian art at the time of its origins—an art characterized by the same perfect fusion of dogmatic content, inner prayer, and artistic creation. Complying with the demands of Orthodoxy, the art of this period reached its apex. Certainly, in Byzantium as in Russia, neither all painters nor all the clergy understood hesychast teaching or put it into

43 N. K. Goleizovskii, "Message to an Iconographer," *Vizant. Vremen.* XXVI (Moscow, 1965), 238.

44 *Ibid.*, 237.

45 *Ibid.*, 238.

practice. But it was hesychasm that played the decisive role in the spheres of man's spiritual and practical activity.[46] As has been said, the development of Russian art was not the result of a struggle. But what lay at the heart of Byzantine theology at that time was made manifest on Russian soil in its practical, existential aspect. It is here that the fullness of its incarnation was revealed in life and art.[47]

As in Byzantium, iconographic subjects in Russia became more complex and richer. In particular, the general interest of the period in man's emotional world, his soul, shines through.[48] It is typical that both in the

46 Hesychasm, whether Russian or Byzantine, can certainly not be viewed as an "anti-ecclesiastical" phenomenon, even "to a certain extent" (see D. S. Likhachev, *The Culture of Russia* [Moscow-Leningrad, 1962], 85, 131), except on the basis of a misunderstanding. It certainly had nothing to do with "rifts," profound or not, "in the dogmatic view of the world" in the fourteenth-fifteenth centuries (See V. N. Lazarev, *Rublev* [in Russian], [Moscow, 1966], 54-5; *History of Russian Art* [in Russian] vol. 3 [Moscow-Leningrad, 1955], 175). What appeared as being "anti-ecclesiastical" or as "rifts," was in reality nothing but a normal manifestation of this "dogmatic view of the world" corresponding to the life of a given epoch. In other words, this is how such a view unfolded itself in the multiplicity of phenomena and of human experiences.

47 In practice, the application of the hesychast doctrine about the divine uncreated light is reflected, among other things, in the consecration of a large number of churches dedicated to the Holy Trinity and to the Transfiguration, and also in the wide diffusion of these two subjects in iconography.

48 In Russian painting of the fourteenth and fifteenth centuries, two trends emerge: one represented by Theophanes the Greek, the other by Andrei Rublev. Among the various opinions about their associations, the theory predominates according to which Rublev was, if not a direct disciple of Theophanes, then at least a painter whose art matured under his influence. Moreover, it was from Theophanes that Rublev inherited the "hesychast insight into the meaning of phenomena, the ability to translate the spiritual by means of sensory images" (N. Goleizovskii, "Message to an Iconographer," *Vizant. Vremen.* XXVI [Moscow, 1965], 223). Such statements seem questionable to us, all the more since they are based neither on facts nor on works that would demonstrate the dependence of one painter on the other: they are based on the painters' collaboration in the decoration of the Cathedral of the Annunciation (in 1405), and on the manner in which Epiphanius the Wise describes the personality of Theophanes and his influence on the Russian painters. Epiphanius' enthusiastic appreciation should be viewed with greater caution, it seems to us. He was a great admirer of Theophanes, and in such cases, exaggerations are hard to avoid. As "a most wise philosopher," Theophanes the Greek, to judge from his works, was a typical representative of the Paleologan Renaissance, when it was common for quite a few hesychasts to mix traditional Orthodox thought with concepts of the period. The dramatic tension so typical of Theophanes' painting, "the passion and dramatic pathos" of his saints (V. Lazarev, *Theophanes the Greek and His School* [Moscow, 1961], 41), their inner tension and lack of serenity are due not only to his temperament or character traits, but also to the characteristics of the Paleologan Renaissance—peculiarities which can be detected in the subjects of the frescoes he painted in the church of the Transfiguration at Novgorod (provided the assumptions of the specialists are correct), namely an Adoration of the Victim, the Tree of Jesse, Sophia, and so forth (none of which have been preserved).

Theophanes has unquestionably left a profound mark on Russian art. However, his

lives of saints and the figurative arts made an effort not merely to show holiness, but also to disclose it to the fullest possible extent. They show "the Kingdom of God within" man in all the complexity of human nature illumined by the divine, uncreated light.[49] They present the integrity, the fullness of a life guided by a Christian teaching that flourished once again in hesychasm. The expression of the inner harmony of man reconciled with God, with self and with the world, reached its highest perfection in Russian art. This is the best demonstration of what is called "sacred stillness" (hesychia): when, through the power of the Spirit, as St Gregory Palamas said, "we fasten His law to every power of the soul and each bodily member."[50] What is shown by the Russian icon is not so much the struggle against fallen nature as the victory over it—freedom recovered, when "the law of the Spirit" creates the beauty of body and soul which are no longer subject to "the law of sin" (Rom 7:25; 8:2). The center of gravity does not lie in the hard struggle, but in the joy of its harvest, in the sweetness, the lightness of the burden of the Lord spoken of in the Gospel pericope read on the feast days of the holy ascetics: "Take my yoke on your shoulders, and learn from me, because I am gentle and humble in heart, and you will find rest for your soul, for my yoke is easy and my burden light" (Mt 1:29-30). In the domain of art, the Russian icon is the highest expression of humility learned from God Himself. This is

manner of painting and creating stands in sharp contrast to the serene harmony, the contemplative peace, so typical of the art of Andrei Rublev. We are in the presence of two very different spiritual paths. Even if Andrei Rublev was not shaped directly by the Trinity-St Sergius Monastery, he was in any case molded by the environment of St Sergius' immediate circle of friends. From this derives the hesychast character and the "insight into the meaning of the phenomena" which so vividly mark his life and creation. We know that Rublev's environment was of such a high spiritual caliber and of such intensity that its influence must have been decisive, and that Theophanes could hardly have counterbalanced it. On the contrary, judging from the change which Theophanes' art underwent during the years he spent in Russia, he himself must have been influenced by the Russian hesychasts, provided it can be proved that the icons in the Cathedral of the Annunciation that are attributed to him are really from his hand (see A. N. Grabar, "Some Remarks About the Art of Theophanes the Greek" [in Russian] *Trudy Otdela drevnerusskoi literatury* XXII [Moscow-Leningrad, 1966], 86).

49 This is seen most distinctly in the icons of the Mother of God called "Lovingkindness" (*Umilenie, Eleousa*), one of the main subjects, and one of the summits of Russian art. The most profound human feelings, the most intense emotions are shown there, transfigured: these, connected with motherhood, embrace the psychic as well as the physical life, and link the human being to the whole of the created world.

50 *First Triad, second answer.* St Gregory Palamas, *Défense des saints hésychastes*, Introduction, Critical Text and Notes by J. Meyendorff (Louvain, 1959), 76-7. (Partial English trans. by N. Gendle, *Gregory Palamas: The Triads* [New York: Paulist Press, 1983]).

why the extraordinary depth of its content is associated with childlike joy, with intimacy and serenity.

We can say that if Byzantium primarily gave theology its verbal expression, Russia gave it above all its visible, figurative form. In the realm of the artistic language of the Church, it was Russia's lot to reveal the depth of the icon's content, and the highest degree of its spirituality.

One of the most important results of the development of hesychasm in Russia—a period of the flowering not only of holiness and sacred art, but also of liturgical creation—is the iconostasis in its classical form (Fig. 33 and Fig. 34).

As in Byzantium, there were attempts in Russia during this period to make the meaning of the sacrament of the Eucharist more explicit by illustrating various moments of the Liturgy. However, parallel with these attempts, one sees the development of the altar screen separating the sanctuary from the nave. The screen was transformed into an iconostasis, with several rows of icons, and became one of the essential elements of an Orthodox church. It became a partition, hiding the sanctuary from the eyes of the faithful. In our time this partition seems useless, even offensive, not only to non-Orthodox but sometimes even to some Orthodox. This is why it seems useful briefly to discuss the iconographic content and meaning of the iconostasis, in an attempt to show the precision and power of expression proper to hesychasm revealed there.[51] In its classic form, elaborated in the fifteenth century, the

51 In churches of the early Christian centuries, the sanctuary was separated from the nave by a screen or a curtain, or even by a row of columns with an architrave. "The use of curtains seems to be older than that of screens. Curtains are mentioned in the first centuries of the Christian Liturgy" (G. Filimonov, *Questions Regarding the Initial Form of the Iconostasis in Russian Churches* [in Russian], [Moscow, 1859], 29. The use of a curtain instead of a screen is preserved in Armenian and Ethiopian churches). The oldest known reference to the screen and the colonnade dates back to Eusebius of Caesarea (for the first, see his *Ecclesiastical History*, Bk 10, ch. 4, PG 20: 846; for the second, see his *De Vita Constantini*, Bk 3, ch. 38, PG 20: 1097-1100). The development of the iconographic subjects on the screen, and its transformation into an iconostasis began very early. Initially, the architrave carried a cross that was either placed above it or carved into the stone itself. But already in the sixth century, having placed twelve columns in Hagia Sophia in Constantinople, Justinian has bas-relief representations done of Christ, the Mother of God, angels, apostles and prophets. This is about all we know about the iconographic content of the screen before iconoclasm. Afterwards, a new period began in the development of the iconostasis. In the eleventh century, there apparently already were two-story iconostases in Byzantium (K. Weitzmann, "Byzantine Miniature and Icon Painting in the Eleventh Century," *Main Papers*, 13th International Congress of Byzant. Studies [Oxford, 1966], 17). The screen spread to Russia in this form and with the same liturgical significance. The Fathers explained its meaning as being not a separation but a type

iconostasis consists of five rows of icons. It is topped by a cross.

The upper row, depicting the patriarchs, represents the Old Testament church from Adam to Moses—the period before the Law. The patriarchs are wearing unfolded phylacteries (*tephillin*) with appropriate passages. At the center of the row is placed the image of the Trinity, appearing to Abraham near the oak of Mamre. This is God's first covenant with man, and the first revelation of the one triune God.

The row of prophets underneath represents the Old Testament church from Moses to Christ—the period of the Law. It includes images of prophets, who are also carrying scrolls containing texts of their prophecies about the Incarnation. At the center of this row is the icon of Our Lady of the Sign, the Mother of God with the child on her bosom. She is the sign announced by the prophet: "The Lord himself will give you a sign. Behold, a young woman shall conceive and bear a son, and shall call his name Immanuel" (Is 7:14), "which means God with us" (Mt 1:23).

These two rows represent the preparation for the New Testament church among the ancestors of Christ according to the flesh, as well as its prefiguration and announcement by the prophets. Thus the icon of the Incarnation in the middle of the row of prophets indicates the direct link between the Old and New Testament.[52] Each row corresponds to a well-defined period of sacred history, to a time of preparation; and each of the figures seen there is connected to the central image representing the culmination of all these prophecies and preparations.

of union between the two parts of the church. Thus Symeon of Thessalonika wrote: "Above the transom on top of the columns, in the center between the holy icons, are representations of Christ, and on His side of the Mother of God, of the Forerunner, the angels, apostles and other saints. This tells us that Christ dwells at the same time with His saints and presently with us, and that He is still to come" (*De sacro templo*, PG 155: 345).

In Russia, a series of modifications had to be made to the screen, both because of an increase in the number of rows of icons and because of their dimension and distribution. Within the evolving framework of Christian worship, it is significant that the sanctuary screen has not been preserved anywhere in its original form: either it developed as in the Orthodox church or it disappeared, as in the West. (For further details, see our study, "The Question of the Iconostasis" [in Russian], *Messager de l'Exarchat du Patriarche russe en Europe occidentale*, no 44 [Paris, 1963]. In English, in *St Vladimir's Seminary Quarterly* 8, 4 [New York, 1964]).

52 These two upper rows show the pre-Christmas liturgical cycle, or more precisely, the two Sundays that precede the feast, consecrated to the memory of the patriarchs and fathers. The subjects were divided into patriarchs and prophets out of a concern for better visual expression. However, on rather low iconostases, they are represented on the same row.

The next row of the iconostasis, containing the feasts, represents the New Testament period, the time of grace. It shows that what had been announced in the upper rows has become reality: "one [of the testaments] declared the divine works of Jesus to come, and the other accomplished them; as the former described the truth in figures, so the latter revealed it as present."[53] Here are represented the New Testament events that make up the liturgical year, and which are celebrated by the Church with special solemnity as steps of God's providential activity in the world, the progressive unfolding of salvation.[54]

Further down is the row of Deesis (Δέησις), which means "prayer." The angels and the saints, the apostles and their successors—the bishops, monks, martyrs, and so forth—are linked to the central object according to a well-established order: at the center is the Deesis proper, the tripartite icon of Christ, with His mother to the right and the Forerunner in a position of prayer to the left.[55] This entire row is nothing but a developed Deesis. It shows the result of the Incarnation and of Pentecost, the fullness of the New Testament church, the fulfillment of what is shown on the three upper rows of the iconostasis. It is therefore its central, essential part. The main theme of this row is the prayer of the Church for the world: this is the eschatological aspect of the Church.[56]

53 St Dionysius the Pseudo-Areopagite, *De ecclesiast. hierarchia*, ch. 3, 5, PG 3: 460; English trans. by Thomas L. Campbell, *The Ecclesiastical Hierarchy* (University Press of America, 1981), 38. It is possible that the Areopagitica, which were highly popular and influential in Russia at the time of the formation of the iconostasis, contributed to the distribution of the rows. These writings appeared in Russia in the form of a copy made by Metropolitan Cyprian from a Bulgarian translation of 1371.

54 This row usually consists of the icons of Easter (the myrrh-bearers at the tomb or the Descent into Hell) and those of the twelve major feasts: six of Christ (Nativity, Theophany, Entrance into the Temple, Entry into Jerusalem, Ascension, Transfiguration), four of the Virgin (Birth, Presentation in the Temple, Annunciation, Dormition), and two essentially ecclesiological icons (Pentecost and the Exaltation of the Cross). Where there is space, icons of other, less important feasts are added, as well as the icon of the Crucifixion. As a rule, the icons are arranged according to the order of the liturgical year, but they sometimes follow the chronological order of the events commemorated.

55 The Deesis is known in literary documents from the seventh century. In the eulogy to St Cyrus and St John, written by St Sophronius of Jerusalem, we read: "We have entered the church... We saw a great and marvellous icon where in the middle were represented in color the Lord Jesus Christ. To the left was the Mother of God, our Sovereign Virgin Mary; to the right was John the Baptist, the Forerunner of the Savior... Here were also represented some of the glorious choir of the apostles and prophets and some of the martyrs, among them were Cyrus and John, martyrs" (*SS. Cyri et Joannis Miracula*, PG 87, 3:3557).

56 This is why on the classical Russian iconostasis, the holy warrior-saints and princes are never

The lowest level of the iconostasis is called "local": a large icon is placed on either side of the Holy Door. Customarily, this includes the images of Christ and, to His right (left with regard to the viewer) that of the Mother of God with the child. It is true that there are exceptions to this rule: the icon of Christ is sometimes replaced by that of a saint or of a feast to which the church has been dedicated. It is in front of these that, since the end of the iconoclastic period, the entrance prayers are recited. These include a confession of the image of Christ before the icon itself, and a prayer to the Virgin in front of her icon. These local icons are the object of a most direct and intimate veneration: they are kissed, candles are lit before them, and so forth. On the side doors, north and south, archangels or saintly deacons are represented, since deacons play the role of angels ("messengers") in the celebration of the Liturgy. On the south door, the archangel is sometimes replaced by the Good Thief, which emphasizes that the sanctuary is a symbol of paradise: "Today you will be with me in paradise" (Lk 23:43). If additional space remains on each side of the doors, it is occupied by other icons. This row does not have the order or the rhythm of the others; it is often asymmetrical, and adorned with icons that vary widely, depending on local needs and on the character of the church.

The central door, called "Royal" or "Holy," has existed as long as the altar screen; it has been adorned with icons from the earliest times.[57] Customarily, the Annunciation is represented here, with the four evangelists underneath. St Basil and St John Chrysostom often appear holding in their hands the book of the Gospels, or phylacteries with texts from their liturgies.[58] On the symbolic level, this doorway to the sanctuary preeminently represents the entrance to the Kingdom of God. The Annunciation is the starting point, the beginning of our salvation, opening the gate to the Kingdom. It represents the good news announced by the evangelists. Their preaching is addressed directly to the one who comes to this spot to partake of His Kingdom. It is on the solea, the dividing line between the sanctuary and the nave, that the faithful receive communion. This is why the

represented in armor or with weapons. The reverse is true in the case of murals. No exceptions to this rule are found, except during the period of decadence in the eighteenth and nineteenth centuries.

57 A. Grabar believes that the Royal Door had been so decorated from the fifth-sixth centuries ("Un portillon d'iconostase sculpté au Musée National de Belgrade," *Recueil des travaux de l'Institut d'Etudes byzantines* no 7 [Belgrade, 1961], 16).

58 Sometimes one also finds Royal Doors with images of numerous saints on them.

Eucharist is often represented above the Holy Door (Fig. 35). It is the liturgical transposition of the Last Supper, when Christ Himself gave communion to the apostles. On one side He gives them the Bread, and on the other the cup. This two-fold representation expresses that communion must be given under both species. The image of the communion of the apostles emphasizes the ministry of Christ, the sovereign Sacrificer. This ministry is directly expressed here by His priestly actions.

As an image, this iconographic structure of the iconostasis, the order of its rows, corresponds to the liturgical prayer immediately preceding the epiclesis: "You and Your Only-begotten Son and Your Holy Spirit, did bring us from non-existence into being, and when we had fallen away did raise us up again, and did not cease to do all things until You had brought us back to heaven and had endowed us with Your kingdom which is to come."

On a flat surface facing the faithful, easily seen from any distance, the iconostasis unfolds the ways of the divine economy: the history of man created in the image of the triune God and the working of God in history. The ways of divine revelation and the work of salvation descend from top to bottom, beginning with the image of the Holy Trinity, the eternal counsel, the source of the life of the world and of divine economy. The Old Testament preparations, the prefigurations and prophecies gradually lead to the row of feasts—the actualization of what had been prepared. From there they extend to the coming completion of the divine economy—the row of the Deesis. All this is centered on the person of Christ, One of the Holy Trinity. The central image of Christ is the key to the entire iconostasis. For "Christ is never alone. He is always the Head of His Body. In Orthodox theology and devotion alike, Christ is never separated from His Mother, the Theotokos, and His 'friends,' the saints. The Redeemer and the redeemed belong together inseparably."[59] Thus the Deesis shows that "the final purpose of the Incarnation was that the Incarnate should have 'a body,' which is the Church, the new Humanity, redeemed and reborn in the Head."[60] The row containing the Deesis therefore represents the culmination of the historic process. It is an image of the Church in its eschatological dimension. The entire life of the Church is found on it, epitomized, as it were, in its supreme, unvarying destina-

59 Georges Florovsky, "The Ethos of the Orthodox Church," *The Ecumenical Review* 12, no 2 (1960), 195.

60 *Ibid.*

35. A 16th-century Russian Holy (or Royal) Door

tion: the intercession of the saints and of the angels for the world. All the figures represented are united in one body. It is the union of Christ with His Church: the total Christ, the Head and the body (*totus Christus, Caput et corpus*), a union accomplished by the sacrament of the Eucharist.

In response to divine revelation, the paths of the human ascent lead from the bottom to the top through an acceptance of the preaching of the apostles (the evangelists on the Holy Door), by the conformity of the human will to the divine (as represented by the Annunciation on the Holy Door), through prayer, and finally by partaking of the eucharistic mystery—man accomplishes the ascent to the reality represented on the row of the Deesis: the unity of the Church. Indeed, the Church is the ongoing Pentecost; and through the power of the Holy Spirit, man is part of this Body of which Christ is the Head. The Eucharist builds up this Body of Christ. The iconostasis shows this by placing before the eyes of the faithful an image of the organism which they join as members. It shows the Church formed in the image of the divine Trinity, an image found at the top of the iconostasis: a multi-unity, in the image of the Tri-unity. This is the icon to which the icon of Christ leads the believer. "Another revelation unfolds before his eyes...the heavenly Liturgy, the eternal eucharistic sacrifice which originated for all eternity in the bosom of the Holy Trinity, which continues now, and forever unto the ages of ages."[61]

One scholarly point of view holds that the iconostasis somehow replaced, or repeated, the mural decoration of the church. Indeed, the essential elements of this decoration equally find their place on the iconostasis, and quite a few subjects are found in both. However, the connection that exists between mural decoration and the iconostasis can be understood only if one considers the purpose of the one and the other, the respective role of each, which is entirely different.

As a place of worship, a church in its totality is a liturgical space for the gathering of the faithful. Symbolically, it includes the entire universe, and thus it represents the *cosmic* dimension of the Church. Even if the mural decoration conforms to an overall scheme that requires certain fixed subjects in certain parts of the building, it nevertheless allows for a great variety of subjects in other parts of the building, the choice of which is more or less left to discretion, depending on the needs of the place and of the moment.

61 Archimandrite Cyprian, *The Eucharist* (in Russian) (Paris, 1947), 342.

By contrast, the subjects on the iconostasis are strictly defined for the whole as well as for each of its parts. The iconostasis shows the development of the Church in time, its life until its fulfillment in the Parousia, its gradual realization from Adam to the Last Judgment. It thereby discloses the significance of the time process, the meaning acquired by time through its participation in an act outside time, the Eucharist. The Eucharist "incorporates every age and all generations...It is history 're-duced to unity,' the renewal of the salutary event which makes us encounter all the ages before and after us."[62] The iconostasis shows what is created by the cooperation between man and God. It reveals this synergy: people and events give history its meaning and sanctify it. It thereby indicates how everyone has a place in this historical process and defines the significance of the present moment for each person. The meaning of the boundary between the sanctuary and the nave, between the eternal and the temporal, is thereby pointed out—a meaning that consists of the interpenetration of the one by the other, their union. The believer enters the Holy of Holies of the New Testament, the Kingdom of God, "through the veil that is the flesh of Christ" (Heb 10:20)—this flesh that replaced the torn veil of the temple.[63] We recall how, according to St Gregory Palamas, "His deified flesh has received and communicates the eternal glory of the Deity; it is represented on the icons and worshipped insofar as it manifests the divinity of Christ, and it is that too which is offered to us in the sacrament of the Eucharist."[64]

The iconostasis therefore has more than merely a didactic meaning. It represents the ontological link between sacrament and image, and shows this glorious body of Christ, the same real body given in the Eucharist and represented on the icon. This is why, during the iconoclastic period, the Orthodox defenders of images viewed the icon not only as a proof of the Incarnation, because it pointed to the historicity of Christ, but also as witnessing to the reality of the sacrament of the Eucharist. "If that witness

62 J. Tyciak, *Maintenant Il vient*, 34, translated from the German (1963), 34.

63 The fact that St Paul compares the flesh of Christ to the veil of the Temple could certainly have led people to put a veil in front of the Holy of Holies in New Testament churches. This analogy, with all the richness of its meaning, was subsequently extended to the sanctuary screen (at the Church of St Sophronius in Jerusalem, for example, the architrave) and later to the iconostasis as a whole. The analogy in the latter case, with the Old Testament veil torn at the time of the Crucifixion, remains alive within the consciousness of the church.

64 J. Meyendorff, *A Study of Gregory Palamas*, trans. G. Lawrence (New York, 1974), 138.

is impossible, the Eucharist itself loses its reality."[65] Indeed, the true theological dimensions of the iconoclastic controversy are seen here. This also explains the intransigence of the defenders of the icon.

From this perspective, the function of the iconostasis at the very edge of the sanctuary is precisely to show what *is not* an image, but is real and by its very nature different from an image. Christ does not show Himself in the holy gifts: He *gives* Himself. He *shows* Himself in the icon. The visible aspect of the Eucharist is an image which can never be replaced, either by the imagination or by a mere contemplation of the sacrament.

What Russian hesychasm contributed to the development of the classic iconostasis was a living, existential interiorizing of the sacrament of the Eucharist, of the content of the icon of Christ. Hence the awareness and the uncommonly eloquent indication of the link between the two. There is first the slow growth of the body of Christ in the Old Testament (comparable to the care with which Matthew and Luke specify the genealogy of Christ) and its actuality in the New. In other words, it is a proof of its historicity through images, a proof that excludes all abstract thought. We recall that for the iconoclasts, the sacrament of the Eucharist was an image, the only possible one. Thus, by rejecting the icon and therefore implicitly the reality of the Incarnation, they necessarily denied the reality of the eucharistic body and blood. Significantly, the period that witnessed the formation of the iconostasis coincided exactly with a new questioning by Russian heretics of both the image and of the sacrament of the Eucharist. In our time, as has so often been the case in history, this issue takes on great importance.

But the crucial contribution of hesychasm was undeniably the expansion of the tripartite Deesis into an entire series of intercessory saints, with Christ of the Last Judgment at its center (Fig. 36). This development was deemed so important that the iconographers greatly enlarged the size of the Deesis (3.15 meters high in the Cathedral of the Dormition, in Vladimir). They gave it a dominant place, no doubt understanding the impact of this rank of the iconostasis, placed in close proximity to the communicant (the Deesis created by the hesychasts Andrei Rublev, Theophanes the Greek, and their companions). Indeed, to the reality of the

65 J. Meyendorff, *Christ in Eastern Christian Thought*, trans. Y. Dubois (New York: St Vladimir's Seminary Press, 1987), 190.

36. *Christ in Glory*, 15th century.
The Metropolitan Museum of Art, New York (no. 44.101).

eucharistic body corresponds the reality of the judgment. This is clearly emphasized in all the prayers before communion ("I eat and drink my judgment"). The communicant becomes one body with Christ (*syssoma*, "a joint-body," Eph 3:6), the body of the Second Coming. This is why this row is presented exactly above the place where the faithful receive communion. It emphasizes this aspect of judgment and intercession. Only by passing through communion-judgment is one able to interiorize the reality depicted on the iconostasis—a reality that corresponds to the eucharistic prayers for all those who are united by the sacrament of the Body and Blood: the patriarchs, fathers, and prophets fallen asleep in the Old Testament faith; the apostles, martyrs and confessors (who fell asleep in the New); and finally the living, including the faithful present in the church. It is therefore the reality of the Body joined to that of the image which, together with the word, ensures fullness in liturgical participation: the physical union and the union of prayer through the image.

Thus the iconostasis is far from being a mere recapitulation of decorations on the walls. Nor is it a haphazard collection of icons lacking didactic significance—a collection "that has become a false focal point of the Byzantine church," unrelated to the eucharistic sacrament, and "creating an obstacle to keep the lay people, unworthy creatures, at a distance" (*sic* !).[66] Such a point of view is still widespread. However, as P. Florenskii states,

> the iconostasis does not conceal any fascinating, strange secrets from the faithful, as some imagine in their ignorance and self-conceit. On the contrary, the iconostasis shows them, the half-blind, the mysteries of the sanctuary. It opens the gate to another world for them, the limping and disabled—a door that is closed to them because of their stagnation. It announces the Kingdom of Heaven by shouting into their ears that remain deaf.[67]

Clearly, when it is materially impossible to have a complete iconostasis in a church, it can undoubtedly be limited to the Deesis itself, or even to the single icon of Christ. However, deliberately to forgo the fullness of the iconostasis is to repudiate what the Church teaches through it.

66 Julian Walter, "The Origins of the Iconostasis," *Eastern Churches Review* 3, no 3 (1971), 261, 266, 267.

67 P. Florenskii, "The Iconostasis," (in Russian), *Bogoslovskie Trudy* 9 (Moscow, 1972), 97.

37. *St Cyril of Beloozero.* 16th-century Russian icon.
A. Rublev Museum, Moscow.

14

The Muscovite Councils of the 16th Century: Their Role in Sacred Art

The sixteenth century is one of the most complex periods in the history of Russian sacred art. On the one hand, it remains one of the most brilliant, especially during the first five decades; the dominant trend in art still preserved all the spiritual richness, the simplicity, the sobriety and monumental character of the image (Fig. 37). On the other hand, a noticeable change takes place around mid-century. This change develops, forms a trend that clearly crystalizes in the seventeenth century and gradually leads to a break with the tradition. This change is due to a variety of external and internal reasons rooted in the preceding epoch. We have already noted how the period that followed Rublev already witnessed a gradual disappearance of the meaning of the spiritual basis of the image. The hesychast spirit weakened, spiritual development declined. What happened was not unlike what had occurred in Byzantium where, "since the official triumph of hesychasm and the canonization of Palamas himself, the response to his doctrine became merely routine, devoid of any true understanding of its spiritual, creative essence."[1] Because of this decline, the creative living tradition in Byzantium gave way to a conservatism that would subsequently be defenseless against the external influences coming from the West. In Russia, in the period under scrutiny, hesychasm gradually ceased to play a leading role. In the spiritual life, the trend headed by St Joseph of Volokolamsk achieved dominance. Though a hesychast himself, St Joseph accorded great importance to outward asceticism and to intense activity, whereby prayer became subordinate to social service. For his followers and successors, it was education that occupied the first place. The spiritual life dwindled and grew more narrow; it was oriented above all to the external. Parallel with the orientation of spirituality in the direction of a ritualized, strictly regulated piety, the same, formalistic

1 Alexander Schmemann, "An Unpublished Work by St Mark of Ephesus on the Resurrection" (in Russian), *Pravoslavnaia Mysl'* (Paris, 1951), 144.

orientation is found in art. The dogmatic content of the image begins to lose its predominant significance, and is not always understood to be its very basis. The preference of the Josephites for well-ordered beauty and well-arranged harmony encouraged quantity, to the detriment of quality.

The external historical conditions of Muscovite Russia likewise contributed to a decline of the spiritual life and a corresponding change in art. With the fall of Constantinople (1453) and the occupation of the Balkans by the Turks, the slow reorientation of Russia began: from the circle of Orthodox countries in the East it turned toward the sphere of western culture.[2] This was the beginning of the influence of western ideas. At this time, this influence upon sacred art was expressed merely by the borrowing of certain subjects and details of an iconographic character, revamped in the spirit of traditional painting. These influences, which entered Russia by way of the border cities (above all Novgorod and Pskov, which had intense relations with the West) gradually intensified, and found a fertile soil in the "intellectual stagnation" so typical of the period.

In Russia, the middle of the sixteenth century was a time of compilation and conservation. Just as Moscow moved to the forefront of the united principalities, so the Muscovite metropolis became the center toward which the local spiritual traditions converged. Civil as well as church life was organized, the situation was assessed, and everything received from the

2 The beginning of this process, which took its definitive form in the sixteenth century and reached completion under Peter I, goes back to the end of the fifteenth century, the reign of Ivan III (1462-1505). When he married Sophia Paleologus, who had been educated by the Pope in Rome, the princely court experienced a true infatuation for the West. When Gennadius, the Archbishop of Novgorod, undertook a new translation of the Bible, the work was directed by a Dominican friar called Benjamin; and it was the Vulgate that was used as a reference. Translations from the German and Latin of western spiritual literature, made in "the archbishop's residence," appeared in Novgorod ("On the Veneration of Sophia, Divine Wisdom in Byzantium and in Russia" [in Russian], *Trudy V siezda russkikh akademicheskikh organizatsii za granitsei*, vol. I [Sofia: 1932], 497). At this time, the anti-heretical struggle bore the stamp of western methods. The struggle against Latinism, while being characteristic of the period, got on well with a certain leaning toward the West. Western influences keep increasing and present a very complex phenomenon in the sixteenth century. At the time of the Renaissance in the West, the arts and sciences were inseparable from magic and all sorts of occult lore. What foreigners such as the Roman Catholic Nicholas the German, private physician of the great prince, imported to Russia were astrology, a belief in the Wheel of Fortune, and other superstitions which St Maximus the Greek, a great defender of the true faith, labeled as "Greek, Latin, and Chaldean teachings." To this unhealthy amalgam should have been opposed the vigilance, sobriety of thought and of the heart found in hesychasm, but it had already weakened in Russia.

historical and spiritual past was recorded. But what was thus compiled already contained some elements foreign to the Orthodox tradition, elements that had been introduced as a result of the decline of the spiritual life, and also because of the contemporary historical situation.

The "Hundred-Chapters Council" (Stoglav)

On June 21, 1547 Moscow was devastated by a terrible fire that destroyed cathedrals, monasteries and palaces. After this disaster everything had to be rebuilt, and the burned icons had to be replaced. Such a task could not be faced solely with the means the Muscovite iconographers had at their disposal.

> The sovereign Orthodox tsar...sent people to Novgorod the Great, Smolensk, Dmitrov and Zvenigorod to find holy, precious icons. Numerous holy and wondrous icons were brought from several cities. They were placed in the Cathedral of the Annunciation to be venerated by the tsar and all the Christians, until new icons could be painted. The sovereign sent for iconographers from Novgorod the Great, Pskov, and other cities. The iconographers arrived, and the sovereign tsar ordered some to paint icons, others to decorate the walls of the palaces...[3]

In the Kremlin, the work of the iconographers was supervised by Sylvester, archpriest of the Annunciation Cathedral, born in Novgorod, and the private tutor of Tsar Ivan the Terrible. It was probably on his orders that the iconographers created a whole series of symbolic icons which were subsequently characterized as "theological-didactic." The themes of these compositions became the topic of discussions and conciliar decisions in the sixteenth and seventeenth centuries. They reflected the beginning of the change that had made itself felt both in iconography and, much more importantly, in the consciousness of the faithful, in their attitude toward and their understanding of the icon. At the beginning, this transformation was not interpreted in a positive manner, by a definition of principle, but rather through a lack of clarity and preciseness in reasoning.

In 1551 a council, known in history as the "Hundred-Chapters Council" (*Stoglav*), was held in Moscow, presided over by Metropolitan Macarius.[4] The

3 *Communications of the Imperial Society of Russian History and Antiquities* (1847), 19. Quoted by N. Andreev, "The Affair of Diak Viskovatyi" (in Russian), *Seminarium Kondakovianum* V (Prague, 1932).

4 The name is derived from the fact that the decisions of this council are divided into one hundred chapters. The Russian text was edited in 1890, in Moscow. There is a French

council was convoked to bring order into various aspects of Church life, including art, and because, in the words of the tsar, "morals are wavering, arbitrariness has set in, and everyone acts according to his own will." Among the regulations of the *Stoglav* concerning art, some addressed specific, concrete questions (chapter XLI, questions 1 and 7), while others dealt with the basis and the very principles of icon painting and with the painters themselves.

Of the two specific questions discussed by the council, one (question 7 of chapter XLI) dealt with the possibility of representing on icons persons, living or dead, who were not saints. By way of example, the tsar, in asking this question, mentioned the icon with the inscription, "Come, O peoples, let us adore the Divinity in three Persons."

> There, at the bottom, tsars, princes, prelates, and people of lower standing are represented while they were still alive...They are painted even on the icon of the All-pure Mother of God in Tikhvin, which describes her miracles...We must reflect on this, remembering the writings of the holy Fathers. Is it proper on icons to include both the living and the dead at prayer?

The council replied that the traditions and "the writings of the holy Fathers," as well as the icons themselves, attested to such practice.[5] Indeed, we know that the tradition of painting persons who are not saints on icons and mural church decorations, where required by the subject, goes back to the earliest Christian times. Such representations were therefore not a novelty but common in sacred art. By way of examples, the council enumerated the following as contemporary illustrations of such iconographic subjects: the Exaltation of the Cross, the Protection of the Virgin, the Procession of the Wood of the Cross, and the Last Judgment. In the latter case, "not only are saints painted, but also a great number of unbelievers from various countries."[6] The custom of representing non-

translation by M. Duchesne, *Le Stoglav ou les Cent chapitres* (Paris, 1920).

5 *Stoglav*, 111.

6 *Ibid.*, 174. Nonetheless, the very existence of this problem leads to questionable statements about the reasons why it arose in the first place. It has been attributed to the fact that in the sixteenth century, "secular painting" began to infiltrate Russian iconography (N. Pokrovskii, *The Monuments of Christian Art and Iconography* [in Russian] (St Petersburg, 1900), 347), or to ideas from portrait painting (N. Andreev, "Metropolitan Macarius and Religious Art" [in Russian], *Seminarium Kondakovianum* VII [Prague, 1935], 241). It is assumed, therefore, that this question posed by the tsar presupposed the principle of representing on icons portraits of non-saints, both living and dead. Consequently, the answer of the council is considered inadequate in relation to the scope of the question asked (N. Andreev, *ibid.*, note 70). But at

saints on icons and wall paintings must have been widespread at the time, due largely to new subjects and compositions, particularly in the case of icons of saints containing illustrations of scenes from their life. But the balance had been upset, and the non-saints often occupied too much space in the composition. Naturally, the question of the propriety of such representations had to arise.

Another question, the first in chapter XLI, is more significant for us. It deals with the iconography of the Holy Trinity:

> On icons of the Holy Trinity, some represent a cross in the nimbus of only the middle figure, others on all three. On ancient and on Greek icons, the words "Holy Trinity" are written at the top, but there is no cross in the nimbus of any of the three. At present, "IC XC" and "the Holy Trinity" are written next to the central figure. Consult the divine canons and tell us which practice one should follow. The Reply: painters must paint icons according to the ancient models, as the Greeks painted them, as Andrei Rublev and other renowned painters made them. The inscription should be: "the Holy Trinity." Painters are in no way to use their imagination.[7]

As we can see, this deals with the traditional Orthodox representation of the Trinity in the form of three Angels.

Though we do not know why, some scholars believe that the council's reply to the question lacks precision,[8] or that "the question remained without solution, since the Fathers of the council were only able to make a general statement concerning the need to follow ancient models,"[9] especially the icon of Andrei Rublev. But in fact, if one takes into account the sense of the question, the answer is very clear and specific: the council decided that there should be only one general inscription, "the Holy

this time, portraits that imitated nature did not exist. Whether a man was alive or not, a saint or not, his image was made in the style of an icon; if not, the image would be meaningless. Thus, for the council, there could not have been another type of image-portrait. Moreover, the very manner in which the question was formulated does not in our opinion justify giving it a scope it did not have. Indeed, the question was not on how to represent people who were not saints (as a portrait or not), but whether their representation was allowed on the icon at all. The question's precise wording is, "Is it proper to paint them?" It seems to us, therefore, that N. Pokrovskii's position is justified when he gives as reason for this question the fact that the presence of non-saints in icons, as well as their great number, could perturb and scandalize the faithful. One should add the possibility that such representations could be criticized by the heretics.

7 *Stoglav*, 107 (There are some errors in this French translation, due to the translator's lack of knowledge about iconography).

8 N. Pokrovskii, *Monuments*, 356-7.

9 A. I. Nekrasov, *Figurative Art in Ancient Russia* (in Russian) (Moscow, 1937), 278.

Trinity," and that none of the figures depicted should have either an inscription or a cross in the nimbus.[10] It is true that the council did not give a theological explanation to its ruling: it limited itself to referring to the authority of Andrei Rublev and to ancient models. Here, as in other instances, the weakness of the Hundred Chapters Council can be seen—a weakness which was later to have disastrous consequences for Russian iconography.

Returning to the question at hand, one should note that most of the representations of the Trinity that have come down to us have neither a cross in the nimbus nor any identifying inscription. However, in both Greek and Russian iconography, before and after Rublev, but particularly in later works, the angel in the middle—always interpreted by the iconographers as symbolizing the second Person of the Trinity—is sometimes depicted with a cross in the nimbus bearing the inscription *ho ôn*,[11] IC XC, and with a scroll in its hand instead of a staff.[12] As the reference of the *Stoglav* indicates, the icon by Andrei Rublev contained no such specification. At the time of the struggle against the heresy of the Judaizers, who denied the divinity of Christ and the Orthodox doctrine of the Holy Trinity, all three angels were sometimes represented with a cross in their nimbus. Moreover, though indeed very rarely, icons are found in which

10 N. V. Malitskii, "Contribution to the History of the Composition of the Old Testament Trinity" (in Russian), *Seminarium Kondakovianum* II (Prague, 1927), 43, shared this opinion. The decision of the council has certainly helped to stabilize the iconography of Andrei Rublev's Trinity by making it "a canonical model," in a certain sense. However, there is no reason to view this decision as the fixing of an unchangeable iconographic outline, as is sometimes said.

11 There is an inaccuracy in the study made by N. Pokrovskii of the council's decision on this subject. In *Monuments*, 353, he views the cruciferous halo as an attribute of the Divinity. In truth, the cross in the halo is an attribute belonging exclusively to Jesus Christ: it designates the sufferings he underwent in His humanity. The inscription *ho ôn*, "The Being," (*ho* is the article, *ôn* the present participle of the verb "to be") indicates His Divinity. This "Son of man" represented in the icon is the same God who, in the Old Testament, spoke to Moses (Ex 3:14). Gregory the Theologian writes: "This name is the one He gives Himself when He speaks to Moses on the mountain. He concentrates in Himself the fullness of being which has neither beginning nor end, which is like an ocean of being, unlimited and infinite, transcending the boundaries of every concept of time or of nature" (*Oratio* XXXVII, PG 35: 317BC). This inscription is explained in the same way by Maximus the Confessor in his commentary on the halo of the Lord.

12 The oldest examples of images where the angel in the middle is understood as Christ are in a tenth-century Greek Bible (where His halo is cruciferous) in the Bilbiothèque Nationale (Paris), and in an eleventh-century Cappadocian fresco (see M. Alpatov, "La Trinité dans l'art byzantin et l'école de Roublev," *Echos d'Orient* [April-June, 1927]).

the inscription "IC XC" appears not only next to the angel in the middle, but also next to the two others. Both cases can be interpreted as an attempt to emphasize the equal honor of the Three, though such attempts falsify Orthodox doctrine. It is true that many patristic commentaries give a certain theoretical justification for specifying the angel in the middle. Nonetheless, the inscription "IC XC" on this image is an error, because the name of the God-man is applied there to an image that is not His direct, concrete representation. "When the Word became flesh...then He received the name of Christ," St John of Damascus wrote.[13] It is then that He also suffered. This is why it is wrong to put a cross in the nimbus of the middle Angel in the Holy Trinity. To depict such a nimbus, and the inscription "IC XC," on the other two angels is even more erroneous. Indeed, in this case the signs of the Incarnation and Passion of the Son of God would be attributed to the other Persons of the Holy Trinity, thereby assigning to them the specific economy that is proper to the second Person. The common will of the Trinity, that makes the three Persons share the economy of the redemption, is one of the basic truths of the Christian faith. But

> this same unity of nature and of the divine will of the God-man with His Father and the Holy Spirit excludes any possibility of transmitting His sufferings, accepted in His human nature and human will, to the common will and nature of the Holy Trinity. It is not the Holy Trinity that suffers with the Son, nor is it the Divinity of the Son consubstantial to that of the Father and the Spirit that suffered and died. It is the Hypostasis of the Son that suffered on the cross according to His humanity, by accepting this through the human will which only in Christ is distinguished from the one divine will common to the Father and the Spirit.[14]

Thus any specification, whether through an inscription or by a cross in the nimbus, is either an absurdity (in this case there would be three Christs) or a heresy condemned by the Church: "You fools, who attribute the passion to the Godhead, be silent!"[15]

Chapter XLIII of the conciliar decisions contains a question that is directly related to the iconography of the Holy Trinity, that of the "representation of the Godhead":

> The prelates, each in his own diocese, will carefully and with unflagging attention see to it that the good iconographers, and their apprentices, paint according to

13 *De fide orthodoxa* I, 4, ch. 6, PG 94, 1:1112.

14 V. Lossky, *The Discussion About Sophia* (in Russian) (Paris, 1936), 77.

15 Canon of Tone 7, Ode 9.

> the ancient models, and do not depict the divinity according to their own concept or assumptions. If Christ our God can be depicted in the flesh, He is not depictable according to His Divinity; as John of Damascus has it, "Do not represent the divinity. You, blind ones, do not lie because the Godhead is simple and indivisible, inaccessible to the eye. But in representing the image of the flesh, I venerate and believe, and I glorify the Virgin who gave birth to the Son..."[16]

As can be seen, this text is not conspicuous for its clarity. In its obvious sense, it seems to refer to the divinity of Christ. But Christ is represented in His humanity, and no one has ever attempted to depict or describe His divinity, His undescribable Divine nature. In Orthodox thought, the question of whether one could depict the Godhead or not had never arisen, as making no sense. Yet here we have an Orthodox council that strongly accuses the iconographers of trying to represent the divinity "according to their own conception." The contrast between the depictable flesh of Christ and His divinity, which is undepictable, seems to suggest that there was some representation of the Deity other than the image of the incarnate Son of God. Indeed, at the time of the *Stoglav,* there already existed three iconographic representations of the Trinity: the traditional Old Testament Trinity, the image called "the Paternity" (God the Father with the Son in His lap, and the Holy Spirit in the form of a dove), and the "New Testament Trinity," the Father and the Son seated on a throne, with the dove between them. At the council no question was asked, at least not directly, about the iconographic content of the last two representations. The lack of clarity in the conciliar decision has led some scholars to conclude that "the precise iconography of the Trinity was passed over in silence" by the council.[17] However, as we have seen, the council gave a clear response about the iconography of the Old Testament Trinity, about which a question had arisen. Thus an iconographic subject

16 *Stoglav,* 136. This text does not appear literally in the writings of John of Damascus, but it may derive from liturgical texts. The Hundred-Chapters Council generally treated sources with a great deal of freedom, as is known. Metropolitan Philaret of Moscow went so far as to entertain doubts: "Does a council that resorts to lies to support its opinions and attributes to the holy Fathers and Apostles non-existing doctrines and canons, deserve the name of Church Council?" ("Conversation With an Old-Believer," *Works,* vol. 1 [Moscow, 1835-1836], 180-205). Cited by V. Nikonov, "The Stoglav" [in Russian], *The Journal of the Moscow Patriarchate,* no 9 [1951], 46).

17 N. K. Goleizovskii, "The *Message to an Iconographer* and the Echoes of Hesychasm in Russian Painting in the Fifteenth and Sixteenth Centuries," (in Russian) *Vizantiisky Vremennik* 26 (Moscow, 1965), 220.

that was apparently hard for the council to define, and which was not connected to the historicity of the Gospel—this basic principle of Orthodox iconography—was "passed over in silence." A comparison of the regulations concerning the Old Testament Trinity with the context of chapter XLIII has allowed certain scholars to conclude that the council attempted to limit the representation of the Trinity to this one iconographic type and thereby "to prevent any attempt to depict God the Father in icons of the Trinity, as was done in the West."[18] Indeed, the quoted text, as well as the instruction given to iconographers at the beginning of chapter XLII to "apply themselves to paint the corporeal image of Our Lord God and Savior Jesus Christ" and the decision concerning the Old Testament Trinity (chapter XLI), allow us to conclude that the "representation of the Divinity" refers precisely to the icon of God the Father—an image which, two years later, would provoke impassioned discussions that continue to our day. Let us recall that the image of God the Father on frescoes and icons ("the Paternity") was still unusual at the time of the *Stoglav.* Moreover, and this certainly is essential, this image remained ambiguous for a long time, as we shall see when we study this iconographic subject: it lacked precision and lent itself to diverse interpretations.[19]

In Russia, the first known example of the so-called "New Testament Trinity" is found in the famous quadripartite icon in the Cathedral of the

18 G. Ostrogorsky, "Les décisions du Stoglav au sujet de la peinture d'images et les principes de l'iconographie byzantine," *Orient et Byzance*, Recueil à la mémoire de Th. Ouspensky I (Paris, 1930), 402.

19 N. K. Goleizovskii detects, in the attitude taken by the council on the subject of the representability of the Deity, the influence of certain texts in the second and third treatises of the *Message to an Iconographer*, that comment on the image of the Trinity and which justify, according to him, "almost any representation of the Divinity" (*op. cit.*, 228). If certain texts of the third treatise permit such a conclusion, the second treatise categorically prevents it. We have seen that a very clear line was drawn in it between prophetic visions and sensory manifestations—elements that are totally confused in the third treatise. It is stated there specifically that God "does not appear as He is, but as the viewer may see Him," that is, in very different ways. Such a commentary can indeed justify any representation of the Deity. It should be added that, in spite of certain sometimes literal coincidences between the second and third treatises, there is a clear difference between them not only in content but also in the manner of exposition. In the one, such content is expressed briefly and with great precision; in the other, with prolixity and emphatically. In the latter, the author tries hard to make his text more pompous and to express his thought in a more sentimental, emphatic way, but the thought itself loses clarity. This leads us to believe that these two texts were written by two different authors.

Annunciation. It was painted after the fire by iconographers from Pskov on order from the archpriest Sylvester, the closest collaborator of Metropolitan Macarius. This image could hardly remain unnoticed, especially since it was to one of the themes of this same icon ("Come, O peoples, let us adore...") that the tsar referred to in his question concerning the representation of non-saints. We must believe that the council had its reasons for "passing over in silence" all iconography of the Holy Trinity aside from the Old Testament Trinity. First, it is possible that neither the fathers of the council, nor Metropolitan Macarius himself, had any clear concept about the subject of representing the Divinity. But then, it is not clear why, two years later, the same Macarius would suddenly defend so harshly the representation of God the Father. Certainly, his view on this question may well have changed. On the other hand, some scholars believe that there was less than total unanimity on all points between the council and the metropolitan.[20] There may not have been agreement on this point either. One may venture this hypothesis: did the lack of precision of the conciliar judgments not derive from the fact that the fathers could not decide whether to adopt the metropolitan's attitude or to challenge it directly, and that they were satisfied with merely making allusions? On the other hand, the thinking of the council may have been influenced by the third treatise of the *Message to an Iconographer* which, in contrast to the second treatise, shows evidence of confusion and a lack of clarity about the prophetic visions and the apparitions in the Old Testament. At any rate, the inaccuracy of this text may have introduced uncertainty in the argumentation of the councils, which clearly avoids naming an image that seems to it incomprehensible.

The questions dealing with the very basis of iconography and with the iconographers are grouped together in this same chapter XLIII. Here, the essential principles seem to evanesce into secondary considerations: on morality, on the supervision of painters, on their relationships with their apprentices, and so forth.

The council required that icons be painted according to ancient models,[21] "in the image and likeness, according to the essence, by looking

20 For example, I. N. Zhdanov believed that Macarius did not exercise a great influence on the decisions of the council. See N. Andreev, "Metropolitan Macarius and Religious Art" (in Russian), *Seminarium Konkokovianum* VII (Prague, 1935), 239, note 59; also, G. Ostrogorsky, "Les décisions du Stoglav," *Orient et Byzance* (Paris, 1930), 402.

21 *Stoglav*, 107, 118, 133, 134.

at images by ancient painters, and by keeping to good models." Such rules are repeated on several occasions and in various contexts. A new icon must present its prototype, the person or what is represented (be "in the image"), the similarity of features ("in the likeness"), and finally, must be "according to the essence"—since an Orthodox icon should correspond to the Tradition, to the iconographic canon established by the Church.[22] In art history, such demands—to follow the ancient iconographers, "not to invent anything according to one's imagination," also "not to depict the Godhead according to one's own concepts"—are usually viewed as an expression of the council's tendency to restrict the painter's creative initiative, even as an obligation to copy the models literally. One scholar goes so far as to say: "At the council of 1551, named *Stoglav*, the decision was made to introduce painting manuals—stereotyped models for the representation of saints and of entire compositions," by means of which, it is argued, the Church "endeavored to subordinate art to its regulations and established canons."[23] It is true that iconographic manuals (*podlinniki*) were widely disseminated after the *Stoglav*. However, such "collections adapted to those of the saints' lives arranged by month appeared only at the end of the sixteenth century, and were never either printed or approved legally."[24] The content of such manuals was determined by the printers themselves, not by the church authorities. They were books of drawings, of schematic models, serving as documentation used at various epochs by iconographers. Such sketches had nothing to do with the artistic quality of their works.[25] Their role was purely informational: they imparted data, and anyone who knows their content and is not blinded by prejudice certainly sees their place in the creative process. They prescribed nothing. They presented models, that is, the schematic characteristics of the saint (Fig. 38) or the event to be depicted, and

22 While speaking of ancient models, in chapter 27, the council ordered that old icons are to be cared for, preserved and repaired (pp. 82-3).

23 N. E. Mneva, *History of Muscovite Russia* (in Russian) (Moscow, 1965), 115. We have not found any such decision in the 1890 Moscow edition of the conciliar decisions, nor is it found in the Duchesne translation, *Le Stoglav* (Paris, 1920), which uses several editions of these texts. Moreover, the "inventions" and "imaginations" the council refers to are not deviations from artistic models but from the doctrinal foundations of the Orthodox image. As we have seen, they are concerned only with certain iconographic subjects, even their details: errors in the iconography of the Trinity, and "the representation of the Deity."

24 A. I. Nekrasov, *Figurative Art in Ancient Russia* (in Russian) (Moscow, 1937), 316.

25 A. Grabar, *Byzance* (Paris, 1963), 54.

38. Page from painters' manual.

thereby made the painter's work easier by preserving it from historical errors concerning any given person—in sum, they prevented the iconographer from falsifying the memory and the tradition of the Church.

We will return later to the issue of the connection between rules and artistic creation. Suffice it to say here that neither manuals (*podlinniki*) nor the ancient models the painters had to follow could limit the freedom of their creation.[26] The obligation to conform to ancient models is perfectly normal and in keeping with the foundations of sacred art. It has always existed in the Church. "Iconographers paint icons modelled not on poor images, but on beautiful ones that are noted for their antiquity," Theodore the Studite wrote in the ninth century.[27] Painting according to ancient models does not mean reproducing them literally. Such a requirement—even when it is expressed in a still more emphatic manner as, for example, in the Russian *Pedalion (The Rudder: Kormchaia Kniga)* cannot harm the painter's creativity in the least. We know that the *Stoglav* frequently referred to this work while pondering various issues, perhaps including the question about iconographers and about the painting of icons. At any rate, there is such a similarity between the *Pedalion* and the conciliar decisions that it is impossible not to see a direct influence. The *Rudder* states: "Let the iconographer's skills resemble those of the ancient models, the first painters, men of divine wisdom...Let him not add anything new himself, not even an iota; even if he thinks he knows many things, let him not dare transgress the tradition of the Fathers."[28] The request "not to add an iota" and the council's "not to invent anything according to one's imagination" essentially mean the same thing. What they proscribed is not artistic creation but departures from "the tradition of the Fathers," that is, from Orthodox doctrine, even if such departures seem inspired by the painter's great knowledge. During its entire existence, sacred art has always obeyed "rules

26 It should be added that no manual can keep a painter from making alterations if his creativity deviates from the Tradition of the church.

27 *Ad moniales*, PG 99:1176.

28 The chapter from which this passage is borrowed presents an almost complete analogy with the decisions of the Hundred Chapters Council concerning iconographers (their moral caliber, and so on). The text of the *Pedalion* used by the council was hand-written and was composed by Metropolitan Macarius just before the council. The chapters that deal with icon painting were not part of the printed edition of the *Pedalion*, but are found in the iconographic Manual (*podlinnik*) of Bolchakov, which appeared under the direction of Uspenskii (Moscow, 1909).

and canons," or more precisely, it is always guided by them. It has never been hampered by them, as this art itself clearly demonstrates.[29]

Aside from concrete issues and iconographic principles, the *Stoglav's* essential prescriptions aimed at raising the level of quality of iconography and the moral level of iconographers. Chapter XLIII, the longest, is devoted to these two topics. It sometimes deals in great detail with the most varied aspects of life and daily relationships. Unlike what happened with matters of principle, here the council expressed itself in a much more concrete and prolix fashion.

At this time, there was undoubtedly intense artistic activity, particularly in the towns and villages removed from the cultural centers. The council said:

> Let those who up to now have painted icons without having learned to, who paint fancifully, without either practice or conformity to the image...be obliged to learn from good masters. Whoever, by the grace of God, will start painting according to the image and likeness, let him paint. Let the one from whom God has withheld such a gift abandon painting altogether, so that the name of God may not be blasphemed by such paintings.[30]

Taking into account the overall situation in which sacred art found itself in the middle of the sixteenth century, the Hundred-Chapters Council endeavored to place it under the supervision of the higher church authorities.

> In all towns and villages and monasteries of their diocese, the archbishops and bishops will inspect the icon painters and will personally examine their works...The archbishops and bishops will personally assess the painters they have charged with supervising the others, and will control them rigorously.[31]

The council imposed supervision not only over the quality of sacred art, but also over the iconographer's moral life. It ordered bishops to forbid the painting of icons by any painter, master or apprentice, who "does not live a well-ordered life, but lives in impurity and in disorderly fashion.[32]

The control by the church hierarchy over the painting of icons, established by the *Stoglav,* has been judged in many different ways by

29 It is fair to say that certain present-day scholars have a rather "original" concept of the canon, which corresponds neither to its sense nor to its purpose. Since they inevitably and constantly are faced with facts that contradict their view, they explain such facts as so many "aberrations" ("*in spite of* the canon"), as resistance to the "constraining role of the Church," and so forth.

30 *Stoglav,* 135.

31 *Ibid.,* 136.

32 *Ibid.,* 135. At the same time, the council pays high regard to the iconographers who live up to such demands: they "will be highly respected and will receive special esteem...The great lords and the people of humble estate will honor such painters because they paint venerable icons" (p. 136).

scholars. Some considered such a measure perfectly normal and rational, the clergy being more able, if not to evaluate an icon's worth then at least to decide on its Orthodoxy or heterodoxy, on its conformity to the teaching of the Church or the lack of it.[33] N. Kondakov, by contrast, held the opposite view: "The degree to which spiritual censorship, established on principle, yielded nothing was, and still is, not worth talking about. Indeed, it was clear to all that the bishops were able neither to keep a close watch over iconography nor to teach iconographers anything."[34] And indeed, the situation did not change in the least, neither immediately after the council nor subsequently. During the seventeenth and eighteenth centuries, a whole series of authors describe the situation in the same terms as did the *Stoglav,* and they repeat the same demands.[35]

In the decisions of the *Stoglav,* "one no longer really sees that the work of the painters is viewed as spiritual asceticism, which was typical of the *Message to an Iconographer.*"[36] Nor does one see in them the view of the icon held by the author of the *Message.* He addressed himself to men who shared his views on the spiritual *praxis* of hesychasm, and, more generally, to all those to whom they served as models, people whose life conformed to theirs. By contrast, the council addressed itself to the great number of contemporary iconographers and their apprentices. It only gave them a minimum of moral rules, and established norms concerning their faithfulness to those rules and the production of icons. As we have seen, it was precisely in Russia that what constituted the very heart of Byzantine theology found its more complete incarnation, as much in life as in art. Russian theology expressed itself not so much in words as through the image, in an existential fashion, so to speak. But now this practical application of theology began to weaken: the spiritual attitude concerning the icon and its creation that characterized the *Message to an Iconographer*

33 G. Ostrogorsky, "Les décisions du Stoglav," *Orient et Byzance* (1930), 407; N. Pokrovskii, *Monuments,* 350.

34 *The Russian Icon* (in Russian), part I (Prague, 1931), 44.

35 J. Vladimirov, Symeon of Polotsk, Tsar Alexis, as we shall see. At the time of Peter the Great, the author I. T. Posochkov wrote: "From now on, illiterate peasants should be strictly forbidden to paint icons without having received written permission." After describing the very low level of icon painting, he concludes, "This is why in this domain more than in that of the other arts, tight supervision should be established" (*A Book About Wealth and Poverty* [in Russian] [Moscow, 1951], 146).

36 N. Goleizovskii, "The *Message to an Iconographer,*" *Vizant. Vremen.* 26 (Moscow, 1965), 225.

is altogether absent from the decisions of the *Stoglav*. Theoretically, the council formulated reasonable demands—"to follow the ancient iconographers," that is, to conform to the tradition. But deprived of its vital foundation, spiritual asceticism, such a demand degenerated into mere outward regulations that were imposed and accompanied by controls.

The Hundred-Chapters Council may appropriately be described not by what it was, but by what it lacked. It deviated from the essential. This council was certainly faithful, at least in theory, to everything Orthodox theological thought demanded of sacred art; but its judgments on specific iconographic subjects, like those on matters of principle (creation, the moral life, and so forth) lacked what was essential, an exposition of theological reasons. In principle, from the viewpoint of the Church, a reference to the traditions in the form of models "of great painters" was certainly normal—references to ancient classical masters always carried great weight—but the way this principle was understood and the lack of any criticism of existing models led the council to promote passive conservatism, instead of creativity within the Tradition.[37] If, on the one hand, it made a solid effort to prevent the play of the imagination, on the other hand, it did not take notice, or seemed not to take notice, of the existence of eccentricities in a whole series of new compositions. Hence the contradiction between the council's theoretical decisions and its practical attitude toward existing icons. Indeed, an entire series of images painted during this era, and which were at the council's disposal, contained embellishments by Russian painters, as we shall see. These fantasies were based not only on Byzantine models, but also on direct borrowings from Roman Catholicism. The *Stoglav* passively adopted all such departures from Orthodox doctrine—deviations which it was precisely supposed to correct. It thus allowed them to pursue their course and by doing so, it ratified "wavering morals."

The Hundred-Chapters Council appears as a phenomenon typical of an epoch of transition. It had serious consequences for the subsequent path of sacred art, not only in Russia but in the Orthodox Church in general. It reflected the theological powerlessness of its epoch, when the criterion of authenticity was

37 Similar measures were adopted by the *Stoglav* regarding liturgical music. In this area, as in the case of all ecclesiastical life, the council, using the same terminology, refers to existing practice—thus legitimizing all the deviations which existed in this period (see N. D. Uspenskii, *The Art of Ancient Russian Chant* [Moscow, 1965], 204.

replaced by conservatism, and the living, creative tradition by superficial regulations. The innovations, passively accepted by the *Stoglav*, continued to spread, and this led to opposition on the part of those who continued to view the icon in the traditional Orthodox fashion. Beginning with the second half of the sixteenth century, discussions started on the content of sacred art and the direction it should take. As we shall see, the ideas expressed in these discussions were symptomatic of the changes that were taking place.

The Council Of 1553-1554: The Trial Of John Viskovatyi

Two years after the Hundred-Chapters Council, the case of John Viskovatyi, Chancellor of the Foreign Office (*diak*),[38] required conciliar deliberations known under the title, *Instruction or Document on the Blasphemous Writings and the Doubts About the Holy and Venerable Icons of Chancellor John Mikhailov, Son of Viskovatyi, in the Year 1553.*[39]

What led Viskovatyi to speak out and begin discussions with Metropolitan Macarius were the new icons painted after the fire of 1547 by iconographers from Pskov in the Cathedral of the Annunciation, as well as the wall paintings done in the palace of the tsar.

> In the year 7062 [1553], on October 25, a discussion took place between the sovereign tsar and John Vasilievich, the crown prince, sole Ruler of all Russia, and his father, Macarius, Metropolitan of all Russia, the archbishops and bishops, the nobles and the entire holy assembly...The metropolitan said, "Sovereign, here in Moscow, your capital, four iconographer-syndics have been appointed, in conformity with the conciliar decision [by the *Stoglav*]. They were charged with

38 "Diak" means civil servant, in this instance, Minister of Foreign Affairs. His trial has been edited (in Russian) by O. Bodianskii in *Chteniia imperat. Ob. Istorii i drevnostei rossiiskikh*, Bk 2 (Moscow, 1858), based on the Volokolamsk monastery MS. This is the edition we have used here. The best and most detailed work on the subject is that of N. Andreev, "The Trial of Diak Viskovatyi" (in Russian), *Seminarium Kondakovianum* V (Prague, 1932). See also, "Metropolitan Macarius and Religious Art" (in Russian), *Semin. Kondak.* VII (Prague, 1936), and "The Monk Zenobius of Otnia on Iconography" (in Russian), *Semin. Kondak.* VIII (Prague, 1935). Viskovatyi's trial is sometimes attributed (twice by I. Grabar, Schweinfurth, Alpatov and Brunov) to the Hundred-Chapters Council, which is not correct. As N. Andreev points out, the mistake comes from an error in chronology. The council which studied this case convened at the end of 1554.

39 Of humble origin, having arrived at the high position of Minister of Foreign Affairs, Viskovatyi was an exceptional person: "In Moscow at the time, he was second to none"; "His intelligence, and his art as an unlearned Muscovite, amazed the foreign ambassadors," stated Rüssow, author of the *Livonian Chronicle*, (Andreev, *op. cit.*, 217).

> the supervision of all the iconographers, so that they paint according to the image and likeness...At this moment, chancellor John Mikhailov said, "It is not proper to represent either the invisible Godhead or the bodiless powers, as we see it done these days in the icon 'I believe in one God.'" When the metropolitan asked, "How should this be painted?", John replied, "One should write on this icon the words, 'I believe in one God, the Father Almighty, Maker of heaven and earth, and of all things visible and invisible.' Only the elements which follow this may one paint and represent iconographically." The metropolitan abruptly replied, "You speak and reason falsely on the holy icons. Such reasoning is the heresy of the Galatians who prohibit the painting in the flesh of the invisible bodiless powers, on earth." Also, "You are not allowed to express any opinion about God and the divine actions...You should mind your own business, the one entrusted to you. And do not lose your manuscript."[40]

In spite of this reply by the metropolitan, Viskovatyi did not keep quiet. In November he brought him a manuscript "of his thoughts and opinions about the holy icons," asking that it be examined by the council then being held in Moscow to deal with the heresy of Matvei Bashkin.[41]

Viskovatyi formulates the reason that had prompted him to speak in the following words:

> Lord, all my zeal has to do with the fact that the image of our Lord and Savior according to His economy in the flesh, as well as those of His All-pure Mother and of the saints that were well pleasing to Him, have been removed. Personal comments on the parables have been put in their places. It seems to me, Lord, that this expresses individual understanding, and not Holy Scripture.[42]

Viskovatyi ends the explanation of his doubts by asking the metropolitan for pastoral directives: "I bow before you, my Lord. Consider all my doubt, and instruct me in what is or is not according to God."[43]

The icons which contained the subjects that offended Viskovatyi and led to his protest were a series of new, symbolic compositions on the Creed, the Trinity and its works, the eternal Counsel, and the quadripartite icon in

40 O. Bodianskii, *op. cit.*, 1-2.

41 The council was not "summoned because of the trial of Viskovatyi," as N. Pokrovskii and N. E. Mneva state in *The Art of Muscovite Russia* (Moscow, 1965), 116. See also, Y. A. Lebedev, *Ancient Russian Art of the Tenth to the Seventeenth Century* (in Russian) (Moscow, 1962), 186.

42 O. Bodianskii, *op. cit.*, 11.

43 *Ibid.*, 12. When Viskovatyi brought his manuscript "and asked the metropolitan and the entire holy assembly to be so good as to verify it according to Holy Scripture," Macarius sent "this manuscript...to the autocrat of all Russia, asking what the pious tsar ordered him to do about this." The tsar sent the manuscript back to the metropolitan and ordered the council to discuss it, and to let him know the result (pp. 2-3).

the Cathedral of the Annunciation, which can still be found at the same place and included four subjects: "God rested on the seventh day," "Only-begotten Son and Word of God," "Come, O people, let us adore God in three Persons," and "In the tomb, in your flesh (Fig. 39)." Viskovatyi characterized some themes of these icons as "inventions," others as "Latin concepts." What was of concern was the image of God the Father, that of Christ "in the image of David," that of the young Christ as a warrior or naked, covered by the wings of the cherubim, and also that of the image of the Holy Spirit, "standing up, alone, in the likeness of an incomprehensible bird." These were precisely the subjects that the *Stoglav* had avoided, either by using imprecise terms or by passing over them in silence.

In his manuscript, Viskovatyi based and developed his point of view on the iconographic subjects that had offended him. "It is by basing himself on this manuscript that the metropolitan gave his answers to the council."[44]

Most of the contested subjects are no longer reproduced today and have lost their topicality. Nonetheless, they reveal the changes that were taking place in Russian sacred art, and this specific cast of mind that corresponded to the decay in the Church's awareness, of which we are not yet entirely free in our day.

The dispute began with one of Viskovatyi's most important points: "It is not proper to portray the invisible Deity." This had never been required of the icon, and the icon had never dared to do so. Now, however, iconographers began to depict the invisible Deity according to the vision of the prophet Daniel[45] in the icon depicting the Creed, or more precisely, its first article (God the Father), as well as in other compositions.

We have seen that the issue of representing the Deity had already been raised at *Stoglav*, though in a very imprecise form. The council had spoken out strongly against iconographers who, "according to their own imaginings," had portrayed the Deity in a form other than Christ, who is God representable in His flesh. If, in terms of chapter XLIII, it is possible

44 *Ibid.*, 3

45 "I saw in the night visions, and, behold, one like the Son of man came with the clouds of heaven, and came to the Ancient of Days..." (Dn 7:13). "I beheld till the thrones were cast down, and the Ancient of Days did sit, whose garment was white as snow, and the hair of his head like pure wool" (7:9).

39. The four-part icon from Cathedral of Annunciation, Moscow.

to conclude that this text was directed against the image of God the Father, here, by contrast, there can be no doubt. What had remained imprecise at the *Stoglav*, insufficiently expressed or simply passed over in silence, now came to the fore without ambiguity. The metropolitan and the council now began explicitly to defend the image of God the Father and the subjects which represented the "imaginative embellishments" that had theoretically been condemned two years earlier by the *Stoglav.*[46]

The metropolitan began his defense of the contested image with a long, detailed list of examples found in various churches. Referring to these models, he stressed their antiquity and above all their Greek origin. In order to confirm the legitimacy of the image of God the Father, he appealed to the testimony of the Athonite monks present at the council: there are twenty-one great monasteries on the Holy Mountain, "and in the holy churches it is impossible not to see the painted image of Lord Sabaoth or the Holy Trinity."[47] "In our Russian land," the metropolitan concluded, "ever since our enlightenment by holy baptism, the painters do not represent the Godhead invisible according to His essence, but they portray and represent according to the prophetic visions and the ancient Greek models."[48] But "Viskovatyi's 'doubts' centered precisely on the point that one should not paint *according to prophecies*, which have already been fulfilled and surpassed, but *according to the Gospels*, i.e., according to the fullness of the historical Incarnation."[49] According to Viskovatyi, the prophetic visions could not serve as models for depicting God. The Old Testament knew no direct, divine revelation; and the prophets "did not all receive the same vision, which was not of the essence, but of the glory" of God.[50] Viskovatyi drew a sharp demarcation line between the revelations of the Godhead in the prophetic visions, and the revelation fulfilled in the

46 The iconographic subject of God the Father will be studied singly, in conjunction with its proscription by the Great Council of Moscow. Here we limit ourselves to a brief analysis of the argumentation of both parties.

47 O. Bodianskii, *op. cit.*, 14.

48 *Ibid.*

49 Georges Florovsky, *Ways of Russian Theology*, Part One, trans. R. L. Nichols (Belmont, MA: Nordland Publishing Co., 1979), 30.

50 O. Bodianskii, *op. cit.*, 7. It is accurate that the Old Testament revelations, even when they take concrete forms as, for example, with the prophet Isaiah, are visions not of the essence but of the divine glory: "I saw the Lord seated on a high and lofty throne" (6:1); "my eyes have seen the King, Yahweh Sabaoth" (6:5). This revelation is explained by Christ Himself as a vision of the divine glory (Jn 12:41).

Incarnation. "Everything that is old has passed away; everything is new."[51] He did not deny the scope of the Old Testament, but placed it in the general perspective of the Church: the latter lovingly accepts the Old Testament prefigurations, but prefers their fulfillment, grace and truth. To support his position, he referred to the eighty-second canon of the Council *in Trullo,* to the Seventh Ecumenical Council, to the Synodikon of the Triumph of Orthodoxy, and to the writings of John of Damascus.

Viskovatyi contrasted the Old Testament prefigurations with their fulfillment: the true vision of God, the appearance of the Son of God in the flesh. In the prophetic visions, including that of David, the Church sees manifestations of the Word of God announcing His Incarnation (see, for example, at Vespers on the Sunday of the Patriarchs, the fourth sticheron after "Lord, I call upon thee"). The significance of the prophetic visions was precisely to be "types and shadows," stilled by the appearance of the authentic human image of God. This does not preclude the Old Testament prohibition of the image: God remains unrepresentable, "for no one has seen God anywhere." Only in His Incarnation is God visible, and thus portrayable. "Who can make an imitation of God who has neither flesh, nor a description, nor an image?", Viskovatyi asked, referring to St John Damascene. This is why the representations of God the Father, who did not become man, can only be based on the imagination; they "are not based on any witness."

In the image of God the Father, Viskovatyi saw an attempt to represent the unrepresentable divine essence. He says this in his self-criticism: "I believed that they had represented the unrepresentable Deity."[52] The prophets did not see the divine essence, he argued; and this is what allowed the metropolitan to refute Viskovatyi's main reproach of the iconographers, that of painting according to the imagination. They represent God, Macarius emphasized, not according to the essence, but according to the visions. "The Lord Sabaoth is depicted according to His humanity, as he was seen by the saints and the holy Fathers."[53]

As with the image of God the Father, Viskovatyi saw flights of fancy in

51 *Ibid.*, 6.

52 *Ibid.*, 32.

53 *Ibid.*, 36. The metropolitan's argument seemed so irrefutable that it appears, quite recognizably, in the arguments of all the defenders of the image of God the Father. It has lost none of its value, even in our time.

the representations of the Son of God other than in His human form. He stated: "I have seen that, while depicting the creation of heaven and earth, that of Adam and others, they painted our Lord Jesus Christ in the form of an angel."[54] "Holy Scripture convinces me that the Word of God, our Lord Jesus Christ, is truly visible to us in His fleshly economy. But as born of the Father before all ages, He is neither visible nor representable."[55] To this, Metropolitan Macarius replied, "While portraying the creation of Adam and of all creation, Christ our God, invisible according to His divinity, is represented on icons in the flesh, under the form of a winged angel according to the prophecy of Isaiah, the Angel of the Great Counsel, for God is with us..."[56] According to Viskovatyi, God the Son can only be represented in "the economy of the flesh," His humanity. Only through such an image can He be known. But according to the metropolitan, He can also be represented "in the flesh, in the form of an angel." To support his contention, he referred to the icon of the Holy Trinity where the Three that appeared to Abraham are portrayed "in their human form...with wings, according to the great Dionysius."[57] Viskovatyi was troubled by the image of Christ in the form of an angel: it could be interpreted as if Christ had assumed the angelic as well as the human nature, or even as proclaiming the superiority of the angelic order over the Incarnation.[58] It is true that certain Old Testament texts speaking of the Messiah call him "Messenger," in Greek, ἄγγελος (angel). Thus in Isaiah, He is the "Angel of the Great Counsel"; in Malachi, "the Angel of the Covenant" (3.1). But the name "angel" refers to His ministry, not to His nature. He is the divine Messenger (angel) because he became incarnate. The Messiah is known only in His human aspect, not in an angelic form. Furthermore, if the Word of God "by whom all things were made" is depicted, in His creative act (the creation of the world), in the form of an angel, then the angelic order is truly considered as superior to the Incarnation. In other words, the One who was incarnate and suffered is not considered to be the Creator. Taking into account heresies and "unstable minds," Viskovatyi could well have concrete reasons to justify such fears.

54 *Ibid.*, 10.

55 *Ibid.*, 8.

56 *Ibid.*, 22. "For unto us a child is born, unto us a son is given: and the government shall be upon his shoulder: and his name shall be called, Wonderful, Counsellor..." (Is 9:6).

57 *Ibid.*.

58 *Ibid.*, 10.

The metropolitan's reference to the image of the Old Testament Trinity contradicted the perfectly traditional decision of the *Stoglav:* the inscription IC XC, the name of Jesus Christ, was identified as an error when applied to an angel. The image of the Trinity is not that of the persons of the Father, and the Son, and the Holy Spirit: it is that of the tri-unity of God. This is why, for the *Stoglav,* the only possible inscription on this icon could be the general name, "Holy Trinity." What was at stake here was the giving of the name of Christ to a symbolic image, that of an angel, understood as a hypostatic image of the second person of the Trinity before His Incarnation—an image, so to speak, parallel to His human image. This clearly contradicted canon 82 of the Quinisext Council (*in Trullo*), which prohibited the substitution of a personal image by a symbolic one.

In the new iconographic subjects, Viskovatyi saw a move away from the truth of the Gospel, a return to the Old Testament, to the prophetic "types and shadows." Referring to canon 82, he stated that it was not proper to venerate the prefiguration more than the truth. If God is portrayed according to the prophetic prefigurations in the same manner as He is represented in the Incarnation, "the glory of the economy of our Lord Jesus Christ in the flesh is diminished."[59]

Moreover, according to Viskovatyi, the icon must be iconographically correct and recognizable in order for it to be an authentic witness: "In order not to create controversy, things should be painted in the same manner. There is one icon in the narthex and another one in the church. The same subject is depicted on them, but from a different aspect."[60] (For example, when the creation of the world is portrayed, Christ is sometimes painted in the form of an angel, sometimes in that of the Ancient of Days.) In other words, the painters extrapolated the visible or verbal prophetic images from their context and adapted them in a different manner to a different context, "according to their idea," whereby their witness lost its authenticity.

By contrast, in the eyes of the metropolitan, the portrayal of God according to the prophetic visions had the same power of witness as the image of the Incarnation. He saw no difference between them. Alongside

59 *Ibid.,* 7.
60 *Ibid.*.

the historic image of Jesus Christ, the Son of God, there can be a representation of God because

> He does not appear as He is, but in a manner accessible to the viewer. This is why he appears old, then young, sometimes in the fire, sometimes in the cold, in the wind or the water, or dressed in armor. He does not thereby change His nature, but adapts His features to the different persons to whom He appears.[61]

This quotation, taken from the third treatise of the *Message to an Iconographer,* indeed justifies any representation of the Godhead. According to the metropolitan, "the glory of our Lord Jesus Christ in human form" not only is not diminished thereby, but glorified even more. For him, the incarnate Son of God is only one of the possible prototypes. His image is on the same level as the prophetic visions, and thereby loses its uniqueness. Macarius put all these on the same level: the icon-witness to the Incarnation, the portrayal according to the prophetic prefigurations, the illustration of biblical stories, the various transformations into images of the symbolic-poetic descriptions of divine power, wrath, and so forth, as well as the mystic, didactic allegories which he used abundantly to justify the compositions objected to by Viskovatyi. His explanations and justifications illustrate even more abundantly than the images themselves the changes that had occurred in the understanding of the icon. We find here a complete break with the patristic underpinnings of the image.

Thus, in one of the icons ("God rested on the seventh day"), the body of Christ on the cross is covered by the wings of the cherubim. Viskovatyi saw in this "a Latin heretical concept." He said, "In conversations with Latins, I have often heard that the body of our Lord Jesus Christ was covered by the cherubim to avoid shame"[62]—to which the metropolitan replied that a testimony coming from "enemies of the truth" is not acceptable. "As for the wings of the cherubim in the Eternal Counsel, there is sure and authentic witness from the great Dionysius."[63] Macarius interpreted these two wings as the "logical and spiritual soul" of Christ by which He redeemed our darkened, corrupted soul, just as by the flesh He assumed, He redeemed the flesh of Adam.

61 *Ibid.,* 19.

62 *Ibid.,* 7. Viskovatyi's position continually put him in touch with foreigners and, according to the testimony of Heinrich Staden, "he was very hostile to Christians" (N. Andreev, "The Trial of Diak Viskovatyi" [n Russian], Semin. Kondakov. V [Prague, 1932], 217). Indeed, the text indicates that he clearly saw the dangers of corruption heterodox influences presented for Orthodoxy.

63 O. Budianskii, *op. cit.,* 19-20.

Another detail of the same icon is commented on by Macarius as follows:

> As for God the Father, the Lord Sabaoth who pours the content of a vessel on the standing Christ in the Crucifixion [naked and covered by the wings of the cherubim. L. O.], this prefigures holy baptism and the chalice He accepted in His flesh at the Crucifixion, that is the vinegar mixed with gall. The prophet Daniel witnessed to this when he said, "They gave me gall to eat and vinegar to quench my thirst." The four Gospel writers also testify to this.[64]

Indeed, this composition is close to that of baptism, but since this "prefiguration of baptism" is presented as an "aspersion," that is, in "a Latin form," the metropolitan added comments about the chalice.

In the icon "Only-begotten Son and Word of God," one detail represents "the young Jesus Christ, dressed in armor, holding a sword in one hand, and seated on the cross." The metropolitan explained this as follows: "He will put on the armor of justice and a helmet. He will render just judgment, and will whet his wrath against His opponents...whom He will kill with the breath of His mouth." In his comments, Macarius referred to the prophets, the Book of Wisdom, the psalms and various hymns, as well as to the commentary of John Chrysostom on Psalm 44 ("At Thy right hand stood the queen"). He supported his reflections by the text already referred to, that of the third treatise in the *Message to an Iconographer*.[65]

Thus, Viskovatyi attempted to clarify the meaning of the image, the very intent of the new icons, and their compliance or non-compliance with Orthodox tradition. By contrast, the metropolitan, as we have seen, was satisfied with external signs, with references to words taken from "the divine Scriptures." As soon as Viskovatyi expressed his dissatisfaction with this way of justifying these images, he was accused of "fantasies" for failing to ground himself in the "divine Scriptures." This literal correspondence of the images with texts, even words, was constantly supported by references to Greek models. For the metropolitan, the infallibility of the Greek iconographers was never in doubt. A painter himself, he had clearly understood the psychology of these painters who worked according to accepted models, without any verification or assessment.[66]

64 *Ibid.*, 21.

65 *Ibid.*, 19.

66 See N. Andreev, *op. cit.*, 231, note 245.

In some cases the metropolitan and the council agreed with Viskovatyi, in particular on the issue of the hands of the crucified Christ which were shown clenched. This image had to be modified.

As for Christ portrayed in the "image of David," that is, wearing royal vestments and the pontifical *omophorion*,[67] no prophet, Viskovatyi maintained, had confessed the economy in the flesh of our Lord Jesus Christ in the image of David. With regard to this image, as well as that of the Holy Spirit, "represented alone in the form of an incomprehensible bird," "of whom he could not even think without being horrified," the council recognized that its grounding was inadequate. "We will search the Scriptures for evidence on this subject. After conciliar discussion, we will render our decision."[68] Apparently, no evidence for this image of the Holy Spirit was found, for it disappeared, and we do not know what this representation looked like.[69]

Aside from the issues raised in the manuscript, the metropolitan replied to Viskovatyi's oral protest against the depiction of the bodiless powers. At the time of the chancellor's first intervention, the metropolitan's reaction had been violent and enigmatic: "You speak and reason falsely about the holy icons. Such reasoning is the heresy of the Galatians, who prohibit the painting in the flesh of the invisible bodiless powers, on earth."[70] At the council, the metropolitan interpreted the portrayal of the angelic choirs by references to Dionysius the Areopagite, and other Fathers and prophets. It is generally admitted that in his protest against the portrayal of "the Divinity and the bodiless powers," Viskovatyi understood by such bodiless beings the world of angels in general. This conclusion is justified mainly on the basis of the metropolitan's reply. On the other hand, it is true that, while quoting the decision of the Seventh Ecumenical Council that enumerated the objects to be represented,

67 This image is undoubtedly due to a legend about the episcopacy of Christ, which appeared in Russia precisely in the sixteenth century.

68 O. Bodianskii, *op. cit.*, 19.

69 As to the icon of Christ "with the features of David," it spread widely in the seventeenth century under the names of "Christ the High Priest," "King of Kings," and "The Queen stands at Your right hand."

70 See Andreev, *op. cit.*, 233. There are various scholarly hypotheses about the enigmatic heresy to which the metropolitan refers. Some scholars believe "that one should perhaps not look for a specific meaning in the accusation of Metropolitan Macarius... What was essential was the accusation of heresy; that such a heresy... never existed was of little importance" (N. Andreev, *ibid.*, 224, note 188).

Viskovatyi omitted mention of the angels. In his manuscript, however, he did not speak of the unrepresentability of the incorporeal beings; and replying to the metropolitan at the council, he maintained that he did not have in mind the representation of angels.

> I only spoke to you, Master, of the one indivisible Godhead, not of angels...Master, you have now asked the bishops what I said, and they have told you that I had spoken of the incorporeal beings and of angels. Now, Master, I do not remember having said this. But if the bishops say so and I am guilty of this, I ask you Master, for the love of God, to forgive me, together with the entire holy assembly.[71]

There seems to be no reason to doubt the sincerity of Viskovatyi on this matter.[72]

Aside from objecting to certain icons, Viskovatyi was offended by the wall painting in the palace of the tsar where "the image of the Lord is portrayed; and next to it is depicted a woman, in sleeveless garment, as if she were dancing; above are the inscriptions 'fornication,' 'jealousy,' and other mockeries."[73] The context indicates that Viskovatyi was perturbed not so much by the tasteless nature of such juxtaposition, and thus by the lack of respect for the image of Christ, as by the fact that the image of Christ "according to his human economy" was drowned here in allegories and parables. As frequently happened, the metropolitan's reply was limited to a detailed description of the subject of the decoration, supported by a reference to the life of St Basil the Great.[74]

71 O. Bodianskii, *op. cit.*, 33.

72 There certainly is no way one can conclude from the metropolitan's reply that Viskovatyi was a "semi-iconoclast," as V. Riabushinskii does in "Un tournant dans le développement de l'iconographie russe au XVIe siècle: l'affaire du diak Viskovat," *Russie et Chrétienté*, nos 3-4 (1948), 9. He detects in the words attributed to Viskovatyi "a departure from the spiritual and a return to the corporeal."

73 O. Bodianskii, *op. cit.*, 11.

74 "In the largest hall, he says, the Savior in heaven is painted in the middle, surrounded by cherubim, with the inscription 'Wisdom Jesus Christ'; to the Savior's right is a door with the words: 1) courage, 2) intelligence, 3) purity, 4) justice; on His left, another door with the words: 1) fornication, 2) folly, 3) impurity, 4) injustice; between the lower doors is a seven-headed devil; above him stands Life holding a torch in its right hand, and in its left, a lance; above all this stands an angel—the spirit of the fear of God. Behind the right door are represented the foundations of the earth and sea and everything invisible in it, and then an angel, the spirit of piety; around this are the four winds surrounded by water, above which is the dry land...An angel, a spirit of great understanding, holds the sun; underneath him, to the south, night hunts down day; still further down is virtue and an angel with the inscription, 'zeal,' together with jealousy, hell and a hare. On the left side behind the doors there is also the dry land

It is clear from the trial that, before going to the metropolitan, Viskovatyi had for three years "shouted to the people," that is, had openly proclaimed what was false in these new icons. He probably began to "shout" well before the *Stoglav.* He certainly made the mistake of not addressing himself at once and directly to the metropolitan to tell him of his doubts: it is for this that the latter reproached him.[75]

"Although a council charged him with heresy and disorderliness, it did not give any satisfactory answer to his questions and bewilderments."[76] It condemned him, describing his writings as "perverse and blasphemous." In January 1554, two meetings were devoted to his condemnation. Since the council had been called to judge heretics, the case of Viskovatyi was automatically put in the same context. The council neither studied nor discussed: it denounced and accused. "As if they were out to confound Viskovatyi at all cost, the ecclesiastical powers attached great importance

on which the Lord is painted in the form of an angel, holding a mirror and a sword; an angel is putting a crown on His head; the entire scene carries the inscription: 'bless the crown of the year of your goodness.' Below, there is the wheel of the year with still another wheel; and to the right are love, a hunter, and a wolf. On the left side, jealousy says to the hare, 'jealousy is a terrible evil which has begotten and produced fratricide.' Jealousy stabs itself with a sword. There is also death, and around all this is the dry land and angels who serve the stars" (*ibid.*, 27-8).

The metropolitan explained these composite paintings by means of the story of the conversion to Christianity of Ebbulius, the tutor of St Basil the Great. However, as N. Pokrovskii correctly observes, "This explanation...does not really explain any of the representations mentioned" (*op. cit.*).

75 In Viskovatyi's behavior there certainly are things that are not clear. This has led some scholars to suspect him of heresy, and to see in his intervention motives of a personal nature (hostility toward Sylvester) or of political character (the struggle of political groups surrounding the tsar). It is possible that such considerations played a certain role in the discussions. However, they should certainly not be viewed as the discussions' overriding concerns. What led Viskovatyi to speak out was precisely the danger he saw to the purity of Orthodoxy. "Viskovatyi's 'doubts' disclose a very profound and penetrating religious understanding" (G. Florovsky, *Ways of Russian Theology*, Part One, trans. R. L. Nichols, 29), which could be prompted only by intense and sincere convictions of faith. Hence his obstinacy, his logic, and the maturity of his theological argumentation. On the other hand, the position of Metropolitan Macarius in this affair is not very clear either. How can one explain the violence of this "sweet and lovable bishop" (A. Kartashev, *History of the Russian Church* [in Russian], vol. 1 [Paris, 1959], 426), and his desire to condemn Viskovatyi at any price: Was his ideological attitude in defense of new icons not also accompanied by personal interest? In this matter, he was a most competent person: as an iconographer himself and a builder of churches, one who especially loved the beauty of the Liturgy, he must at least have permitted the subjects of the new icons in the church of the tsar, the Cathedral of the Annunciation. Indeed, he felt responsible for them.

76 G. Florovsky, *Ways*, 29.

to various secondary errors, in word choice or quotations. Using the great weight of its authority, the council forced Viskovatyi to submit."[77]

Despite all the respect due to Metropolitan Macarius, to his talents and his remarkable and multiple activities, it must be said that the case of Chancellor Viskovatyi leaves a hardly flattering impression of those who judged him. Even before he began to answer the questions raised by Viskovatyi, the metropolitan clearly took pains to discredit him by creating an unfavorable climate against him. He tried to find out whether Viskovatyi acted alone or had accomplices. He pointed out imprecisions, unfortunate or wrong expressions in his manuscript, and he suspected willful errors in it, even though Viskovatyi recognized at once that Macarius was right. All this, in connection with the trial of heretics (Kossoi, Bashkin) cast a shadow over Viskovatyi.

But the metropolitan's stubbornness in defending the new trend in iconography can certainly not be explained only by his desire to condemn Viskovatyi for having caused trouble among the faithful. Nor can it be explained only by the fact that a believing layman, who had intervened in theological matters and had adopted a critical attitude, had vexed Macarius. On several occasions, the latter repeated: "You are forbidden to scrutinize matters of the Divinity and divine actions. You must only believe and venerate the holy icons with fear." This already shows a Roman Catholic view of the Church, representing it as divided into a "teaching Church" (*ecclesia docens*) and a "learning Church" (*ecclesia discens*). But the real problem was undoubtedly that Macarius, in all his sincerity, did not understand the essence of the issues raised by Viskovatyi. In reality, two essentially different views of sacred art were taking shape in the discussions that took place between them.

For Viskovatyi, all appreciation of iconography was based on the essential truths of Orthodoxy. He was far from being a conservative, "fiercely attached to the past."[78]

> Viskovatyi did not defend the past, he defended "truth," that is, iconographic realism. His quarrel with Metropolitan Macarius was a clash of two religious and esthetic orientations: traditional hieratic realism as opposed to a symbolism nourished by a heightened religious imagination.[79]

77 N. Andreev, "The Trial," *Semin. Kondak.* V, 240.

78 N. Pokrovskii, *Art*, 335.

79 G. Florovsky, *Ways*, 30.

For the metropolitan and the council, the determining principle was the practice existing in the Church, supported by a nebulous and powerless theological argumentation, and also by references to Russian and Greek monuments, used injudiciously and unscrupulously. In answering Viskovatyi, Macarius constantly invoked the holy Fathers, but he had not truly assimilated the spirit of their teachings. He limited himself to piling up quotations, sometimes, as we have seen, only isolated words, provided there was an outer correspondence to what was depicted. His entire argumentation showed a fidelity to the letter, but not to the patristic spirit.

The patristic foundation of the icon—to witness to the Incarnation, that is, the realism of the Gospels, which is basic to Orthodox theology—became blurred. It ceased playing its crucial and decisive role. The new trend in iconography "constituted a break with hieratic realism and its replacement by decorative symbolism or, more accurately, allegorism... The decisive dominance of 'symbolism' signified the decline of iconography."[80] The focus shifted from the face or fact to be depicted to the abstract idea. The theological and spiritual content gave way to intellectualism and pictorial virtuosity. What found an ideological defender in the person of Metropolitan Macarius was a deviation from sacred art; it was this deviation that was defended by him and by the council. "In the sixteenth-century atmosphere, charged with the electricity of Protestantism and of free inquiry,"[81] such a deviation proved to be fertile soil for western influences. The case of Chancellor Viskovatyi represents the clash between the traditional Orthodox understanding of the image and the growing western influence. "Paradoxically, such 'Westernism' achieved victory under the guise of 'antiquity' and 'conservatism.'"[82]

It must be said that Viskovatyi was neither the first nor the only one to be perturbed by the "embellishments" of the iconographers.[83] Similar compositions had prompted doubts and discussions much earlier. Thus a letter written by the interpreter Dimitrios Gerasimov to chancellor Mi-

80 *Ibid.*, 29.

81 A. Kartaschev, *History*, vol. 1, 515.

82 G. Florovsky, *Ways*, 30.

83 A contemporary of Viskovatyi, Artemius the monk, abbot of the Monastery of the Trinity, objected to the image of Sabaoth with the features of an old man because it was "western" (Ustrialov, *The History of Ivan the Terrible, the Prince Kurbsky* [in Russian], 3rd ed., [St Petersburg, 1869], 17-9); in 1592, the Brotherhood of Lvov did the same (A. I. Nekrasov, *Figurative Art* [Moscow, 1937], 290).

chael Misiur-Munekhin at Pskov states how, since 1518 or 1519, a composition similar to the ones contested by Viskovatyi had been submitted to St Maximus the Greek for evaluation. At the time, it was "an unusual image which was found nowhere in the Russian land except in one city." St Maximus replied that he had never seen anything like it "anywhere," and that the iconographers must have composed such an image "on their own." Apparently, a written commentary had also been submitted to him. He adopted a negative attitude towards icons of this type. "To paint such images that scandalize the heterodox and our simple Christians is most unnecessary"; one should "paint and venerate the images that correspond to our feasts, established by the Fathers and the councils." Otherwise, "if anyone would want to paint images by borrowing lines from Scripture, he could make an unlimited number of them." In this same letter Gerasimov added that, long before this, there had already been a great discussion about this image at the time of Archbishop Gennadius (archbishop from 1484 to 1504). A disagreement had arisen between him and the iconographers of Pskov concerning their "incorrectly painted images." The iconographers alleged that they painted images "according to the models of the masters with whom they had studied, who reproduced Greek models." They limited themselves to this vague reference, "without submitting any documentation on this subject." The inhabitants of Pskov "then listened more to the iconographers than to the archbishop."

In the 1560s, about ten years after the discussion with Viskovatyi, a similar composition was submitted to the monk Zenobius of Otnia for evaluation.[84] They asked him what he thought of the icon "God the Father," which some "did not accept for veneration, while others praised it and said that it has been composed with profound wisdom."[85] Apparently, the question must have been painfully urgent, and, to judge from the insistence of Zenobius' interlocutors, it had lost nothing of its acuteness since the discussion with Viskovatyi. "I beseech you, for the

84 According to tradition, Zenobius (d. 1568), a disciple of St Maximus the Greek, was a writer and a polemicist of great authority among his contemporaries. The questions and Zenobius' answers are included in his work, *A Demonstration of the Truth to Those Who Asked About the New Doctrine*. A portion of it was later included in the collection of his works edited in Moscow in 1642.

85 N. Andreev, "The Monk Zenobius of Otnia on Iconography" (in Russian), *Semin. Kondak.* VIII (Prague, 1935), 268.

love of your neighbor; had there been no quarrel about this icon, no one would have brought this up. But since some do not accept this icon for veneration, I beg you, speak."[86] Zenobius was undoubtedly not aware of this icon, as he did not understand the question. "What is the icon you call 'God the Father'? I do not understand." He was told that it was an icon of "God the Father Sabaoth," and was given a "commentary," that is, an explanatory description.

To judge from this "commentary," the incriminated icon, based on a combination of biblical texts, was a variant of the composition "Only-begotten Son and Word of God," which had earlier offended Viskovatyi. God the Father was depicted on it as David, king and pontiff ("with a miter on his head and an *omophorion* on his shoulders," a sword in his iron-gloved hand), the young Christ wearing armor, seated on the cross, and so forth.

Having listened to this commentary, Zenobius expressed himself forcefully and unambiguously:

> The model as well as the commentary on this icon are far removed from the thought of the holy and apostolic Orthodox Church. They are totally alien to faith and pious thought. They are a great blasphemy against the divine nature, a lie about Jesus Christ.[87]

According to the commentary, Sabaoth was represented "as David," because the latter was an ancestor of Christ according to the flesh; he is called "the ancestor of God," and, in the Gospel, the Savior is often called "Son of David." Zenobius reacted to such confused reasoning by stating that, according to the same line of thought, one should represent God the Father as Abraham. An image of Sabaoth resembling David is "a blasphemy against the glory of God. If a corruptible man, born and mortal, has to be viewed as the origin of the One who is without beginning, this would be an impiety that has not yet been found in any heresy."[88] Zenobius sarcastically noted that "if God had been represented as king and pontiff, to whom would he, as bishop, have to address himself, since He himself is God the Father?"[89] In general, "this icon in the likeness of David corresponds to nothing in Holy Scripture, whether apostolic or prophetic, or even in the Gospel itself. Rather, that image of God the

86 *Ibid.*, 271.
87 *Ibid.*, 269.
88 *Ibid.*, note 65.
89 *Ibid.*, 290.

Father as David, and the image of Christ as David, was composed on the basis of numerous heresies."[90] We remember that what had prompted Viskovatyi's protest was precisely the image of Christ in the form of David. In his rebuttal, Zenobius referred to canon 82 of the Council *in Trullo.* As for the details of the image, in particular the iron glove and sword, he said: "It is not proper to represent God the Father, incorporeal and invisible, who brought all things from nothingness into being, as an avenger." If this is how "the power of the punishment of God" had to be "portrayed on icons," then one would have to "represent the bowels of God in the form of a lute or that of a threatening bear" on the basis of texts such as "my bowels shall sound like a harp on Moab," or "I will be for them like a devouring bear."[91] Zenobius said nothing about the very principle of whether or not it is possible to represent God the Father; he limited himself strictly to the concrete question that had been submitted to him. Nonetheless, from his surprise and disapproval, one may conclude that an image of the "incorporeal and invisible" God the Father in human appearance was to him utterly inconceivable.

Zenobius condemned the representation of the young Christ, seated on the cross, a sword in His hand, as an arbitrary modification of the Gospel record: "Not one of the theologians has presented, and none of the Fathers has celebrated a Christ who vanquished hell by descending from the cross, wearing iron armor and a copper helmet"; likewise, "the young Christ seated on the cross is alien to Orthodox thought and is a diabolical blasphemy."[92] Indeed, in this representation one does not see the Christian concept of the supreme humiliation of the cross as a victory. The victory of the cross is depicted by means of weaponry, and the realism of the Gospel is replaced by allegorism.

Zenobius objected with no less indignation to another detail of the same icon: a crucified seraphim ("as deriving from a heresy," Maxim the Greek had said on the same subject) and cherubim of whom the commentary spoke as follows: "the white cherubim is His [that is, Christ's] holy soul. The two red cherubim are the word and the spirit." All this probably represented a development of the same subject already commented on by

90 *Ibid.*, 271.

91 *Ibid.*, 270, note 69.

92 I. Mansvetov, "The Crucifixion Represented on a Spoon of the Monastery of St Antony in Novgorod" (in Russian), *Trudy Mosk. Ob.*, vol. 4 (Moscow, 1874), 44.

Metropolitan Macarius. Some scholars speculate that the crucified cherubim was a variant of the vision of Francis of Assisi on Mt Alverno.[93] However, as G. Florovsky believes, this could equally have resulted from the influence of German mysticism. In the fourteenth century, the image is seen in Suso, the well-known Roman Catholic mystic who had become highly influential, especially beginning with the fifteenth century. His mystic-erotic works, with his own illustrations, were certainly known to the iconographers of Pskov, who had close connections with the West.

Having analyzed the details of the incriminated iconographic subject point by point, Zenobius found in it traces of Gnosticism, Manichaeism, and Sabellianism. He stated that the entire composition was the outcome of "heretical thinking, of the deviation of mad frenzy." "I reject all this according to the rule of the Sixth Ecumenical Council," he wrote.[94]

Zenobius did not speak of the western origin of certain details in the compositions which he rejected. Unlike Viskovatyi, he may simply not have know their origin. In his judgment of principle concerning the icon, he displayed a strong, unwavering fidelity to the patristic tradition. In his rebuttals he relied especially on the decision of the Quinisext Council: the council has ordained "that icons be painted according to grace and truth," he said, to commemorate "the life of the Lord in the flesh, His salutary passion and death, the divine deliverance thus given to the world."[95]

The appearance and above all the wide dissemination of new "theological didactic" compositions is generally interpreted by scholars as one of the means used by the Church in its struggle against heresies. However, we find no confirmation of this in contemporary documents. Not one of the anti-heretical writings composed during this period warrants such a conclusion. Such subjects are missing from the enumeration of what is depicted on the icons made by St Joseph of Volokolamsk, the great enemy of heretics. If the intent of such images was to fight heresy, it is strange that such fierce opponents of heresy as Gennadius, Bishop of Novgorod, or St Maximus the Greek adopted such a negative attitude toward them. Even when defending such compositions, Macarius himself did not view them as anti-heretical

93 L. Mastulevich, "The Chronology of the Reliefs of the Cathedral of St Dimitrius in Vladimir" (in Russian), *Ezhegodnik Rossiiskogo Instituta Istorii isk*," vol. 1 (St Petersburg-Moscow, 1922), quoted by N. Andreev, "The Trial," 235-6.

94 I. Mansvetov, *op. cit.*, 44 and N. Andreev, "Zenobius the Monk," 274.

95 N. Andreev, *ibid.*, 274.

weapons. What could such "mystic-didactic" compositions teach or prove? This is all the more difficult to admit since even then no one could understand them without special explanations. "There is no inscription on them," Viskovatyi told the council;

> "Our Lord Jesus Christ is portrayed in the form of an angel, or seated on the cross wearing armor; or one sees the Eternal Counsel—all this without an inscription." The metropolitan told John, "There certainly are inscriptions on all these holy icons. On the Eternal Counsel is written 'the Lord Sabaoth,' and the image of the crucified Christ in the lap of the Father carries the inscription 'Jesus Christ.'" And John said, "My Lord, I have indeed seen the inscriptions 'Jesus Christ' and 'Sabaoth' on all these icons; but there is no written explanation of these parables, and no one of those I asked knew anything about it."[96]

This dialogue illustrates how impossible it was to find one's way through such compositions without an explanation, or to see the meaning of what was represented. Toward the end of the sixteenth century, all these subjects had become so common that they are viewed as normal phenomena even in our day. Thus, in Lebedev's *The Science of the Liturgy in the Orthodox Church*, one reads about the sixteenth-century representations,

> The pastors of the Russian Church have always accepted and approved such representations not only because of their inner meaning, but also because they saw in them a system of teaching through the image, and because the essential symbols that are part of the composition of such images have been used in the Greek church since ancient times.[97]

As we can see, this last argument is the same as that used by Metropolitan Macarius: the practice of the Greek church is a criterion of truth. However, the "inner meaning" of a great number of these images reveals an incredible amount of embellishment and is expressed in a choice of symbols and allegories so "profound" that it not only did not form "a system of teaching through the image" but remained simply incomprehensible. Hence the profusion of inscriptions on such icons in the second half of the sixteenth and seventeenth centuries. "Without them, such icons would have remained incomprehensible," a nineteenth-century author stated. The meaning and the content of these images were simply inaccessible to the people. "Experience has shown that icons without inscriptions became the object of various commentaries that often caused the people to become agitated."[98]But inscrip-

96 "The Trial," *op. cit.*, 35.

97 (In Russian), Part One (Moscow, 1900), 128.

98 Ia. Lebedinskii, "The Measures Taken by the Russian Government to Improve Iconography in the

tions were not always the solution. Even a man as cultivated, and a theologian of such repute, as Metropolitan Philaret of Moscow wrote on the subject of the icon "the Burning Bush": "In the composition of this icon quite a few things seem incomprehensible."[99] One can easily imagine what this "system of teaching through the image" would produce among the simple believers.

It is certainly possible that heresies were somehow linked to these "symbolic" icons. It is a matter, however, not of polemical intent, but rather of a clear inner affinity. The creators of the new icons were mystics no less pretentious and nebulous than the Judaizers themselves. Both were nourished by the same unhealthy "heightened religious imagination." In its polemic, the Church could certainly not make use of icons "composed of numerous heresies," according to the evaluation of Zenobius the monk.

In the second half of the sixteenth century, however, this decadence in sacred art was far from predominant in ; on the contrary, its achievements were only slightly inferior to those of the preceding epoch. But the general erosion of spirituality deprived art of the foundation it had when hesychasm played a crucial role. In this period, a disparity was created between the ascetic life and prayer on the one hand, and creation and theological thought on the other. There was a gradual departure from the Orthodox view of the image, and from its doctrinal foundations formulated by the Sixth and Seventh Ecumenical Councils. The art trend championed by the Council of 1553-1554 would gradually cease to recast foreign borrowings into an artistic language proper to Orthodoxy. This would subsequently lead to a direct imitation of the West, and to a break with the Tradition.

Seventeenth Century" (in Russian), vol. 12 (Kharkov: Dukhovnyi Vestnik, 1865), 53-4, note 1.

99 Quoted by L. S. Retkovskaia, *The Universe in the Art of Ancient Russia* (in Russian) (Moscow, 1961), Trudy Gossud. Istor. Muzeia, "Pamiatniki Kultury," no. 33, 15. The "Burning Bush" is one of the "theological-didactic" compositions found in the list of subjects given to the council by Metropolitan Macarius.

15

The Art of the 17th Century: An Art Divided, the Tradition Abandoned

In the seventeenth century, artistic activity in Russia experienced an extraordinary flowering. Never had as many works of architecture or mural decorations been created as during the second half of the century. It was an epoch of great acquisitions in the artistic domain, but also of great losses.

> The loss of the grand style, of the deep meaning of the pictorial image, in short, the absence in seventeenth-century painting of the expression and spiritual intensity proper to the works of the twelfth to the fifteenth centuries, was compensated by intense liveliness of color, a superbly decorative character, and great ornamental richness.[1]

Nonetheless, this art, the painting of icons in particular, was still of a rather high spiritual and artistic quality. The patriarchal workshops, the monasteries, as well as the great majority of the iconographers, continued to create strictly traditional art. Russian art spread widely beyond the country's borders. At the request of church and civil authorities, Russian painters were sent to decorate churches in Georgia, Serbia, Moldavia, and Walachia. The higher clergy and the nobility of various Orthodox countries particularly appreciated Russian icons: these were ordered or brought back as gifts. Greek painters tried to get "recipes" from iconographers in Moscow.[2] Thus, the technical procedures and the style of Russian painters were disseminated, as well as the subjects adapted by Russian sacred art in the sixteenth century.

In accord with the taste of the epoch, what was most appreciated was mastery of execution. Since the sixteenth century, the art of numerous talented painters had become a type of virtuoso performance: it began to resemble that of the miniature. In icons, such virtuosity was regarded, if not as the essential, then at least as its main quality. In the seventeenth

1 Periodical, *Ancient Russian Art, the Seventeenth Century* (in Russian) (Moscow, 1964), 7.

2 André Grabar, *L'expansion de la peinture russe aux XVI et XVII siècles, L'art de la fin de l'antiquité et du moyen âge*, vol 2 (Paris, 1968), 946-63.

century, Deacon Paul of Aleppo made a tour of Russia with Macarius, the Patriarch of Antioch. He became ecstatic upon seeing such icons. "You should know," he wrote,

> that the iconographers of that city [Moscow] are unequalled anywhere in the world as concerns the artistry, the finesse of the painting, and ability in artistic mastery. They make little icons that make the heart of the viewer beat fast. On them, each saint, every angel has the dimensions of a lentil or of an *osmani* [a small coin]. We were thrilled when we saw them.[3]

The absence of the essential qualities of the great art of the preceding epochs in seventeenth-century art was largely the result of spiritual decay, but also of the historical conditions which had arisen already in the sixteenth century. In other Orthodox countries, interest in Russian art was due not only to the decline of artistic life under the Turkish occupation; there was also a concept of sacred art that was essentially the same, and a common attitude toward such art caused by the circumstances that marked the history of Orthodoxy at this time.

By progressively moving away from the hesychast spiritual attitude, the creative tradition of the Orthodox world became lifeless, the level of theological thought sank. This spiritual decadence affected all of Orthodoxy (though not simultaneously, it is true), independently of the extremely diverse historical conditions in which the local churches found themselves. In their inner life, all these churches were in the same situation when confronted by the new times—new times that brought a showdown between Orthodoxy and the non-Orthodox West, between the vision of the Orthodox world and the rationalism of western culture. Despite the variety of circumstances, not only did the historical conditions not contribute to bringing an end to this spiritual decay; on the contrary, they deepened it, thereby opening wide the door to foreign influences on Orthodox spiritual life. As much in the countries under Turkish domination as in Russia, the pressure from the western confessions increased. "Entire armies of propagandists well-trained in special schools[4] were sent to the East...A network of Roman dioceses covered the

3 *The Journey of Patriarch Macarius in Russia,* (henceforth, *Journey*), translated from the Arabic into Russian by G. Murkos, published in *Chteniia Imper. Ob. Istorii i drevnostei rossiiskikh,* Bk X, ch. 10 (Moscow, 1889), 43.

4 The most famous of these was the College of St Athanasius in Rome, opened by Pope Gregory XIII in 1577. See Alexander Schmemann, *The Historical Road of Orthodoxy,* trans. L. Kesich (New York, 1963), 323ff.

entire Orthodox East." Since the level of instruction among the Orthodox was low, people were sent to the West for their schooling. They returned under the influence of a western theological and spiritual atmosphere.

In Russia, this century, the last before the time of Peter I, began with "the Time of Troubles" and ended with this emperor's brutal reform. During the Time of Troubles, the decisive role in the reconstruction of the state fell once more upon the Church: only its voice had sufficient authority to put an end to anarchy and to rally the Russian people. However, by the middle of the century, the situation changed. The historical development of the Russian state brought it within the orbit of western culture. For lack of its own system of education, a western type of teaching was introduced. Southwest Russia played the greatest role in this. "The Orthodox monk of southwest Russia, educated either in a Latin school or a Russian one of the same type, was called to Moscow and was the first to promote western learning."[5] Together with such learning, a scholastic theology was instilled. Not only did the Russian southwest live in close proximity to the peculiarly western problems of this time, it also had to live through them and to seek a solution for them. Itself already contaminated by occidentalism, it infected the Russian Church with the diseases of the West.

The withering of the creative theological tradition in Orthodoxy weakened it to such a degree that, in its defense against the attack by the western confessions, it was "forced to arm itself with western scholastic arguments" which, in turn, gave rise to a new and dangerous influence upon Orthodox theology, one that derived not merely from the use of improper theological terms but from theological and spiritual doctrines." What certain theologians such as Florovsky call "a pseudo-morphosis of Orthodoxy"—an Orthodoxy "dressed in improper thought forms and expressions"—had arrived.[6] Russian as well as Greek theology were permeated with scholasticism; Orthodox thought was paralyzed. It was a subservience, the Latinization of a defenseless Orthodoxy; and this Latinization encompassed theology, the vision of the world, and religious psychology itself.

5 V. O. Kliuchevskii, *Works* (in Russian), vol. 3. (Moscow, 1957), 275.

6 Archbishop Basil (Krivochéine), "Les textes symboliques dans l'Eglise orthodoxe," *Messager de l'Exarchat du Patriarche russe en Europe occidentale*, n. 49 (1965), 11-2.

In the spheres of both artistic creation and theological thought, the creative life in the Tradition became weaker. The evaluatoin in the light of the Tradition of everything heterodoxy had brought with it, as had happened earlier, now came to and end. The changes that had occurred in the religious psychology of the epoch were expressed by a break between prayer and asceticism on the one hand, and creation and theological thought on the other. The creative tradition was replaced by two opposite trends: a conservatism (which had also occurred in Byzantium, as we have seen) and, under the influence of western culture, a rallying of the painters around the art of western culture.

The Orthodox countries under Turkish domination saw their artistic life, if not disappear, then at least greatly diminish. The imitation of western art gained ground in the great cities, in areas open to western influence. Traditional Orthodox art was relegated to the monasteries and the provinces. A split occurred, for the simple people continued to hold firmly to traditional art, seeing in it both a defense against heterodoxy and a proclamation of the national spirit.[7]

In seventeenth-century Russia, under the pressure of western civilization, culture became separated from the Church, and became an autonomous sphere. Until then, the Church had embraced all aspects of life, all domains of human creativity. Certain areas of creative activity now freed themselves, and this caused a split in Russian society. Formerly, despite all differences in social standing, the spiritual mentality of the Russians had been homogeneous, but now western influence broke "the moral unity of Russian society. Just as glass cracks when it is heated unevenly in various parts, so Russian society, unevenly touched by western influences, cracked."[8]

Such influences increasingly penetrated the very life of the Church and its art. Russia was flooded by western religious art works as well as by

7 This plight of traditional Orthodox art was already obvious on the Adriatic coast in the fourteenth century, where it found itself face to face with the strong western influence coming from neighboring Italy, the center of the Renaissance. The painters were forced either to imitate the Italians in order to satisfy their clients, or "to return to Byzantine forms to please conservative taste, and to work in small churches where the Byzantine forms were identified with the highest expression of the sacred" (see J. Djuric, *Icônes de Yougoslavie* [Belgrade, 1961], 52).

8 V. O. Kliuchevskii, *op. cit.*,361-2.

"copies, drawings, and pictures reproducing original western works, introduced by the Jesuits."[9] Russian painters made great use of all this; in decorating churches they borrowed entire compositions. They were most strongly attracted by the anecdotal, everyday manner in which such western reproductions represented biblical subjects. The illustrated Bible of Piscator, published in Amsterdam in 1650, became highly popular among the Russians. It should be added, however, that while using all this material, the Russian painters still recast it in the organic language of Orthodox sacred art. From the artistic point of view their works, such as the wall paintings on the churches of Yaroslavl, Kostroma, and Rostov, far surpass their originals. Nonetheless, this art was only minimally "illuminated by fleeting gleams of the great traditions."[10]

Beginning with the fourth decade of the seventeenth century, painters in the Ukraine used western reproductions as models.[11] As for the second half of the century, according to Paul of Aleppo, "While painting Orthodox images, Cossack painters, now skilled and educated, borrowed beautiful things from Frankish and Polish painters when doing the faces and the coloring of the clothing."[12] The influence of western models no doubt explains why on Mount Athos, where at this time the monks were fiercely loyal to the Orthodox tradition, they were very hostile to Russian and especially to Ukrainian icons. They suspected Latin heresy in them and "preferred the most modest local image to the best Russian icon."[13]

In Muscovite Russia, in the circles of first class painters—especially in the tsar's iconographic atelier and among painters who were somehow attached to it—a new trend surfaced, revealing new aesthetic ideas, and a new type of art arose. The historical and spiritual conditions of this stage in the life of the Russian Church and its art were such that it was this trend that became dominant and turned its back on tradition.

Nowhere did the break with tradition cause such acrimonious discussions, such impassioned commotion, and such a painful sundering as in

9 M. Sychev, *An Icon of Simon Ushakov in the Diocesan Storeroom of Novgorod* (in Russian), Collection dedicated to the 25th anniversary of the scholarly work of P. Ainalov (St Petersburg, 1915), 96.

10 I. Grabar, *History of Russian Art* (in Russian), vol. 6 (Moscow), 492.

11 V. Sventsitskaia, "The Works of Ivan Rudkovich" (in Russian), in the journal *Iskusstvo*, no 6 (1964), 65, note.

12 *Journey*, Bk IV, ch. 12, 41.

13 A. Grabar, *L'expansion de la peinture russe*, 941.

Russia. Nowhere had the question of art been raised with such clarity. This "century of lost equilibrium"[14] manifested a particular unease, which became apparent in a series of measures taken by church and civil authorities, as well as in written documents. The second half of the seventeenth century has left us more than a dozen of these,[15] devoted to sacred art either completely or in part. We have seen how in the sixteenth century the discussions that agitated large segments in Russia dealt with the doctrinal basis of the image, with the conformity, or the lack of it, of certain iconographic subjects with Church teaching. In the seventeenth century also, certain texts continue to focus on the same problem. They are the *Acts* of the Great Council of Moscow, the writings of the monk Euthymius, and (partly) the *Testament* of Patriarch Joachim. Another series of documents is of special interest to us. These documents are the first Russian treatises devoted to aesthetics and the theory of art. They

14 G. Florovsky, *Ways of Russian Theology*, Part One, trans. R. L. Nichols (Belmont, MA: Nordland Publishing Co., 1979), 87.

15 The most important of these are: 1) Joseph Vladimirov, "Letter of a Certain Iconographer Joseph to the Iconographer of the Tsar, the Wise Simon Theodorovich (Ushakov)," edited in Russian by E. Ovchinnikova in *Drevnerusskoe Iskusstvo XVII veka* (Moscow, 1964). Hereafter, "Letter"; 2) Simon Ushakov, "Discourse to the One Who Has Zeal for the Painting of Icons," edited in Russian in the collection *Mastera iskusstva ob iskusstve*, vol. 4 (1937). Hereafter, "Discourse"; 3) Symeon, Bishop of Polotsk, "Request or Message to the Tsar during the Great Council of Moscow," partially published in Russian by L. N. Maikov in *Ocherki iz Istorii russkoi literatury XVII-XVII stol.*, (St Petersburg, 1889), and in *Simeon Polotskii o russkom ikonopisanii* (St Petersburg, 1889); 4) *The Acts of the Great Council of Moscow of 1667*, edited in Russian (Moscow, 1893); 5) "The Writing of the Three Patriarchs of 1668," written at the request of the tsar and signed by Patriarchs Paisius of Alexandria, Macarius of Antioch, both visiting Moscow, and by Joasaph of Moscow. Text edited by P. P. Pekarskii, *Materialy dlia istorii ikonopisaniia v. Rossii* (St Petersburg, 1865); 6) "Edict of the Tsar" of 1669, in the same edition; 7) Euthymius the monk, "Questions and Answers Concerning Russian Seventeenth-Century Iconography," edited by G. Filimonov in *Vestnik Ob. drevnerusskogo iskusstva* (Moscow, 1874-1876); 8) *La vie de l'archiprêtre Avvakoum*, edited in part by P. Pascal, *Avvakoum et les débuts du Raskol* (Paris, 1938). (Partial English trans. by H. Iswolsky, "The Life of Archpriest Avvakum by Himself," in G. Fedotov, *A Treasury of Russian Spirituality*, vol. 2 [Belmont, 1975], 136-81); 9) Patriarch Joachim, "Testament" (fragment that appeared in Russian in the iconographic manual edited by Bolshakov, with text edited by Th. Uspenskii in Moscow); 10) Karion Istomin, "Discourse to the One Who Has Zeal for the Painting of Icons," written at the end of the seventeenth century. This is a compilation of the works of Ushakov, Symeon of Polotsk, and of the Writings of the Patriarchs and the Tsar. Let us also mention the collection published in 1642 under the title *Florilegium. Selected Writings on the Dignity of Holy Icons and Their Veneration.* It contains no original works, but includes a series of older texts of a polemical nature against the Protestants and reflects the discussions with them. It has not been reprinted since.

express the totally new concept of art that appears at this time. Directly or indirectly, they are devoted to a defense of the new trend which has become entrenched in Russian art practice, and they give it a theoretical justification. These are the works of master iconographers Joseph Vladimirov and Simon Ushakov, as well as those of Symeon of Polotsk, the *Writing* of the three patriarchs and, in part, the *Edict* of the Tsar. Lastly, a third group of documents expresses opposition to the new trend: the *Testament* of Patriarch Joachim, and the *Life* of Archpriest Avvakum. The importance of all these documents lies in the fact that they illustrate the changes that have occurred, as much in art itself as in its conception. They show how the new trend was understood by its followers, and how its opponents judged it. All of them reflect the complex, even contradictory, conceptions of art in the seventeenth century. Even the documents that defended traditional painting reveal the decay that had begun in the sixteenth century, but now in a more dangerous and advanced form.

Most of the seventeenth-century documents are rooted in the anxiety caused by the poor condition of contemporary sacred art, and they attempt, more or less insistently, to improve its quality. Beginning with the sixteenth century, as we have seen, the ever-growing demand for icons had led to a significant increase in the number of iconographers.[16] Men who sometimes lacked even the necessary technical skills come to swell their ranks. The regulations of the *Stoglav* already witness to this, and then the documents of the seventeenth century. It is clear that, under such

16 Let us note that nowhere was the icon so widely spread, nor did it play such an important role, as in Russia. The chronicles mention the building and decorating of churches, the creation, transfer and even the restoration of icons, together with events of national importance. The icon was organically linked to the life of the people. It accompanied them in all the events of their life; all of life, and especially the agricultural calendar, was structured around feast days; and this naturally translated itself into the veneration of certain icons and in their dissemination. Icons were an indispensable element in the layout not only of the interior, but also of the exterior of all public and all private buildings. It is hard for us to imagine today that "Tsar Alexis Mihailovich had 6200 icons in his hall of icons, received as gifts...In addition, there were more than 600 old icons, and also a great number in storerooms, images that had been removed from the rooms to protect them from thieves" (N. P. Kondakov, *The Russian Icon*, III [in Russian] [Prague, 1931], 30-1). The Cathedral of the Annunciation had no less than 3000 icons, as did the Cathedral of Our Lady of Smolensk in the Novodevichii Monastery. Of all these treasures, only a few fragments are left. "What neither devastating fires nor invasions which destroyed all the decorations in the cathedrals and the wooden churches, and the icons in private homes, were able to accomplish, was accomplished through neglect" (*ibid.*, 38). Then, of course, there was the premeditated destruction for ideological reasons.

conditions, the general level of sacred art could not be maintained appropriately.

In their struggle against poor painting the authorities, religious as well as secular, required that icons be painted "according to the ancient models." Such "ancient models" became the only criterion for judging the correctness of an image. They replaced the theological criterion, and perfectly satisfied church and civil authorities. To remedy the existing situation, the Great Council of Moscow formulated a similar decision, without entering into as many details as the *Stoglav*. It instituted control over the iconographers, exercised by a syndic, a painter belonging to the clergy. Thus it repeated an approach to fighting bad painting which had already proved unsuitable and had failed totally. One year later, the *Writing* of the three patriarchs tackled the same problem, though in a more general way. It required that skilled painters oversee the others and testify to their abilities in signed affidavits. Following the patriarchs, the 1669 *Writing* of the tsar created a type of state diploma: "After examination, we want to grant our tsar's charter to all the best iconographers, to each according to his ability, by way of confirmation."[17] This is how the supervision of the work of the iconographers moved from spiritual teaching, asceticism, and prayer to the control of the church, and then to that of the civil authorities. The Hundred-Chapters Council had already relied upon the latter by threatening to use "the tsar's wrath." The art of the Church was now regulated by both church sanctions and official decrees from the tsar.

Among the seventeenth-century documents, it is above all the writings of Joseph Vladimirov and Symeon of Polotsk that address the quality of icon painting. The latter presented a special note to the Tsar, to be studied at the council. The *Letter* of Vladimirov, the first document in chronological order, provided source material for several later writings and influenced them to a greater or letter extent. Symeon of Polotsk used it extensively. More than the other documents, this *Letter* described in detail the defects of the icons themselves and of the attitude of the faithful toward them, all the while lacing this description with biting criticism which was formulated intelligently, ingeniously, and coherently. Vladimirov used wit and a fiery temper to assail the manufacturer of bad,

17 "Edict of the Tsar," 17.

cheap icons, and those who bought them. "Where else," he wrote,

> can we see such indecencies as can be recognized here and now? The lowering and profanation of the venerable, sound art of the icons have been caused by ignoramuses for the following reason: everywhere in the villages and hamlets, wholesale merchants bring icons by the basketful. They are painted in a most ridiculous manner. Some of them do not even resemble human images; their aspect is like that of savages.[18]

According to the author, such icons were resold in great quantities from one merchant to the other. They were taken to remote villages and "exchanged, like children's whistles, for an egg, an onion, or all sorts of things." Vladimirov did not limit his criticism to "the simple folk," who acquired an icon for an egg or an onion. He went to war against the rich who had bought these same icons cheaply. He maintained that the evil did not only come from the merchants who earned a living by selling icons, but "especially from negligent priests who lack zeal and care in administering church matters." The greatest encouragement for bad painting came from people "whose mind is bent on gold and silver, who build luxurious homes and love to keep high-priced horses in their stables—but who buy bad icons in churches."[19] According to Symeon of Polotsk, such paintings are a blasphemy against God himself, and the ones who paint them are called "God's scribblers."[20] The mass production of icons, the authors state, results in unemployment for the good iconographers, who live in poverty or change jobs.[21] "All this leads to a decline of God's churches," Symeon of Polotsk exclaimed.[22] What was at stake was not just the popularity of handcrafted icons: there was also the situation of the average iconographers. In addition to their occupation, they had to perform the mandatory labor imposed upon all citizens by the state. This is why the *Stoglav,* as well as a series of seventeenth-century documents, asked that iconographers be given a higher social standing in order to improve their way of life.

The criticism of sacred art by the seventeenth-century documents is certainly well-founded. The massive buying and reselling and the commercialization of the icon led to inevitable carelessness and abuse, which

18 Joseph Vladimirov, "Letter," 33.
19 *Ibid.*, 36.
20 Maikov, ed., 8.
21 J. Vladimirov, "Letter," 35.
22 Maikov, ed., 5.

could only lower the quality of icons. It is certainly not without reason that an order of the tsar in 1688 prohibited icon painting by the inhabitants of the villages of Mstera and Kholui. Vladimirov blamed particularly the merchants, and rightly so: it is they who, in their own interest, suggested to buyers that "salvation cannot be gained by good painting, and that among the miraculous icons there were many that were badly painted."[23] He also blamed the faithful who, out of naivete, or "in order to save money, buy bad icons cheaply and then wait for signs and miracles. In truth, such people tempt God and do not really venerate the icons of the saints."[24] Vladimirov recognized that miracles are not dependent on the images, just as He "works through unworthy persons" and through the forces of nature. But if He acts this way, it is not because of the unworthiness of the icons but *despite* it. Thus, "when a miracle occurs through one of these unsuitable images, this will not protect us before the just Judge."[25]

And yet, despite all these good points, the all-too-generalized criticism of artisanal icons by the above authors is somewhat suspect. What did they understand by "bad icons?" According to what criterion did they judge their quality? Was it only a matter of poor workmanship? A great number of seventeenth-century icons have come down to us; they are extremely diverse in character and quality. However, we do not know of any "unsuitable images" whose aspect is like that of "savages." It is difficult to imagine that they all have disappeared without leaving a trace, while others remain. Certainly, in the eyes of the painters of whom Paul of Aleppo spoke, and in the eyes of their clients, the customary trade icon must have looked like a daub. But this was not the only problem. In an article devoted to some of the documents we have mentioned, G. N. Dmitriev correctly notes that they fought the production

> of cheap icons used by the people, the simple folk. It goes without saying that the authors of these documents viewed the painting of icons as poor, as not corresponding to what they required of art. However, we are in fact dealing here with two different arts existing side by side: that of the leading classes and that created by the people, or, at any rate, spread among the people and accepted by them. The struggle against that art was but a manifestation of the class struggle. It was not only the

23 "Letter," 33.
24 *Ibid.*, 36.
25 *Ibid.*, 34.

> pretext, but the reason behind the first Russian "treatises" on art history—treatises that justify and praise the "superior" art of the leading classes as well as their struggle against the art used by the common people. To a greater or lesser degree, the authors of the "treatises" (not only Simon Ushakov, but also the others) were advocates of the new style of painting that was established at this time.[26]

Indeed, what was at stake was not merely the quality of the icons, and polemical impetuosity was not the only reason that led the authors to exaggerate the faults of artisanal painting. They too had appropriated the ideology that sustained the new trend in painting.

By its very nature, the art of the Church, sacred art, did not and could not have a class character. On the contrary, independent of its artistic qualities, it has over the centuries served as a unifying element, not only on the social and political, but even on the national plane. It obeyed only one criterion; and in it the doctrinal aspect was not differentiated from the aesthetic. The aesthetic appreciation of a work, as we have stated, coincided with its theological appreciation. Indeed, art was theology revealed by means of aesthetic categories. In some of the seventeenth-century documents this theological criterion remained decisive, but only in the realm of iconography. As for the followers of the new trend, for them the aesthetic criterion gradually separated from the doctrinal and acquired an independent value. It is no surprise that the unqualified criticism of the artisanal icons derives from the ideologists of this trend. And thus, for Vladimirov, the aesthetic criterion was the only decisive one: it was better to have a well-painted image of Christ than many bad, "unsuitable" icons. What is more, if one could not have a beautiful icon, it was better not to have one at all rather than to pray before a "bad one."[27] The attitude of Symeon of Polotsk was more flexible. On the one hand, he vehemently criticized the production of bad icons; on the other, he defended these same icons in his discussions with the Protestants.[28] It is clear that from the doctrinal perspective such "bad icons" nonetheless conformed to their intention. Is this not the reason why the official documents (the *Acts* of the Great Council, the *Writing* of the three patriarchs and of the tsar) were more muted in their criticism than the above authors, and were limited to

26 I. N. Dmitriev, "Art Theory in Ancient Russian Literature," [in Russian] *Trudy Otdela drevnerusskoi literatury* IX (Moscow-Leningrad, 1953), 108-10.

27 "Letter," 42-3.

28 Maikov, ed., 137.

general considerations about iconographers? Euthymius the monk, Patriarch Joachim, and Archpriest Avvakum say nothing about the quality of icons. As for the people, an aesthetic appreciation of the icon was entirely foreign to them. Paul of Aleppo, who judged sacred art precisely from the aesthetic point of view, wrote: "As all Muscovites are known for their great affection and love of icons, they consider neither the beauty of the image nor the art of painting. For them, all icons, beautiful or not, are the same."[29] For the mass of the people, therefore, artistic quality was not the decisive factor. Whatever changes had occurred in the consciousness of the Church, the icon remained an expression of faith, independent of its aesthetic quality.

What, then, was the decisive factor that controlled the opinions of the authors of our innovating documents? In the work cited above, Dmitriev states:

> It would not be correct to suppose that the opinions expressed in the treatises were justified by "western ideas" that had penetrated among us in the seventeenth century. Anyone who knows the writings of the Byzantine theoreticians devoted to the question of art will certainly easily recognize the intimate link between our treatises and these works.[30]

Such a conclusion can only be the result of a purely superficial juxtaposition of texts. Certainly, the ideologists of the new art did not openly break with the Orthodox tradition: they even stressed their fidelity to the Tradition of the Church. This is why in their theological reasoning they often appealed to the thinking of the "Byzantine theoreticians" and repeated their classical exposition on the image. However, both in practice and in theory, as we shall see, they had recourse to ideas and they elaborated theses that were diametrically opposed to the tradition, and therefore to the "Byzantine theoreticians." Most certainly, "western ideas" do not fully explain their treatises; but the culture in the making, the way of thinking and of viewing life, and also theology "had put on a western dress."

This radical modification in culture and world vision, which appeared among the "elite" and the ruling circles of Russian society, had to bring with it an equally radical modification in art, a new attitude toward it, and

29 *Journey*, Bk IX, ch. 3, 136.
30 Dmitriev, "Art Theory," 110.

new aesthetic categories. This new vision of the world was peddled by a desacralized culture of the western type, a class culture. The art of this new culture was also desacralized, foreign to the masses. This very art and the way of understanding it revealed an artistic vision and new aesthetic categories that were no longer founded either on doctrinal premises or on the Orthodox spiritual experience, but which came from that desacralized culture. Faith itself was viewed as an aspect of culture; and in the appreciation of art the aesthetic factor became decisive. It is this factor, this new concept of art, which is the basis for the critical attitude toward the artisanal icons among the ideologists of the new style of painting.

Art historians have often observed that the treatises of the seventeenth century represent a defense of art. To a greater or lesser extent, all endeavor to justify art and prove its usefulness. But if the subject of these treatises is wider than the framework of sacred art, it is certainly the defense of the latter that caused their appearance. The work of Vladimirov is openly addressed to a well-defined antagonist (the defenders of traditional art and of the artisanal icon). The other documents, by contrast, do not name their opponent. Nonetheless, in the course of their argumentation, their apology assumed a clearly anti-iconoclastic character. "The creation of icons," Simon Ushakov wrote, "has been greatly praised in all centuries, countries, and social environments since it has been much used everywhere because of its great usefulness." He develops at length the classical argumentation against the iconoclasts using references to the Old and New Testaments. Describing the creation of icons as originating with God himself, he concluded: "If God forbids the making of images in the Decalogue, the one who reasons soundly will see that He forbids the fashioning of idolatrous images, venerated instead of God—not images that bring beauty, spiritual well-being, and that represent the divine economy." Referring to the Holy Face, he concluded: "Why should we not paint that of which God himself has given us an example?"[31]

The *Writing* of the patriarchs opens by stating that iconic art was not invented in India, as Pliny thought, nor by Pyrrho: "It is neither the Egyptians nor the Corinthians, nor the inhabitants of Chios, nor the Athenians who first invented this honorable art, as some have thought. It is indeed the Lord himself who is said to be the creator of all the arts and

31 S. Ushakov, "Discourse," 22.

of all matter."[32] In other words, the creation of images is not a pagan invention, "as some would think," but an aspect of human creation introduced by God himself. The patriarchs closed their argument as follows: to show in detail all the praises due this art would indeed be the same as "emptying the Atlantic with a cup."[33] Ushakov, on his part, concluded his account with the word:

> Hating this beauty of the Church and God's grace, the devil created through his servants an intolerable calumny of the holy icons by calling them idols, just as through a clever ruse he has smitten the image of God in Adam with a flaw, a great defect.[34]

But to defend icons and prove their usefulness to the Orthodox, especially to the Russians, was like breaking through an open door. At this time, the sin of the Muscovites was a somewhat exaggerated, occasionally even falsified, veneration of icons, rather than any leaning toward iconoclasm. It can therefore not be denied that these writings, devoted to aesthetic theory and which, according to the expression of Dmitriev, "justified the superior art of society's privileged circles," reflected at the same time the struggle against Protestantism—the Protestantism outside the Church as well as the protestantizing trends within the Church. Beginning in the sixteenth century, the iconoclastic danger became more acute because of the infiltration of Protestantism into the Muscovite state, and above all because of the rapid, conspicuous success of the Reformation in Poland and Lithuania. It was precisely at this time that Maximus the Greek wrote his anti-Protestant works (*Treatise Against the Lutherans Concerning the Veneration of Icons, Writing Against the Heretics*). The Protestant refusal to venerate images is the Judaizing heresy, against which the first treatise of the *Message to an Iconographer* had been written. As for the seventeenth century, Protestant pressure was felt very strongly in the entire Orthodox world, especially after the Calvinist and iconoclastic profession of faith by Cyril Loukaris, Patriarch of Constantinople, appeared within the Church itself. This profession of faith caused great upheaval, as much in the Greek-speaking East as in southern Russia. In Muscovite Russia, the question of Protestantism posed itself with great intensity early in the 1640's when the *Anthology* in defense of the holy

32 "Writing of the Three Patriarchs," 8.

33 *Ibid.*, 9.

34 "Discourse," *op. cit.*

icons was published (1642). The discussions became especially acrimonious when Valdemar, Prince of Denmark, asked for the hand of the Russian Princess Irene. Later, the authors of our treatises must certainly have been in continued contact with the Protestants residing in Moscow, as is known from the polemical disputes of Symeon of Polotsk with them.[35]

Aside from their anti-Protestant argumentation, our documents at the same time defended the new art that had become rooted in the Church and in the daily life of its members—the art of a culture independent of the Church. This new art, on the one hand, caused a blind infatuation and, on the other, provoked an equally blind opposition. The apology of the theoreticians of this new art is characterized by a particularly revealing trait: it uses the traditional anti-iconoclastic argumentation, both against those who denied icons and against the opponents of the new art and of new ideas. Thus, to its followers, this new trend in art became indistinguishable from the art which the Church had defended against the iconoclasts. Vladimirov simply equated the iconoclasts with those who opposed innovations in art.

Among the seventeenth-century documents, it is the *Writing* of the three patriarchs that is the most important for us since it best reveals the changes that had occurred in the concept of sacred art. The patriarchs viewed art above all from the perspective of its social, civil, and moral usefulness; therein lie the content and the basic meaning of their *Writing*. They did not analyze art from the perspective of the Church, but from that of creation pure and simple. For them, "the art of images" was art in general, independent of its ecclesial or secular character. Such confusion is not limited only to the *Writing* of the patriarchs: it is typical of all the documents in this group. Thus, in their argumentation, the patriarchs referred indiscriminately both to the Church Fathers and to pagan thinkers. In their reasoning and in the examples they cite, they put both on the same level. For example, while demonstrating that icons ought to be venerated on account of their link to the prototype, they naturally referred to St Basil the Great. But then they immediately added that even before him "the Stagyrite philosopher" (Aristotle) had found that the movement

35 In 1660, there were three Lutheran churches and one Reformed Church in the so-called German quarter in Moscow (see V. O. Kliuchevskii, *Works* [in Russian], III, 270).

toward the image and its prototype was the same. Thus the Christian doctrine of a Church Father on the personal link that exists, in the realm of grace, between the image and its prototype was reduced to an abstract philosophical concept. Speaking of the aim of art, the patriarchs explained that it consists, above all, in representing everything: the sacred and the profane. Images, they said, are like "learned instructors." Referring to St John Damascene, they likened the image to a book for the "unlearned." In agreement with the Seventh Ecumenical Council, they spoke of the correspondence between word and image: but this council spoke of the word of the Gospel, while the patriarchs referred to the word in general, and by way of example, cited the judgment of pagan philosophers:

> Simonides was not wrong in saying that the painting of images was silent poetry, whereas poetry was painting in words. Plato, the greatest of philosophers, did not miss the truth either when stating that the art of painting was alive but silent, voiceless because of the very excellence of its honor.[36]

For the patriarchs, as can be seen, the word, whether pagan or Christian, had value as such. They did not distinguish between the natural intelligence of the philosophers and the intelligence of the Fathers illumined by grace, by an understanding of revelation. The same holds true for their judgments concerning the image. Patristic theology was totally absent from their thought: the essential basis of sacred art, which witnesses to the Incarnation, eluded them altogether. It is true that in their text a certain distinction is made between the art of the Church and secular art.[37] But artistic quality is the only criterion they applied to the one and to the other. Their criterion was therefore exclusively aesthetic. On this plane there was for the patriarchs no difference, not only between the art of the Church and that of the world, but also between Christian and pagan art, as there had been none between the holy iconographers and the painters of pagan antiquity. By considering Orthodox iconography within the general domain of the creation of images, the patriarchs erased the demarcation line; as they had done in the realm of the word, they removed the fundamental differences that exists between the sacred and the secular image. The one remaining distinction was the subject:

36 "Writing of the Three Patriarchs," 12.

37 Let us note that the patriarchs, while stating that the origin of art goes back to God Himself in order to prove the sublimity of this human activity, refer to the sages of Antiquity: "The wise Greek sages," they say, "have left written commandments so that no slave or prisoner may learn the art of the image, and only the children of nobles and the sons of counsellors may be initiated into this art" (*ibid.*, 8).

Christian or not, sacred or profane. The very concept of sacred art is thus desacralized in the same manner as within Roman Catholicism. In this way the patriarchs supported the new art trend represented in Russia by Ushakov and Vladimirov. For such ideologues of innovation, there was no longer any difference between an Orthodox and a Roman Catholic image, as many examples indicate.

In this sense, the most telling documents are the *Letter* of Vladimirov and the work of Simon Ushakov. The motive that led Ushakov to take up the pen had been his discussions with John Pleshkovich, the Serbian archdeacon, concerning the innovations that had appeared in the painting of Russian icons. The content and the outlook of this writing are especially typical of the atmosphere in the seventeenth century. Articulate and concrete, this text reflects, more than the others, the thought pattern of the innovators, and the sources that nourished it. The two parts of the *Letter*—the first devoted mainly to a criticism of bad painting, the second to the discussion itself—are written forcefully and with passion. The author repeatedly uses violent expressions and polemical tricks that are not always entirely honest. The second part is entitled: "A Reply to Those who Humiliate the Painting of Holy Icons, or Answer to a Certain Blasphemer, John of the Wicked Mind."

The sense and context indicate that Pleshkovich was utterly hostile to western art and to the imitation of western models by Russian painters. Upon seeing at Ushakov's an image of Mary Magdalene painted in the western fashion, Pleshkovich spat at it, saying that "he did not approve of such clear images."[38] This provoked the discussion. We do not know Pleshkovich's reasoning, and evaluating it on the basis of Vladimirov's refutations is difficult. Because of Pleshkovich's hostility toward the new style of painting and his predilection for "bad" icons, Vladimirov accused his opponent of iconoclasm, that is, of nothing less than heresy. He even compared him to Constantine Copronymus: "In vain are you vehemently opposed to the beauty of the Church, and do you provoke anew the ancient struggle."[39]

38 This attitude of the Serb Pleshkovich is quite understandable if one remembers the importance that Orthodox art had for the Serbians of this time in the face of heterodoxy.

39 "Letter," 45. Such accusations of heresy were at times absurd. Thus a certain priest Loggin was accused of iconoclasm: he had "blasphemed the icon" because he had severely criticized a woman with too much white makeup, while the color white was used in the painting of icons. (see A. V. Kartashev, *History of the Russian Church* [in Russian], vol. 2 [Paris, 1959], 152).

In his evaluation of contemporary icons and in his attacks on Pleshkovich, Vladimirov showed how convinced and logical a partisan of western art he was, just as were Simon Ushakov and Symeon of Polotsk.[40] While praising western art, Vladimirov mentioned that he did not do this to praise the faith of other peoples. However, as people "of little faith," the westerners so greatly love wisdom and "very sophisticated painting" that they paint not only Christ, the Virgin and the saints, but also their kings, "as if they were alive."[41] As for Orthodox art, foreigners "do not denigrate icons that imitate the light, nor do they mock images of the saints—but they sneer at bad painting and at the ignorance of the truth."[42] What, then, was this truth, the ignorance of which caused the reproach of foreigners? Where did Vladimirov see it? Foreigners ridiculed not only badly painted icons but also the very concept of the image, that through which its authenticity is seen—and here, it seems to us, we approach the doctrinal question. The rest of Vladimirov's reasoning indicates that this is indeed the case. Russian iconographers must have heard reproaches like those about which Savvatii, the monk from the Solovki, spoke in his petition to the tsar in 1662: "Strangers laugh at us, saying that up till now we do not even know the Christian faith."[43] Indeed, the sympathy of the iconographer Vladimirov for western art colored his artistic reasoning with conceptions of the image and of its meaning that were proper to Roman Catholicism, not to Orthodoxy.

Let us recall that Vladimirov did not speak of secular but of sacred art, of the icon. But while defending it, he systematically referred to western painters who represented Christ, the Virgin, and portraits of kings "as if they were alive," without distinguishing between them. Gradually, Vladimirov himself adopted this attitude. In the method of representation, he no longer saw any difference between an icon, a cultic image (that

40 E. S. Ovchinnikova, who edited the "Letter" of Vladimirov, disagrees with G. Filimonov, who detected "a strong sympathy for western painting" in Vladimirov's attitude. Having made an exhaustive study of Vladimirov's treatise, Ochinnikova writes in the Preface to her edition that the question is apparently more complex (p. 13). She interprets the question as an expression of the perfectly legitimate struggle of the new art trend against the old, outdated tradition (p. 19). In fact, Vladimirov's sympathy extended far beyond western painting; as we shall see, it embraced the ideological content of which such painting was the expression.

41 "Letter," 45.

42 *Ibid.*, 41.

43 Cited by V. O. Kliuchevskii, *op. cit.*, 311.

of Christ or of a saint) and the common portrait of a person. "*The saints and other people* are represented by the lovers of wisdom not to obtain signs or miracles, but to have a true image of them, and to keep their eternal memory through the great love one has for them."[44] Vladimirov did not see how the confusion between a cultic image and a secular portrait results from a doctrinal attitude, and how it contradicts the Orthodox concept of the sacred image.

He insisted that images, above all that of Christ, must be historically true. He referred to the "image-not-made-with-human-hands" (the Holy Face), left to us by Christ himself. He explained with great clarity which representation of Christ is authentic, which one false and leading to error. He condemned those "who slap on the paint according to their own will, in an ugly, inappropriate manner, one not in conformity with the real face of Christ,"[45] which is, no doubt, according to the imagination. He indignantly mentioned the painter who, at the time of Leo the Great, had painted Christ "in the image of Zeus,"[46] that is, had copied an idol. Such a copy, just as one made from the imagination, was strangely associated for him with "bad painting." He also considered such a copy as a deviation from the image of Christ that was historically authentic. According to him, a "badly painted" image was false. "An inappropriate and badly painted image is unacceptable and contradicts its prototype."[47] To this Vladimirov added a very correct theological reasoning. While relying, no doubt, on St Basil the Great's well known work on the Holy Spirit, which he does not name, he stated that "God can only be adored through an authentic image of Christ." God is spirit, and only an image of the incarnate Son of God shows, in the Holy Spirit, both the divinity of the Lord and, through it, the Father.[48] Thus the authenticity of the image of Christ is indispensable to the adoration of the Holy Trinity. However, this traditional Orthodox judgment is contradicted by its practical application. For Vladimirov, an image of Christ is authentic when it imitates life, nature. "In every icon or human portrait, reasonable painters represent the aspect proper to each part, each joint, and thus every image or new

44 "Letter," 37.
45 *Ibid.*, 34.
46 *Ibid.*, 35.
47 *Ibid.*, 41.
48 *Ibid.*, 43.

icon is painted with light colors, rosy cheeks, and shadows—as in life."[49] Vladimirov was convinced that the Holy Face, the "Image-not-made-with-human-hands," was precisely such a naturalistic image.[50] In his opinion, then, authenticity meant fidelity to what the painter saw in the life surrounding him. "When he sees something or hears a description of it, he retraces this in images, that is, in his personages, making them resemble what one sees or hears."[51]

The theoretical foundation of such a concept of the image is found in the work attributed to Simon Ushakov. For him, the image as such is based on the same principle as that of a reflection in the mirror. Ushakov, too, cites the example of the Holy face, and then continues:

> Not only is the Lord himself the creator of the image, but every object to which sight has access possesses the secret and most amazing power of this art. For every object, when placed before a mirror, paints its image on it by a decree of divine wisdom. O miracle without miracle! A wondrous image appears that moves when man moves...laughs when he laughs, cries when he cries...and seems fully

49 *Ibid.*, 52.

50 A drawing made by him has been preserved, "representing the Holy Face with a living, humanly expressive face, with wrinkles on the forehead and around the eyes" (E. S. Ovchinnikova, *The Portrait in 17th Century Russian Art* [in Russian] [Moscow, 1955], 20). In 1663 this drawing was used in Vienna to make an engraving which bore the following caption in Polish: *A long time ago, upon returning from their pilgrimages, the Jesuit Fathers brought back to Rome the true image made without hands, the linen of Abgar. A copy of it has been engraved in Vienna, through the courtesy of Joseph Vladimirov, Muscovite iconographer.*

The iconographic manual of Siva reproduces this same engraving with the following explanation: *The transfer of the Holy Face from Edessa to Constantinople occurred in the year 6452 from the creation of the world, the year 944 since the Incarnation of Christ... This image is presently in Rome, at the church of St Sylvester, Pope of Rome.*

Now, we know that the Holy Face preserved in Constantinople disappeared during the sack of the city by the Crusaders in 1204. The Roman Catholic version according to which the Jesuits 300 years later (the order was founded in 1534) supposedly rediscovered it has replaced the Orthodox tradition about the fate of this image. Had it really been found and preserved in Rome, this would have increased this city's authority. Consequently, this Latin version did not arise by chance: it would play a leading role in the strong western pressure exercised in the spheres of theology, art, and everyday life. The very fact that a work of a Russian Orthodox iconographer had appeared in Vienna under the patronage of the Jesuits is already significant. For this, protection was needed and great practical ability. It is hard to determine the role played by Vladimirov himself in this reorientation. At any rate, this proves that in addition to his "strong sympathy" for western painting, he also had concrete contacts with the West. We should also note that the "Writing of the Three Patriarchs," after referring to the Orthodox tradition about the origin of the Holy Face, adds to it the western legend of Veronica, which appeared in the fifteenth century. To our knowledge, this is the first time this legend appears in an Orthodox context; it is repeated subsequently in the "Edict of the Tsar."

51 "Letter," 58.

> alive without having either a human body or soul. Is it not God himself who teaches us the art of painting icons through the intermediary of nature?[52]

The natural property of reflecting objects is compared by Ushakov not only to the creation of the Holy Face: he proposes this property as a model for human creation. To create means to imitate the mirror which reflects the divine order. To say this differently: for Ushakov as well as Vladimirov, the image, like a reflection in the mirror, should represent people and objects in their visible, daily condition,[53] that is, according to what is disclosed to the eye, to the emotions, and to reason.

This principle was applied to a realm that lies beyond the limits of such a natural concept. A concrete example will allow us to see how traditional Orthodox concepts were falsified by such re-interpretation. In the image of the Nativity of Christ, he states, the child "must absolutely be white and pink, but especially beautiful—not deprived of beauty since the prophet has said, 'The Lord has entered into his kingdom. He is adorned with splendor,' And, 'Lord, we will walk in the light of your face.'" "How then," he asks, "could one paint his face dark?"[54] But the two prophecies cited by Vladimirov have an eschatological meaning. The

52 "Discourse," 22-3. In ancient Russian manuscripts, one comes across the phrase "as if he were alive," which is used to characterize what is represented in the icon. In no case is this expression to be understood in the sense given to it by the seventeenth-century apologists of the new art trend. As Dmitriev has noted correctly (*op. cit.*, 113), this expression, as a form of praise, is applied to works of art of a totally different nature. Indeed, when the ancient Greek pagan writers as well as some Orthodox wished to praise an image, they said that it was "alive." The words are the same in the two cases, but the art they characterize is entirely different. This is because here the term "life" ("living") has two entirely different meanings. For both, the image represents life, but this life is not the same for each. For the advocates of the new art, the artistic translation of life—life being the inner, spiritual *praxis*—has been replaced by the direct representation of the life that is accessible to the eye, "as one sees something, or hears a description of it." What was alive in the art of the eleventh to the sixteenth centuries, has for them perished. The same is true for the concept of "remembrance" ("recall"). The advocates of the new art understood this term in a subjective, psychological sense, while to Orthodox consciousness (a term often referred to during Iconoclasm), it meant not merely a commemoration, but an ontological participation in the prototype.

53 Ushakov has painted an entire series of icons of the Holy Face in which he attempted to render the human flesh, a living body and details of various psychological states as well as the natural folds in the linen, with the greatest possible accuracy (see Plate 43). This painter undertook the composition of a type of illustrated manual, "an alphabet of this art; all the members of the human body which our art needs." That is, he demonstrated the manner in which the members of the human body are to be represented in a naturalistic instead of an iconographic fashion. See the end of his "Discourse."

54 "Letter," 57.

first is the prokeimenon of Sunday, that is, an image of the eighth day of creation, of the age to come. The second is used at the feast of the Transfiguration, that is, of the uncreated divine light. A better choice could not be made, since these two prophecies reveal precisely the essential character of the Orthodox icon, its eschatological orientation. But, we know, the icon can only render this eschatological meaning of the prophecies symbolically, and this is what eluded Vladimirov. In his view, vivid colors were needed to render the uncreated light; and to correctly transpose the prophetic words concerning the divine beauty and the uncreated light, one should, he believed, represent the new-born child with a white and rosy face, in the style of western painting.

He applied the same reasoning when speaking of the images of the saints.

> Where is the rule to be found stating that all the faces of the saints are to be represented equally tanned and dark? Not all the saints had a thin, drawn face. And if during their life certain saints did not look healthy because they neglected their body, they must exchange this face for a clear one after their death, having received their crowns. But even during their life many saints were noted for their striking beauty. Should one therefore represent them with dark faces?[55]

To buttress his reasoning, Vladimirov cited examples from Scripture:

> When Moses, the great one among the prophets, received the law from the Lord in Sinai...the children of Israel could not look at the face of Moses because of the light that rested upon him...Should one therefore depict the face of Moses as dark and tanned?

Or also,

> When the elders saw how very beautiful Susannah was, they coveted her. They slandered her because of it, and brought her before the court, ordering her to uncover the head so that they could absorb the beauty of her bright face...And in our time, you, Pleshkovich, ask iconographers to paint dark images that do not resemble the beauty of their prototype. You teach us to give the lie to ancient writings.

Now, first of all, we know that the faces on icons were not always dark: they were painted dark or bright, independent of the color they had during the saint's life. But what is utterly absurd in Vladimirov's reasoning is that he puts on the same level the face of a saint illumined by grace (that of Moses), physical beauty (which he likens to a bright face, following the taste of his time), the physical, sensuous beauty of Susannah which

55 *Ibid.*, 58.

prompted the lust of the elders, the bright aspect of the flesh in bloom, and the divine light. Vladimirov saw no difference between the two types of beauty. In order to transpose the one and the other into an image, it is appropriate to use bright colors, and above all to approach visible reality as much as possible.[56] Thus Vladimirov no longer viewed the beauty of holiness in the traditional Orthodox manner, that is, as a divine likeness. For him, it consisted of physical beauty, and the divine light was the physical light. He saw in both merely natural properties that did not surpass the limits of the created. Through this, he introduced the concept of created grace into the icon. It is precisely this beauty, "similar to the one seen in life," which the opponents of innovation "had begun to hate," Vladimirov states. "They maintain that the beauty of the saints is depicted to tempt the Christians."[57] He became indignant when artistic paintings prompted his opponents not to prayer but to guilty feelings, and he compared them to sodomites. "Listen. How dare you look with evil intent at images of saints, harboring seductive thoughts in your heart?" "A true Christian," he taught "should not be tempted even when looking at prostitutes, and should not be overcome with passions when looking at icons of the saints." Vladimirov required that one take a spiritual, not a carnal, attitude before man's physical beauty, and that one should not let oneself be tempted. In other words, according to his reasoning, an image that reproduces nature puts one in the same situation as if one were looking at a prostitute, and one should have the same reaction. Thus, one is supposed to pray no longer *thanks to* the icon, but *in spite of* it.

According to Vladimirov, an image that imitates nature ought to reflect the various physical and psychic states corresponding to the circumstances in which the person represented found himself. Thus, before Pilate, Christ "stood perturbed." On the cross, "His senses had withered."[58] As for Ushakov, leaning on the well-known sermon delivered by St Basil the Great on the day of St Barlaam, he said: "We strive to represent the

56 Among the saints, there were certainly persons of great physical beauty. But what the church presents to us as an example is not this fleshly beauty but the saint's inner life. Is this not the reason why the Gospel does not give us any physical descriptions, and why it exalts neither the beauty nor the strength of the human body? Is it not the goal of Holy Scripture, like that of the icon, to lead us to a state opposite to the one in which the old men found themselves when they looked upon Susannah?

57 "Letter," 61.

58 *Ibid.*, 57.

sufferings of the martyrs in a vivid manner so that the viewers, their hearts moved by pity, might share their merits." Here we find the unequivocal influence of western spiritual concepts.[59] We detect not only the Roman Catholic concept of "merit" but also that of the image as a stimulant for natural emotions. It is true that an image which reproduces the physical and emotional life of man in a naturalistic manner can only claim to prompt a corresponding emotion in the viewer, a natural emotion.

Thus, even if in the theoretical reasoning of our authors there is a certain formal link with "the Byzantine theoreticians," even if they lean on them, in reality—let us repeat—they reveal a diametrically opposed attitude in their concept of the image (its content, its beauty, the light, and so forth). We are confronted here with two views of the sacred image that are radically different: the Orthodox concept and that of Roman Catholicism. It is toward the latter that the concept of the image and its pictorial language are now oriented.

Their new concept of the image has led the authors of the treatises to view traditional Orthodox art as a stage that has been surpassed. Manuscript G of the same *Letter* of Vladimirov contains a typical variant that clearly illustrates his attitude toward the art of the past (or at least that of the trend to which he belonged). Here we read: "That there have been bad icons in Russia from ancient times is not surprising, since a people that has been led from darkness into the light only recently could not, in such a short time span, fully absorb an art of such great wisdom,"[60] that is, the art that seemed ideal to Vladimirov, as it represented the truth with greater accuracy. Thus he was concerned not merely with his contemporary iconographers and their errors, but with the Russian art of the preceding periods in its entirety, with this art which Vladimirov viewed as being "an ancient usage." But a usage is not a written law:[61] it perpetuates itself thanks to ignorance and lack of understanding.

It should be said that such reasoning was somehow supported by the

59 In the same realm of ideas, Ushakov executed a representation of the seven deadly sins, which was but a reworked copy of an illustration of Ignatius of Loyola's "Spiritual Exercises," with a purely Roman Catholic "classification" of sins (see Sidorov, *The Drawings of the Ancient Masters* [in Russian] [Moscow, 1955], 45; and *History of Russian Art* [Moscow, 1959], vol. 4, 498-99).

60 "Letter," 25.

61 *Ibid.*

reactions prompted by the reforms of Patriarch Nikon. Indeed,

> It was the abrupt and indiscriminate rejection of all Old Russian ceremony and ritual which gave Nikon's reforms their sharp quality. Not only were these rites replaced by new ones, but they were declared false and heretical, almost impious.[62]

True, things were different with respect to sacred art. Nonetheless, within the overall context, the "corrections" of the rites by Nikon, on the one hand, "scandalized and wounded the conscience of the people," leading to protests and a schism. On the other hand, for people leaning toward innovation, they offered a pretext to doubt the Orthodox tradition and its art, and to criticize them. Archpriest Avvakum, for example, mentions the following words of the innovators, uttered during a discussion: "Dear Avvakum, do not be stubborn. Why do you mention Russian saints? They were stupid, our saints. They could neither read nor write—why believe them?"[63] Such a negative attitude was seen particularly among those painters who were most influential.

What then was the reaction of the Church and of the defenders of traditional art? In what positive ways did they fight this abandonment of Orthodox doctrine about the concept of the images, this distortion of its language?

Before all else, one should say that, because of the loss of the authentic, traditional criterion and the implantation of scholastic theology, the defenders of Orthodox art found themselves, when faced with new theories, without defense on the theological plane.

Characteristically, the Great Council of Moscow did not react to the appearance of radical modifications in sacred art, despite the pressing actuality of the question, just as the sixteenth-century councils had not reacted to deviations from the Orthodox teaching concerning icons. Certainly, the council showed its concern for the quality of sacred art and required that icons be painted according to ancient models. But Vladimirov and Ushakov also painted according to ancient models. The council's silence is all the more strange since the petition of Symeon of Polotsk, an advocate of the new art, was completed precisely to be discussed there. Yet there is no echo of it except on one point: the representation of the Deity. The right to pronounce judgment on sacred

62 G. Florovsky, *Ways of Russian Theology*, Part One, trans. R. L. Nichols (Belmont, MA: Nordland Publishing Co., 1979), 95.

63 *The Life of Archpriest Avvakum* (the Russian text) (Moscow, 1960), 139 and 156.

art was no doubt reserved for the patriarchs of the East. But as we have seen, their judgment was not only not opposed to the introduction of alien elements into Orthodox art, but, on the contrary, supported it with its authority. In his work cited earlier, Dmitriev writes:

> In his argumentation, Ushakov refers to the phenomena of nature, to man's natural properties, and to the social dimensions of art, but he loses sight of the interests of the Church. This oversight, so typical of the development of Russian thought in the seventeenth century, is also characteristic of the *Writing* of 1668 [namely, that of the three patriarchs].[64]

With a painter carried away by new ideas, such an omission is understandable; it is more than strange with patriarchs. As much in content as in overall orientation, their writing is unquestionably the least ecclesiastical document of all. As for the Writing of the tsar, it essentially followed that of the patriarchs and also contained no reaction against the innovations.

Nonetheless, the break of the new trend with the Tradition provoked a violent reaction, characterized by the unhealthy rending proper to the seventeenth century. According to the defenders of the Tradition, neither western art itself nor its imitation was acceptable to the Orthodox Church because they had been contaminated by ideas of the non-Orthodox West. Those who defended the innovations viewed them as a legitimate succession to the Orthodox tradition, and the new art forms introduced by Vladimirov and Ushakov as the normal development of traditional sacred art. By contrast, for the defenders of the Tradition, the issue was not "a development" but a break: alien elements had been introduced into Orthodox art, thereby denaturing it. The "imitation of nature," the portrayal of what was directly visible inspired "fear" in them. Vladimirov asked Pleshkovich: "You say that the image of the Lord scares you. Is it because you have seen it painted in the imitation of man as he is?...It is the image of Emmanuel...but your blasphemous tongue has called it that of a German woman."[65] This is because the human flesh, deprived of the spirituality of the represented prototype, became associated in the eyes of the defenders of the Tradition with everything "German," that is, heretical. To them it seemed repulsive. "On the hill they have painted a German on this cross," Pleshkovich said, referring to a cross made in 1654-1655 and placed at the gate of Iaroslavl. As for Archpriest Avvakum, he expressed himself in the spontaneous

64 Dmitriev, "Art Theory," *Trudy Otdela* IX (Moscow-Leningrad, 1953), 102-3.

65 "Letter," 50-1.

and picturesque fashion that is typical of him:

> The image of the Savior, Emmanuel, is painted with a puffy face, red lips, curly hair, fat hands and muscles...He looks altogether like a German, pot-bellied and corpulent; the one thing lacking is a sword on his hip. But all this is painted according to unspiritual thoughts, for the heretics themselves have begun to love the coarse flesh. They have abandoned the sublime.[66]

As is known, it is Patriarch Nikon whom Avvakum held responsible for all such innovations, though this opinion is contested in a passage by Vladimirov. In their discussion, Pleshkovich referred to the violent measures against the new art taken by Nikon. Vladimirov replied by saying that

> the honorable, most reverend Nikon...shows great zeal for the very judicious painting of icons...He does not condemn the art of painting, but he does not praise crude, unsuitable iconographers—not only Latins but also the Russians when they are bad...As for beautiful painting, he does not repudiate it.[67]

Nonetheless, according to Pleshkovich and the testimony of Paul of Aleppo, the patriarch destroyed icons, not because they were badly painted, but precisely because of their western, heterodox character, saying that this painting "resembled Frankish portraiture."[68] Thus what Vladimirov says about Nikon's fight against so-called badly painted icons, regardless of their Latin or Russian character, does not agree at all with the patriarch's real attitudes. Furthermore, the icons Nikon destroyed belonged to nobles and high dignitaries: they could therefore hardly have been of poor artistic quality.[69] We may state with certainty that Patriarch

66 The Letter of Archpriest Avvakum, *ibid.*, 4th sermon, 135.

67 "Letter," 55.

68 *Journey*, Bk IX, ch 3, 137.

69 There is not the slightest reason to ascribe to Nikon a resistance only to Latin and Lutheran iconographic subjects, and a sanctioning of westernized painting (see *History of Russian Art* [in Russian], vol. 6 [Moscow], 426). Paul of Aleppo is very clear in his description. In 1654, Nikon ordered that the icons painted by Muscovite painters "according to Frankish and Polish models" be collected, "removing them even from the houses of functionaries of the State." He had their eyes gouged out and had them paraded through Moscow, threatening to punish all those who would paint icons according to such models. In 1655, on the Sunday of the Triumph of Orthodoxy, after the Liturgy in the cathedral, the patriarch had these icons brought to the middle of the church. He gave a long address, saying that such painting was "inadmissible," using explanations borrowed from a collection of patristic sermons (this undoubtedly was the *Florilegium*, edited in 1642). Then taking the icons one by one, he showed them to the people, saying, "This icon comes from the house of such and such a dignitary, the son of so and so." He broke them and threw them on the stone slabs. Together with Patriarch Macarius of Antioch and Metropolitan Gabriel of Serbia who were present, he anathematized all those who would paint such images or keep them at home (see *Journey*).

Nikon was aware of the limits of sacred art.

As for the apologists of the new art, the artistic quality of the western art works was for them a sufficient reason to venerate them on par with the Orthodox icon. Thus, in the eyes of Vladimirov, both a naturalistic image, and even its printed reproduction, could be blessed and replace an icon.

> When we see among our compatriots or among foreigners an image of Christ or of the Virgin which is well printed or painted with this very sagacious art...we prefer such salutary objects to all the things of the earth. We buy them from strangers with love...and receive a representation of Christ on sheets of paper or on boards, kissing it lovingly. Following the rules, we bring such icons to the priests who recite the necessary prayers, praise God, and bless His image by sprinkling it with holy water, as is prescribed by the rubrics for the consecration of church objects.

A little further, after enumerating various cultic objects made with materials of foreign origin, he continues: "And as all this is blessed by the hands of the bishop and the words of prayer, why should one also not bless this image of Christ painted in imitation of life, even if it is made by foreigners?"[70]

These words of Vladimirov indicate that there was a ritual blessing not only of icons painted "according to Frankish and Polish modes," which were destroyed by Patriarch Nikon, but also of western art works and reproductions, as if they were Orthodox icons. This shows the degree of indifference toward the doctrinal content of the icon reached by the Muscovite clergy. This indifference, indeed this forsaking of the doctrinal criterion, provoked a violent reaction on the part of Patriarch Joachim. In his *Testament*, he wrote:

> In the name of the Lord, I command that icons of the God-man, of the most holy Mother of God and of all the saints not be painted according to Latin and

70 "Letter," 50. In his argumentation, Vladimirov put the various objects used in worship (sacred vessels, priestly vestments) on the same level as a cultic image. However, as far as the Orthodox icon is concerned, such an assimilation is impossible. We find here a confusion which points, once again, to the total loss of the Orthodox concept of the image. Furthermore, this sin exists also in our own time: witness the list of subjects to be discussed at the council (*Journal of the Patriarchate of Moscow* [in Russian], 11 [1961], 25). Such confusion places the question of the icon back to the stage which preceded its solution at the Seventh Ecumenical Council. Let us recall from the *Acts* of the Council that what was asked was, "How should icons be venerated? In the same manner as sacred vessels, ornaments and other cult objects, or differently?" We know that the Council answered this question as follows, both in the *Acts* and in its decision: the icon must be venerated on the same grounds as the cross and the Gospel. In other words, the image was placed not in a utilitarian but in a dogmatic context.

> German representations. They are tainted and unacceptable, newly invented according to individual fantasies; they corrupt our Church tradition. If churches have any that are incorrectly painted, they must be removed.[71]

With regard to prints of foreign origin, Patriarch Joachim wrote in his *Testament*:

> Numerous merchants buy German printed sheets of paper, sold by German Lutheran and Calvinist heretics. On them, one sees people portrayed as people from their own country, clothed in foreign German dress, according to their blasphemous opinions and not according to the ancient models found among the Orthodox. These heretics do not venerate icons, and because of these sheets of paper the veneration of icons is neglected.

This led the patriarch to forbid completely both the printing of sacred images on paper and their sale, and even more their use in churches or houses in place of icons.[72]

In spite of the inadequacy and the weakness of the arguments of the defenders of traditional art ("The Church does not allow such new expressions. This is not our custom," Patriarch Joachim said), one senses in them, if not an understanding, then at least a sure instinct of what an Orthodox image is. For them, it was not a question simply of denying what was incomprehensible or of rejecting "the new." They repudiated what was foreign, even hostile, and clearly destructive to Orthodox art, and more generally to spirituality as such. This refusal was not expressed in rational terms: rather it was instinctive, and thus all the more violent. Patriarch Nikon smashed icons painted in the new fashion and poked out their eyes. The "ascetic" reasoning of Archpriest Avvakum is lacking in the rational arguments. He limited himself to insults which, it is true, were spirited and humorous. Though he attacked Nikon, whom he held responsible for the innovations in iconography, the fact remains that these two men were, on this point, of the same opinion. A convinced grecophile (at least during his patriarchate) and an enemy of western culture, Nikon was accused by his enemies of being an advocate of "German" customs. Such an accusation, at least with respect to icons, is absurd. The principles of sacred Orthodox art were as dear to him as to Avvakum and his followers. If the latter tried to accuse Nikon, it is because they viewed the

71 The book entitled *Shield*, quoted in the Iconographic Manual of Bolshakov (in Russian), edited by Uspenskii (Moscow, 1903).

72 Mentioned by N. Pokrovskii in *The Monuments of Christian Iconography and Art* (in Russian) (St Petersburg, 1900), 370.

changes in art within the overall context of the reforms undertaken by him. For Avvakum and his followers, everything in this domain was sacred to the same degree, immutable like the Deity itself.

Only Patriarch Joachim clearly defined what he was fighting against, even if his definition falls rather within the province of ascetic spiritual practice, and lacks a theological terminology. Such images, he says, are "perverted." They are "newly-invented according to individual fantasies." They "corrupt the Orthodox tradition." Joachim and Archpriest Avvakum took the same approach in judging the new art: they viewed it, above all, from the perspective of ascetic practice, and condemned it as a "new invention" according to "the vague impulses of the flesh." Nevertheless, the very concept of such ascetic practice and of the judgments it inspired were different in each case. For Joachim, this new art was unacceptable in worship, in the church; for Avvakum it was likewise unacceptable, but on the national level, on the level of the state which, from his perspective, included the Church as a component of its life. "Alas! Alas! O unhappy Russia! What is this craving for German customs and mores that has taken hold of you?"[73] For Avvakum and his supporters, the sacred character of the state extended to everything; in it, there could be nothing that was not sacred. Salvation, for him, dwelt not in a creation inscribed in the Tradition but in the intangibility, the immutability of everything that exists, whether authentically traditional or not, whether in form or in content. "What has been established before us, let this remain so unto ages of ages."[74] This immutability thus included everything that had been introduced into sacred art: all the fantasies of Russian painters, all the borrowings from the West covered by the authority of the sixteenth-century councils, as well as the borrowings that had been accumulated since. All this was viewed as an inviolable heritage *in toto*, and to our day the old-ritualists remain attached to this, at least in principle.

It should be noted that, aside from Avvakum, the advocates of traditional art did not defend it by reason of its venerable antiquity: not one of them speaks of it in such terms. Only their opponents (Vladimirov) and contemporary art historians attribute to them this attitude of attachment to "the old."

73 *The Life of Archpriest Avvakum* (in Russian) (Moscow, 1960), 136.
74 *Ibid.*, 109.

In the seventeenth century, the corruption of sacred art followed two paths. On the one hand, there was a a re-orientation of the Orthodox concept of the image and of its pictorial language in the Roman Catholic sense. On the other, there occurred a deterioration of iconography under the influence of western representations and the fantasies of Russian painters. We have seen in the previous chapter that the abandonment of the realism of the Gospel initially provoked strong protest. But in the seventeenth century such allegorism—such painted parables that betrayed Gospel realism—multiplied. Beginning with the sixteenth century, "There remained not one single idea, however unimportant, belonging to the poetic view of the world in Christianity, not a single liturgical chant, not a single psalm, for which no attempt was made to personify it in iconography."[75] Certainly, among the numerous new iconographic subjects, some can be justified by their theological content (for example, "All of creation rejoices in you, full of grace," and "Let every breath praise the Lord," and other icons of cosmic character); but for the overwhelming majority it was a question of fantasies which corrupted Orthodox iconography. We have already said that errors occur in all periods, as much in iconography as in theology, but earlier we dealt with exceptional phenomena. Now, however, they become legion, caused as much by borrowings from outside Orthodoxy as by "departures of a drunken folly," in the words of Zenobius the monk.

Certain seventeenth-century documents are devoted to the struggle against this corruption of Orthodox iconography: the Acts of the Great Council of Moscow, the works of Euthymius the monk, in part that of Patriarch Joachim, and also those of Vladimirov. In this domain also, we come across a phenomenon that is typical of this period: on the one hand, certain iconographic subjects are well studied and critiqued according to a theological criterion (particularly by the Great Council); on the other hand, no light is shed on the incompatibility of the very principle of such painting with Orthodox tradition.

For Vladimirov, the iconographic errors were but one indication of the low level to which, according to him, Russian painting had sunk. He criticized such errors in the same way that he criticized the "bad icons," and on the same plane. He saw a similarity between errors in the old icons and

75 G. Filimonov, "Surveys of Russian Christian Iconography: Sophia the Divine Wisdom" (in Russian), *Vestnik Ob. drevnerusskogo iskusstva pri Mosk. Publichnom Muzee* (Moscow, 1976), 131.

errors contained in the liturgical books, and he often referred to the correction of the books which was then taking place.[76] Vladimirov's criticism is justified only when he attacks subjects due to the "frenzy" and the "fables" of Russian iconographers such as, for example, Archangel Michael represented as a monk wearing the great schema,[77] "or something still worse and blasphemies against God still more impious: Christ in the lap of the Father on the Cross, as if He were in the folds of the garments of the Lord Sabaoth"[78]—a subject borrowed from Catholicism and already criticized in its own time by Viskovatyi. However, the criterion on which Vladimirov based himself was neither the Tradition of the Church nor theology: it was "reason." Who, then, "being endowed with reason will not mock such folly?," he asked.[79] In the examples we have cited, the criterion of reason is justified by the patent absurdity of what he criticizes. But this criterion is insufficient and powerless where the evidence is not as absolute, and where a theological understanding, however elementary, is indispensable. What was important for Vladimirov was to bring out the "frenzy" that contradicted the natural reason, but whether any particular style of iconography was Orthodox was for him no longer significant. Thus, in his controversy with Pleshkovich, he constantly invoked historical realism, but he did not understand this in the Orthodox sense. For him, only the fact as such was important, independent of its meaning. Where will you find, he asks, the image of the Mother of God in the icon of the Descent of the Holy Spirit? One does not find her there, he replies, "believing her excluded from the reception of the Holy Spirit."[80] Indeed, before the direct borrowings from Latin iconography, no image of Pentecost with the Mother of God at the center can be found in Orthodoxy. But this is explained neither by an ignorance of Scripture nor by the content of this feast, a content that eluded Vladimirov. In accordance with his ideas, he created an image of the Descent of the Holy Spirit according to a Catholic model, with the Virgin at the center.[81] For the

76 "Letter," 25.

77 "For these idiots say that when the archangel Michael became a monk, he was not yet able to defeat Satan until he had received the great habit [great schema]," *ibid.*, 59.

78 "Letter," 60.

79 *Ibid.*, 59.

80 *Ibid.*, 60.

81 See L. Ouspensky, "Quelques considérations sur l'iconographie de la Pentecôte," *Messager de l'Exarchat du Patr. russe en Europe occident.*, nos 33-4 (Paris, 1960).

same reason—the decisive importance of the historical fact as such—he omitted the Apostle Paul in the iconography of this feast, since he was absent from the event.

The iconographic question that most seriously preoccupied the Great Council of Moscow was the "representability" of God the Father, or rather the impossibility of representing Him. This question, as we have seen, had already been raised at the Hundred-Chapters Council, and at the 1553-1554 Council. For these councils, the decisive criterion had been the practice existing in their time, regardless of whether or not it conformed to the Tradition of the Church. Now the question was raised differently; the Great Council judged current practice in the light of doctrine and of Gospel realism, as the opponents of this iconography had done in the sixteenth century. To prohibit the representation of God the Father, the Great Council used extremely harsh terms and required conformity not to words, but to the sense of Orthodox doctrine.[82] Unlike Metropolitan Macarius, who had justified this image on the basis of prophetic visions, the Great Council commented on these visions in the traditional Orthodox way, which totally excluded the possibility of using them to represent God the Father. By this conciliar decision, all the subjects defended by Metropolitan Macarius were banned. In its essentials, the decision of the Council was limited to subjects associated with the representation of the Deity.

The same subject was at the core of the preoccupations of the monk Euthymius. According to him, "it is quite proper to paint the image of God the Father," but for him this image was the incarnate Word, Christ represented as a Child in the arms of his Mother, as a twelve year old adolescent in the temple, then as an adult "as He lived in the world and performed miracles," and as He had been seen by the patriarchs and prophets. Euthymius severely condemned the image called the "Paternity," seeing in it, "as much on the part of the painters as on that of those who had commissioned it, an audacity deprived of all sense." As the monk Zenobius had done in his time, he brought to its logical conclusion the transposition of a verbal image into an icon, thereby bringing its absurdity to light. Thus iconographers depicted Christ "seated, wearing episcopal

82 In view of the great importance of this subject and the relevance of the decision of the Great Council, we will study this question separately in the next chapter.

vestments." But the Lord is also called priest, hegumen, lamb, shepherd, king of kings, "and there still is a great number of other ascriptions. If the iconographers were to begin painting Christ as a priest wearing a phelonion, an epitrachilion and the rest, or else in the image of a monk hegumen, could anything be more absurd than this?"[83] The thought of Euthymius is characterized by an intolerance toward any alteration of the historical truth, any deviation from Orthodox doctrine. Christ and each of the saints must be represented "according to what they looked like when they lived and walked upon the earth." But the iconographers were painting "the most holy Mother of God wearing the vestments of a queen, and with wings"; and St John the Forerunner "wearing a royal, winged crown on his head." Is this in agreement with the Tradition of the Church? Euthymius asked. "The most holy Mother of God is indeed called a Queen, but not because she wears royal vestments. It is because of the birth of her Son, the eternal King of kings, and also because she now lives in the Kingdom of Heaven and reigns eternally with her Son." As for the representation of St John in the form of an angel, with wings, Euthymius said that the title of "angel", is given to numerous saints ("an earthly angel, a heavenly man"), and although the word "angel" means "messenger" and suits the Forerunner especially well, such a portrayal with wings contradicts the historical truth, since he had no wings during his life.

While Patriarch Joachim limited himself to criticizing typically "German" iconography, the monk Euthymius blamed Russian iconographers for truncating and occasionally falsifying the meaning of the Orthodox image through their fantasies and their use of foreign iconography. In short, Euthymius rejected private "visions" and concepts that were not based on the catholic teaching of the Church, on doctrine.

"The iconographers have recently begun to paint the most merciful Lord according to Latin and Lutheran models, holding an apple or a globe in His hand, which the holy Fathers do not accept." Certainly, all of creation is in the Savior's power, but "the power of the Lord is not a globe. It is His divine, life-giving word that delivers us from eternal torment," and this word is represented by means of a phylactery or a book. Also, "At present, certain iconographers begin painting the holy apostles according

83 "Questions and Answers Concerning Russian Iconography" (in Russian), ed. G. Filimonov, *Vestnik Ob. drevn. iskusstva* (Moscow, 1874-1876). See "Materials."

to German models, with instruments of torture according to the torments they suffered." And not only the apostles, but

> the holy martyrs themselves are represented to this day according to the ancient tradition, holding not instruments of torture, even if they had suffered various torments, but the cross of Christ. They show thereby that they suffered for the One who was crucified, that they were fortified by it in their sufferings, and that they are now still glorified by it and not by instruments of torture.

In other words, what is important is not the method of execution itself but its meaning. The essential trait of Orthodox iconography, especially Russian, has always been to deepen the meaning, not to reduce it to an episodic aspect, so typical of western iconography. What is important for the Orthodox consciousness is not the type of death inflicted upon the saints, but their witness to Christ, to His Incarnation and redemptive mission.

Like Patriarch Joachim, Euthymius reacted vehemently against an abandonment of the tradition in the representation of the Mother of God, whom "the iconographers also paint according to Latin models, with unveiled head and disheveled hair..." "As soon as she was betrothed to Joseph, the holy Mother of God no longer left her hair loose. She wore a veil, even though she was, and remained, a virgin." In other words, such a representation of the Mother of God did not correspond historically to her social situation.[84]

But it was the image of divine Wisdom, Sophia, which Euthymius attacked most severely:

> The hypostatic Wisdom, as the Word and Power, is the Son of God. And if one dares to paint Wisdom under an invented form, one will soon begin to dare painting the Word by means of another invention, and the Power by still another one. What, therefore, could be more absurd than that?[85]

84 One of the borrowings mentioned by Euthymius is the image of the Virgin "standing on the moon." The reference is probably to the image named "St Sophia of Kiev." This subject appeared in the West at the end of the fourteenth century, with a precise theological content: as a symbol of the Immaculate Conception. "How widely the Catholic opinion about the Immaculate Conception had spread among the seventeenth-century theologians in Kiev is well known...The members of the congregation of the Academy of Kiev were required to confess that 'Mary was not only without actual sin, but also free from original sin'" (G. Florovsky, "The Veneration of Sophia Divine Wisdom in Byzantium and Russia" [in Russian], "Works of the Fifth Congress of Russian Academic Organizations Abroad, Part One" [Sofia, 1932], 498, 500).

85 Euthymius undoubtedly had in mind the image of Sophia of Novgorod. For centuries, this image had provoked explanations of its "mysterious meaning" that were as varied as they were arbitrary. That gives us food for thought; it certainly indicates how unclear the image was.

"Concerning all this," Euthymius said,

> one should ask the wisest men to explain with greater precision, provided the explanation be according to Holy Scripture and not according to human syllogisms, that is, untrue reflections. For according to the tradition of the holy apostles, the saints command us to flee from syllogisms that lead to lies. If [according to the saints] we abandon our faith for syllogisms, our faith will be lost, for we will no longer believe in God, but in men.

The monk Euthymius ended his exposition by expressing the desire to have the Church decide such questions.

> Everything that has been written should be presented to the consecrated bishops so that they give a sure testimony of the truth, so that everything that must be kept be kept, and everything not suitable for keeping be rejected. As to what is doubtful, let this be corrected by the judgment of the Church.

The world of learning, both before and after the Russian Revolution, has greatly, sometimes even enthusiastically, appreciated the seventeenth-century treatises on art history and the role they have played. Scholars before the Revolution saw in them a rejuvenation of worn-out concepts and principles, and of art itself which was imitating ancient models. In the treatise of Vladimirov some scholars even saw "a ray of light in the development of the artistic ideas of old Russia."[86]

For contemporary scholars, the value of these treatises lies in the fact that they contributed to the genesis of the aesthetic concepts of an emerging secular art, this within the framework of the changes to which the regime and the culture were subjected at the time. The treatises contributed to the ingrafting of a practically new way of viewing artistic creation, and to the desacralization of church art.

Despite all the differences between the presuppositions of the two groups, their general attitude toward church art is the same. The old scholars, educated to the norms of academic painting with its proportions, its anatomy, its perspective, etc., and the scholars of our day, starting from ideological premises, view sacred art in the same way the authors of the seventeenth-century treatises: for them, it is an art that is characteristic of a certain historical period; its secularization corresponds to an organic evolution.

It must be said that the seventeenth-century treatises, especially those of Vladimirov and of Ushakov, were in fact constructive in the sphere of

86 G. Filimonov, "Simon Ushakov and his Age in Russian Iconography" (in Russian), *Sbornik Ob. drevnerusskogo iskusstva* (Moscow, 1873), 81.

secular art, that is, the art that went hand in hand with the culture emerging in Russia during this epoch. But at the same time, these treatises were unquestionably destructive of sacred art: destructive because, while they did not leave its domain, they broke with its principles. They applied to sacred art the principles that are at the basis of contemporary western art, and thereby undermined the very foundations of sacred art. This was not a question of separation of church and state,[87] which would be normal; the evil lay precisely in the absence of separation. While becoming secular, art still pretended to be religious. The emerging secular art certainly asserted itself and acquired its independence—but its principles were also applied to the art of the Church, and they distorted it. The change that occurred in sacred art is certainly neither a development nor an evolution. The evolution of this art corresponded, as it still does, to the orientation of the spiritual life, and to the general condition of the Church. As long as the Tradition of the Church was lived in a creative manner, new forms constantly emerged from within and developed according to their own inner, spiritual laws. In the seventeenth century as well, church art that had remained traditional also evolved. But this evolution, by being attuned to the life of the Church during this epoch, was oriented toward conservatism and artistry. It was not "the last century of ancient Russian art," of the icon, nor was it the inner depletion of sacred art, as is often thought. Just as the Church itself can neither disappear nor become exhausted, nor can its art either wither or disappear. But for a long time this art ceased to play the leading role of being the mouthpiece of Orthodox faith and life.

The vision the Church has of the world does not evolve. It remains the same in our day, just as the Church remains the Church. But within the context of the reforms of government and culture, two different cultures and two different visions of the world collided under the common aegis of Orthodoxy. The world vision distinctive of the new culture made its way into the consciousness of the faithful and into their spiritual life. And with it "was implanted a foreign, artificial, external tradition that blocked the paths of creativity."[88] It obstructed the paths of both theology and of art. Orthodoxy experienced the introduction of a concept of the image,

87 See *History of Russian Art* (in Russian), vol. 4 (Moscow, 1959), 54.

88 G. Florovsky, *Ways of Russian Theology*, Part One, trans. R. L. Nichols (Belmont, 1979), 86ff.

and of its creation, that was independent of the spiritual life. The piety of the faithful remained Orthodox, but their thinking and creativity broke loose from Orthodoxy. They lived in an Orthodox way, but thought in a heterodox manner. Their attitude toward the holy icon remained the same, but they created it according to the western fashion. Spiritual wholeness disintegrated. Seventeenth-century man remained profoundly believing, but in his creativity he felt attracted to a non-Christian understanding of the world—a world the meaning of which his faith no longer disclosed. The painter's social experiences, varied and multiple, mingled with his faith, marked his art.[89] This is the ambiguity so typical of the seventeenth century: a defense of the traditional art forms and their destruction are often found side by side, not only in the same social class, but even in the same person. What is tragic in the attitude of Simon Ushakov and of Joseph Vladimirov is that they undermined the very reality they defended so passionately and with such great conviction.

When considering sacred art as a whole, we can see how in the seventeenth century the spiritual decay that ravaged the entire Orthodox world resulted in a complete loss of the Orthodox conception of the image, in a total lack of comprehension of its content. This is the main reason for its decay on the one hand, for its secularization on the other. External efforts were made to raise its artistic level, but its decomposition was spiritual—and in this respect it is the official documents of the Church authorities themselves that are most revealing. We have seen that the *Writing* of the three patriarchs was marked by the total absence of any theological basis for the image. The professions of faith that appeared in the seventeenth century as a reaction to the Calvinist profession of faith by Patriarch Cyril Loukaris are equally characteristic. These include: the confession of faith of Metropolitan Peter Moghila, reworked and later signed by four patriarchs and twenty-two bishops, and known under the title of the *Orthodox Confession; The Message of the Patriarchs of the Eastern Catholic Church Concerning the Orthodox Faith* (the confession of Patriarch Dositheus of Jerusalem); and the *Catechism* of Peter Moghila. All

89 Hence the anxiety one perceives, among other things, in the contracts made with iconographers at the time: "Let nothing that is incompatible with the holiness of the church be introduced" (see G. Brusov, *The Frescoes of Yaroslavl* [in Russian] [Moscow, 1969], 15). Such clauses are frequently found in Roman Catholic documents; it is hard to imagine them in the Orthodox Church at the time of Dionysius or Rublev.

these documents have a markedly latinized character. In the domain of sacred art they just blindly followed the ways of thinking imposed by Protestantism. They limited themselves to justify this art and to refute the accusation of idolatry. Their content and spirit did not go beyond the framework of the Council of Trent (1563); and the *Catechism* of Peter Moghila only offered an abbreviated recapitulation of the decision of this council. What is most distinctive of these documents is the absence of any theology. It is as if the patristic theology of the image had never existed. Even when they refer to the Seventh Ecumenical Council, the authors and the signatories only explain how icons ought to be venerated, just as the Council of Trent had done. Equally typical is that, precisely in the seventeenth century, everything concerning the doctrinal content of the icon disappeared from the Russian Synodicon of the Triumph of Orthodoxy.

The patristic heritage ceased being a criterion, and this was made apparent at times in an absurd way. Thus in the sixteenth century (in 1512) a compilation of various translations by an unknown author appeared in the "Chronicle" under the title "Prophecies of the Hellene Sages." Here, prophecies invented to defend the Incarnation and the dogma of the Trinity were put in the mouth of philosophers from antiquity, Sybils, even pagan gods. These "prophecies" were subsequently introduced into various collections and became widely disseminated, especially during the seventeenth century.[90] Corresponding to this literature, these "Hellene Sages" appeared on the walls, doors, even on icons in Russian churches. Later they were at times even depicted on the iconostasis, below the row of local saints. These images were accompanied by "prophecies" corresponding to those in the collections, written either on phylacteries or on the background of the image. Thus "Hermes-the-Thrice-Great...explains his theology. To understand God is difficult; to explain Him impossible, for He is tri-personal, ineffable, a being and a nature the likeness of whom is not found among men." Menander: "The Deity cannot be investigated. It is ineffable and indestructible, composed and glorified in three persons, heard by man and glorified. God must be

90 Thus they are included in certain editions of a polemical nature, such as the *Book of Cyril* (1644), containing patristic works that explain Orthodox doctrine. Articles against heretics (Arians, iconoclasts, Latins, Armenians) were included, among which were the "prophecies of the wise Hellenes," intended no doubt for the anti-heretical struggle.

born of the pure Virgin Mary, and in Him I also believe." Homer: "A star will shine on mortals: it will be Christ among the nations. He will live strangely, seeking to unite the earthly to the heavenly." Aphrodition ("the Persian of the perverse spirit," who was earlier vehemently accused by St Maximus the Greek): "Christ will be born of the pure Virgin Mary. I too believe in Him,"[91] and so forth. Taking into account the renewed interest in antiquity, it is possible that the "Prophecies of the Hellene Sages" represented, in the eyes of the seventeenth-century people, an attempt to combine "the history of natural revelation given to the pagans in the persons of their best representatives"[92] with the fullness of the Christian revelation. But in fact these contrived "proofs" were part and parcel of the "inventions" and the "frenzy" in iconography which had flooded sacred art, and by means of which an attempt was also made to prove something. It is striking and revealing of the condition of seventeenth-century thought that these "prophecies" prompted no reaction, even though they appeared in the main churches of the Kremlin (the cathedrals of the Assumption and the Annunciation). Even the documents devoted to a criticism of bad painting and iconographic errors said nothing against such doctrinal "proofs." On the contrary, some of the iconographic manuals gave instructions on how properly to paint the "Hellene Sages" with their "prophecies."

The growing interest in antiquity, in wisdom from the outside, contaminated the ecclesial consciousness and distorted it. This is expressed, on the one hand, under the unhealthy form of false prophecies and, on the other, through an amalgamation of concepts based on the natural reasoning of the philosophers and on texts by the Church Fathers. A perfect example is the *Writing* of the patriarchs, in their argumentation concerning art. In the properly theological realm, the same assortment can be seen, for example, in Symeon of Polotsk, a latinizer and and advocate of the new art. Thus in his work *The Crown of Faith*, which Patriarch Joachim called "a crown of baleful thorns grown in the West,"[93]

91 N. A. Kazakova, "The Prophecies of the Greek Sages and Their Representations in Russian Painting" (in Russian), *Trudy Otdela drevnerusskoi literatury* XVII (Moscow, 1961), 368.

92 N. A. Speranskii, "Ancient Russian Iconostases" (in Russian), *Khristianskoe Chtenie* (September-October 1893), 330.

93 A. V. Kartashev, *History of the Russian Church* (in Russian) (Paris, 1959), vol. 2, 247. Like some of our contemporaries, "Symeon did not attach great importance to the differences between the Greek Orthodox and Catholic churches" (A. M. Panchenko, "Word and Knowl-

Symeon referred indiscriminately to the Church Fathers and to a series of pagan authors. Such appeals to Antiquity provoked a severe criticism from certain quarters. For example, Metropolitan Isaiah of Kiev, driven from his see by Peter Moghila, wrote:

> The reasoning of this world is one thing, the reasoning of the spirit another. All the saints studied the spiritual reasoning coming from the Holy Spirit and, like the sun, they have illuminated the world. But now one acquires his power of reasoning not from the Holy Spirit, but from Aristotle, Plato, Cicero, and other pagan philosophers. This is why people are utterly blinded by falsehood and seduced from right understanding.[94]

The realm of ritual and liturgical order was also affected by the general decline of spiritual life. In Russia during the seventeenth century, this was occasionally expressed in totally unhealthy phenomena. Thus, chanting was frequently performed "in several voices" (that is, two or three parts of the office were celebrated simultaneously, and sometimes even five or six, which created a terrible cacophony). There was also what was called *khomonia*, that is, the introduction of vowels and sometimes of entire syllables into the chanted words, which distorted the text completely. "While listening to such nonsense, some who admitted not one critical thought in matters of religion saw in it a mysterious meaning, which eluded their understanding,"[95] just as they saw such a meaning in the inventions of the iconographers on subjects taken from liturgical texts, the psalms, and so forth. It is symptomatic that every attempt to return to the norm by correcting errors, even in the most flagrant cases, met with opposition and was classified, without the slightest embarrassment, as "heresy." It is all the more surprising that, alongside all these unhealthy phenomena, most icons (except, naturally, those affected by the new trend and by deformations) still remained on a high spiritual and aesthetic

edge in the Aesthetics of Symeon of Polotsk" [in Russian], *Trudy Otdela drevnerusskoi literatury* XXV [Moscow, 1970], 236).

94 Cited by G. Florovsky, *Ways of Russian Theology*, Part One, trans. R. L. Nichols, 70.

95 N. D. Uspenskii, *The Art of Ancient Russian Chant* (in Russian) (Moscow, 1955), 205. In the domain of sacred chant, something analogous to the phenomenon of new art happened. The ornamentation of the sixteenth and the beginning of the seventeenth centuries gradually gave way to theatrical melodies brought to Russia by foreign masters. Patriarch Nikon himself, although he had destroyed icons painted according to "Polish models," invited Polish singers who sang "like an organ." For his choir, Nikon ordered the compositions of Martin Mielczewski, the director of the Rorantist chapel in Cracow, who was famous in his day (see G. Florovsky, *Ways of Russian Theology*, Part One, 105).

40. *The Meeting of Our Lord.* 17th-century Russian icon. Korin Collection, Moscow.

level (Fig. 40). What is more, the painting of icons represented the most healthy element of the liturgical life of the Russian church.

The general decay of spiritual life in Orthodoxy left it defenseless against pressure from the western confessions. Faced with this new situation, Orthodoxy was unable to express its vital, creative strength, either in the face of the West with its inner warfare (the crisis of the sixteenth-seventeenth centuries) or in its own life. In opposing the western confessions, Orthodox theologians fought blindly, employing Protestant arguments in their struggle against Catholicism, and Roman Catholic ones in their struggle against Protestantism. This does not mean that Orthodoxy itself had changed. While theological thought became paralyzed, spiritual life continued. The Church did not modify its doctrine in the least and adopted no false dogmas.

> However low the level of theological training may have been as a result of historical circumstances, and despite the heterodox influences that had penetrated it, the Orthodox Catholic Church continued to keep, as its basis, the faith of the Ecumenical Councils and of the holy Fathers. More precisely, it was the Church of the Ecumenical Councils and of the holy Fathers.[96]

The Orthodox Church certainly kept its independence from Roman Catholicism and Protestantism, but its theology and its art did not. It is in art that this dependency revealed itself in the most pronounced and long-lasting manner and was therefore the most fraught with consequences. For a long time this state of affairs produced a kind of "inferiority complex" toward western art, and uprooted it for a long time from its living, creative tradition.

The new art trend modified not only the very concept of the image and its content; not only did it divert the Orthodox image from its direct, immediate purpose—it naturally also modified the artist's consciousness.

In the traditional sacred image both content and form are defined by the prototype represented, the inner state of which radically differs from sinful man's actual condition. It is its participation in the divine life, its holiness, that defines both form and content. In Orthodox sacred art man is the primary, not to say the only, subject. No art is so devotedly attached to him, no art raises him as high as the icon. Everything the icon

96 Archbishop Basil (Krivochéine), "Les textes symboliques dans l'Eglise orthodoxe," *Messager de l'Exarchat du Patriarche russe en Europe occidentale*, no 49 (1965), 11.

represents refers to man: the landscape, the animals, the plants. In the hierarchy of beings, man occupies the dominant position. He is the center of the universe, and the surrounding world is presented in the condition that man's holiness confers upon it. The painters of the new trend, however, endeavor to portray the saint as if he were not a saint.

Man's body and his emotional world appear not to be destined for sanctification. Everything that refers to man's nature and all things surrounding him are portrayed as being alien to spiritual sanctification, to the transfiguration. The human being continues to be the main subject of the image, but in his actual, non-transfigured condition. "This image of man in all its inner significance becomes lost in the abundance of things, animals and plants. Man merely becomes a fragment of the big, bustling world, and is no longer able to occupy a dominant position in it."[97] Man is lowered to the level of the rest of creation. The hierarchy of being is broken.

In the sixteenth century it was the image of the Incarnation, the image of Christ, that became lost in allegories, parables, and so forth. At present, the image of deified man, the outcome of the Incarnation, disintegrated into a *mimesis* (imitation) of the present life. First, the economy of the second Person of the Trinity became indistinct, then that of the Holy Spirit. The authentic link between the image and its prototype—a link disclosed with such depth and insight in the Orthodox icon—was broken. In the formula, "God became man so that man might become God," the second half seems to have slipped away from the artist's awareness: it was no longer perceived existentially. Life and self-awareness were severed from the very purpose to which man is called: divine likeness. This eliminated the eschatological orientation of the icon, deprived it of all dynamism. In other words, the image ceased to be a revelation of God, "a revelation and manifestation of what is hidden": it was deprived of its Christian meaning and goal. From this point on, there was no longer an image that was specifically Christian insofar as it expressed Christian life and doctrine. There was only the use by Christianity of an image which was alien to it. Just as for the secular mind there is no human reason illumined by a knowledge of God, but only the use by Christianity of man's natural, unaided reason. Art gradually ceased to be the Church's own language; it

97 *History of Russian Art* (in Russian), vol. 4, 39.

only served the Church from the outside. This has always been, and still is, the case in Roman Catholicism; and this way of seeing also began to enter the Orthodox consciousness.[98] Thus one arrives at a conscious break with the principle established by the Seventh Ecumenical Council, according to which only the artistic aspect properly belongs to the artist. In this manner, the principle formulated in the *Libri Carolini* was adopted: the image is the fruit of the painter's imagination, and he is responsible for it as its author. The integral catholic experience of the Church was broken into the multitude of the particular notions of isolated painters.[99] The concept of authorship became the same as in our time; the road was cleared for the principle which, owing to the new trend, was later to dominate and express the official life of the Church. Such art would remain alien to the people until the moment when the ruling circles, secular and ecclesiastical, imposed it by administrative means.

98 Hence the statement which is often heard not only among Roman Catholics but even among Orthodox bishops, that the councils, supposedly, did not define a special type of ecclesiastical image.

99 This situation is clearly illustrated by the appearance of signed icons in the seventeenth century. Certainly, the example of Greek painters who began signing their icons in this age may have influenced the Russian iconographers. Also, E. Ovchinnikova, who edited the "Letter" of Vladimirov, is right in linking this question "to the theories expressed by him about the need for a personal signature or a painter's seal under his work" (*ibid.*, 10), precisely as an expression of his personal responsibility for the content of his work. On the traditional icon, an author's signature as such is a phenomenon that is extremely rare, if not exceptional.

41. "*The Paternity.*" 15th-century Russian icon.
Tretiakov Gallery, Moscow.

16

The Great Council of Moscow and the Image of God the Father

Chapter 43 of the *Acts* of the Great Council of Moscow is devoted to the question of the image of the Divinity, in particular that of God the Father. The chapter is entitled, "On the Iconographers and the Lord Sabaoth."[1]

> We decree that a skilled painter, who is also a good man (from the ranks of the clergy), be named monitor of the iconographers, their leader and supervisor. Let the ignorant not mock the ugly and badly painted holy icons of Christ, of His Mother, His saints. Let all vanity of pretended wisdom cease, which has allowed everyone habitually to paint the Lord Sabaoth in various representations according to his own fantasy, without an authentic reference...We decree that from now on the image of the Lord Sabaoth will no longer be painted according to senseless and unsuitable imaginings, for no one has ever seen the Lord Sabaoth (that is, God the Father) in the flesh. Only Christ was seen in the flesh, and in this way He is portrayed, that is, in the flesh, and not according to His divinity. Likewise, the most holy Mother of God and the other saints of God...
>
> To paint on icons the Lord Sabaoth (that is, the Father) with a white beard, holding the only-begotten Son in his lap with a dove between them is altogether absurd and improper, for no one has ever seen the Father in His divinity [Fig. 41]. Indeed, the Father has no flesh, and it is not in the flesh that the Son was born of the Father before all ages. And if the Prophet David says, "from the womb, before the morning star, I have begotten you" [Ps 109/110:3], such generation is certainly not corporeal, but unutterable and unimaginable. For Christ himself says in the Holy Gospel, "No one knows the Father except the Son." In chapter 40, Isaiah asks: "What likeness will you find for God or what form to resemble his?" Likewise, the holy Apostle Paul says in chapter 17 of Acts: "Since we are God's offspring, we ought not to believe that the Godhead is the same as gold, silver or stone shaped by human art and thought." St John of Damascus likewise says: "Who can make an imitation of God the invisible, the incorporeal, the undescribable, and unimaginable? To make an image of the Divinity is the height of folly and impiety" [*On the Heavens*, Bk IV, chapter 17, on the image]. St Gregory Dialogos forbade it in a similar way. This is why the Lord Sabaoth, who

1 The original appeared in the *Acts of the Councils of Moscow of 1666-1667* (Moscow, 1893). Some passages that do not deal with the subject treated are omitted here.

is the Godhead, and the engendering before all ages of the only-begotten Son of the Father must only be perceived through our mind. By no means is it proper to paint such images: it is impossible. And the Holy Spirit is not, in His nature, a dove: He is by nature God. And no one has ever seen God, as the holy evangelist points out. Nonetheless, the Holy Spirit appeared in the form of a dove at the holy baptism of Christ in the Jordan; and this is why it is proper to represent the Holy Spirit in the form of a dove, in this context only. Anywhere else, those who have good sense do not represent the Holy Spirit in the form of a dove, for on Mount Tabor He appeared in the form of a cloud, and in another way elsewhere. Besides, Sabaoth is not the name of the Father only, but of the Holy Trinity. According to Dionysius the Areopagite, Sabaoth is translated from the Hebrew as "Lord of Hosts." And the Lord of Hosts is the Trinity. And if the Prophet Daniel says that he has seen the Ancient of Days sitting on the throne of judgment, that is not taken to mean the Father, but the Son at His Second Coming, who will judge all the nations with His fearsome judgment.

Likewise, on icons of the Holy Annunciation, they paint the Lord Sabaoth breathing from His mouth, and that breath reaches the womb of the Most Holy Mother of God. But who has seen this, or which passage from Holy Scripture bears witness to it? Where is this taken from? Such a practice and others like it are clearly adopted and borrowed from people whose understanding is vain, or rather whose mind is deranged or absent. This is why we decree that henceforth such mistaken painting cease, for it comes from unsound knowledge. It is only in the Apocalypse of St John that the Father can be painted with white hair, for lack of any other possibility, because of the visions contained in it.

It is good and proper to place a cross, that is, the Crucifixion of our Lord and Savior Jesus Christ, above the Deesis in the holy churches in place of Lord Sabaoth, according to the norm preserved since ancient times in all the holy churches of the eastern countries, in Kiev, and everywhere else except in the Muscovite State. This is a great mystery kept by the holy Church...

The Council concludes with the words: "We say this to shame the iconographers so that they stop making false and vain paintings, and from now on paint nothing according to their own ideas, without an authentic reference."

The main subject of this chapter is therefore a question of principle. Is it possible to represent the Divinity, in particular God the Father, in human form? We recall that in sixteenth-century Russia, this question had been raised at the Hundred-Chapters Council. Raised in relation to the image of the Old Testament Trinity, it probably dealt with New Testament icons of the Trinity (the "Paternity," the "Synthronon"), though this is not formulated specifically. As much in the discussion between Metropolitan Macarius and Viskovatyi as at the Council of 1554, the question of the portrayal of the Divinity focused above all on the image of God the Father. The defenders of this image, like its detractors, agreed in saying that it was impossible to portray God in His essence. But while the opponents saw in it an attempt to do so anyway, and consequently as a "fantasy," its advocates replied that God is represented not according to His nature but according to the prophetic visions. Metropolitan Macarius based his justification on widespread church practice. For partisans of the portrayal of God the Father, this last argument has remained decisive to our day. This image "had become a custom."[2] Sergius Bulgakov has stated that "the icon of God the Father...though not foreseen by a direct decision of the Seventh Ecumenical Council, is nonetheless legitimated through its accepted use in the Church."[3] This "legitimization" by practice has shown such resilience that, in spite of the decision of the Great Council of Moscow, it was mentioned even recently in official handbooks for the clergy.[4] Explaining the symbolism of the hand reaching out of heaven, the author states: "The introduction of this symbol in sacred art is explained by the desire the Church has to preserve its flock from errors concerning God the Father."[5] Another customary symbol to represent God the Father was the image of an old man or the Ancient of Days. But, as we have seen, the Great Council of Moscow not only did not recognize the accepted usage but condemned it with an abruptness so typical of the epoch, stating that this representation originated in "a mind deranged or absent."

2 Archpriest Anatolius, *On the Painting of Icons* (in Russian) (Moscow, 1945), 82.

3 Sergius Bulgakov, *The Icon and Its Veneration. A Dogmatic Survey* (in Russian) (Paris, 1937), 137.

4 For example, Lebedev, *The Science of the Liturgy* (in Russian) vol. 1 (Moscow, 1901), 119-20.

5 The explanation, given by certain authors, of the hand as a symbol of God the Father is rather arbitrary. For example, I. N. Bogoslovskii states on p. 16 of *God the Father, First Person of the Trinity, in the Monuments of Ancient Christian Art* (in Russian) (Moscow, 1893), that "in the language of painters, the right hand is, as it were, a monogram of God the Father." Such a statement is refuted by iconography itself. In the Old Testament and in Jewish art (for example, in the synagogues of Beth Alpha and Dura-Europos, third century A.D.), the hand is generally a symbol of the Divinity. It signifies that God is present and addresses Himself to man: "There the hand of Yahweh came on him" (Ez 1:3); or that God speaks, "The word of Yahweh came to me, saying" (Jer 1:4; 2:1), and so forth. This meaning of the hand has remained the same in Christian art. If, in some cases—for example, in the images representing an action of the Trinity—one can see in it the symbol of God the Father, in the icons of saints, by contrast, the hand is often accompanied by the inscription IC XC; or Christ himself is represented instead of the hand. There is, therefore, no reason to see in the image of the hand the exclusive symbol of the person of the Father, without taking into account the iconographic subject where it is found. This symbol is explained well by W. Loeschke in "Neue Studien zur Darstellung des tierköpfigen Christophoros," *Beiträge zur Kunst des christlichen Ostens*, vol. 3 (Recklinghausen, 1965).

Nonetheless, this decision prevented neither the dissemination of the image nor, as shall be seen, its theoretical justification.

From the beginning of the quarrel about the image of God the Father down to our time, this image was justified by prophetic visions: that of Isaiah, "I am a man....[and] my eyes have seen the King Yahweh Sabaoth" (6:5), and especially that of Daniel, which gives a more concrete, descriptive image, "one that was Ancient of Days took his seat; his raiment was white as snow, and the hair of his head was like pure wool" (7:9, see also 7:13). These visions of the Lord Sabaoth and of the Ancient of Days, understood as figures of God the Father, were not themselves the subjects of icons, but the representation of God the Father was considered possible because of them. They served as the basis of this representation, accompanied by corresponding inscriptions: "We portray the Father without beginning in the form of an old man, as Daniel saw him," as the manual for iconographers by Dionysius of Phourna puts it,[6] "or for depicting God the Father in the form of an old man or of the Ancient of Days."[7] At the beginning of the twentieth century, teachers in schools of iconography taught the delineation "of the Lord Sabaoth" in icons of the Holy Trinity (we are dealing here no doubt with the subjects called "Paternity" and "New Testament Trinity") "according to the indications in Scripture and his apparitions to certain elect in the Old Testament."[8] This indication is also found in certain manuals for iconographers (*podlinniki*), in which the very image of God the Father appeared from the seventeenth century on.

Thus God, who could not be represented in His divinity, could be portrayed in human form. For some He could be portrayed only in His Incarnation (as the Son of God); but for others, it was also possible to represent God the Father, in accordance with the Old Testament visions.

But if we consider the patristic commentaries on the Old Testament prophecies, as well as the liturgical texts, it becomes clear that to see visions of God the Father in such prophecies is flagrantly to contradict the manner in which the Church viewed them. The Church related such prophetic visions not to God the Father but to the Son of God. All of them prefigure His Incarnation and have no other aim than its preparation, including Daniel's

6 M. Didron, *Manuel d'iconographie chrétienne grecque et latine* (Paris, 1845), 451.

7 I. N. Bogoslovskii, 65.

8 *Iconographic Collection* (in Russian) (St Petersburg, 1907), vol. 1, 84-5.

eschatological song ("I saw in a dream at night") which prefigures the Second Coming of Christ. John of Damascus has left us the most systematic account of the patristic view on theophanies and Old Testament visions:

> And Adam saw God, and heard the sound of His feet as He walked in Paradise in the cool of the evening, and hid himself (Gen 3:8). Jacob saw and struggled with God (Gen 38:24), for it is evident that God appeared to him as a man sitting upon a throne (Is 6:1). Daniel saw the likeness of a man, and one like a son of man coming before the Ancient of Days (Dan 7:13). No one saw the divine nature, but the image and figure of what was yet to come. For the invisible Son and Word of God was to become truly man, that He might be united to our nature, and be seen on earth.[9]

It is precisely in this sense that the Church explains the visions in the liturgical texts that celebrate the prophets, in those of the Sunday of the Patriarchs, and especially in the Liturgy of the feast of the Presentation of the Lord in the Temple. This feast celebrates the encounter between the Old and the New Testaments, thus revealing the meaning of the Old Testament prophecies in the most concrete and clearest way. In the person of St Simeon, the Old Testament prophetic ministry "departs in peace" and the New Testament Church greets its founder, announced by the prophets as the "Head of the Old and the New" (sticheron of the aposticha). In this feast, the Church seems to summarize the prophetic prefigurations. "You have been seen by the prophets, Jesus, as much as it was possible to see You then" (second sticheron of the aposticha). "The one who created Adam" (Matins, oikos), the same who is "the Ancient of Days who formerly gave the law to Moses, is seen today as a child" (first sticheron of the lite), and so forth. The vision of the Lord Sabaoth (the title applied in images to God the Father) by the Prophet Isaiah is

9 *De imaginibus oratio* III, ch. 26, PG 94(I): 1345; *On the Divine Images*, trans. David Anderson (New York: St Vladimir's Seminary Press, 1980), 80. As far as is known (see, for example, Joseph Barbel, CSSR, *Christos Angelos* [Bonn, 1941]), Hippolytus of Rome (third century) represents the only exception among the ancient fathers in the way he comments on the theophanies and visions of the Old Testament. In his *Commentary on Daniel* (Paris: Editions du Cerf, 1947), ch. 11, 282, while predicting the Second Coming, he states: "For Daniel, the Ancient of Days is none other than God and the Lord of all things, the Father of Christ Himself...." By contrast, certain fathers expressed themselves very strongly in the opposite sense. Thus Hilary of Poitiers writes: "The one Son who is in the bosom of the Father has proclaimed God to us, whom no one has ever seen...This is what the words of the prophets tell us, what is announced by the Gospel and indicated by the apostle, and what the church confesses: the one who has appeared is the true God. But let no one pretend he has seen God the Father" (*De Trinitate* 5, 34, PG 152: 153A).

included as one of the readings of the Liturgy of the Presentation and it is commented upon as follows: "When in a vision Isaiah saw God who will be incarnate, O never setting light who rules the world" (irmos of the fifth ode of the canon). The vision of the prophet Ezekiel is likewise commented upon: "You appeared as a prophet of God, O wondrous Ezekiel, for you announced to everyone the Incarnation of the Lord, the One who is the Lamb and Creator, the Son of God, who appeared for eternity" (Liturgy of the feast of the Prophet Ezekiel, July 21, kontakion). "And Daniel, the just and marvellous among the prophets, clearly showing forth your Second Coming, says, 'I see thrones set up and the judge seated, and the river of fire flowing'" (Sunday of the Patriarchs, fourth sticheron on "Lord, I call upon Thee").

Thus, all these theophanies and prophetic visions of the Divinity are revelations of the future. They are understood by the Church in a christological context, and the name "Ancient of Days" is applied not to the Father but precisely to Christ. There is not one liturgical text that ascribes the prophetic visions or the title "Ancient of Days" to God the Father.

It is the imagery-filled content of the prophecy of Daniel that served as a pretext for its use in portraying of God the Father. There is a vision of two different beings each with his own designation: the Son of Man and the Ancient of Days: "And behold, one like the Son of Man came with the clouds of heaven, and came to the Ancient of Days" (Dan 7:13). What is not clear is the relationship between the two characters, who were understood as two different persons. Since the Son of Man was Christ, then the Ancient of Days, who is seated on the throne, and into whose presence the other is brought, was understood as God the Father. Here also we should rely on patristic commentaries and on the Liturgy. Cyril of Alexandria states: "'He came to the Ancient of Days.' What does that mean? Is this a reference to a place? This would be absurd since God is not in one place but fills everything. What then does this mean, 'He came to the Ancient of Days'? It means that the Son attained the glory of the Father."[10] As we have already stated, there is no direct revelation of the Divinity in the Old Testament, and all the prophetic visions are visions not of the nature or of the divine Persons, but of the *glory* of the Divinity. Even a vision as concrete as that of Isaiah, "My eyes have seen the king, the Lord of Hosts" (6:5), is explained by Christ himself as a vision of glory:

10 *In Danielem prophetam*, PG 70: 1462.

"Isaiah uttered these words because he had seen his glory, and it was of him that he spoke" (Jn 12:41). This is why the Council explained that the inscription "Sabaoth," which normally accompanied the image of God the Father (on icons of the Trinity or when He was portrayed alone) is false: the name Sabaoth "who is the Divinity," means not the Father, but "the Lord of Hosts," and refers to the entire Trinity, that is, in the vision of Isaiah, to the glory of the Divinity common to the three Persons, Father, Son, and Spirit—a glory manifested by the One who was to become man.

Thus, according to St Cyril, "the Son attained the glory of the Father" means that the Son in the humanity assumed by Him attained the glory of the Father from whom, in His Divinity, He was never separated. And the vision of Daniel prefigures the two states of the same Son of God: humility in the Incarnation (the Son of Days). This is precisely how the Orthodox Church understands the vision of the two characters: "Daniel spiritually learned Your mysteries, O Lover of man; for in purity of his spirit he saw You walking on the clouds as Son of Man and Judge of all the peoples and kings" (Feast of the Prophet Daniel and the Three Youths, December 17, fifth ode of the canon). This is why the prophecy of Daniel "is not taken to mean the Father, but the Son who, at His Second Coming, will judge all the nations with His fearsome judgment."

Thus the anthropomorphic image of the Godhead, the beholding of His glory by the Old Testament prophets, can only refer to Christ, either in the context of the Incarnation or in that of the Second Coming. This is how the Orthodox Church interprets the Old Testament visions, and this understanding nullifies the basic argument of those who advocate the possibility of representing God the Father. To detect the two different persons in the vision of Daniel would be to apply to a prophecy the logical categories it transcends. From this derives the false interpretation allowing one to see the image of the Father in the Ancient of Days.[11]

The Great Council of Moscow examined the principle of the portrayal of the Deity not in an abstract manner, but in the context of specific iconographic subjects, in particular of the representation called "Pater-

11 Moreover, only the way in which the Church understands the Old Testament prophecies elucidates the antinomian character of the biblical texts about seeing God—texts which seem contradictory to us: on the one hand, "I am a man...and my eyes have seen the King, Yahweh Sabaoth" (Is 6:1); on the other, "No man can see me, and live" (Ex 33:20 and Jg 13:22).

nity." The Council's opinion on this would-be trinitarian image is preceded by a judgment on the portrayal of God the Father: "No one has ever seen the Father in the flesh" and "no one has ever seen the Father in His Divinity." The Council did not develop this principle further; limiting itself to a brief formulation of the argument, it categorically prohibited any image of God the Father "without an authentic reference," that is, having no foundation in revelation. The Council started from a classical Orthodox premise by contrasting the non-incarnate Father to the incarnate Son. God cannot be represented except in the incarnate second Person of the Holy Trinity. The Council viewed the depiction of the non-incarnate and therefore invisible Father as a representation of the Divinity. Basing itself on the apophatic thesis of the inconceivable and therefore unrepresentable God, the Council essentially translated the same principle used by the Orthodox apologists in the iconoclastic period. "Why do we not represent the Father of our Lord Jesus Christ?," the Fathers of the Seventh Ecumenical Council asked through Pope St Gregory II. "Because we do not know what He is...and if we had seen and known Him as we have seen and known His Son, we would have tried to describe and represent Him in art."[12] The Ecumenical Council, as can be seen, not only rejected "through a direct decision" the icon of God the Father, as Sergius Bulgakov thought, but it contrasted the impossibility of representing the non-incarnate Father to the possibility of portraying the Son of God. It indicated, and this is particularly important, that from the doctrinal point of view, there can be no image of God the Father.[13] The

12 Mansi XII, 963E. Also see the above chapter, "The Iconoclastic Teaching and the Orthodox Response."

13 We must note here the two radically antithetical attitudes toward this text from the *Acts* of the Seventh Ecumenical Council, expressed by two Greek authors of the eighteenth century: Macarius of Patmos and St Nicodemus the Hagiorite. The first, while attacking Roman Catholics, asks: "Are they Christians, the ones who in contradiction to the Seventh Ecumenical Council represent the Father who cannot be seen?" ("Homily on the Day of the Three Hierarchs," in the collection *The Gospel Trumpet* [*Euaggelike salpigx*], eighteenth cent., 323). On the other hand, St Nicodemus objects: "The Father without beginning must be represented as He appeared to the prophet Daniel, that is, as the Ancient of Days. And if Pope Gregory, in his Letter to Leo the Isaurian states that we do not represent the Father of our Lord Jesus Christ, he says this so that we would not represent Him according to His divine nature" (*Pedalion* [in Greek] [Athens, 1957], 320).

On this subject, as can be seen, Nicodemus shares the point of view accepted since the time of Metropolitan Macarius; like him, he moves away from the way in which the Church understands the prophetic visions. It is true that, for the Church, holiness has never been

first Person of the Holy Trinity, who did not become incarnate, is indeed the bearer of the divine nature, "for the word Divinity means nature," as St John of Damascus explained (therefore, an image of the Father, bearing only the divine nature, would be an image of the Divinity), "and the word Father means Hypostasis."[14] Representing the one or the other is impossible, "since no one has seen the Father in His Divinity." St John of Damascus insisted on this on several occasions: "If anyone should dare to make an image of the invisible, formless and colorless Divinity, we reject it as a falsehood."[15] For the Seventh Ecumenical Council and the Orthodox apologists, the lack of an image of the Father follows directly from the Incarnation, the latter being the only basis for the New Testament image and for the possibility of portraying God. For the Orthodox sensibility, any representation of God, aside from the Incarnation, is excluded. "I boldly draw an image of the invisible God," said John of Damascus, "not as invisible, but as having become visible for our sakes by partaking of flesh and blood. I do not draw an image of the invisible Godhead, but I paint the image of God who became visible in the flesh."[16] Although He is the Image of the Father, Christ Himself cannot as such be captured in matter before His Incarnation; according to His Divinity, He is as unportrayable as His Father. "Limiting the unincarnate Word in space is not only senseless and absurd...It is idolatry," Theodore the Studite wrote.[17]

For the Orthodox defenders of icons the image was not only a proof of the Incarnation, a testimony to the historicity of Christ, it also witnessed to the reality of the eucharistic sacrament. If such testimony through the image is not possible, then the sacrament of the Body and Blood itself loses its reality.[18]

synonymous with infallibility. As Mark of Ephesus, commenting on the subject of the Origenism of St Gregory of Nyssa, has stated judiciously: "It happens that someone is a master and still does not say everything completely accurately. For what need would the Fathers have of Ecumenical Councils, if none of them could not in anything stray from the truth?" (Archimandrite Ambrose, *St Mark of Ephesus and the Union of Florence* [in Russian] [Jordanville, NY, 1963], 128).

14 St John of Damascus, *De fide orthodoxa*, Bk. I, ch. 9, PG 94 (1): 1028A.

15 *De imaginibus oratio* II, ch. 11, PG 94 (1): 1293; *Oratio* III, ch. 9, *ibid.*: 1322; *On the Divine Images*, trans. D. Anderson (New York: St Vladimir's Seminary Press, 1980), 58.

16 *Oratio* I, ch. 4, *ibid.*: 1236; trans. Anderson, *ibid.*, 16.

17 *Antirrheticus*, PG 99: 457D. This certainly does not mean that Christ can be represented only after a particular historic moment and cannot be represented, for example, in illustration of the Old Testament (the creation of the world, etc.). What it means is that Christ can only be represented according to the human nature he assumed, and in no other way.

18 Cf J. Meyendorff, *Christ in Eastern Christian Thought*, trans. Y. Dubois (New York: St Vladimir's Seminary Press, 1987), 190.

The Godhead only reveals itself through the veil of the Body of Christ. Participation in His Divinity, and knowledge of Him, can only become real by sharing in the Body and Blood of Christ; and this reality of the sacrament of the Eucharist excludes any image of God aside from that of Christ. It is undoubtedly in this context that the Great Council of Moscow required that "a Cross, that is the Crucifixion"—not an image of the Lord Sabaoth—be placed on the iconostasis, for the iconostasis discloses the economy of the second Person. It is probably also in the same context that one should understand the special ruling of the Holy Synod of the Russian Church in 1722, which ordered that the image of God the Father on the antimensia be replaced by the inscription of the name of God in Hebrew, as a testimony to the divinity of Christ.[19]

In speaking of the image called the "Paternity," the Council did not designate it by any name, neither that of the "Trinity" which was sometimes attributed to it, nor that of "Paternity" (this latter designation is sometimes applied by scholars to the image called the "New Testament Trinity" or "Synthronon"). It must be said that to our knowledge the name "Paternitas" is never found on icons. Its origin is uncertain. Not applying to this image any of the proper names given to it, the Council only had recourse to descriptive expressions and exclusively considered the content of this image.

As an alleged image of the Trinity, this composition has no basis either in the prophetic vision, or in revelation in general. It is not a direct unveiling of the Holy Trinity as is the apparition to Abraham near the oak of Mamre. It is an amalgamation of three elements of a totally different nature: a prophetic vision arbitrarily interpreted as a vision of God the Father, a vision of the incarnate Son in the form of Emmanuel, and a portrayal of one of the manifestations of the Holy Spirit. This image, one supposes, was an attempt to "concretize" and give a visible form to the New Testament revelation of the Holy Trinity. Indeed, all that is known about the Trinity is known through the Incarnation: "God the Father is known by us precisely since the Incarnation...as Father, as God the Word,

19 N. Pokrovskii, *The Gospel in Iconography, Especially Byzantine and Russian* (in Russian) (St Petersburg, 1892), 389. Ref. to the Complete Collection of the Decisions of the Department of the Orthodox Confession, 2, 163-4, no 516. This ruling is repeated in *The Clergy's Manual* (in Russian) by S. Bulgakov (Kiev, 1930): "On the antimensia...it is strictly forbidden to represent the Lord Sabaoth in the form of an old man, and the holy evangelists in the form of animals" (note, 780).

incarnate for us, as Son of God."[20] The Holy Spirit appeared in the form of a dove above the Jordan. But the three images that form the composition of the "Paternity" are based on revelations concerning the plan of economy; but here they refer to the inner life of the Trinity. In other words, each of the three images was removed from its proper context and artificially linked with the others to form an image of the Holy Trinity with the names inscribed above: Father, Son (or Jesus Christ), Holy Spirit. Furthermore, this representation sought to indicate, aside from the triunity of God, the intratrinitarian relationships: the eternal begetting of the Son by the Father and the procession of the Holy Spirit. The Council focused its attention on the first of these two aspects, the begetting. "It is not in the flesh that the Son of God was born of the Father before all ages. And if the Prophet David says, 'From the womb, before the morning star, I have begotten you,' such generation is certainly not corporeal, but unutterable and unimaginable." Procreation is the transmittal of the Father's nature to the One He begets; this is why the generation of the Son of God according to Divinity is as unrepresentable as the Father Himself. Here we are faced with a new contradiction with regard to the teaching of the Church. The liturgical texts speak as follows: "The indescribable word of the Father [the Son of God in His Divinity] became describable by taking on flesh from you, O Mother of God..." (kontakion of the Triumph of Orthodoxy); also: "The One who, being invisible in the bosom of the Father, is presently resting, describable in your womb, O All-pure One, clothed in your appearance" (irmos of the seventh ode of the canon, tone six, Wednesday). Christ possesses the properties of His two births. As Theodore the Studite explained: "The One who came forth from the uncircumscribed is indescribable. By contrast, the one born of a circumscribed mother is describable."[21] But in the image of "Paternity," since the Father Himself is represented in human form, the birth of the Son is also portrayed by analogy with human birth. The "Uncircumscribed" who is "in the bosom of the Father" is described by an image of the Incarnation: Christ Emmanuel (the name given to the adolescent Christ), born of the Virgin, obedient to the laws of human development in time, is introduced to the bosom of the Father.

20 St Symeon the New Theologian, Critical Edition with an Introduction by A. A. Darrouzès (Paris, 1966), vol. 1, 105.

21 *Antirrheticus* III, ch. 2, PG 99: 417.

The portrayal of the second, incarnate Person is here an image of His generation outside time (according to His Divinity). But "the engendering before all ages of the only-begotten Son of the Father must only be perceived through our mind. In no case is it proper to paint all this in images: it is impossible." Thus, as a trinitarian icon, characterizing the divine Hypostases and accompanying them with corresponding descriptions, the composition called "Paternity" introduced anthropomorphism into the mystery of the Trinity. This was done by representing in human form not only the Father, but also the Son. Finally, the simultaneous presence of an old man and an adolescent applied temporal categories proper to the created world to the life of the Holy Trinity, uncreated and outside the categories of time. This could be misinterpreted as a statement that there was a time when God the Father had no Son and was therefore not a Father—which is "worse than all blasphemies," as John of Damascus wrote concerning a similar rationalization,[22] thinking perhaps of the Arian heresy.

Finally, "the Holy Spirit is not, in His nature, a dove. He is by nature God. And no one has ever seen God." These words may seem like strange caviling on the part of the Council; indeed, it would never enter anyone's mind to identify the Holy Spirit with a dove. However, since the "Paternity" is a "trinitarian" image that has to represent the three divine Persons, why is the Holy Spirit depicted in one of His manifestations? According to the wording of the Seventh Ecumenical Council, "the Holy Spirit did not become incarnate in a dove, but manifested Himself in the form of a dove."[23] As is pointed out by the Muscovite Council, His manifestations varied: at the Baptism, He appeared under the form of a dove; on Mt Tabor, in the form of a cloud; and on Pentecost, in the form of tongues of fire. This is how His manifestations are to be represented. But one form of manifestation cannot be the image of a divine Person. The non-revealed Hypostasis of the Holy Spirit is manifested only in its actions. It is such actions that one identifies with the dove, and this is what was adopted by iconographic usage. Thus the Hermeneia required that a dove be painted in the most diverse iconographic subjects, wherever the operation of the Holy Spirit is shown, even in the ordination of St Nicholas; in

22 *De fide orthodoxa*, Bk I, ch. 8, PG 94 (1): 812A.

23 Mansi XIII, 181A.

an icon of Pentecost, together with the tongues of fire, a dove absurdly doubled the divine manifestation. The Council apparently saw the presence of the dove on a would-be trinitarian icon as an attempt to fix this symbolic image as the icon of the third Person of the Holy Trinity, as is indicated by the inscription "Holy Spirit," referring to the Hypostasis.[24]

Thus the portrayal of the incomprehensible, unrepresentable God the Father was, in the view of the Great Council of Moscow, a representation of the Divinity: "No one has seen the Father, except the Son, as Christ Himself says in the Gospel." These words are followed immediately by a reference to the prophecy of Isaiah and to the words of St Paul, who applied this prophecy to the idols he saw in Athens. By means of this reference, the Council seems to remind us that the portrayal of the Deity is typical of paganism, not of Christianity. "Paganism," Sergius Bulgakov writes, "starts from the immediate conviction, from the evidence, so to speak, that the Godhead can be portrayed, that it has an image."[25] This is the reason why Bulgakov viewed the pagan idol as the ancestor of the Christian image.[26] For Orthodox theology, however, the origin of the icon is not the idol, but the lack of an image in the Old Testament, before the Incarnation. St John of Damascus states: "In former times God, who is without form or body, could never be depicted. But now that God is seen in the flesh conversing with men (Bar 3:31; 1 Tim 3:16), I make an image of the God whom I see."[27]

The radical difference between paganism and Christianity in the portrayal of God consists in that, for Christendom, God is represented not according to "a human concept"—that is, a concept of God, certainly, but anthropomorphic nonetheless, and not according to an abstract

24 Let us recall that there had already been an attempt to create an icon of the Holy Spirit "in the incomprehensible form of a bird," and that this icon had been presented to the council of 1554 (see above, chapter 14, "The Muscovite Councils of the Sixteenth Century and Their Role in Sacred Art").

25 *The Icon and Its Veneration*, 9.

26 "...Pagan iconography is, so to speak, the Old Testament of Christian iconography" (*ibid.*, 10-1). "Paganism bestowed upon Christianity an already articulated concept of the icon" (*ibid.*, 14). Bulgakov is here in complete agreement with the art historians and in total contradiction to the way in which the Church understands the origin of the Christian image.

27 *De imaginibus oratio* I, ch. 16, PG 94 (1): 1245; *On the Divine Images*, trans. D. Anderson (New York: St Vladimir's Seminary Press, 1980), 23. Cf *Oratio* II, ch. 5, PG 94(1): 1288; ch. 7 of the same *Oratio*; *Oratio* III, ch. 4, PG 94(1): 1321; ch. 8, col. 1328; and ch. 24-25, col. 1344.

idea—but in accordance with the reality of His revelation in the Son of God. Let us repeat that the Old Testament prohibition keeps all its force. But God who imposed this ban becomes depictable Himself in the Person of the incarnate Son, who is "the image of the invisible God" (Col 1:15). This is not a portrayal of the unrepresentable God: it is the image of God become flesh. The Council concluded its critique of iconographic subjects depicting God the Father with a categorical prohibition against painting them: "This is why we decree that from now on such mistaken paintings cease, born as they are of unsound knowledge."

Nonetheless, the confused thinking typical of this epoch is apparent even in this decision of the Council. Indeed, to the injunction not to make an image of the Father is added: "It is only in the Apocalypse of St John that the Father can be painted with white hair, for lack of any other possibility, because of the visions contained in it." Certainly, the Council had reason to view the representations from the Apocalypse as illustrations, since they were not cultic images. But since what was at stake was the possibility or impossibility of a representation, the Council's own explanation became self-contradictory. On the one hand, it interpreted the vision of Daniel as a vision of Christ, Judge of the Second Coming. On the other, it applied to God the Father the attributes of the apocalyptic "Son of Man" (white hair and clothing), those of the Ancient of Days, and of Christ, the Judge of which the Apocalypse speaks. Moreover, the thought of the Council is expressed in such a general way that one no longer sees the difference between the two visions, which in the Apocalypse are clearly differentiated: the first vision, "one like unto the Son of Man" with white hair (1:13-14), and the second vision, "one who sat on the throne" (4:2-3), which has no anthropomorphic image. A commentator of the Book of Revelation explained this second vision as follows: "Since he [St John] presents the Father in his second vision, he does not apply to Him any corporeal stamp, as he had done in his preceding vision, that of the Son. He compares Him to precious stones." That is, he describes the One on the throne in a symbolic way.[28] The lack of distinction between these two visions introduces into the evaluation of the Council an uncertainty approaching a contradiction. Even if the interpretation of the second

28 *Commentary on the Apocalypse* (Russian edition) (Moscow, 1889), 51, by Andrew, Archbishop of Caesarea (eleventh century). Another commentator, Arethas, Archbishop of Caesarea, repeats the former (PG 106: 568).

apocalyptic vision as that of God the Father is acceptable, nothing allows one to give Him an anthropomorphic image, that of an old man. Nonetheless, the incongruity in the thought of the Council does not in the least diminish the significance of its decision concerning the portrayal of the Godhead in a cultic image.

Despite the outright proscription of the Great Council of Moscow, representations of God the Father continued to multiply; and with the passage of time they came to be justified, apart from the prophetic visions, by considerations of a theological and philosophic order. We are thinking especially of the works of I. N. Bogoslovskii, *God the Father, the First Person of the Holy Trinity, in the Monuments of Ancient Christian Art* (in Russian) (Moscow, 1893), and of that by Sergius Bulgakov, *The Icon and its Veneration: A Theological Essay* (in Russian) (Paris, 1937). Bogolovskii's reasoning takes as its point of departure the accepted usage in the Church; for Bulgakov, such usage confirms and supports his philosophical-theological system.

Bogoslovskii does not deny "the doctrine of the inconceivable and incomprehensible spiritual nature of God the Father, excluding all corporeal likeness and therefore not allowing any depiction." He quotes St Athanasius of Alexandria: "Let us not assign to the Father a body capable of suffering, like the one the Son bore for the salvation of the whole world."[29] But despite this, Bogoslovskii considers the representation of God the Father as entirely normal. It is acceptable because Holy Scripture and patristic doctrine, while asserting the truth of the inconceivability of the divine essence, speak of the vision of God by the prophet Daniel,[30] and the Fathers express the truth about the first Person of the Trinity by resorting to anthropomorphic language (Father...). In Bogoslovskii's view, this is what authorizes art to make such truths "visible."

Bogoslovskii completes his justification of the image of God the Father by what he calls "a psychological law," which is in agreement with the thought of his time. He says:

> Man is in the image and likeness of God, and this is why our knowledge of God must naturally assume an anthropomorphic character, especially since we do not know God except in relation to ourselves. Now, as we can see in the real world, when the son is an adult, his father is usually an old man. At a certain point of

29 St Athanasius, *Expositio fidei*, PG 25: 203; I. N. Bogoslovskii, *God the Father* (in Russian) (Moscow, 1893), 21.

30 "The Ancient of Days seen by Daniel is unquestionably God the Father" (Bogoslovskii, *ibid.*, 63).

our intellectual development, we adorn the concept of the fatherhood of the first Person of the Holy Trinity with such traits, and this all the more since such a concept is not alien to the divine Word, no doubt because of the psychological law we have indicated.[31]

According to this author, three ways of representing God the Father correspond to the stages of intellectual development:

The ways of representation are: *symbolic* (the hand from heaven); *allegorical* (as when, starting with the image of God the Father which God the Son is, our mind ascends to the prototype); and lastly, *historical* and direct (when God the Father is portrayed in the image of an old man or the Ancient of Days).[32]

But if Scripture and the Fathers express the truth in the form of anthropomorphic concepts, this does not mean that such concepts can be represented. St John of Damascus says:

If Holy Scripture clothes God with forms which appear to be physical...these forms are still immaterial in an important sense, because they were not seen by everyone, nor could they be perceived with the unaided eye, but they were seen through the spiritual sight of prophets or others to whom they were revealed.[33]

According to Bogoslovskii's reasoning, it would appear that since "in the real world" an adult son has an old man as a father, we receive at a certain point of our intellectual development (sic!) a concept of God as father through the image of an old man; in this case, then, the image would be "historical and direct." The very concept of historicity is perverted here. For Bogoslovskii, the image no longer points to an event that occurred at a certain moment: it is the expression of a certain concept by means of traits of our surrounding world. The cornerstone of the theology of the icon—to witness to the entrance of God in the history of the world—eludes Bogoslovskii's thought. For him, there is but one pictorial expression of "the concept of God." As for the icon of the Son of God, as an image of the Father, it is, in relation to the Father, allegorical.

If Bogoslovskii applies a "psychological law" and "stages of intellectual development" to the knowledge of God, this is the typical result of scholastic theology infected by Protestantism and Roman Catholicism. In the realm of the knowledge of God, Orthodoxy is not aware of "psychological laws": it only knows revelation, accessible in varying degrees, apart from all dependence on stages of intellectual development. The Orthodox

31 *Ibid.*, 63.

32 *Ibid.*, 65.

33 *De imaginibus Oratio* III, ch. 24, PG 94 (1): 1344; On the Divine Images, trans. Anderson, 78-9.

theology of the image does not know representations of God through analogies with "the real world."

One aspect of Bogoslovskii's work, found also in other authors, must be noted. He does mention the council of Metropolitan Macarius in 1554, which recognized the image of God the Father "in conformity with ancient models," but he says nothing about the Great Council of Moscow, and totally ignores the liturgical texts that deal with the way in which the Church understood the prophetic visions.

Bogoslovskii's writing is a polemical work apparently directed against certain types of protestantizing intellectuals who denied sacred images in general, and especially that of God the Father. According to these, with Christianity, the human race has reached a higher stage of its intellectual development as compared to the sensual concepts of God in paganism. Consequently, only an abstract concept of God is proper, and every religious image is excluded. Bogoslovskii attempts to prove the opposite, but he begins from the same basic principles: it is precisely mankind's higher degree of intellectual development which, according to him, allows for a knowledge of God the Father, as well as His anthropomorphic portrayal.

More serious is the theological-philosophical justification given for the portrayal of the Godhead in the work of S. Bulgakov. It is part of this author's entire theological system and is significantly different, as much from the concept generally admitted by the defenders of the image of God the Father as from the teaching of the Orthodox Church. Bulgakov justifies the representation of God the Father by basing himself neither on a false interpretation of the prophecies nor on a "psychological law," nor on abstract allegorizing. This representation is part of his system and represents one of its axioms. By making use of generally accepted theological concepts and terms found in Holy Scripture, Bulgakov justifies the possibility of representing the Godhead as such; the image of God the Father is but a particular instance that confirms his thesis.

In his teaching on the possibility of depicting the Divinity, as well as on the icon in general, Bulgakov starts, as he says, "not from the *apophatic thesis* concerning the invisibility of God, and consequently the impossibility of representing Him, but from the *doctrine of sophiology*, according to which God has an image to which the world conforms. God has drawn His image in the creature; consequently, *this image of God can be repre-*

sented"(italics by Bulgakov).[34] In general, Bulgakov views the apophatic thesis concerning the impossibility of portraying the Godhead as a false premise which the Orthodox, during the iconoclastic period, borrowed from their opponents, "inadvertently and through misunderstanding."[35] This is why he paraphrases the eucharistic prayer addressed to God the Father in the Liturgy of St John Chrysostom ("for Thou art God ineffable, inconceivable, invisible, incomprehensible"[36]) as follows: "In relation to His creature, God is not without image, invisible, unknowable, and therefore unrepresentable."[37]

The teaching of Bulgakov on the possibility of depicting the Godhead is based on the following reasoning: man is created in the image of God, and this "concept of man bearing the divine image carries within itself, *as its basis* [italics mine], the reverse notion, namely, that the human befits the image of God." This "image of God in God is heavenly humanity," *Sophia*, eternal, divine humanity.[38] The Godhead is eternally divine-human, and the image of God is drawn in man precisely because the human image is proper to God Himself. By this conformity of God to the creature, the human image of the Creator is known by man; this is why God revealed Himself to the Old Testament prophets and could be seen by them in this form. This is also why

> in paganism, the concept of the unrepresentability of God as invisible and lacking an image was quietly rejected...The basis of divinity can be known and represented by man; because it is, in a certain sense, human.[39]

Such is, in brief, the main thesis, the starting point, of Sergius Bulgakov.

One should say, first of all, that "the divine image proper to man, understood as a result of the creation of man in the image of God, is not at all the same thing as a conformity between the Godhead and mankind."[40] The fact that man was created in the image of God does not signify the opposite: that the human image is proper to the Divinity. The divine image of man means that such an image is characteristic of the human person—not that

34 *The Icon and Its Veneration* (hereafter, *Icon*) (in Russian) (Paris, 1937), 82.

35 *Icon*, 83.

36 See also the Liturgy of St Basil: "Thou who art without beginning, invisible, inconceivable, indescribable, without change... Father of our Lord Jesus Christ."

37 *Icon*, 82.

38 *Ibid.*, 83.

39 *Ibid.*, 9.

40 V. Lossky, *Controversy about Sophia* (in Russian) (Paris, 1935), 38.

the nature of the Divinity and the nature of man define one another in "Sophia."

Bulgakov's disagreement with the apophatic thesis concerning the unrepresentability of God prompted him often to make very cutting statements about the Fathers of the iconoclastic period, especially those of the Seventh Ecumenical Council, for whom this thesis was the basis for all their reasoning. According to Bulgakov, they thereby took the wrong road in their defense of the icon and misinterpreted its content. The error made by the apologists, he says, consisted in an erroneous view of the link between the dogma of Chalcedon (one Person and two natures in Christ) and the image. Thus it is the image of Christ which is the starting point of Bulgakov's reasoning about the representability of the Godhead. "According to His human nature, or more precisely according to His corporeal essence, Christ has a visible image, said the defenders of the icon. He can be represented; but according to His divine nature, He has no visible image and cannot be represented."[41] It is this thesis of the Orthodox which, according to Bulgakov, resulted from an erroneous understanding of the dogma of Chalcedon. According to him, the Divinity can be described precisely in its eternal, divine humanity. "As God-man, Christ has a human image; in it, He enclosed His human life on earth."[42] He possesses "doubly an image that is one and the same: according to His divinity, in a manner invisible to created eyes; according to His humanity, in a manner visible."[43] The icon of Christ is possible "precisely according to His human, visible image which, nonetheless, is identical with His invisible, divine image."[44]

It follows that the image of Christ is an image of God, not because it is the image of the divine Person who "has united the separate natures" (irmos of the ninth Ode of the canon, tone four), divine and human, but because Christ is a manifestation of uncreated humanity in created hu-

41 *Icon*, 94.

42 *Icon*, 120. According to Bulgakov's doctrine, the Incarnation itself actualizes the eternal humanity of the Word (*The Lamb of God* [in Russian] [Paris, 1923], 211). The possibility, even the necessity of the Incarnation of God, belongs to the very nature of things. "God has created the world precisely for His Incarnation; it is not the world which, through the fall of man, has impelled God to become incarnate" (*ibid.*, 139). From Bulgakov's point of view, the Incarnation is the purpose of the world's existence, and not the means of its salvation. He sees in it the final act of creation: "The eternal humanity is joined to the earthly humanity, the divine Sophia to the created Sophia" (*Icon*, 151).

43 *Icon*, 94.

44 *Icon*, 95.

manity. "For man, *God is representable* [Bulgakov's italics] in such humanity which is His."[45] Through the created "bodily essence" taken from His Mother, the eternal divine-humanity was actualized, "became concrete"; and Bulgakov emphasizes the possibility of representing not the Person, but the eternal divine humanity. But the Orthodox apologists viewed the representation of God not in some original and eternal "divine humanity," but in the image of the person of Christ, bearer of the human and divine natures. "Thus," Theodore the Studite writes, "Christ is circumscribed in respect to His hypostasis, though uncircumscribable in His divinity; but the natures of which He is composed are not circumscribed. In fact, how would it be possible to represent a nature which was not visible in a person?"[46] According to St John of Damascus, "a person possesses what is general, together with distinctive particulars, as well as an independent existence. Nature, however, has no independent existence, but is visible in persons."[47] It is the person of Christ that is represented with His individual features, according to His "bodily essence" taken from His Mother. This concept of the person which, in this context, is missing in Bulgakov, is a key concept, as much for the dogma of Chalcedon as for the theology of the icon. In patristic theology, it is precisely this concept that allowed the solution of the fundamental dilemma of the iconoclastic debate by moving beyond it, thereby giving a solid basis for the veneration of icons.[48]

If one accepts the thesis that Divinity is representable, then one would think that each of the three Persons of the Trinity should have a direct, suitable image. However, according to Bulgakov, the non-incarnate Persons (the Father and the Holy Spirit) cannot have a direct image. But since divine humanity, made concrete in the Son (one of the Trinity), can be presented in Him, it is possible to represent the humanity proper to the Trinity itself. Bulgakov states:

> If God is sometimes presented in the form of an old man, we find there a human image of the *one*, personal, tri-hypostatic God (Elohim). There is no reason to see in this a distinct icon of the Father...As such, this human image in the representation of God the Creator (outside any direct link to the Incarnation) already

45 *Ibid.*, 106.
46 *Antirrheticus* III, PG 99: 405.
47 *De fide orthodoxa*, PG 94 (1): 1004A.
48 Cf. J. Meyendorff, *Christ in Eastern Christian Thought*, trans. Y. Dubois (New York: St Vladimir's Seminary Press, 1987), 188-9.

> clearly points out that the image of God was drawn in man at his creation, or, inversely, [Bulgakov repeats], that the human image is proper to God. The humanity of the Creator's image is a testimony of eternal humanity, or of Sophia, divine Wisdom, the eternal divine icon in God himself.[49]

Thus, according to Bulgakov, one should see in the old man, when He is portrayed alone, not an image of God the Father (as is usually understood) but of the tri-hypostatic God, that is, of the Holy Trinity. According to the doctrine of Bulgakov, such a depiction of the Trinity in a single image is possible because "the Holy Trinity is a tri-hypostatic Person" (sic!).[50] Thus, God the Father, being transcendent, has no independent image; but the Trinity, as a "Tri-hypostatic Person (!)," can have one, and this image is that of Sophia, humanity eternal and divine. Thus the nature common to the three Persons of the Trinity is endowed with a personal principle that has its image: that of an old man, image of the tri-hypostatic, anthropomorphic God (thus, Father, Son, Holy Spirit, plus the old man "Elohim"). What does this image mean? A fourth Person of the Trinity? Certainly Bulgakov rejected the accusation that Sophia was a fourth hypostasis in God. Nonetheless, if one applies his reasoning to the image, this is precisely what one arrives at, and this is an essential distortion of the Christian doctrine of the Holy Trinity. The fundamental error of Bulgakov—a confusion between nature and person—is evident in his teaching about divine nature as a personal principle, Sophia.

Despite all the above, God the Father, according to the sophiology of Bulgakov, can be represented personally, but only in relation to the Son in the icon of the Holy Trinity: "the Father is represented here under the aspect of an old man." Bulgakov asks: "What does the representation of the Father in human form mean, although He did not become incarnate?"[51] God is not represented here to witness to the resemblance between Father and Son. Bulgakov, perhaps thinking of Bogoslovskii, considers such an explanation as insufficient, not justifying the Incarnation of the Father in the

49 *Icon*, 138. At one time, N. Berdiaev criticized Bulgakov for multiplying the meanings of Sophia: "She turns out to be everything: the most Holy Trinity, and each of the hypostases of the Holy Trinity, and the universe, and humanity, and the Mother of God" (N. Berdiaev, "Sophiology," *Put'* XVI [in Russian] [Paris, 1929], 99). Sophia is also the Divinity of God, or the Divinity in God; and also the eternal icon of God in God.

50 *Icon*, 45. "God is a tri-hypostatic Hypostasis" (*The Lamb of God*, 215). "The unity in the Trinity is not only the Divinity (*ousia* or Sophia), but also the tri-hypostatic subject, the triune I" (*The Comforter*) [in Russian] [Paris, 1936], 42, note).

51 *Icon*, 138.

icon. "In that case," he says,

> one should simply avoid any icon of the Holy Trinity. But...this human representation of the Father points out...that humanity is a direct image of God, as the vision of the Prophet Daniel (Dan 7:9) *before* the Incarnation, as well as that of the Prophet Ezekiel (Ez 1, *passim*), equally state.[52]
>
> However, this humanity proper to the Holy Trinity is revealed concretely only in the Son, who already has an individual, human image, that of Jesus, Son of David, Son of Abraham. The Father has no such [that is, personal, human] image, other than the through the Son. It is only in relation to this image that the first Person of the Holy Trinity, as Father of the Son, is depicted. Strictly speaking, what is represented is not the human person of the Father: He has none—but humanity as an image of the Trinity, assumed in a personal way by the Son. In this sense one can truly say that the icon of the Father is the representation, in the Father, of the Son He has revealed to man.[53]

What is the outcome of such convoluted reasoning? In the image of the Trinity, the first Hypostasis, not having a personal image, can only be represented in relation to the Son, "as the Father of the Son." However, since the Father has no human person (the Son has none either!), the image of the old man in the icon of the Trinity represents not the Father, but the humanity of the Trinity, that is, always Sophia. But in relation to the Son, this human image of the Trinity (Sophia) appears to be the Father (thus, the first Hypostasis nonetheless?), and at the same time "the representation, in the Father, of the Son He has revealed to man" (as an image of the Father?). But according to the Orthodox faith, Christ, as an image of the Father, cannot be described because He is His Consubstantial image according to His Divinity.[54]

> Certainly, the concept of the Son as the Image of the Father implies a personal relationship. However, what is shown through the Image is not the person of the Father, but His nature, which is identical in the Son...As *eikon*, the Son honors the Divinity of the Father.[55]

As to the reasoning of Bulgakov, one may conclude that, from the moment that the humanity proper to the Holy Trinity reveals itself only in the Son, the depiction of "the Son of the Father" reveals, in concrete

52 *Icon.* We have, Bulgakov states, "a concealed manifestation of the Father in the divine-human form, that is to say, resembling that of the Son, precisely in the vision of the Prophet Daniel, in the manifestation of the Ancient of Days toward whom the Son of Man is led, and also in the apparition of the three Angels" (*The Lamb of God*, 190-1).

53 *Icon*, 138-9.

54 St Theodore the Studite, *Antirrheticus* III, PG 99: 408.

55 V. Lossky, "La théologie de l'image," *Messager de l'Exarchat du Patriarche russe en Europe occidentale*, No 30/31 (1959), 130.

terms, the humanity of the Father under the aspect of an old man. Thus the justification of the image of God the Father by means of sophiology, as "the internally justified way out of an impasse,"[56] does not remove the impasse. It does not lead to a Trinitarian image since, in order to represent the Trinity, the image must be a personal one, that is, it should represent the persons of the Father, Son, and Holy Spirit, or else be a symbolic image (such as the Old Testament Trinity)—but not an amalgamation of a personification of nature (the old man), of the person of the Son, and of an allegory of the Holy Spirit in the form of a dove. Bulgakov considers such a portrayal of the Holy Spirit in the image of the Trinity as normal.[57]

Thus the anthropomorphic image of the Godhead aside from the Incarnation is used as a proof by Bulgakov for his teaching on Sophia-eternal humanity in God; and one might think that the portrayal of God-Trinity under the form of "Sabaoth" awaited its justification in his teaching. But in order to accept the thesis of Bulgakov, according to which the Deity can be represented, one has to accept his entire teaching about Sophia. However, as Metropolitan Sergius expressed it, this doctrine "can either replace the doctrine of the Church or yield to it, but it cannot be combined with it."[58] This is why it was condemned by the Holy Synod of the Russian Church as a doctrine solely derived from philosophic thought and from the author's creative imagination.

56 *Icon*, 139.

57 Proceeding from his doctrine, Bulgakov wishes to see the image of the Holy Spirit "in the faces of the holy, God-bearing saints," and, "in an exclusive sense," in the icon of the Mother of God. In an exclusive sense, because in his doctrine of Sophia as the eternal humanity in God, he distinguishes in her two principles, through analogy with created humanity: the masculine principle (the Son) and the feminine principle (the Holy Spirit). Thus Bulgakov asks the question: Is the icon of the Mother of God, as the pre-eminent Spirit-bearer, not "a hidden icon of the third Hypostasis in the human image" (*Icon*, 140)? A little further, he replies, "The icon of the Mother of God, especially if she is without the Child, is the human image of the Holy Spirit." Further on, it is true, Bulgakov states a reservation: one should understand by this "that for Him [the Holy Spirit], Her [the Virgin's] human face is fully transparent" (*ibid.*, 151). However, this reservation hardly brings any clarity. To understand by "the supreme manifestation" of the Holy Spirit His action in man, the human being's deification through Him, is one thing. It is quite another to see in the hypostatic image of the Mother of God an icon, even a "hidden one," of the third Hypostasis of the Holy Trinity, a "human image of the Spirit." Here again, the concept of hypostasis is erased in Bulgakov, so that for him the hypostatic image of the Mother of God becomes at the same time an icon, a "hidden one," it is true, but nonetheless an image of the third divine Hypostasis. Lastly, it is hard to understand why an image of the Mother of God without the Child is an icon of the Holy Spirit to a greater extent than when she is represented with the Child.

58 The future patriarch. Decree (in Russian) of September 7 (1935), 1.

The Great Council of Moscow realized that a custom introduced into the Church, even validated by a council, does not always express the truth. As St Cyprian of Carthage said: "A practice that has been introduced surreptitiously among some cannot serve as an obstacle to the assertion and triumph of the truth. For a custom without truth is but an inveterate error."[59] Not accepting the concept of justification through custom, the Great Council considered the question of the portrayal of God the Father by basing itself on the truth, on the Orthodox faith. As the comparison of the Council's decisions with patristic and liturgical texts has shown, this decision cannot be viewed as arbitrary or insufficiently supported.

There can be no anthropomorphic image "of the Lord Sabaoth (that is, the Father)." The old man Sabaoth represents a personification of the Deity which is identified with the Father and understood as His image. But there can be no image of the Godhead apart from a person, and the non-incarnate person of the Father cannot have a human image, "because the Father has no flesh."

> Faithful to the word of the Gospel, "no one has ever seen God" (Jn 1:18), the Church did not demand: "show us the Father" (14:8), so that we might know Him through our earthly knowledge. The glory of God is to be "God ineffable, invisible, inconceivable" (anaphora of the Liturgy of St John Chrysostom)...For the believer this is a sacred reality he can only approach by "taking off his shoes" (Ex 3:15), having purified himself not only from sin but also from every perceptible, material image ("the inaccessible darkness of the vision").[60]

"God has no outline: He is simple. Do not imagine His structure...do not fence in God with your corporeal concepts, do not limit Him through the measure of your understanding," said St Basil the Great.[61]

Likewise, the eternal begetting of the Son by the Father in the bosom of the Holy Trinity cannot be represented through the image of His human birth from His Mother.[62] It is the thesis of Orthodox dogma that "The Father, sole principle in the Trinity, who begets the Son and spirates

59 Letter to Pompeius against Stephen's letter about the baptism of heretics, *Sancti Caecilii Cypriani opera* (Venice, 1758), Epistola LXXIV, col. 337.

60 Same Decree of September 7 (1935), 2.

61 "Premier entretien sur la création de l'homme à l'image" (Paris, 1970), ch. 5, 176-9.

62 V. N. Lazarev is wrong in disputing the influence of the image of the Nicopean Virgin upon the "Paternity" because the content contained in it is supposedly entirely different ("On an Icon from Novgorod and the Anti-trinitarian Heresy" [in Russian], *Drevnerusskaia kultura* [Moscow, 1966], 107-8). The content is not different since it shows the same relationship, in one case with the Mother, in the other with the Father.

the Holy Spirit, is a hardly perceptible allusion to new mysteries in the bosom of the Godhead, rather than an attempt to disclose them,"[63] much less to transpose them into an image. It is precisely the apophatic concept of the utter inconceivability of God that forms the basis of the Orthodox doctrine on the impossibility of depicting the Deity. This is what essentially characterizes the entire patristic tradition of the Orthodox Church. In its knowledge and representation of God, Orthodoxy knows neither "psychological laws," "stages of development," nor "conformity between the Godhead and humanity." The theology of the icon knows no image of God apart from revelation, an image-witness to the fact. We can only agree with H.-J. Schulz, who writes:

> A visible representation of what is essentially invisible is, for this theology of the icon, not merely ostentatious or foolish. It is heresy and sacrilege, because it is an arbitrary addition to revelation and to the divine economy and, in this present case, also a heresy asserting an incarnation of the Father and of the Holy Spirit.[64]

In its discussion on the portrayal of the Godhead, the Great Council limited itself to only a few iconographic subjects and paid no attention to other iconographic errors, which were numerous at the time. Nonetheless, the basic principle it formulated greatly overshadowed the enumerated subjects. A whole series of subjects which had aroused debate already in the sixteenth century and, more generally, all subjects that were not based on the realism of the Gospel (that were "without authentic reference") fell under the Council's ban as a result of its decision of principle.

63 Metropolitan Sergius, the same Decree of September 7 (1935), 3. It seems to us that we cannot view as positive the mention Metropolitan Philaret of Moscow makes of the "Paternity" while explaining the iconostasis of the Cathedral of the Dormition in the Kremlin to the successor to the throne: "The series of patriarchs on both sides of the Lord Sabaoth who, from his bosom, engenders the eternal Word" (as quoted by I. Snegirev, "Memories of the Visit of his Highness the Dauphin to the Muscovite Sanctuary" [in Russian] [St Petersburg, 1838], and in *Monuments of Muscovite Antiquities* [in Russian] [Moscow, 1841], 11). The traditionally Orthodox utterances of Metropolitan Philaret on the subject of the icons of the Holy Face and of the Dormition do not allow us to surmise that he, great theologian that he was, did not see the contradiction between "Paternitas" and the liturgical texts. Here we have to take into account, it seems to us, that the metropolitan explained the content of the iconostasis as a whole, without going into a dogmatic analysis of the image contained in it. The usage that existed, then, had invaded minds to such a degree that it had obscured the true understanding of the image; a theological explanation of "Paternitas" would have been superfluous and could have been confusing.

64 H.-J. Schulz, "Die Höllenfahrt als Anastasis," *Zeitschrift für katholische Theologie*, vol. 81 (1959), no 1, 12.

42 *The New Testament Trinity.* 17th-century Russian icon. Korin Collection, Moscow.

These were above all the other New Testament compositions depicting the Trinity which, through their content, are closely related to the "Paternity," the "Synthronon" or "New Testament Trinity," (Fig. 42)[65] and the "Throne of Grace."[66] Though the origin and meaning of these images differ, they falsified the Orthodox faith just as much as the "Paternity." Moreover, the image of the New Testament Trinity was later also prohib-

65 This iconographic subject was based on an illustration of Psalm 109 (110): "Yahweh declared to my Lord, 'Take your seat at my right hand, till I have made your enemies your footstool.'" The oldest known illustration is found in the tenth century Utrecht Psalter. Here, as in later examples, Christ is represented twice, in accordance with the commentary on these words by St Jerome (*Breviarium in Psalmis*, PL 26: 1163), as expressing two different conditions of our Lord: glorious-heavenly, and humiliated-terrestrial. In the West, both the poem itself and the commentary were used in church doctrine to oppose Arianism; at the feet of the two persons represented were placed the vanquished enemies, Judas and Arius. However, the transposition of Jerome's commentary into imagery led to a personification of the two natures of Christ. After the East-West schism, already at the beginning of the twelfth century, one of the persons represented was transformed into God the Father, and a dove was added to the composition. This is how this illustration became a representation of the Trinity. From the twelfth century on, this image spread widely in the West in Bibles, Breviaries, Antiphonaries and other liturgical books. In the fourteenth century, it appears as an independent, pious image (see the work of W. Braunfels, *Die Heilige Dreifaltigkeit* [Düsseldorf, 1954]). From the West, this iconography passed into Orthodox art. The oldest example of it in Russia is the quadripartite icon in the Cathedral of the Annunciation in Moscow. After appearing in Russia toward the middle of the sixteenth century, this image "ended up no longer seeming to be 'a Latin invention,' but even became one of the important components of the Last Judgment" (L. S. Retkovskaia, "On the Appearance and Development of the Composition 'Paternitas' in Russian Art" [in Russian], *Drevnerusskoe iskusstvo XI-XVI vekov* [Moscow, 1963], 257).

66 The image of the Trinity in the form of an old man representing God the Father, with the crucified Christ on his lap, and the dove, is of Roman Catholic origin; in its finished form, it dates back to the end of the eleventh or the beginning of the twelfth century. In the West, the traditional name of this composition is "The Holy Trinity." But the fact that it is sometimes accompanied by the opening words of a Latin eucharistic prayer, and that it is also called "Throne of Grace," indicates that its meaning is above all eucharistic, as W. Braunfels explains. The aim of this image is to show that the eucharistic sacrifice, like that of Golgotha, is offered to the Father and accepted by Him, effecting the reconciliation between God and man. This image "gradually moves from the altar, through the cross and the sacrifice, to the Holy Spirit and the Father" (*op. cit* p. 42). This subject, so typically Roman Catholic in its translation of the concept of satisfaction, has variants that are no less typically Roman Catholic. Thus the dead Christ is sometimes represented without the cross, held up by God the Father, as in the composition of the "Pieta," where He is sustained by His mother. This must express the suffering of the Father, which is analogous to that of the Mother (*ibid.*, p. 41). In Russia, the first known example of this type is found agian on the same quadripartite icon in the Cathedral of the Annunciation. The crucified Christ, in the bosom of His Father, is covered by the wings of the cherubim (see above, chapter 14, "The Muscovite Councils of the Sixteenth Century"). Despite its clearly non-Orthodox meaning, the subject of the crucified Christ became so popular in Russia that it was still represented in the nineteenth century, as for example in the Cathedral of St Vladimir in Kiev.

ited in the Greek Church, without theological discussion, simply for being Latin. In the time of Patriarch Sophronius III, the Holy Synod of Constantinople (1776) said: "It has been decreed by the Synod that the icon allegedly of the Trinity is an innovation. It is alien to the apostolic Orthodox Catholic Church and is not accepted by it. It infiltrated the Orthodox Church through the Latins."[67]

An important question arises concerning these icons of the New Testament Trinity. On the one hand, accepted practice in the Church indicates that they exist. On the other hand, the Orthodox rite of "the Blessing and Sanctification of the Icon of the Most-holy and Vivifying Trinity" adopted by the Russian Church, and hence constituting an ecclesial act, does not know such icons either in its enumeration of Orthodox trinitarian icons, or in the theological content of the prayer of blessing. The Rite of Blessing mentions the following icons:

> As recounted in the Old Testament, Your apparition in the form of three angels to Abraham, the glorious patriarch; in the new Dispensation, the manifestation of the Father through a voice, of the Son in the flesh in the Jordan, and of the Holy Spirit in the form of a dove. Also, when the Son, after ascending to heaven in His flesh and being seated at the right hand of God, sent the Comforting Spirit to the apostles in the form of tongues of fire; and on Mt Tabor, the Father revealed himself to the three apostles through a voice, the Holy Spirit through a cloud, the Son through a supraluminous light.

Thus the ritual of blessing recognizes four trinitarian icons: one from the Old, and three from the New Testament—icons of Theophanies, revelations of the Holy Trinity in the New Testament (Theophany, Transfiguration, and Pentecost). Only at the blessing of the Old Testament icon is the following sticheron chanted (tone 8): "Come, O peoples, let us worship God in three Persons." At the blessing of other trinitarian icons the troparion and kontakion of the corresponding feasts are sung. The events which are represented are, of course, manifestations of the Holy Trinity in the world, but they do not show Its image. Aside from the enumerated trinitarian icons, the ritual of blessing knows of no others. Is this not because in the New Testament it is not possible to have an image of God "glorified in the Holy Trinity, the One no mind can reach and no word can express, the One never seen by men anywhere" (The rite of blessing for trinitarian icons)? A visible image of the divine Trinity, in whatever iconographic variant, according to whatever

67 Sethad, *Bibliotheca graeca medii aevi* (Venice, 1872), vol. 3, 317.

abstract concept, is impossible.[68] Of the three Persons of the Divinity, only the second hypostasis can be represented in human form in the Son of God who became the Son of Man. The world only knows God in the Son through the Holy Spirit. In the New Testament, Pentecost is the apex of the revelation of the Trinity—a revelation not in image but within man himself, by his deification. Divinization, then, is "the action of the Spirit...through Whom the Trinity is known."[69] In other words, the dogma of the Trinity is not an abstract doctrine, a formula or a truth knowable through a process of abstraction, like a scientific truth. Knowledge of the Trinity is not gained by external teaching but by an inward, living experience of the Christian life. It is an existential experience of divine knowledge, of which testimonies are found in the lives of the saints and in patristic writings. It is not by chance that it is precisely in the wake of St Sergius of Radonezh, himself a "dwelling place of the Trinity" (troparion of the saint), that this image of the Old Testament Trinity is shown with a new fullness, a new vision and a new theological content in the icon of St Andrei Rublev. The icon of the Old Testament Trinity links the beginning of the Church in the Old Testament, the promise made to Abraham, to the moment at which the New Testament Church was founded. The beginning of divine revelation is joined to its consummation on the day of Pentecost, to the supreme revelation of the tri-hypostatic Divinity. It is precisely in this image that the "action of the Spirit" unfolded to Andrei the monk the meaning of the Old Testament revelation, a new vision of the trinitarian life.

This image turned out to be so powerful that, in the words of P. Florenskii, "among all the philosophical proofs for the existence of God, what is most convincing is the conclusion: the [icon of the] Trinity of Rublev exists; therefore, God exists."[70]

68 An image of the Trinity can only be symbolic, as, for example, that of the Old Testament Trinity—a revelation of the Trinity in impersonal angels, or, as was the case in early Christian art, in the form of a throne, a book, and a dove. At the beginning of Christian art, there was also the symbol of the triangle.

69 Ode 7 of the first canon of Pentecost. See also the kneeling prayers at Vespers for the same day.

70 P. Florenskii, "The Iconostasis" (in Russian), *Bogoslovskie Trudy* 9 (Moscow, 1972), 100. Despite the opinion of certain scholars and theologians for whom the main Person of Rublev's "Trinity" must be in the center and the Son at the Father's right (by analogy no doubt with the New Testament Trinity), it bears repeating that the Trinity of Rublev strictly follows the order of the Creed (from left to right): Father, Son, and Holy Spirit. What seems incontrovertible to practicing painters is not taken into consideration by the theologians. For neither the symbolism of the colors nor that of the iconography leaves any room for doubt. We have made a brief analysis of this icon in *Der Sinn der Ikonen* (Bern, 1952); *The Meaning of Icons*, trans. G. E. H. Palmer and E. Kadloubovsky (New York:

Scholars have seen a link between the appearance of images of "Paternity," in Byzantium and the Balkans as well as in Russia, and the spread of anti-trinitarian heresies (Bogomilism, the Strigolniki, and the Judaizers). According to some scholars, the fight against such heresies prompted the search for new iconographic subjects supporting the trinitarian dogma, "to come to the aid of anti-heretical writings."[71] The icon of the Old Testament Trinity, it was felt, was not sufficiently convincing to express the equality and consubstantiality of the Persons, being too speculative. It was in order to complete this icon, so to speak, and to express the trinitarian dogma in a more concrete fashion, that the iconographic subject called "Paternity" appeared as an antidote to heresy. Rather rare in Byzantium and in the Balkans, this subject was disseminated particularly in Russia. Here it appeared at the end of the fourteenth or during the fifteenth century (this, at any rate, is the date attributed to the first known icon of Novgorodian origin). Rare at first, this composition became highly popular in the sixteenth-seventeenth centuries. Its appearance led to a wide dissemination of images of God the Father on frescoes and icons representing the Trinity or other subjects.

It is certain that the period during which these heresies spread coincides with the apparition of this composition. On the surface, the icono-

St Vladimir's Seminary Press, 1982). Here we will merely repeat that the garment of the angel in the center has the colors of the Incarnate Word, to which the very visible clavus on the *himation*, a symbol of the message, is related. A certainly less vivid clavus is visible in the hue of the garment of the angel on the right—a symbol of the third hypostasis. As to iconographic symbolism, this icon illustrates the fundamental ecclesiological thesis, that the Church is a revelation of the Father in the Son and the Holy Spirit. The edifice, the house of Abraham, above the angel of the first Person, is an image of the Church. The oak of Mamre—tree of life and wood of the cross, above the angel of the second person—indicates the economy of the son of God. Lastly, above the angel of the third Person, there is a mountain, a symbol of the spiritual ascent. It may be added that the meaning of this icon centers on the eucharistic cup, the divine Meal. But in the representation of meals, beginning with the first Christian centuries, the main person was placed as a rule not in the middle but to the right, that is, in relation to the viewer, to the left. There are rare exceptions: certain Serbian frescoes from the thirteenth-fourteenth centuries, the Last Supper of Simon Ushakov, and some later representations (see K. Wessel, *Abendmal und Apostelkommunion* [Recklinghausen, 1964]). As to the Last Supper on the iconostasis in the Cathedral of the Trinity (Lavra of the Trinity-St Sergius Monastery), attributed if not to Rublev himself then at least to his circle, there is no exception to the rule: Christ, the main person, is represented, as is customary, to the left in relation to the viewer. It is useless to refer to the one known exception, as is sometimes done—the image of the Holy Trinity called "Zyrian," where the angel in the center is accompanied by the inscription "Father." Even if this icon can be attributed, as is conjectured, to the circle of St Stephen of Perm, this exception does not rescind the rule.

71 See L. S. Retkovskaia, "On the Appearance," *Drevn. iskusstvo XI-XVI Vekov* (Moscow, 1963), 239.

graphic content of the image seems to be opposed to heretical statements. Indeed, all these heresies denied the divinity of Christ, and consequently, the dogma of God as Trinity. By indicating the eternal begetting of the Son by the Father, the composition called "Paternity" witnessed to the tri-unity of God, and served as a clear proof of the divinity of Christ. Thus, the generally accepted scholarly point of view appears to be supported by an adequate and convincing argumentation.

However, written documents contain not the least indication allowing one to conclude that the Church used this iconographic subject to fight heresies. (At any rate, none have been discovered so far, despite the abundance of writings devoted to this struggle.) Whether official Church documents or writings of the most tenacious opponents of heresy, not one of them mentions this subject by way of argument. In his discussion with Viskovatyi at the council of 1553-1554, convoked precisely against the heretics who had denied the divinity of Christ and the dogma of the Trinity, Metropolitan Macarius himself, while defending the image of God the Father, nowhere mentions "Paternity" as a means of fighting heresy. Such an argument would certainly not have been superfluous in supporting his position. The debate with the heretics dealt not with the iconography of the Trinity, but with the very dogma of the tri-unity of God. Even if the Church had wished to fight heresy by means of this image, and to prove the divine tri-unity, not one iconographic variant, including the "Paternity," would have been convincing; this all the more since the icon itself could not have served as an argument, because the heretics were iconoclasts.

In the polemical writings against heretics and in the expositions of their anti-trinitarian attitudes, only the icon of the Old Testament Trinity is ever mentioned. The entire third treatise of the *Message to an Iconographer* is devoted to it,[72] as is the letter of St Joseph of Volokolamsk to Archimandrite Vasian concerning the Holy Trinity.[73] What is more, the sixteenth-century *Chronicle,* an official document, illustrates the victory over heresy by means of a miniature accompanied by a corresponding text; it uses not the "Paternity," but precisely an isocephalic Old Testament Trinity.[74] Lastly, the supreme organ of the Russian Church, its local council, prohibited the image of the

72 Edited by N. Kazakov and Ia. Lurié, *Heretical Anti-Feudal Movements in Russia in the Fourteenth and Early Sixteenth Centuries* (in Russian) (Moscow-Leningrad, 1955), 360-73.

73 *Ibid.,* 306-9.

74 Published by L. S. Retkovskaia, 241.

"Paternity" because it is not possible for the Church to change its own doctrine. Besides, the ultimate defeat of heresy did not prevent the development and dissemination of this iconographic subject.

What interests scholars the most is the layout of the "Paternity"—a portrayal of three in one: "The three Persons are brought so close together that they form but a single group, framed as they are by the silhouette of the Father."[75] As soon as the Judaizers denied the image of the Old Testament Trinity because they considered that Abraham saw not the Trinity, but God with two angels, some scholars concluded that it was the "Paternity" that was to show the trinitarian dogma with the greatest fullness and precision. "In this type of image, the unity and quality of the three persons of the Trinity have received their clearest expression, one not allowing any misunderstanding."[76] But what is the unity that is depicted here? The heterogeneous figures are unable to show either the equality of the Persons or the unity of Their Nature. And if this image is understood as expressing a purely symbolic unity, where then are the persons of the Holy Trinity, since a personification, or a symbol, is not the image of a person? The unity of the Trinity, in its Orthodox understanding, is the unity of Its Nature. But in this composition, there is no natural unity between the old man, the adolescent, and the dove. For this reason, there is no equality either.

To explain this image, L. S. Retkovskaia cites the words of St Joseph of Volokolamsk: "Let us therefore confess one God and not three; for they are not separated one from another...but together Father, Son, and Holy Spirit, each contained *the one in the other* [italics by Retkovskaia], without confusion or separation." "If we did not know the representations of the 'Paternity' painted well before these words of Joseph of Volokolamsk," Retkovskaia writes, "we could have believed that the image of this composition, in any of its variants, appeared as a literal illustration of the above quotation."[77]

However, in his letter to Archimandrite Vasian and in the second treatise of the *Message to an Iconographer*, St Joseph used classical patristic concepts about the ineffable, unrepresentable Deity. At any rate, he knew theology well enough so as not to consider the Persons of the Trinity as

75 A. Heimann, "L'iconographie de la Trinité," *L'Art chrétien* (Paris, 1934), 39.
76 L. S. Retkovskaia, *op. cit.*, 243.
77 *Ibid.*, 246.

being portrayable in their Divinity, whether in an anthropomorphic fashion (as Father and Son) or in a zoomorphic one (as the Holy Spirit). Joseph's expression, "the one in the other," refers to the uncreated, intra-trinitarian life, but in no case to a plastic art form.

This subject has not ceased to create "misunderstandings," as illustrated by the variance between divergent interpretations, beginning with those of the iconographers themselves, and the periodic discussions that started in the fifteenth century, continued in the sixteenth and seventeenth, and still continue today.[78]

78 The council only considered the image of the "Paternity," representing the Father, the adolescent Son in His lap, and the dove between them. However, the information we have indicates that this iconographic subject was not limited to the variant studied at the council. A study of the development of the iconography of the "Paternity," since its apparition, shows that this iconography fluctuated over the centuries. It is especially significant that these fluctuations reflect not the search for a better expression of a well-defined content, but a search for the content itself: Who is the main person represented? The iconography varies, as do the inscriptions:

1) In certain images (namely the eleventh-century miniature illustrating St John Climacus, *Vaticanus graecus 394*, fol. 2; a twelfth-century Greek illustration of the Gospel, in Vienna, *Gr. 52*, fol. 1), it is the Ancient of Days who is represented with the features of Christ;

2) In other images, the main person is Christ in His conventional appearance of a mature man: thus in the embroidered veils of Sophia Paleologus (1449, with the inscription IC XC) and of Solomonia Saburov (1525, with the inscription "Lord Sabaoth");

3) Sometimes the old man with the white hair (the Ancient of Days) is represented with the inscription IC XC (the thirteenth-fourteenth-century fresco at Kastoria carries the additional inscriptions: Father, Son, Holy Spirit). Alongside these trinitarian representations, there are bi-unitary images with the same iconographic indications and inscriptions (for example, the eleventh century miniatures of the Codex of Mount Athos, *Dionysiou* 740, of the fourteenth-century Serbian Psalter in Munich, for example, of the fourteenth century Bulgarian Psalter of Tomich in Moscow, and so on). In all such images, bi-unitary as well as trinitarian, the Child Emmanuel sits on the lap of Christ (in His conventional appearance or with the features of the Ancient of Days). In certain representations, the two persons carry the cruciferous halo. On the knees of the Ancient of Days, one sometimes sees not the Child, but the adult Christ in reduced dimensions (the twelfth century *Gospel of Vienna, gr. 52*; the frescoes of Kastoria and Grottaferrata). In all these images of Christ, whether He is portrayed in His conventional appearance or as the Ancient of Days, the Lord's Hypostasis is disclosed both iconographically and by means of inscriptions. What does this image mean? In "Über Herkunft und Entwicklung der anthropomorphen byzantinisch-slavischen Trinitäts-darstellungen des sogenannten Synthroni- und Paternitas Typus," *Festschrift W. Sas-Zaloziecky* (Graz, 1956), 60, H. Gerstinger speculates that from the moment the representation of the Ancient of Days contradicts Orthodox doctrine, the images of the super-essential (the Ancient of Days) may be linked to gnostic heretical circles. If in the Ancient of Days one should see the eternal Word, that is, Christ as God, in the Child Emmanuel it would be proper to see Christ in His Incarnation. In this case, it would be a representation of His two natures, separated one from the other, which would be Nestorianism. But since the Son of God, Gerstinger continues, can be represented only in His Incarnation, as the eternal Word, He can be depicted only symbolically, in the form of the

The lack of sure documentary evidence and the contradiction between this image and Orthodox doctrine prevent us from seeing in it a weapon of the Church against heresies. Simultaneity in itself proves nothing. At any rate, there is no unanimity among scholars as to the origin of this image. We note here the work of M. S. A. Papadopoulos about the image of the "Paternity."[79] True, it is not the author's intent to discover the reasons why the image appeared. But in our opinion, his conclusions represent a better approach to this question. Papadopoulos posits that the appearance of this subject in Christendom originated in a rite of adoption which existed in antiquity and which survived in Byzantium until the thirteenth century. An important component of this ritual consisted of having the adopted child sit on the knees of the adoptive father. According to the author, this image evidently contradicted Orthodox theology,

Ancient of Days. Now, as we have seen, the Ancient of Days, both in the vision of Daniel and in the Book of Revelation, is the Christ of the Second Coming and therefore bearer of His two natures, human and divine, like the Child Emmanuel. Whatever the case might be, and despite the presence of the dove, no image of the Trinity results from this since the Hypostasis of the Father is absent;

4) Lastly, the Ancient of Days is understood as the image of the Father, and the inscription that accompanies it is "Father," "Lord Sabaoth" or "Heavenly Father." (To repeat: nowhere have we found the inscription "Paternity.")

We see the same fluctuations on this iconographic subject in the West, up to the fourteenth century. The above-mentioned examples of representations dating back to different epochs make it abundantly clear that for a long time there was no clear understanding of this iconographic subject. The incoherence of its iconography, and the lack of consistency in the inscriptions that accompany it, do not permit us to see in it either unanimity or uniformity. In the image of the "Paternity," there is also fluctuation as to the place of the dove, symbol of the Holy Spirit. In Russia, such variations continued as late as the seventeenth century. In western iconography, these variations are more pronounced than in that of the East, and the dove is found either between the old man and the child, or in the child's lap. The Great Council of Moscow speaks only of the first variant, which Bogoslovskii considers to be the ideal one. Thus he writes, "One could hardly find a more suitable way of personifying the concept of the procession of the Holy Spirit" (*op. cit.*, 3). At any rate, the position of the dove reflects the doctrinal concept of the procession of the Holy Spirit. Thus A. Heimann believes that its place between the Father and the Son "eminently corresponds to Catholic dogma, which states that the Holy Spirit proceeds from the Father and the Son" (*op. cit.*, 47). If the dove is placed in the bosom of the Son, this "is in conformity with Orthodox faith, where the Holy Spirit proceeds only from the Son" (sic!) (*ibid.*, 40). By contrast, L. S. Retkovskaia sees the placement of the dove between the old man and the child as a way of opposing the manner in which Roman Catholics understand the procession of the Holy Spirit, the *filioque*. This author believes that placing the dove in the bosom of the child could be understood as an expression of the *filioque*. A. Grabar understands the position of the dove in the same way (*Cahiers archéologiques*, vol. 20, Notes, 237).

79 "Essais d'interprétation du thème iconographique de la Paternité dans l'art byzantin," *Cahiers archéologiques*, vol. 18 (1968), 121-36.

and he concluded: in the eyes of the Byzantines, this iconographic subject had to express either a close natural relationship (if the ancient pagan meaning of this gesture still survived); or an adoption, which, if applied to the Trinity, would express a heretical concept of the relationship between Father and Son; or else also a spiritual kinship. Without analyzing these conclusions, we may say that the image of the "Paternity" represents a lingering vestige of ancient beliefs. According to the conclusion of Papadopoulos, it is precisely in Russia, where this representation was widespread and is preserved until our day, that it kept its most ancient, original name of "Paternity."

Compositions that falsify Church doctrine usually first appear in illustrations. In trying to illustrate the text as precisely as possible, so as to make it more understandable and accessible, a painter may make an error out of ignorance. But he may also consciously convey his erroneous concept of the Orthodox tradition. At all times in the history of the Church, there have been points of view reflecting various degrees of assimilation to the Orthodox theology faithful to revelation—amalgamations between theology and philosophy. This occurred primarily when, while dealing with theological concepts and terms, gaps or misunderstandings remained that could lead to direct contradictions of Church doctrine. Thus the boundary between what was conceivable and what was not, between what could or could not be portrayed, was no longer clearly felt and faded from consciousness.

To believe that it is possible to portray the Deity is a temptation that has always existed in Christendom. It has never been eliminated, and the question of the limit of what can be depicted has constantly remained on the periphery of the ecclesial consciousness. In certain periods, circumstances helped to nourish this temptation, or rather stimulated it through heresies or remnants of other beliefs or concepts about the Godhead. Here, it seems to us, is where one has to look for the origin of images similar to that of the "Paternity."

The apocryphal texts of early Christianity sometimes contain anthropomorphic concepts of the Divinity. The anthropomorphic representations of the Deity (extremely rare, it is true) also date back to the beginning of Christianity. The oldest known representation of the Trinity in the form of three men is found on a sarcophagus from the end of the fourth century (Lateran Museum), that is, it dates back to the time of the massive influx of pagans into the Church.[80] Sometimes a false conception of the vision of God also emerges—the temptation to view God apart from His Incarnation. Since the Incarnation not only made God visible, but gave man the opportunity to contemplate Him, contemplation has sometimes been confused with prophetic vision.[81]

The "Paternity" appeared at a time when acrimonious discussions took place in Byzantium concerning the vision of God. In Orthodoxy, this vision is not linked to anthropomorphic apparitions; and, in general, the attitude toward all visions has always been one of caution. But in heretical Bogomil circles, anthropomorphic visions of the Trinity were viewed as authentic. The monk Euthymius Zigabenus states in his *Panoplia Dogmatica*: the Bogomils "say that not only in dreams but also in reality they see the Father as a bearded old man and the Son as an unbearded adolescent."[82] Bogomil concepts, their views of the Holy Trinity, were widespread in the Church and in Byzantine society. Even if one cannot positively affirm any influence of Bogomil doctrines on the iconographic subject of the "Paternity," we can only agree with K. Onasch, who is of the opinion that the appearance of anthropomorphic portrayals of the Holy Trinity in Byzantium exactly at this time cannot be accidental.[83]

80 Moreover, is it possible, as is sometimes done, to attribute to the Church a polemic against the Arians by means of these images found on sarcophagi destined to be buried and not exposed to people?

81 M. A. Grabar gives an example: a miniature of the ninth century (thus immediately following Iconoclasm) at the Bibliothèque Nationale in Paris (*Gr. 923*) which represents an unknown man contemplating God the Father's sending the Savior into the world (this miniature is placed near a quotation from St Basil on the contemplation of God in his Homily XV, *De fide*, ch. 1 and opening of ch. 2, PG 31: 465). A. Grabar, *L'iconoclasme byzantin* (Paris, 1957), illustr. 163.

82 *Euthymii Zigabeni Panoplia dogmatica*, XXVII, par. 23, PG 130: 1320. The leaders of the Paulicians, the predecessors of the Bogomils, ascribed to themselves the role of the persons of the Holy Trinity and called themselves Father, Son, and Comforter, as Photius indicates in his account of the new appearance of the Manichaeans. We find the same thing in the eleventh formula of renunciation of heresy concerning the reception of Paulicians into the church. See *Travaux et mémoires*, 4th extract (Paris: Centre de Recherches d'Histoire et de Civilisation byzantines, 1970, 133-4). In addition, Bogomilism was to a large extent sustained by the apocryphal literature of the early years of Christianity.

83 K. Onasch, "Ketzergeschichtliche Zusammenhänge bei der Enstehung des anthropomorphen Dreifaltigkeits-Bildes der Byzantinisch-slavischen Orthodoxie," *Byzantinoslavica* 31 (Prague: 1970), 231. By contrast, Gerstinger sees in it a visible western influence. Indeed, in the West, the representation of the first and the third Persons of the Trinity hardly ever met with opposition. Well before the appearance of the "Paternity," an analogous representation existed in the West: it is a miniature made by an Anglo-Saxon monk in the twelfth century. There is

Bogomil ideas had penetrated Russia as early as the eleventh century, through the intermediary of Bulgarian Bogomils and their literature. Apparently, they were subsequently reflected in the heresies of the Strigolniki and of the Judaizers. Whatever the case, one may "suppose with a high degree of probability that the religious and philosophic ideas of the Russian Strigolniki were basically founded on the same dualistic conception of the world as that of the Bulgarian Bogomils."[84] It is not possible to state with certainty that the image of the "Paternity" derived only from Bogomilism, whether in Russia or Byzantium. In the West, where it persisted among the Albigenses and the Cathars, the anthropomorphic concept of the Deity was more clearly reflected in art.[85] It is significant that, in Russia, the depiction of the "Paternity" first appeared precisely on the periphery, just as did the heresies, in places where contacts with the West were particularly frequent: in the region of Novgorod (the above mentioned icon in the Tretiakov Gallery, the image behind the altar in the Zverin Monastery [1467], and the "Paternity" in the dome of the Tikhvin Monastery from the early sixteenth century)—and only later in Moscow.

As we have said earlier,[86] the heresies of the Strigolniki and the Judaizers are not directly reflected in art. This would not have been possible, since the heretics were iconoclasts. Nonetheless, their unhealthy and excited religious imagination could not help but contaminate Orthodox consciousness and art. There is an inner kinship between the nebulous and abstruse mysticism of the heretics and the disappearance of every theological criterion among wavering Orthodox, even perhaps among certain fervent zealots of Orthodoxy. It is this fertile soil that gave birth to

a great difference in style between this miniature and the Byzantine images, but an equally great iconographic kinship (*op. cit.*, 81).

84 T. A. Sidorov, "The Fresco of Volotovo 'Wisdom has Built Herself a House' and its Relation to the Novgorodian Heresy of the Strigolniki in the Fourteenth Century" (in Russian), *Trudy Otdela drevnerussk. Literatury* 26 (Leningrad, 1971), 228.

85 N. Braunfels (*op. cit.*, ix) mentions a western anthropomorphic representation of the Holy Trinity from the end of the tenth century, in the form of three men standing next to one another and corresponding perfectly to the Bogomil visions: in this image, the Father is an old man, the Son an adult, bearded man, and the Holy Spirit, a young beardless man. K. Onasch conjectures that the appearance of the "three-headed monster," disseminated in the West since the eleventh century, is linked to Bogomil concepts of the anthropomorphism of God (*op. cit.*, 233). This representation was forbidden in Russia by the Holy Synod: "The parish priests will see to it that in the houses of their parishioners there will be no incorrectly painted icons, such as the one representing the Holy Trinity in the form of a three-headed man" (Bulgakov, *The Clergy Manual* [in Russian] [Kiev, 1913], 745-6, note).

86 See above, chapter 13, "Hesychasm and the Flowering of Russian Art."

images about which there had been "great discussion" since the fifteenth century, causing some "to refuse to venerate icons, while others were amazed at the profound wisdom with which the model had been composed." These "models composed with profound wisdom" were indeed the result of an excited religious imagination, of a deviation from the realism of the Gospel, as much in theology as in art. They abolished the distinction between what is representable and what is not. Moreover, we should keep in mind that heresies thrived precisely among the clergy and in the upper class of society (the court of the Grand Prince). Watching over the purity of Orthodoxy was certainly not on the minds of the heretics and of their protectors. The result of all this was the simultaneous expansion both of the Old Testament Trinity as an affirmation of the true doctrine of the Church—the historian Buslaev is right in explaining this phenomenon as an attempt by Orthodoxy to oppose the heresy of the Judaizers[87]—and of changes in this doctrine through images such as that of God the Father, different variants of the "Paternity," and so forth. But the dissemination of the latter images was caused especially "by general changes in the world view of large social milieus."[88] As we have seen, these changes consisted of an infiltration of ideas from a new culture which was emerging in Russia, new ideas with regard to the Church's view of the world and in its art. In the realm of theology, western scholasticism was taught, under the influence of Roman Catholicism and of Protestantism. The theological criterion used to evaluate an image was being lost. This led to a loss of the very meaning of the image, to an abandonment of the doctrinal foundations of the Quinisext Council and of the Seventh Ecumenical Council. A disintegration of the ontological unity between word and image resulted. It is typical that the same iconographers, on the one hand, wrote sentences of an apophatic nature on the phylacteries of pagan gods and ancient philosophers and, on the other, simultaneously represented God the Father: both appeared in the cathedrals of the Kremlin, that is, in the very heart of Russian Orthodoxy. (Thus, in the Cathedral of the Dormition, Christ is represented in the main dome, God the Father in another). If some voices were raised to defend the authentic meaning of the Orthodox image, they were shouting in the desert.

87 F. I. Buslaev, *Works* (in Russian) (St Petersburg, 1910), vol. 2, 331.
88 K. Onasch, 236.

Such a voice was that of the learned monk Euthymius who saw in the image of the "Paternity" "insolence devoid of judgment, both on the part of those who paint and of those who commission it." The general atmosphere was such that there arose no opposition against the dissemination of abstruse images. What satisfied the faithful was no longer the conformity to the meaning of the word, but to "words" in general, or a combination of words artificially removed from their context. Such representations not only spread like wildfire, but they were accepted and considered as the norm. The result of this is still felt today. This was due in part to the fact that church writers and theological works (with rare exceptions) demonstrated a blind faith in the infallibility of the image as such, without taking into consideration the consistency or lack of consistency of such images with the Orthodox faith. In our own day, the return of theology to the patristic tradition is strangely linked to an utter lack of concern for the theological content of the icon.

As we have seen, the Great Council of Moscow reacted in no way to the emergence of profound changes that were evident in sacred art, despite the pressing nature of the problem. But its merit and significance for our time lie in the fact that it helped to clarify the very basis of Orthodox art—the image of the Incarnation, as well as the very basis of its alteration—the depiction of what cannot be represented. Indeed, by losing the criterion of *what* is representable, art gradually also lost the criterion of *how* the sacred is portrayed, and the artistic language of the Orthodox icon deteriorated. At a time when the Orthodox tradition was betrayed, as much in the image itself and in its conception as in thought, the decision of the Great Council of Moscow categorically to prohibit any representation of the Deity is an authentically Orthodox echo of the patristic theology of the icon.

17

Art in the Russian Church During the Synodal Period

In the eighteenth century, the spiritual decline became progressively worse, and allowed the new art to occupy a commanding position.

In Russia, the reaction against the advance of the western confessions and the deformation of sacred art—a reaction which in the seventeenth century had been so violent, though somewhat instinctive and disorganized—ceased at the beginning of the next century. The reform of the state by Peter I did not spare the Church, which was incorporated into the structure of the government by the suppression of the patriarchate and the creation of the Synod. During this synodal period, the new art became a vehicle to express the official piety under the aegis of the state.

In order to better understand the situation, let us briefly recall the main stages of the life of the Church and of its art during the preceding period.

The quarrel between the Josephites and the opponents of land holdings by monasteries led, within the Church itself, to the question of the Church's role and place in the world. The two divergent points of view with regard to the question of monastic possessions, of heretics, and so forth, in fact represented a clash between two different views of the Christian life. There was, on the one hand, the spiritual and contemplative hesychast trend which, among the followers of St Nilus of Sora, was characterized by a complete detachment from the world. Among the followers of St Joseph of Volokolamsk, on the other hand, the emphasis was placed on the social ministry of the Church. The victory of the Josephites brought with it not only a retrenchment and contraction of the spiritual life; it also made the awareness of a clear boundary between the life of the Church and that of the state more difficult. A dichotomy appeared in ecclesial consciousness. The conception of the Church in its integrity became less pronounced. A split appeared in sacred art, and the spiritual level of the image began to sink.

Beginning in the sixteenth century, this dichotomy in the consciousness of the Church led to the victory of the social ideal, which is concerned with the domain of morals. This marked the beginning of the new relationship between Church and state. One hears, as it were, an echo from the West in the confusion that developed between the Church and the world. The dream takes shape to organize another ideal Christian society alongside the Church, a Christian state here below, on earth and with the help of the secular authorities. A confusion arose in the minds of the people concerning the very essence of the Church, its reason for being, its nature and life—human and at the same time divine—as the Body of Christ. As the concept of Church became progressively less clear, and changes occurred in the relationships between Church and state, sacred art likewise deviated from its direct, primordial goal. It began to assume functions that did not correspond to its essence. While continuing to express the doctrine and the life of the Church, it gradually began also to serve social interests and the ideal of a Christian state. The Orthodox sense of the image faded. Its very creation moved from the inner, spiritual place to the external: this was expressed by its moralizing, anecdotal tendencies, by a predilection for ornamentation. A system of outward rules appeared, governing the moral life of the iconographers. The living, creative tradition gave way to conservatism.

The seventeenth century witnessed "The atmosphere of western absolutism more and more obviously penetrating into Moscow." Thus the quarrel of Patriarch Nikon with the tsar was, in a sense, the equivalent of the western dispute about the relationship between empire and priesthood.[1] The theory of the two swords, imported earlier by the Dominican Benjamin, penetrated the minds. There was a general move away from the culture of the Church and a gravitation toward the secularized concepts of western culture. Despite the violent opposition of the advocates of traditional art, a clear break with the Orthodox image and the Orthodox way of understanding it was formulated in theory and occurred, at least partially, in practice. The advocates of innovations used elements borrowed from the West, without in the least understanding their meaning; the confessional aspect of art began to lose its primary importance, giving way to the aesthetic criterion.

1 Alexander Schmemann, *The Historical Road of Eastern Orthodoxy*, trans. Lydia Kesich (Crestwood: St. Vladimir's Seminary Press, 1977), 331.

The growing confusion between the Kingdom of God and the reign of Caesar was resolved under Peter I by a brutal destruction, a violation of the canonical structure of the Church—one that for two centuries would leave its mark on the life of the Church and its situation within the state. To the emperor, the reform of the state also meant the reform of the Church. The political-juridicial concepts he had borrowed from Protestantism carried with them the notion of the primacy of the state over the Church. In the Church, Peter saw, alongside his own power, another power which had to be incorporated into the general structure of the state. By the suppression of the patriarchate, "the Church was decapitated, in the literal, technical sense of the term."[2] A collegial administration, bearing the Latin name of spiritual "Collegium" was imposed—an institution which, according to Metropolitan Philaret, divine Providence and the ecclesial spirit were "to transform into a Holy Synod."[3] At the head of this Synod was "the tsar's eye," the procurator general. But the supreme power in everything that concerned the Church belonged to the emperor.[4] The state viewed all affairs, including those of the Church, as its own.[5] The state "takes on the undivided care for the people's religious and spiritual welfare. Even if the state later "intrusts or reassigns such care to the 'clerical order,' it does so...by its power of delegation,"[6] insofar as the needs and the welfare of the state demanded it. To the emperor, as for the "Old Ritualists,"[7] the Church appeared as one with the political life. But for Avvakum, the ideal was a sacralized state, while for Peter it was a secularized Church. The "Old Ritualists" wished to see a sacred empire serving the Church; Peter, a Church serving the state.

2 A. V. Kartashev, *Essays on the History of the Russian Church* (in Russian) (Paris, 1959), 312.

3 *Ibid.*, 377.

4 Until 1917, all decisions of the Synod and of the Consistory carried the seal: "By Decree of His Imperial Majesty."

5 Creative activity could exist only under the control of the state; only on this condition was it permitted. The "police state" which Peter I created in imitation of western absolutism, "represents the urge to build and regulate a country and a people's entire life—the entire life of each individual habitant—for the sake of his own and the 'general welfare' or 'common good.' Police pathos, the pathos of order and paternalism, proposes to institute nothing less than universal welfare and well-being, or, quite simply, universal 'happiness'" (G. Florovsky, *Ways of Russian Theology*, Part One, trans. Robert L. Nichols [Belmont, MA: Nordland Publishing Co., 1979], 115).

6 *Ibid.*, 115-6

7 We prefer this term to the one generally used, that of "old believers," which seems too imprecise.

At the time of Peter I, the struggle against bad icon painting continued, but it assumed a different character. In the seventeenth century, two trends had confronted one another in this struggle: that of canonical painting faithful to the Orthodox tradition, and the new trend that was budding within the new culture. During this period, the Church still assumed responsibility for the quality of sacred art. And if Tsar Alexis Mikhailovich, and before him Ivan the Terrible, had meddled with the domain of this art, their intervention had clearly been an internal Church matter, aimed primarily at the good of the Church. But when the Church was incorporated by Peter I into the administrative system of the state, sacred art became simultaneously the art of the Church and of the state. The latter assumed responsibility for it, and the measures concerning it were taken on the scale of the entire state. This is why, even if a member of the episcopate was charged with overall supervision, the quality of the art, traditional as well as new, was determined by the legislator. A decree of Peter in 1707 confided "spiritual management" to Metropolitan Stephen Iavorskii; but the immediate supervision of the painting of icons "in the entire Russian state" was confided, by a decree of the same year, to the architect John Zarudnev, "the aforementioned John having to call himself superintendent." "For his administration, let a special building be given to him, several old and young employees from the Armory palace, guardians and soldiers from the Moscow garrison, as well as everything that is needed for this task."[8] A decree of 1710 described Zarudnev's duties in twenty points; in this text, the emperor was guided by practical considerations for the good of the state. "For the greater beauty and honor of the holy icons," Zarudnev had to take the census of "all those who painted icons in Moscow, in other cities, as well as of the foreign painters dwelling in His Majesty's entire Russian Empire."[9] He had to divide them into three categories, each with its own tax scale, and was to give them proper certificates. Bishops, priests, and monasteries were forbidden to accept icons from non-certified painters. "Certified painters had to write on the icon the year, the month, the day, the painter's category, his true name and surname."[10] The relationships between the painter and his apprentices, between clients and painters, were spelled out in detail.

8 "Materials for a History of Icon Painting in Russia," collected by P. P. Pekarskii (in Russian), in *Izvestiia Imperat. Arkheografich. Ob.*, vol. V, publication 5 (St Petersburg, 1865), 4.

9 *Ibid.*, 22.

10 *Ibid.*, 24.

Thus, the general reform of the state included a rigid administrative framework that was imposed on sacred art. The following year, 1711, saw the administration of Zarudnev transferred to the Ministry of Church Affairs. "The soldiers were taken back by the Ministry of War, the employees and guardians were dispersed."[11] "But without offices, without employees, without soldiers, without all that was needed for the Ministry to function, the affairs in question [namely, the painting of icons] cannot possibly be administered."[12]

From the beginning, the activity with regard to art of the Synod founded by Peter I can be seen in two decrees, of April 6 and May 21, 1722. The first, to which we referred in the preceding chapter, concerned the antimensia. Referring to the Great Council of Moscow, the Synod prohibited the portrayal of Lord Sabaoth "with the features of an old man," as well as the use of symbolic animals to portray the gospel writers and bearing their names. The image of Lord Sabaoth had to be replaced by "the inscription of the name of God in Hebrew letters."[13]

The second decree[14] prohibited churches from owning icons carved on wood or sculpted in stone, "invented by inept or ill-intentioned iconographers." Indeed, the decree stated, "we do not have artists chosen by God. Only ignorant and ill-mannered people dare make such things." "This custom has entered Russia through the agency of infidels, especially Romans and our neighbors, the Poles, who follow them." In these last words, one can hear, as it were, an echo of the shifting attitudes toward Protestantism and Roman Catholicism which at this time marked the ecclesiastical politics of the confidants of Peter I. Thus, the "latinizing" Stephen Iavorskii advocated the Roman Catholic type of sculpture. But the above decree appeared after Stephen had been replaced by Theofan Prokopovich, who favored Protestantism.[15]

11 *Ibid.*, 5.

12 *Ibid.*, 6.

13 *The Complete Collection of the Decisions of the Department of the Orthodox Confession* (in Russian), vol. 2, Decision no. 516, 163-4.

14 *Ibid.*, 293-5.

15 Subsequently, on November 30, 1832, the Synod promulgated a new decree forbidding statues. Numerous sculptures were destroyed as a result of this decree; others were hidden and then forgotten. The statues called "Christ in prison," preserved in great numbers in northern Russia, date back precisely to the eighteenth century. This subject appeared in the West at the end of the fifteenth century. Its best known example is an illustration of the Passion of Christ by Dürer (called "Kleine Passion"), where it is found on the cover. It had undoubtedly been imported to the north by Russian and foreign merchants through Arkhangelsk. The version

Aside from sculpture, the decree prohibited a whole series of icons "contrary to nature, to history, and to truth itself." The list is rather bizarre. It mentions "the image of the Theotokos in labor during the Nativity of the Son, with a midwife next to her...; the image of Florus and Laurus with horses and grooms bearing fictional names," that is, traditional Orthodox subjects together with deviations.[16]

With respect to art in general, the Synod stated that such "ugliness resulted from a lack of artistic taste." Proportions were not observed, images were painted "with human heads that are excessively large, and other similar things."

Both decrees mentioned the Great Council of Moscow. But in these Synodal decrees there was no longer even a trace of any theological argument—as was still found in the decisions of the Great Council of Moscow. The Synod's attitude toward sacred art was based on considerations of propriety and on what "is indicated by regulations and sound reason," with the aim of avoiding "mockeries concerning the holy prototypes" and "reproaches on the part of the heterodox against the holy Church." Such were the arguments which, for lack of theological considerations, prompted the decisions of the Holy Synod. In other words, we deal here with the same principles as those which had served as a springboard for the seventeenth-century innovators.

At the time of Peter I, the traditional art of the icon began to coexist with the new trend (Fig. 43 and 44). The state was not concerned with tendencies in art: the one important thing was that art be under its control. It was understood that the essential task of this art was to be useful to the state; it had to contribute to the religious and moral education of the citizens. This is how Peter I viewed art in the general framework of his reforms.

The notion that traditional art represented a bygone era prevailed

found in *History of Russian Art* (Moscow, 1960, vol. 5, 432, note 2) does not explain why this image became widespread precisely in the north.

16 Thus, the martyr St Christopher with the head of a dog; the Mother of God called "with three hands," no doubt with three natural hands instead of a pendentive; the image of the burning bush; "the image of the Wisdom of God in the form of a young girl; the image of the creation of the world in six days by God, in which God is represented reclining on cushions...; the image of Lord Sabaoth in the form of an elderly man with his only Son on his lap and between them the Holy Spirit in the form of a dove," that is, the "Paternity"; the Annunciation with the Father blowing from His mouth, a crucified cherubim, and so forth.

43. *Deesis.* Russian icon.
Beginning of the 18th century. Collection M. Martens, Antwerp.

44. *The Coronation of the Virgin.*
Russian, from 1773.

more and more. Indeed, was such art not a component of the old Russia that was doomed to disappear? Already at the time of Peter I,

> the old traditions had been forgotten to such an extent that when Antropov was named administrator of iconography, succeeding Zarudnev, he admitted that he no longer knew ancient iconography. As is clear from his reports to the Synod, he often protested against ancient images, considering them to be incorrect, and prohibiting their circulation among the faithful.[17]

The rationalistic trend gained an increasing hold on the minds of the people and obscured their understanding of the meaning of the cultic image. For a long time, this tradition obliterated the boundary line separating Orthodox from heterodox art.

The eighteenth-century manuals of iconography—the Russian *podlinniki* as well as the Greek *hermineia*—presented a hodgepodge of Orthodox and western iconography. The great majority of the iconographers still kept to the traditional art (especially in the north, during the eighteenth century), but the modern trend became dominant. The theories of the seventeenth-century innovators, and new artistic views based on the concepts of a secular culture, penetrated deeper and deeper into the awareness and were no longer actively opposed. From the eighteenth century on, the new trend in art followed the same path taken by official religious policy.

Faced with the threat of Protestant iconoclasm, the Orthodox turned to latinizing, anti-Protestant literature. "In order to strengthen the faith and keep it from Lutherans, Calvinists, and other iconoclasts," one author wrote in 1724, "one should print as many copies of the book [by Stephen Iavorskii] *The Rock of Faith* as necessary."[18] While neither this author not the others were advocates of latinism in the field of doctrine, the manual *Alphabet* which the same author (Posochkov), in the wake of Ushakov, proposed for the instruction of the iconographers was nonetheless entirely naturalistic and inspired by western models.[19]

17 N. Pokrovskii, *Essay on the Monuments of Christian Iconography and Art* (in Russian) (St Petersburg, 1900), 371.

18 I. T. Posochkov, *The Book of Poverty and Wealth* (in Russian) (Moscow, 1951), 27.

19 It is advisable to begin with the image of a middle-aged man, standing straight and naked, with an indication of the precise measurements from the heel to the top of the head and of other proportions also. "On the other sheets one should begin the alphabet; a new-born baby should be painted on the first sheet, a year-old child on the second, a two-year-old on the third. One should then paint it one year after the other up to the age of twenty; after which,

Another eighteenth-century document is equally characteristic, namely the *Pedalion*, composed by St Nicodemus of the Holy Mountain (d. 1809). It is a typical example of the evolution that was taking place. St Nicodemus' understanding of sacred art is permeated with western rationalism. For him, there is no difference between an Orthodox and a Roman Catholic image. In his view, if "the Latins act improperly," it is only because they "no longer write the names of the saints on top of their icons." This is the only difference he sees between their art and that of Orthodoxy. The seven reasons for the veneration of icons he enumerates lack all theological significance, and the essential one—to witness to the Incarnation—is missing. Certainly, St Nicodemus refers to the Seventh Ecumenical Council; but for him, the very basis of this council's argumentation—the correspondence between word and image—is limited merely to the illustrative aspect. As was the case earlier with Vladimirov, what is of decisive importance is the mere fact, stripped of its evangelical significance. Thus, he writes that to represent the Apostle Paul on icons of the Ascension and Pentecost, and Christ on that of Mid-Pentecost, as well as other traditional Orthodox details, is "contrary to the Gospel and out of place." As for the Orthodox icon of the descent into Hell (*Anastasis*), he is of the opinion that it should be replaced by the Roman Catholic image of Christ rising from the tomb because, he says, only the soul of Christ made the Descent into Hell, while His body remained in the tomb. St Nicodemus views all such aspects of Orthodox iconography as so much "ineptness," "invented by iconographers because of their lack of knowledge and bad habits...All this is to be eliminated. We should do everything in our power so that iconographers become skilled and dexterous."[20] Within the context of the general concepts of St Nicodemus and those of his time, this means: replace the traditional Orthodox artistic language by the language proper to Roman Catholicism.

In the eighteenth century, as in the seventeenth, the latinization of the Orthodox world continued. In the Near East as well as in Russia, Roman Catholics and Protestants vied with one another to impose their own

between twenty and thirty, two years should be added, and five years between thirty and ninety—this entire alphabet should depict naked subjects. Then begin another alphabet, depicting the subjects clothed, upright and seated, as well as in all sorts of different aspects" (*ibid.*, 145-6).

20 *Pedalion* (in Greek) (Athens, 1957).

influence in the cultural and religious domains. This influence was exercised through the embassies of western countries and through the Jesuit order, who attempted to augment their role in the leading circles of society by all means.[21] On the one hand, *avant-garde* concepts of a secularized culture entered Russia while, on the other, and on the strictly religious plane, non-Orthodox views proper to the western confessions were implanted.

Of all the Orthodox countries, thanks to Dositheos, Patriarch of Jerusalem, only Romania was able to neutralize Latin influence by creating a center of authentic Orthodox culture, together with printing houses. Romania became a stronghold of Orthodoxy, and throughout the eighteenth century it alone stood firm. It is through Romania that a renewal of the Russian spiritual life came into being at the close of this century.

In the words of a church historian, the secularization carried out in Russia by Peter I by political means amounted to a "transfer from the West of the heresy of state and custom."[22] But this "heresy" was more far-reaching: it brought with it a direct influence of western ideas, both Protestant and Catholic, on the relations of Church and state, on the general level of religious education and sacred art, as well as of culture. This confessional influence by means of western culture occurred all the more easily since this culture presented itself as "Christian," even though it derived from a changed and truncated Christianity which, during the Renaissance, had resurrected a type of pagan world-view. Separated from the Church, this culture still wore a mask of truth, and therefore insinuated itself into the dulled awareness of the people who, having lost the criterion of authenticity, were afraid of being "censored by the heterodox" for "not discerning the truth."

In the process of the genesis and formation of this secular Russian culture, and in light of this democratized culture, elements not belonging to it were no longer viewed as culture. Consequently, "a large number of

21 See A. Kartashev, *Essays on the History of the Russian Church* (in Russian) (Paris, 1959), vol. 2, 409. In Constantinople, the western embassies, using political and financial means, intervened decisively in patriarchal elections, and there were numerous instances of depositions. Thus in the eighteenth century, over a period of seventy-three years, forty-eight patriarchs succeeded one another on the see of Constantinople.

22 E. Golubinskii, as quoted by G. Florovsky, *Ways of Russian Theology*, Part One, trans. R. L. Nichols (Belmont: Nordland Publishing Co., 1979), 114.

people blindly accepted that the Church was hostile to culture, and that what was of the Church had to be separate from culture."[23] Cultured society, that is, the entire nobility reformed by Peter I to buttress the empire, broke away from the Church and from the people, from its past, from its history.[24] The Age of "Enlightenment," ostentatious, dreaming, and confused, could tolerate only a "rationalized" faith, the very same faith conveyed by a so-called "Christian" culture. From this perspective, the Church began to look like a body that was estranged from, even hostile to, culture—a type of nursery of superstitions and obscurantism to be combated as much by the state as by enlightened society. "Under Peter's successors, such state 'protection' of the Church became in time an outright and tormenting persecution justified on the grounds of state security and the need to struggle against superstition"[25]—a persecution marked by the direct influence of Protestantism. "Prior to Elizabeth's reign, government authority and even state law extended a certain special and preferential protection for Protestantism."[26] "It was a methodical terror applied by the state...It took on the catastrophic aspect of a foreign invasion."[27]

The reign of Elizabeth marked a period of reprieve in the life of the Russian Church. As for Catherine II, named "most-Orthodox," she was convinced that Orthodoxy in no way differed from Lutheranism, except in the domain of worship, which had become vital because of the backwardness of the people. It was precisely during her reign that the procurator-general Melissino, the "pre-eminent subduer of religious ob-

23 *Ibid.*

24 "Ancient in its family origins and belonging to the military estate, new as a social class, [the cultivated society] claimed the entire treasure of the new culture, absorbing it for itself alone and confining it to its circles, closing in on itself through this new, almost external, force" (A. Khomiakov, "The Opinion of Foreigners about Russia," *Selected Works* [in Russian] [New York, 1955], 94).

25 G. Florovsky, *Ways*, 120.

26 *Ibid.*, 127.

27 A. V. Kartashev, *Essays*, 398. In 1742, on the feast of the Annunciation, Archbishop Dimitri (Sechenov), while speaking of the reign of the Empress Anna (1730-1740) in a homily delivered in the presence of the Empress Elisabeth, said: "Above all, what persecutions of the defenders of piety, of the celebrants of the holy Mysteries! The clergy—bishops, priests, and monks—were tortured, executed, defrocked. Unceasing deportations by land and sea! To where? Why? Monks, priests, and pious men were sent to faraway Siberian cities, to Okhotsk, Kamchatka, and Orenburg. This caused such a fright that the pastors themselves, the preachers of the word of God, kept silence and no longer dared open their mouth to speak of piety. Indeed, it is true: the spirit is willing, but the flesh is weak. The grace of martyrdom is not given to everyone" (*ibid.*, 423).

scurantism,"[28] submitted a project to reform the life of the Church which was fortunately stopped by the Synod and thus had no further consequences. The content of this project is so characteristic of the "Age of Enlightenment" that of its thirteen points we will mention a few that are most typical. Thus point 5 was intended "to purify the Church of superstitions and false miracles associated with relics and icons. In order to study this problem, a special committee is to be formed made up of various people not blinded by prejudice." Point 7: "The prolonged Church rituals" are to be shortened "in order to avoid pagan prolixity in prayer." "The high number of stichera, canons, troparia and so forth, composed in recent decades, are to be eliminated." "Numerous superfluous feast days should be abolished; instead of Vespers and Vigils, short prayers are to be prescribed with sermons useful to the people." Point 11: "Would it not be more responsible to eliminate altogether the custom of reciting prayers for the dead?" Point 13: "One should not allow communion to children under ten years of age."[29] It was with such a mix of disparate elements taken from Protestantism and Roman Catholicism that he intended, through administrative means, to reform the Russian Church.

This enlightened society, fighting prejudices and superstitions, alienated from the Church, hunted for something to feed its religious sentiments and found it above all in the Masonic lodges. "Toward the end of the 1700's freemasonry swept through nearly the entire educated class."[30] At this time, people read a great deal, but without discernment: they read certain authentic Fathers of the Church side-by-side with the Spanish mystics, but particularly Jakob Boehme. In churches built at this time we find Masonic symbols, even on the iconostasis. At the end of the century, the Church was invaded by a sentimental religiosity that suffocated its teaching.

The pressure on the Church exercised by Protestantism and Roman Catholicism had particularly unfortunate repercussions in the spheres of religious education and sacred art.

28 A. Kartashev, *ibid.*, 485.

29 *Ibid.*, 485-7.

30 G. Florovsky, *Ways*, 149. At the same time, the second half of the eighteenth century was the age when "All the basic Russian sects—the Khlysty, Skoptsy [eunuchs], Dukhobors [spirit-wrestlers], and Molokans [milk-drinkers] developed" (*ibid.*, 155). They were persecuted at first, but under Alexander I they infiltrated the upper layers of society and were protected by them.

In the schools of theology, which were established on the western model, scholasticism took firm root, and for a long time. Beginning at this time, the breach between the patristic tradition and the taught theology widened. "Those circumstances became so complex that the fate of Russian theology in the eighteenth century was resolved in an extended debate between the *epigoni* of western post-Reformation Roman Catholic and Protestant scholasticism."[31] The transposition onto Russian soil of a school that was Latin in language and spirit

> signified a break in the church's consciousness: a breach separating theological "learning" from ecclesiastic experience. The rift could be felt all the more keenly when one prayed in Slavic and theologized in Latin. The same Scripture which rang out in class in the international language of Latin could be heard in Slavic in the cathedral.[32]

Metropolitan Philaret of Moscow wrote (before the subsequent reformation of the theological schools) that

> priests knew Latin pagan authors well, but hardly knew religious and Church writers. They could speak and write in Latin better than in Russian. With their exquisite phrases in a dead language, they were more able to shine in a circle of scholars than illuminate the people with the living knowledge of truth.[33]

Paisii Velichkovskii remembered the school of theology in Kiev, which he had left, "where I often heard of Greek gods and goddesses and pious tales, and heartily despised such teaching."[34] The scholastic theology taught in these schools caused distaste and a profound boredom. This boredom was dangerous for the faith and prepared a soil fertile for atheism. Those who attended theological schools often lost their faith: they learned formulas whose spirit was alien to them, and which corresponded neither to their spiritual experience nor to their piety. Their eyes were opened to contemporary culture, but were turned away from the Church.

In this system of education given to the clergy—a system in which all

31 G. Florovsky, *ibid.*, 139. The Jesuits founded a school in the capital for the sons of the Muscovite high nobility. Jesuit influence was felt most strongly at the beginning of the nineteenth century. "For a short time, from 1811 to 1820, the Jesuits even managed to achieve the creation of a special educational district for their schools within the empire. The Polotsk Academy served as its administrative center. To the south, Odessa became a hotbed of Roman proselytism" (*ibid.*, 170).

32 *Ibid.*, 134.

33 *Ibid.*, 210.

34 *Ibid.*, 160.

creative thought was governed not by the Orthodox faith and life, but by Latin and Protestant scholasticism—there was no longer room for the icon, and this is quite natural. Just as for the "enlightened" man of this era, for the clergy instructed in these schools, their ecclesial sense disabled by scholasticism, the "Christian" image in its Roman Catholic form became more intimate, more understandable than the Orthodox icon. Not that the icon had become alien to him; but its Orthodox content had gradually and systematically been deleted from his awareness. This is why western art forms were imposed, if not with the complicity of the clergy, then at least because of their passive attitude in the face of interventions by official authorities—interventions which, by contrast, were very energetic.[35]

In 1767, Catherine II issued a decree prohibiting the painting of icons "with unusual, scandalous features." What she understood by this is not clear. We do, however, have some idea about her attitudes, because it was she who ordered that the iconostasis of Andrei Rublev be removed from the Cathedral of the Assumption in Vladimir, to be replaced by one in the Baroque style, with her own image on it as an icon of St Catherine. In the eighteenth century, only Lomonosov showed interest in the ancient icons, perhaps foreseeing what lay in store for them. In 1760 "he addressed himself to the government, and proposed to have copies made of the best ancient icons in order to save them for posterity."[36]

As the new culture, a class culture, gained ground, the break with the Orthodox image deepened. From the very beginning of this new trend, the traditional image was brought into question as "an antiquated custom," as "blindness to the truth." Already in this period, as we have seen,

35 The following is a typical example of the attitude toward traditional Orthodox art, in a cultivated hierarch on the one hand and, on the other, artisan iconographers. The reference is to a letter written by Archbishop Simon of Kostroma (1760-1782) to the archpriest of the Cathedral of the Dormition in that city: "Father Archpriest John! On this 6th day of June, when I visited the cathedral church of the Dormition where the wall frescoes are being renovated, I noticed that the faces of the saints are painted by the artisans with much darkness, which resembles what the schismatics who fell away from the church because of their superstitions, praise...But I had already recommended to the painters that in their painting they accommodate for the resemblance to nature and stories, as well as for the appropriate beauty, but they find false pretexts to defend themselves" (Lebedinsky, "The Measures of the Russian Government for the Improvement of the Painting of Icons" (in Russian), ***Dukhovnyi Vestnik*** (Kharkov, 1865), vol. 12, 59.

36 A. I. Zotov, *The National Foundations of Russian Art* (in Russian) (Moscow, 1961), vol. 1, 13. No action was taken on this proposal.

the general concept of art was gradually differentiated into "fine arts" and "simple things" (see the *Writing* of the three patriarchs, 1688). In the eighteenth century, the very concept of art was definitely and exclusively reserved for the new trend, and the icon was excluded from it. As the attitude toward the Church changed, so did the attitude toward its traditional art: separated from the culture, the Church could not have any art that could respond to the demands of an enlightened society. "Even to recall the Byzantine arts was shameful—pictorial art moved forward and occupied the first place."[37] In the leading circles of society, the very word "iconography" became pejorative; neither art nor the artist has anything more to do with the Orthodox icon or the iconographer, "that pious dauber." The fascination with the new culture of which the West was the herald (and, in the realm of art, Italy) exercised its pressure on the painter's consciousness. The traditional art of the Church was replaced by painting that was secular but had religious subjects, and which became a "genre" among others. Because of the premises underlying this culture, this art acquired an autonomous life, independent of the Church, and already depending entirely on the painter. Together with architecture and sculpture, this new religious art entered the mainstream of western art, alongside all secular art. Adapting itself to the cultural demands of society and to the paths taken by religious and philosophic thought, it passed through all the main stages of contemporary western art: the Baroque, Classic, Romantic, and so forth.

Thus the art of the icon was, quite naturally, almost totally replaced among cultivated circles by fashionable religious salon painting, an imitation of western models, of little worth. This art was called "icons in the Italian style" or "according to Italian taste," as corresponded to the taste of the age and seemed flattering to enlightened society. A bishop of the Russian church wrote:

> This century [the eighteenth] has witnessed how as a result of trying to cater to the popular taste, painting and architecture in Russia became humble imitators of Italian painting and architecture, servile most of the time and sometimes ridiculous; and this to such a degree that, whatever their artistic merit, they lost all value if they did not resemble Italian works.[38]

However, had the painters gone to the heart of the matter, the author

37 Sakharov, *A Study on the Russian Painting of Icons* (in Russian) (St Petersburg, 1849).

38 Archbishop Anatolius, *On the Painting of Icons* (in Russian) (Moscow, 1845), 38.

sadly continues,

> they would have found errors in the famous works that were hailed as masterpieces of the Italian schools—flaws so unforgivable that these models would have appeared to them as so many products of the pitiful excitement and of the unhealthy imagination of the Italian painters.[39]

The nineteenth century was an age in which national Russian culture, a culture of synthesis, was in full development and enriched the artistic, creative life. It was an epoch that was extremely rich, but also self-contradictory and confused.

The concept of a universal Christianity, proclaimed by Joseph de Maistre, spread widely. The "religion of the heart," popularized by the advent of Freemasonry at the end of the eighteenth century, was transformed, at the time of Alexander I, into a new type of mysticism, usually called "inner Christianity," indifferent to all confession, and in reality a denial of the Church.

While "the Petrine state subordinated the church from without, and in the name of a secular cause, 'the common good,' extorted toleration for secularized life," by contrast, "During Alexander's reign, the state once again conceived itself to be holy and sacred, proclaiming religious leadership and imposing its own religious ideas."[40] According to this conceptualization, the Church seemed to be a "worn out garment" covering the true, "inward" Christianity. It is in the direction of this "inward Christianity," of such a "religion of the heart," that efforts were made to reform Russia as well as the Church. On the administrative level, a new level, a new step was taken in the development of the Church reform begun by Peter I. A new organism, called "the double ministry," was created. Under the supervision of the Over-Procurator of the Holy Synod, the Ministries of National Education and of Confessions were combined. This "combined ministry was to join, if not unite, all confessions or 'churches,' not only in a common task but with a single inspiration."[41]

The spirit that prevailed at the time of Alexander I may be illustrated in a striking way by the initial project of the Church of Christ the Savior in Moscow, a project chosen from among many by the tsar. Its author, the

39 *Ibid.*, 60.
40 G. Florovsky, *Ways*, 168.
41 *Ibid.*, 168.

Freemason A. Vitberg, proposed that this church was not to be "merely Orthodox," but should express "a universal idea." Vitberg wrote: "That this temple should only satisfy the demands of the Greek Russian church seemed unsatisfactory to me. It should meet the needs of all Christians because its consecration to Christ has indicated that it belongs to all of Christendom."[42] It is true that circumstances did not permit the construction of the church according to Vitberg's project.[43] But a review which appeared in the *Journal of the Ministry of National Education* indicates to what degree such ideas ruled the minds. The project was described as a "living, inspired, perfect expression of the trend which then prevailed in Russian society."[44] Such efforts to unify all religions were made at the expense of Orthodoxy, at the expense of the Church, which was in danger of being dissolved into a vague confession, some type of "eclectic Christianity," and this in the name of "general" religion. "Dogmas, and even the sacraments, are less important than this life of the heart."[45] Anyone who tried to defend Orthodoxy was persecuted, because "under the pretense of defending the outer church, he attacks the inner one,"[46] as Over-Procurator Golitsyn wrote about the author of such a book.

In 1813, during the construction of the Cathedral of Our Lady of Kazan in St Petersburg, the sculptor Martos presented models of statues representing the four evangelists, destined for this cathedral, to this same Golitsyn. The procurator of the Synod had enough good sense to refuse these models. The reason for his refusal is revealing. Unquestionably, Golitsyn said, connoisseurs and art lovers

> would be thrilled at the sight of such statues. But all types of people enter a church of God. It is possible that someone who has no idea about elegance in art might be offended on seeing the evangelists completely naked and in such awkward positions.[47]

At the time of Tsar Nicholas I, the projects of Peter I in the realm of church reform were completed. The state organized church administration into one "department" among others. "Henceforth (and until the end of the Synodal period), the Church was known as the 'Department of

42 The periodical *Starye Gody* (February 1912): "A. Vitberg and his Project of the Church of Christ the Savior on the Mount of Sparrows" (in Russian), 8-9.

43 The church was built in 1839-1883 according to the plans of the architect Ton.

44 *Starye Gody, op. cit.*, 3. Ref. to the Journal of the Ministry of National Education (1859).

45 G. Florovsky, *Ways*, 171.

46 *Ibid.*, 186.

47 *The Masters of Art on Art* (Moscow-Leningrad, 1937), vol. 4, 70, note.

Orthodox Confession.'"[48] The change of the administrative organization of the Church into a public department transformed its sacramental and ritual life into an obligatory state service; and any non-compliance was considered as a lack of political loyalty.

The bondage to which the Church had been reduced, the anti-canonical order which had been imposed upon it, the lack of freedom and of independence of its spiritual power, all this led the Church to resemble a mere ritual institution. The educated circles thus moved away from the Church, seeing in it a hotbed of obscurantism and superstitions, an obligation imposed by the state. A true betrayal of the Church took place, beginning with the upper classes of society, followed by the majority of the educated and "free-thinking" population. An educated man "is ashamed of being a believer," wrote Leskov; "In this past century, the entire history of the Russian intelligentsia was marked by a religious crisis."[49] This crisis was often externalized by a movement from passionate faith to atheism, and a fight against God that was equally passionate. The absence of faith in educated circles and their indifference contributed to the spread of sectarian movements among the people, movements that often showed the earmarks of a struggle against the Church and its rituals. It was a period of disintegration, divisions, of imbalance and distress.

But neither the massive exodus from the Church nor the yoke of the state that weighed upon it destroyed its inner, spiritual life. The sacramental essence of the Church could not perish; as much in Russia as in the East, the liturgical life was the core that preserved its vital forces. In reaction to its official condition of humiliation and powerlessness, the Russian Church of the Synodal period responded with unprecedented missionary activity among non-Christians, not only within the Russian empire to the extreme north and the extreme east, but also beyond its borders.

Concurrent with indifference and the absence of faith, a rebirth of the spiritual life took place. It began during the second half of the eighteenth century among the Athonite monks, and entered Russia via Romania. The end of this century and the beginning of the nineteenth were marked by the restoration of numerous monasteries (among which were those of

48 G. Florovsky, *Ways*, 239.
49 *Ibid.*, 292.

St Barlaam, St Cyril of Beloozero, and others) and the foundation of new ones. A great, if not decisive, role in this spiritual renewal was played by the Russian translations of ascetical works (the *Philokalia*), made by the elder (*starets*) Paisii Velichkovskii.[50] This flowering of the spiritual life occurred in the very heart of the Church, within its canonical framework, even if, at the beginning, it remained outside the official piety, outside the theology of the schools infected by heterodoxy. This was not an abstract doctrine which could be taught in a school: the renewal marked "a return to the living sources of patristic theology and thinking about God,"[51] to the living Orthodox experience. The tradition of spiritual direction resurfaced and was revived. A center of spiritual culture, a great school of Orthodoxy, was created at Optina Pustyn. The translations of the Fathers made there were widely disseminated. But this renewal was far from easy or painless. The monks of Optina, as well as other ascetics, St Seraphim and earlier Paisii Velichkovskii, had to endure accusations of heresy, even persecution on the part of certain "enlightened" bishops who upbraided them for practicing inner prayer and spiritual direction. "The prayer of the heart has been destroyed and derided as a pestilence and a ruination," Metropolitan Philaret stated.[52] Despite all this, the unity of the people was being restored, as much in Optina as around the elders in other centers.

The spiritual life of the *startsy* was so intense that all social and cultural barriers fell before them. Men and women of all walks of life and cultural levels, separated in their daily lives, found togetherness around the *startsy* in monasteries; they sought, and found there, the meaning of their lives. The *startsy* of Optina directed the elite of Russian culture (Gogol, Khomiakov, Dostoevskii, and many others). With personages like Metropolitan Philaret, Khomiakov, and others, theological thought likewise experienced a certain renewal.

Nonetheless, even though an authentic spiritual renewal had taken place, it was not directly linked to the traditional Orthodox image, the icon. The break between art and the Church, and the fact that art belonged in the realm of secular culture, had become so deeply anchored

50 During the nineteenth century, the *Philokalia* was reprinted seven times in Russia.
51 G. Florovsky, *Ways*, 160.
52 *Ibid.*, 206-7.

in society's awareness that the painter could not imagine how his art could be linked to spiritual direction and inner prayer, nor was the ascetic *starets* aware that his inner spiritual activity could have a link with the creation of an image. Such was the outcome of the path that had been traveled since the time of Master Dionysius and of the *Message to an Icongrapher.*

The nineteenth century witnessed a series of reforms in the theological schools, one of which was the replacement of Latin by Russian as the language of instruction. Nonetheless, even if the Orthodox tradition was gradually re-emerging despite the use of Roman Catholic and Protestant textbooks in teaching, the schools still remained under the sway of western scholasticism.[53] In the theological academies, Christian archeology was taught. But when

> one of the first pioneers of academic Christian archeology introduced a section on Christian iconography in his course, he received, upon examination, a severe reprimand from Metropolitan Philaret, who pointed out to him that he had been appointed to teach Church archeology, not the painting of the icon.[54]

Such was the character of the epoch.

There is a remarkable mid-century document which not only has not lost any of its importance, but seems to be especially timely for our age. This document, the *Encyclical of the Patriarchs of the East* (1848),[55] addressed to all Orthodox Christians, was a reaction to the appeal of Pope Pius IX. Did the pope consider Orthodoxy sufficiently weakened to be ready for union? Or was he afraid, on the contrary, that the spiritual awakening might contribute to this emancipation from Roman Catholic influence? Whatever the case, Pius IX had addressed the patriarchs of the

53 Only in the second half of the nineteenth century and in the beginning of the twentieth were initial efforts made to become emancipated from western scholastic theology. But even in 1915, Archbishop Hilarion (Troitskii, the future archbishop), in a discourse to the Moscow Theological Academy, spoke of the tasks imposed by the struggle for freedom in the domain of theology: "I consider it my duty to call upon you to combat the harmful Latin-German enterprise and its sad fruits in our theology" (Archbishop Basil [Krivochéine], "Les textes symboliques dans l'Eglise orthodoxe," *Messager de l'Exarchat du Patriarche russe en Europe occidentale*, no 50 [1965], 75). At the Council of 1917-1918, one of the participants, Bishop Anthony of Volynia, said: "It is the organization of our institutions of theological education which, as far as it has been inherited from the world of western heretics, degrades our schools of theology to the highest degree of the scandalous" (Florovsky, *Ways*, 479).

54 D. K. Trenev, "The Preservation of Monuments of Ancient Russian Iconography," (in Russian), *Ikonopisny Sbornik* I (St Petersburg, 1907), Appendix, 18.

55 "...The text of which seems to have been approved in advance by Metropolitan Philaret of Moscow" (J. Meyendorff, *The Orthodox Church*, trans. J. Chapin [New York, 1962], 99).

East, proposing that they unite with Rome. The *Encyclical* is an answer to this proposal. This document, which appeared in a period of extremely difficult circumstances in the life of the Church, deeply impressed the entire Orthodox world. Khomiakov wrote:

> One can never guess where something might come from. The *Encyclical*...is a superb example of this. It has turned our church world upside down. Who would have expected such a phenomenon? Who would have believed that the instinct for ecclesial truth would have brought such lucid awareness in a poorly educated clergy, seriously damaged by external circumstances and its scholastic learning? What no one dared say or could say or publish openly has been proclaimed to the entire world...and this with such simplicity, such undeniable assurance that anyone who hears this language must recognize at once all the unfettered, inner life of Orthodoxy, unless he willingly blinds himself.[56]

In the critique of Roman Catholicism, the starting point, the crux of the *Encyclical*, was the *filioque* and its consequences. It is precisely this doctrine which, originating in western churches, "had progressively brought with it other innovations," and "had falsified the entire ancient apostolic ritual of the celebration of almost all the sacraments and all the institutions of the Church." "In its very essence and in all its characteristics, such a doctrine has all the marks of a non-Orthodox doctrine." Referring to both eastern and western Fathers, the patriarchs wrote:

> This is why the one, holy, catholic and apostolic Church...proclaims once more, this time in conciliar fashion, that this newly introduced doctrine, according to which the Holy Spirit proceeds from the Father and the Son is in truth a *heresy* [italics in the original], and its followers, whoever they might be, are *heretics*. The societies they form are *heretical* societies [italics everywhere in the original], and any liturgical and spiritual communion of the Orthodox children of the catholic Church with them is an iniquity.

The *Encyclical* states:

> Among us, neither the patriarchs nor the councils have ever been able to introduce any novelty whatsoever because with us it is the very body of the Church, that is, the people, who are the guardians of piety. They always want to keep their faith unchanged, and in harmony with that of the Fathers.[57]

56 A. Khomiakov, *Letter to Samarin of March 1, 1849* (in Russian) *Selected Works* (New York, 1955), 394-50.

57 *Encyclical Message of the One, Holy, Catholic and Apostolic Church to All the Orthodox Christians* (Russian trans., St Petersburg, 1850), 7-8, 36-8. However, Rome did not lay down its arms. In 1894 Pope Leo XIII made a renewed attempt at union by addressing himself to Constantinople and modifying the conditions. The Orthodox can keep their faith, and the union would consist "only" in recognizing the Pope as "the supreme spiritual and temporal head of the

At this time, when efforts were being made to "unite all the confessions and churches," the *Encyclical of the Patriarchs* was an important proof of the vital strength of Orthodoxy which, at the needed moment, was capable of showing "an instinct for ecclesial truth" from the depth of its awareness as a Church.

In Russia, an interest in the nation's past, its history, emerged at the beginning of the nineteenth century. Particular attention was paid to everything old, including the icon. A series of studies devoted to the icon were published. Nevertheless, the icon was viewed apart from its religious context: it was an inheritance of the past, and the main criterion of evaluation was the aesthetic one. The norms of Antiquity and of the Italian Renaissance, viewed as a model for all artistic creation, were applied to it. But some writers had a direct, spontaneous perception of the spiritual beauty of the icon, and were overwhelmed by it. An obsequious imitation of the West was not always satisfactory. In 1846, Khomiakov wrote: "We are beginning to realize more and more that all imitation lacks power and is sterile, whether it be patently servile, that is, tied to any school, or free, that is, eclectic."[58] A marked opposition to the ascendency of western art even arose in certain levels of society, and this opposition assumed an anti-Roman, confessional character. While in the eyes of the advocates of western art, traditional iconography represented an obstacle to creative freedom, "the zealots of Orthodoxy began to move away from everything that was picturesque. They viewed all innovations as a moving away from the Church." Such "picturesque" innovations were regarded as the outcome of a deliberate action by Rome. "Those who came from the West to teach us," the author continued,

> and to enlighten the Russians in matters of art, have repeated for the past one hundred years that the painter's hands should not be tied, that one should leave

entire church spread over the world, and as the vicar of Christ on earth, the dispenser of all grace." The Patriarch of Constantinople, Anthimus, responded in 1895. He again denounced the Latin errors, including the new dogmas: that of the Immaculate Conception (1854) and that of papal infallibility (1870). For union to be realized, he demands above all a common faith. But if the Latins prove that before the ninth century the Eastern church acknowledged the *filioque*, Purgatory, the Immaculate Conception, the temporal power and infallibility of the Bishop of Rome..."Then we would not have anything to say" (*The Patriarchal and Synodical Encyclical Message* of the Church of Constantinople regarding the Encyclical of Pope Leo XIII about the union of the churches, dated April 20, 1894 [from the Russian trans. (St Petersburg, 1896), 4, 8].)

58 A. Khomiakov, *The Opinion of the Russians About Foreigners* (in Russian), *Selected Works*, 133.

> him his freedom...The foreign hosts acted in accordance with the design of Catholicism. They were here only to promote opinions elaborated in Rome, aiming at the destruction of Byzantine iconography.[59]

As the interest in the national heritage became generalized, there began, in this context, a search for a type of art that would be at the same time national, morally edifying, and capable of fostering an aesthetic sense. The government, as well as the Slavophile party and the Church were preoccupied with this search. An effort was made to create "a new iconographic style that would replace the barbaric, unrefined Byzantine style." Painters were sought out who could decorate churches and cathedrals with scenes of a more contemporary, "improved" style, which would correspond to the power and the spirit of the state.[60]

At the very moment when art, severed from the roots which had nourished it, had become a class art, attempts were made to discover and impose upon the people a "national character," dictated from above, to replace the natural, spontaneous expression of its faith and life. Beginning with the end of the eighteenth century, "a struggle began for the creation of a theoretical program of national, Russian art"[61] (sacred and profane), founded on the vast popular masses. Traditional art had never intended to be "national" or "purely Russian": it simply *was* that, reflecting all the complexity of the spiritual, social, and political life of the people, and giving it meaning. It made no efforts to educate the people's aesthetic taste, but gave expression to it. At present, however, an art that was deprived of its organic foundation had to fulfill a series of demands: it had to be "natural," "purely Russian," and had to express "spirituality," "the power and the spirit of the state," and so forth. Traditional art, shaped over the centuries in the depths of the catholic experience of the Church, had always been one of the elements that unified the various levels of society. It was understood by the aristocrat as well as by the common man, by the educated as well as by the unlettered, because it expressed a faith common to all. It conveyed beauty as the people understood it, as

59 Sakharov, *op. cit.* At this time an effort was made to combine the traditional art of the icon with modern painting, but such efforts were not viable. For a cultivated person, such a blend was neither necessary nor sufficient; for a man of the church, it was neither needed nor adequate, although for different reasons.

60 A. Grishtenko, "The Russian Icon as Pictorial Art" (in Russian), *Voprosy zhivopisi* III (Moscow, 1917), 11.

61 A. I. Zotov, *The National Foundations of Russian Art* (in Russian) (Moscow, 1961), vol. I, 116.

much on the aesthetic as on the spiritual level. Moreover, these two planes were not separate, even when their expression operated on different spiritual and artistic levels. Icons were differentiated by a style that was more or less elevated, and by a greater or lesser wealth of ornamentation, but not by the very character of their art.

Now, however, the situation was entirely different. Not only was a peasant, for simple economic reasons, unable to acquire an "icon" created by a fashionable artist, the very psychology of the people had to be turned inside out in order to make them accept what they had not created—an individualized work, in addition imitative, one that was alien to them on the confessional level. In the 1840s Botkin wrote: "See whether there is nowadays any sympathy between the painter and the people. They are strangers to one another. The one does not want to know about the other."[62] It could not have been otherwise. "The painters of our time," an historian said, "always have before their eyes the Pantheons and the Madonnas. How then can they understand what a Russian image, an icon, is?"[63] As a result of having their imagination enslaved by "Pantheons and Madonnas," the painters were no longer able to see the difference not only between a portrait and an icon, but even between mythology and the Gospel. Archbishop Anatolius wrote:

> It is especially painful to the Christian sensibility to see in the workshops of our artists a mixed collection of paintings representing sacred and mythological subjects: a representation of Christ next to one of Bacchus, that of the Theotokos next to a Venus, and so forth. Have our painters become so wise that they combine all beliefs? Where will this lead? To what end?[64]

Clearly, images of Venus and of Bacchus were not put in churches; but such confusion, that is, a total loss of any sense of reality, is typical of the epoch. Sometimes the link of the image to the religion was limited to just the inscription of a name which did not correspond to the person portrayed. This insensitivity in the face of a lie was such that it sometimes led to direct blasphemy.[65] In the upper classes it was highly regarded to order

62 *History of Russian Art* (in Russian) (Moscow, 1964), vol. 8, Bk 2, 37.

63 Cited by Shtekotov, *The Painting of Icons as Art*, Collection "Russkaya Ikona" 2 (St Petersburg, 1914), 130.

64 Archbishop Anatolius, "On the Painting of Icons," 109.

65 This is used in our time by atheistic literature. See, for example, L. I. Emela, *The Origin of Religious Rituals* (in Russian) (Leningrad, 1959). The tradeswoman Chikhacheva is represented with a halo, rays, and the inscription MP ΘY (p. 45). On the order of Minister

an "icon" from a well-known, fashionable painter, while this painter, as the historian Buslaev points out, did not even know how to represent sacred objects, yet would not deign to talk to iconographers.[66] "Icons" were painted according to living models, or based on the painter's imagination, and this continued until the end of the Synodal Period. Indeed, despite his influence, even the great Philaret could merely stigmatize this situation in a rather strongly worded sermon: "The audacity of painting icons according to the painter's imagination is the outcome of the capriciousness of modern times."[67]

The efforts to create a "genuine Russian painting," and

> the nationalistic tendencies generated, as always happens, numerous strange and contradictory phenomena. The painters given commissions, the majority of whom had studied at the German school or at the renewed Roman-Bolognese school, had to make the government's fondest wish a reality. They had to restore sacred art to its ancient splendor, power, and momentum.[68]

The decoration in the great churches of the capitals—the Cathedral of St Isaac in St Petersburg (1818-1858); in Moscow, the Church of Christ the Savior (1838-1883)—was done in collaboration with a group of Roman Catholic and Protestant painters, professors and students of the Imperial Academy of Fine Arts: Brullow, Semiradski, Bruni, and von Neff.[69] It was to them, and to others, that the task of creating a national Russian art was entrusted, "to replace Theophanes the Greek, Rublev, Dionysius, and the great number of anonymous masters of the ancient icon. While deeply disdainful of the precious monuments of ancient Russian art, the new 'sublime' iconographic style gave satisfaction, and not only in official circles."[70] As an example of what was produced, Grishtenko, the same author just referred to, mentions the admiration of the Slavophile Shevyrev (indeed, the Slavophiles had enthusiastically welcomed the new religious painting):

Arakcheev, his concubine was depicted by a painter as the Mother of God, and this image was put in the church of the village of Gruzino (p. 44).

66 See F. I. Buslaev, *General Concepts of the Russian Painting of Icons* (in Russian), *Works* (St Petersburg, 1908), vol. 1, 406.

67 "Sermon for the Assumption" (1846) (in Russian), *Works* (Moscow, 1882), vol. 4, 157.

68 A. Grishtenko, "The Russian Icon," 11.

69 Two years before the consecration of the church, the art historian Gnedich, then a student at the Academy of Fine Arts, gave the competent authorities a declaration saying that this decoration, although made by his professors, was "a scandal for Russia." He suggested that it be scraped away and replaced by another.

70 A. Grishtenko, *op. cit.*, 12.

For his Madonna, Bruni manages to find a new image and a new position. He has portrayed her with the features of a maiden. In these dreamy, languorous eyes, in the paleness of the coloring, in the ethereal lines of the body, in this not yet developed youthfulness which had even been censured as a vice—you see the features of a northern, I would say Russian, Madonna, the concept and the image of which were born on the banks of the Neva.[71]

Indeed, this mixture of sublimated eroticism and vulgar triteness had replaced the icon. A contemporary wrote:

What an abyss separates this Madonna from the banks of the Neva from the great image of the Mother of God born on the shores of the Hellespont. And how difficult and almost impossible it was for men in the 1840s to cross this abyss and return to the beauty of ancient times![72]

From the *Message to an Iconographer*, we know that at the time when the art of the icon flourished, what guided the iconographers in their work was the spiritual direction of the elder (*starets*) in the ways of inner prayer. Where then did one go now to receive directions on how to paint "icons"? To the Academy of Fine Arts[73] and also abroad, in order to obtain "originals." Pobedonostsev, Procurator-General of the Holy Synod (1880-1905), regularly placed orders with the German bookseller Grote in St Petersburg for printed models reproducing western art works. He then distributed them to monasteries to guide the monks in the painting of "icons." He had a strong preference for the art of the Nazarenes in Düsseldorf.[74]

In this context, it is not easy to read without indignation and bitterness the decision made by the Holy Synod (March 27-April 14, 1880):

In order that church painting, while faithfully preserving the tradition, may also meet the requirements of art and thereby exercise considerable influence on the development of an elegant taste in the masses, in addition to its religious significance, the Holy Synod views as very useful the mediation of the Imperial Academy of Fine Arts between the clients and the painters when iconostases,

71 *Ibid.*, 12-3.

72 N. Shtekotov, "The Painting of Icons as Art" (in Russian), Collection "Russkaia Ikona" (St Petersburg, 1914), 130.

73 In 1856, a course in "Orthodox iconography" was introduced at the Academy of Fine Arts. It was "Orthodox" in name only. In actuality, it represented "an eclectic mixture of academic classicism with an imitation of Byzantine painting" (*History of Russian Art* [in Russian] [Moscow, 1965], vol. 9, Part One, 31).

74 In his time, Goethe had called their painting "the new devout anti-art" (*neue frömmelnde Unkunst*). See P. Hauptmann, *"Das russische Altgläubertum und die Ikonenmalerei," Beiträge zur Kunst des christlichen Ostens.* Erste Studien-Sammlung (Recklinghausen, 1965), vol. 3, 34.

icons, and their frames are to be made.[75]

This decision reflects the profound tragedy of Russian art: a people possessing one of the greatest artistic cultures in the world, the creator of an art unequalled in its greatness, found itself faced with the necessity of "developing an elegant taste"—and this in order to accept and understand an art that was foreign to it.

The Orthodox icon, which had expressed the faith and life of the people for almost a thousand years, was assigned to oblivion by the educated classes; and this to such an extent that when Goethe, after seeing the icons made by the iconographers of Palekh in the Orthodox Church at Weimar, was struck by the Byzantine traditions preserved by contemporary painters and asked for information about such painting no one could give him any: neither the circles close to the court, nor the local authorities, nor the historian Karamzin, not even the Academy of Fine Arts.[76] P. Muratov writes:

> Everything that had been accumulated over the centuries was dissipated in a few decades. Baroque or Neo-Classic iconostases replaced ancient Novgorodian or Muscovite ones, wherever possible. The ancient icons were piled up in church basements or in bell towers. Repainted and disfigured, they survived only in forgotten churches in obscure little towns, or in the wooden churches in the areas of Olonetsk or Vologda, which had know neither the proximity nor the solicitude of the landed gentry.[77]

In 1907, the historian Trenev made it clear that "the main reason for the deterioration and destruction of our ancient icons still lies in the indifference with which our enlightened Russian society and the Ortho-

75 S. V. Bulgakov, *The Clergy Manual* (in Russian) (Kiev, 1913), 746, note. There were cases where the church authorities themselves were obliged, out of opportunism, to give their support to traditional painting, despite the dominant trend. Thus, in 1888, the Synod declared: "Given the prejudice of the Old Ritualists against icons done in the new Italian style of painting, the parish priests must see to it that in Orthodox churches, especially in Old Ritualist areas, icons be close to the Greek originals in their painting." In the same decree, one finds the same attitude toward liturgical chant: "Given the antipathy of the schismatics toward singing in parts, the parish priests must see to it that in Orthodox churches, especially in areas with a schismatic population, the singing come as close as possible to the ancient church melodies" (*ibid.*, 742).

76 See the *History of Painting* (in Russian) (Moscow, n. d.), vol. 6, 5, note. (Published before the Revolution).

77 P. Muratov, "The Ancient Russian Icons in the Collection of I. S. Ostroukhov" (in Russian) (Moscow, 1914); cited in the Catalog of Ancient Russian Painting in the Tretiakov Gallery (Moscow, 1963), vol. 1, 11.

dox clergy treat them."[78]

> Icon painting was a great art while Russia was being built by the beneficent power that resided in the church....Afterward, things changed. The corrupting influence of secular grandeur affected the church, enslaving it and gradually turning it into a subordinate instrument of the temporal powers. The royal splendor, in which it had a part, eclipsed the life-giving relations of the church, and its role as sovereign eclipsed its role as community, as *sobor.* Its image faded in our religious consciousness and lost its ancient colors. The icon's darkened face is the very image of the church as prisoner of earthly magnificence.[79]

All this was one aspect: the other was the official art of the Church which expressed "the power and the spirit of the state." The Orthodox icon was accused of being "old-ritualist," while the "humble imitation" of Roman Catholicism was accepted as Orthodox and, as such, is obstinately defended even now by many members of the hierarchy and the faithful.

It should be noted that Russian old-ritualism contributed in an important, if not very obvious, way to the neglect of the icon. That it played an important role in preserving the ancient icon is true: this, in itself, is its great merit. Nevertheless, "the schisms made the ancient times lose their prestige by causing a revolt against the Church in their name, and, consequently, against the state that was linked to it."[80] It was this revolt that played a crucial role in the antipathy toward the icon. While one segment of Russian society, influenced by the West, fully adopted the new vision of the world and the new art, another sector of this society, remaining faithful to the Church, allowed itself to become profoundly indifferent toward the heritage of the past, which for the old-ritualists represented the ideal; moreover, it saw the dangers of such a blind allegiance to the past. In the eyes of the state, the schism was a revolt; consequently, everything that had caused it and continued to play a role in it was under suspicion. In the eyes of the Church, every attitude, even one that was correct in itself, was compromised by the very reality of the

78 "The Preservation of Monuments of Ancient Russian Iconography," (in Russian) *Ikonopisnii Sbornik* (St Petersburg, 1907), 2. The following reservation, however, ought to be made: the entire clergy did not share the attitude toward the icon that was rampant among the cultivated classes; there were numerous priests in the churches and monasteries who endeavored to preserve ancient icons, often in opposition to their learned parishioners and the churchwardens.

79 E. N. Trubetskoi, "Russia and her Icons," in *Icons: Theology in Color,* trans. G. Vakar (New York: St Vladimir's Seminary Press, 1973), 95-6.

80 V. Kliuchevksii, *Works* (in Russian) (Moscow, 1957), vol. 3., 318.

schism, by the fact of breaking away from the Body of the Church. Finally, for a great number of people, the two principles could coincide, and thus arose in society an antipathy toward what the old-ritualists defended. This led to a total lack of interest.

From the first half of the nineteenth century, interest in the icon increased, as did the number of scholarly works devoted to it. The second half of the century witnessed the birth of a science of ancient Russian art. "In our enlightened times, justice had finally been done to the unpolished art of the high Middle Ages," Buslaev wrote.[81] This period is marked by the publication of a whole series of valuable works of the so-called "iconographic school." Nonetheless, since the general concepts of art had been modified, the icon was no longer viewed as a work of art and was studied only from an archaeological perspective. Its main interest lay in the tradition of the Church which was preserved in the subjects portrayed. Icons were, it is true, given some credit: with regard to the religious content, "our ancient iconography presents undeniable advantages over western art."[82] But on the artistic plane, the ancient iconography was the outcome "of the stagnation of ancient Russia until the seventeenth century in the literary domain and, more generally, the intellectual."[83] "It was appropriate for a population of hardened villagers...a down-to-earth people almost unacquainted with the inventions of the mind."[84] It "belonged to a state of the art that was extremely undeveloped, technically poor, and unaware of the essential conditions of an artistic tastes educated by a study of nature and by models from the fine arts."[85]

A curious situation arose: the demands of a modern, enlightened society were not met by the artistic level of the icon. Where indifference was not the rule, "people spoke of it as of something ugly, bizarre, outmoded."[86] Western influences were viewed as a positive factor in the development of crude Russian art. But at the same time the imitation of western models led to discontent and disapproval. In the second half of the century, such imitative art and the "pronounced sentimentality" of

81 F. I. Buslaev, *General Concepts of the Russian Painting of Icons* (in Russian) *Works* (St Petersburg, 1908), vol. 1, 31.

82 *Ibid.*, 10.

83 *Ibid.*, 29.

84 *Ibid.*, 41.

85 *Ibid.*, 21.

86 K. Trenev, "The Preservation of Monuments," 33-4.

academic painting prompted a severe judgment: "The Russian painters of our time are faced with a difficult task: to get rid of the absurdity and the bad taste handed down by the eighteenth century." Sacred art had to be separated from secular art. The painters must "strictly differentiate church painting or iconography from historical painting or the portrait." On this path,

> the enviable fate awaited them of becoming completely original creators by applying to the national needs all the benefits not only of a developed art but also of science, so that the church art of our age, as in times gone by [that is, during the time of "stagnation," L. Ouspensky] may not only lead to prayer but also teach by its concepts.[87]

The widely accepted idea that before Peter I, Russia had been intellectually stagnant produced a most curious result: the conviction that one understood Christianity better if one was enlightened by the new culture. The church historian E. Golubinskii expressed this in plain language: "The St Petersburg period [in the history of the Church] is one during which true civilization was introduced among us, and with it self-evidently, a more perfect understanding of Christianity."[88] Such a view of the role of civilization on the spiritual plane leads to a conclusion that is not less paradoxical on the level of art. An "enlightened" painter, equipped with a "developed artistic sense," thereby understands Christianity better; better than an uneducated monk iconographer, he is therefore able to create a Christian art that is more perfect. From this enlightened painter one expects an art that can combine "religious inspiration," similar to that of the past, with "fidelity to nature." The headiness of this "discovery" of fidelity to nature enthralled the educated Russian for three centuries, and turned him away from the icon.

In their appreciation of art and in their search for new ways, the scholars and theoreticians of the second half of the nineteenth century and of the early twentieth century always base themselves on the same theories as in the seventeenth century. For them, the "feeling for divine beauty" was kindled in the Russian painter "only in the eighteenth century under the influence of western models," which "gave a definite European orientation to the best painters of that time."[89] These scholars

87 F. I. Buslaev, *General Concepts*, 67.

88 E. Golubinskii, *Readings in the Imperial Society of History and Russian Antiquities* (in Russian) (Moscow, 1901), xxi.

89 F. I. Buslaev, *General Concepts*, 423-4.

45. *The Holy Face.* Painted by Simon Ushakov.
Tretiakov Gallery, Moscow.

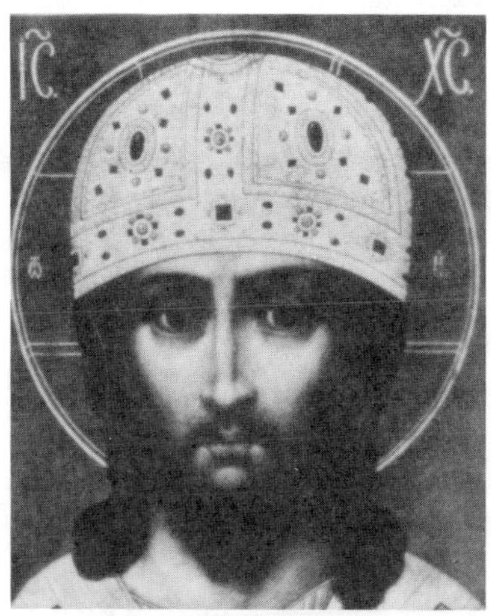

46. *Christ the All-Powerful.* 18th-century.

47. *Christ the Savior.* 19th century.

usually view the work of Ushakov and his group as the beginning of the renewal of Russian sacred art. Trenev writes:

> Had our Russian Orthodox iconography continued to follow the same road of perfection after the seventeenth century, then, by perfecting its artistic forms more and more, and by uniting them so brilliantly to the qualities of its religious inner content, it would have reached the hoped for level of development that would have allowed it, on the artistic level, to satisfy the most demanding and most developed taste of the contemporary enlightened Russian. But the way of this perfection...was interrupted by the historical development that followed, the reforms of Peter I and the all too abrupt turning of Russia toward the West.[90]

In reality, however, the problem was not the reform of Peter I, it was a question of the perfectly logical path followed by the new artistic trend, the sources of which go back to the second half of the sixteenth century. During the eighteenth and nineteenth centuries, this trend progressed along the direction given to it in the seventeenth century. The abrupt changes under Peter I only accelerated the process of desacralization championed by Ushakov and Vladimirov, to which the entire "progressive" literature of their time testified on the theoretical level. In the words of N. Kondakov,

> this entire literature, together with the devices of the iconographers, Simon Ushakov, Joseph the Zoographer and others, only points to one thing: the complete collapse of iconography and, I am afraid, of the entire art of Muscovite Russia [Figs. 45, 46, 47].[91]

Taken to its logical conclusion, "the way of perfection," following in the wake of the West, proved to be in sacred art the worthy inheritance of the "Age of Enlightenment": "absurd and in bad taste"—for some on account of its grossly imitatory character, for others because of its abandonment of the Orthodox tradition, and its "unification of all beliefs."

Thus, neither the *mimesis* of the West nor the ancient icon gave satisfaction, especially on the aesthetic plane. The first was "the ultimate limit of poor taste,"[92] and lacked independence, being an imitation which was, in addition, meaningless; the second, the icon, was still in its infancy on the artistic level and therefore also lacked independence.

If it is strange to present the works of Russian sacred art as works of art, it is still

90 D. K. Trenev, *Russian Iconographic Art and its Desirable Development* (in Russian) (Moscow, 1902), 9-10.

91 N. P. Kondakov, *The Russian Icon* (in Russian) (Prague, 1931), Part One, 48.

92 F. I. Buslaev, *General Concepts*, 26-7.

> more unjust to demote them to the lowest level of artisanry, and recognize the art of iconography as artistic artisanry, an artistic occupation, like all art that has not freed itself from service to the Church and has not yet risen to the level of a completely free creation. Thus, in our opinion, iconography is an art of the Church and for this reason is not an entirely free art. The iconographers are painters of the Church and are therefore not free painters.[93]

Thus, as long as such art "has not freed itself from the service to the Church," it cannot "ascend" to the level of an entirely independent creation, because free creation is a privilege of culture. In the Church, iconography cannot "free itself" as art because "it is fettered by the dogmas of doctrine."[94]

Let us note that all this was written by believing Orthodox persons who loved the icon and who devoted their lives to its study, people who sincerely tried to resurrect an art that would be ecclesiastical in the proper sense, to sketch the paths it would have to follow. But this being said, such art had to be "free"—free precisely from the Church and its dogmas, and from nothing else. Is this not what St Seraphim of Sarov said: "Under the pretext of light we have entered into such darkness that we find inconceivable that of which the ancients had such a clear concept."[95]

The painter Polenov, invited in 1888 by the painter Vasnetsov to help with the decoration of the Cathedral of St Vladimir in Kiev, replied negatively. He explained his refusal as follows:

> The dogmas of Orthodoxy are outmoded and now belong to the domain of scholasticism. We do not need them...It would be to rehash the commonplace, which was expressed back when religion was indeed a living force, when it guided man and supported him.[96]

Such an attitude toward dogma was not a break with the past: it was a severing of the living link with the fullness of the life of the Church, with the fullness of its knowledge. For, in truth, dogmas are as many "divine testimonies of the human mind about what is contemplated and lived, about the data in the catholic experience of the faith concerning the

93 G. Filimonov, *Simon Ushakov and his Epoch in Russian Iconography* (in Russian) (Moscow, 1873), 1.

94 F. I. Buslaev, *General Concepts*, 71. Didron's discovery, made in the 1840s, that sacred art is "paralyzed by dogmas and church doctrine," was totally swallowed by Russian scholars and remains the principal refrain of their writings up to our day.

95 "Entretien avec Motovilov," I. Gorainoff, *Séraphin de Sarov* (Bellefontaine, 1973), 194-5.

96 Cited in *History of Russian Art* (in Russian) (Moscow, 1965), vol. 9, bk 2, 110.

mysteries of life eternal revealed by the Holy Spirit."[97] When dogmas, as expressions of the concrete experience of this faith, cease to be perceived and lived existentially, when they "imprison"—this means that the faith which they express has ceased to be a living force. It was with such an attitude toward the Church and its faith that one attempted to create a sacred art that would "lead to prayer" and "teach by its concepts"!

Certainly, the historians of the period did not know, even in a vestigial way, all the richness of the icon we know today. But this is not where the problem lies. What *is* important is that their opinions about the freedom of the painter and on the Orthodox icon characterized an entire age, that of the eighteenth and nineteenth centuries, and even the twentieth—an age that had adopted criteria that were alien to the art it judged. Entire generations, raised on a *world view* desacralized by a secular culture which had destroyed the integrity of the Christian view of the world, showed themselves to be incapable of seeing the fullness of Orthodoxy, the unity of its teaching, of its spiritual life and artistic creation.

Trenev writes: "In order to perfect the contemporary painting of icons and to paint the saints as we wish, in the spirit of true Orthodoxy, there can for the moment be no other way than a conscientious study of the ancient monuments of our past." Only after this can the iconographer be ready "for his own free creation."[98] Beginning with the nineteenth century, a group of painters, students at the Academy of Fine Arts, attempted to recreate sacred art precisely by starting from a study of ancient iconography, with the help of "a developed artistic sense and learning." They were Solntsev, Vasnetsov, Nesterov, and Vrubel. They sought to realize the dream of an art that would be at the same time religious and "purely Russian." In Russia, it was the art of Vasnetsov that was, and still is, the most popular. In the 1890's Nesterov spoke of his work in the Cathedral of St Vladimir in Kiev in the following terms: "The dream lives there, the dream of a 'Russian Renaissance,' a rebirth of the wondrous and long forgotten art, that of Dionysius and of Andrei Rublev."[99] By way of information for those who admire Vasnetsov's religious art, let us cite here his own view about his effort to resurrect the art of the Russian icon—his

97 G. Florovsky, "The House of the Father," (in Russian) *Put'*, no 7 (Paris, 1927), 79.

98 D. K. Trenev, *Russian Iconographic Art*, 13.

99 A. Mikhailov, *M. N. Nesterov. Life and Work* (in Russian) (Moscow, 1958), 90.

own definition of his work. Let us note the sincerity and the great courage of this celebrated, admired painter. In 1925, in the midst of a circle of friends, Vasnetsov raved about the ancient frescoes in the monastery of Therapontes, the Church of the Savior in Nereditsa, and others. One of those present remarked, "But your icons? Your frescoes? They are masterpieces. They show a deep understanding of the religious spirit in the their interpretation of Russian painters, one could even say, of the entire Russian Church!" Vasnetsov strongly protested:

> Oh no. One could speak this way as long as the ancient Russian icon had not yet been discovered. In my demented pride, it seemed to me that I, I alone, and perhaps also Nesterov, though somewhat differently, had understood the spirit of ancient painting. But when the ancient paintings, these frescoes in the monasteries were restored, and when the pre-Nikonian and even more ancient icons were discovered, an entirely new world appeared, a wondrous world of deep inspiration, of knowledge of the laws of nature—an amazing interaction between colors and painting techniques appeared. Bound by tradition and by certain forms, did these ancient painters not create authentic painting, true in the most profound sense of the concept, that is, a play of color? They were not draughtsmen as we are now: they were real creators, real painters. Russia should not pride itself on its contemporary painting, that is, the painting after Peter I, because we are generally only imitators, original imitators, it is true, in our own fashion. And yet, why hide it, we lag behind Europe. But we should be proud of our *ancient iconography*, of our *ancient painting*. No one surpasses us there...I myself thought that I had understood the spirit of the Russian icon, had expressed the ancient painter's inner world, had mastered in my pride the ancient techniques. I was seriously wrong in this. The spirit of the Russian icon turned out to be much deeper than I thought. The inner world of ancient painting was, spiritually speaking, so much richer than the spirit of our time, be it mine, personally, or that of Nesterov. We are far from achieving their technique, from their effects as colorists. My painting is but a pale and saccharine reflection of the extremely rich world of the ancient Russian icon.[100]

We can do nothing better here than to quote the following observation by Khomiakov: "The possibilities ancient, 'unsophisticated' Russia gave to art are far from being actualized by modern, 'cultivated' Russia."[101] When compared to the icon, the art of Vasnetsov (Fig. 48 and 49), though based on a study of ancient iconography, is but a saccharine reflection, linked to German romanticism, that is, a sort of misinterpreted "Byzantine art." As

100 S. Makovskii, "Iconographers and Painters" (in Russian) *Russkaia zhizn* (3 November 1965), no. 5940, 4.

101 A. Khomiakov, *The Opinion of the Russians About Foreigners* (in Russian) *Selected Works*, 134.

48. *The Korsun Mother of God.*
Russian icon, 16th century.

49. *A Virgin.* Painted by Vasnetsov.

P. Muratov has said, "despite all his attachment to the theme of nationalism, Vasnetsov remained a painter with a German turn of mind."[102] For him, the ancient icon was a subject of external study, not the result of an existential entry into the living texture of the Tradition of the Church. The starting point of his art was not the depth of the Orthodox spiritual experience, but the premises of this same desacralized, secular culture.

In the realm of sacred art, this culture turned out to be sterile. If, on the cultural level, a synthesis between Russia and the West was possible, it could not be achieved where a profession of faith was the issue: a denatured Christianity could not give rise to a synthesis with authentic Christianity. The incontrovertible fact is there: the application of the principles of western art to sacred art, even the creation, on the basis of such principles, of a "national" art founded on a study of ancient iconography, did not produce sacred art. In other words, "the unification of beliefs" (to use Archbishop Anatolius' phrase)—here we are certainly faced with such unification and confusion—turned out to be incompatible with Orthodox doctrines and practices. This is why transplanting the Roman Catholic image onto Orthodox soil only contributed to the gradual divorce between the Church and the awareness of its members.

As we have seen, the spiritual decay first atrophied the awareness of the doctrinal dimension of the image. Then, in general, the importance and the responsible role of the image in Orthodoxy were no longer understood. Carried away by western novelties, educated society easily accepted the substitution of the Orthodox icon by an imitation of the Roman Catholic image—which is to say that it showed an utter indifference toward the fact that the latter image originated in a spiritual experience entirely different from the Orthodox, in dogmatic premises that were different from those in Orthodoxy. If in seventeenth-century Russia there was still an attempt to oppose this foreign image (though the reaction was rather instinctive, and only in the domain of spiritual experience), in the eighteenth century this question not only did not arise, but it lost all its meaning. Indeed, was it not accepted without question that the Christian culture "borrowed" from the West brought with it an image that was equally Christian? Moreover, when faced with the iconoclasm of militant Protestantism, both Roman Catholicism and Orthodoxy certainly confessed the dogma of the Seventh Ecumenical

102 P. Muratov, "Concerning the Icon" (in Russian), *Vozrozhdenie* (27 January 1933).

Council concerning the veneration of icons. Indeed, at the decisive moment when the catholic awareness had perceived a Christian, universal truth, the West and the East confirmed the revealed truth of the veneration of icons, in harmony and mutual agreement. Even if the West did not follow the East in its theological reasoning, the image and its theology were common to both East and West, as long as the latter was joined to the Body of the Church. Nonetheless, this theology remained a dead letter for the West: it was not incorporated into the liturgical life of the Church, it was not assimilated into the ecclesial awareness. Was the almost simultaneous appearance of two concepts, of two attitudes toward the icon that were mutually exclusive, the result of mere chance? By allotting only the artistic aspect of a work to the painter, the Seventh Ecumenical Council viewed the Holy Fathers as the true iconographers, because it was they who considered and revealed what was appropriate to represent. The council based the art of the icon on the Tradition of the Church, "for it comes from the Holy Spirit who dwells there" (oros of the council). In the West, at the same moment, the *Libri Carolini* undermined the very foundation of sacred art. They pulled it away from the Tradition, from the catholic experience of the Church, by delivering it to the painter's capriciousness, while at the same time confirming the *filioque.*[103] When Rome separated itself from the catholic Body of the Church, it was precisely this doctrine that determined the direction of the ecclesial life in the West, and hence its culture. Is it a matter of mere serendipity that the icon subsequently became the patrimony only of the peoples of Orthodox confession, regardless of their geographic situation, regardless of the national or racial group to which they belonged, just as the Roman Catholic image came to be reserved to the people of Latin confession?

Let us recall that the western Church, by moving away from the East, rejected Canon 82 of the Seventh Ecumenical Council (among others), a ruling that abrogated the symbols replacing the human image of Christ. Thus this church remained in the perspective of the "images and shadows" of the Old Testament. Having kept the Old Testament symbols, the West thereby reduced the significance of the image that corresponded to

103 On its part, the Council of Frankfurt, as is known, considers the image to be only a church ornament and a reminder of the works accomplished in times past; this remains the official attitude of the Church of Rome up to our time. Let us recall that Luther too shared the point of view of the *Libri Carolini* and of the Council of Frankfurt.

the Christian revelation, that of the Person of Christ, Image and Word of the Father. This insensitivity toward the personal image, this deficiency in the understanding of it, became the basic flaw of Roman Catholic art—a flaw which was later to be confirmed by scholastic theology.

If no image can be understood apart from the surroundings that created it, this is all the more true when one deals with a Church image. The very basis of the Church and of its art must be the starting point for an understanding of it. For Roman Catholicism as well as for Orthodoxy this basis is the confession of the Holy Trinity. It is of decisive importance for the entire life of the Church: its canonical order, the nature of its theological thought, its spirituality and artistic creation. Indeed, "the Son and the Holy Spirit sent by the Father have revealed the Trinity to the Church, not in an abstract fashion, as an intellectual knowledge, but as a very rule of its life"[104]—a life that is precisely in the image of the Trinity. This is why any change, any dogmatic error in the doctrine of the Trinity can only have corresponding results in the entire life of the Church, and therefore in its art. It is precisely when the *filioque* became a theological system that the desacralization of the sacred in the western Church began. This question certainly requires a special study. In our context, we will limit ourselves to a few words about which consequences of the *filioque* caused a change in Orthodox art.

Two levels that correspond to two distinct aspects in the life of the consubstantial Trinity are expressed directly in art, or, more precisely, determine its content and character. They are: the level of the intra-trinitarian life, that of theology properly speaking; and that of the divine economy, that of the action of God in the created world.

Like all Christian dogma, that of the Trinity can be based only on revelation, the manifestation of one God in three Persons. But the manner in which this revelation is received and understood is not the same in Orthodoxy as in Roman Catholicism. It is this divergence that produced two different triadologies, as well as the difference between Orthodox art and that of Roman Catholicism.[105] For Orthodox theology, the starting

104 V. Lossky, "Du troisième attribut de l'Eglise," *Messager de l'Exarchat du Patriarche russe en Europe occidentale*, nos 2-3 (1950), 65.

105 In the East, Revelation has always been understood as the road to salvation; only on this road can contact with God and knowledge of Him as participation in the divine life, an existential communion, even possibly be conceived. The deification of man is the path to divine knowledge, and the very core of the patristic teaching on salvation. This ascent toward God

point in the confession of the Holy Trinity is the person—the essential mystery of the Christian revelation: the person as possessing the divine nature in its fullness. Consequently, the person is of crucial importance as much for the theology of the icon as for the image itself. It is precisely on the concrete, incarnate person of one of the Holy Trinity that the dogma of the veneration of icons is founded. It is the concept of the person, of *the one who* is represented, that allowed patristic theology to solve the basic dilemma of the iconoclastic controversy, as we have seen. In the relationship established by the image between the human person and the divine person, Orthodox theology sees the beginning of a vision "face to face."[106] Only a personal image creates a way that leads to its prototype, whether the latter be the person of God become man or that of a human being deified by the uncreated grace of the Holy Spirit.

If prayer in the West, as in the East, is addressed to the person, for western theology, by contrast, it is not the Person but the divine nature that is the starting point. This theology receives a clearly delineated form

corresponds diametrically to the descent of God toward man: "The way to divine knowledge ascends from one Spirit through the one Son to the one Father"—to use the words of St Basil the Great (*On the Holy Spirit* [New York: St Vladimir's Seminary Press, 1980], 74-5).

By contrast, in its knowledge and assimilation of Revelation, the West did not choose the road of living and concrete experiences. Roman Catholic triadology takes as its starting point a transposition of the temporal divine economy to the level of the intra-trinitarian life, outside of time; if the Holy Spirit is sent into the world by the Father and the Son, this means that in the bosom of the Holy Trinity He proceeds from the Father and the Son, as Hypostasis. Tertullian, who is viewed as "the founder of the language and thought form of Latin theology" (see J. M. Garrigues, O. P., "Procession et ekporèse du Saint-Esprit," *Istina*, nos 3-4 [1972], 345), already linked the order by which the Persons manifested themselves in their economy to their procession in eternity. Beginning with him, such a transposition of the economy into triadology has remained the norm in western theological thought, due particularly to the prestige of St Augustine, who definitely transformed the analogy into a logical correspondence between the two plans. "This analogy," Berdiaev states, "was to be of prophetic importance for the knowledge and understanding of God. This is particularly evident in the system of Thomas Aquinas. God is known through analogy with the natural world and natural objects. He is like a supreme natural object, endowed to the highest degree with all qualities. God is certainly 'supernatural,' but this 'supernatural' ultimately turns out to be a superlative degree of the 'natural' (the 'natural' being more important than the 'super'). The analogy of God with the power of a natural world is not a Christian analogy. It is on this foundation that theological naturalism was created, which is an inheritance from pagan theological thought. The Church is understood in the same way, through analogy with the state, with the kingdom of Caesar..." ("Thoughts on Theodicy" [in Russian], *Put'*, no 7 [1937], 56).

106 V. Lossky, *The Vision of God*, trans. A. Moorhouse (New York: St Vladimir's Seminary Press, 1983), 168.

with the insertion of the *filioque* ("the Holy Spirit proceeds from the Father *and the Son*") into the official confession of faith, especially with the subsequent specification, "as from one principle."[107] The hypostatic character of the persons becomes of secondary importance; in the Holy Trinity, Its unity, Its nature is the only absolute. As for the Trinity of the Hypostases, their very being becomes relative. They are no longer viewed as possessors of Their nature, but depend on it as Their manifestation. They are understood as "subsisting relations" within this nature. That is, the relationship between the persons is understood not as Their characteristics, but as the persons themselves. As V. Lossky has clearly indicated, "Such diminution of the hypostatic principle constitutes the basic flaw of the theological speculation regarding the *filioque*;"[108] "by the introduction of the (Aristotelian) category of relation into the divine being, the dogma of the Trinity was rationalized..."[109]

But if, in the Holy Trinity, the person (*hypostasis*) is not as absolute as the nature and represents a certain abstract concept, then it loses its absolute, decisive importance also in the image. Whether it be in the divine person or a human being created in the image of God, it loses its predominant meaning as the possessor of its nature. In the image, the person is no longer necessarily the prototype and can be replaced by a symbol, an abstract arrangement, by another person, or by an invention of the painter. The abstract concept of the person, and the failure to understand the personal image, explain why in the West the representation of the unrepresentable (the anthropomorphic images of God the Father and of the Holy Spirit) hardly ever met with opposition. It

107 The natural powers to engender and cause to proceed (*spirare*) are attributed to nature. "From the Father-essence is born the Son, consubstantial to the Father; from the Father and the Son, as from one essential principle, proceeds the Holy Spirit" (V. Lossky, "On the Question of the Procession of the Holy Spirit" [in Russian], *Messager de l'Exarchat du Patriarche russe en Europe occidentale*, no. 25 [1957], 58). In other words, if the Father, as essence, is the cause of the Son, the cause of the Holy Spirit is a certain impersonal principle or a non-personal essence, joining the Father and the Son. The equality of the Persons in their Divinity is thereby violated. Indeed, the Father is the divine nature, having the power to engender and bring forth; this same nature, not having the power to engender but having the power to cause to proceed, is the Son. As to the Holy Spirit, He is of the same nature, but not having the power either to engender or to cause to proceed, He is understood as "the bond of love" between the Father and the Son, that is, as a certain function inside the Holy Trinity.

108 V. Lossky, "On the Question of the Procession of the Holy Spirit," *ibid.*

109 V. Lossky, *Cours d'histoire du dogme*, ch. 5, 32, as quoted by Olivier Clément, "Vladimir Lossky, un théologien de la personne et du Saint-Esprit," *Messager de l'Exarchat du Patriarche russe en Europe occidentale*, nos 30-31 (1959), 197.

could not meet with any because abstract concepts can only be transposed through invented images, devoid of a real foundation.

As we have seen, the change in Orthodox sacred art began precisely with the representation of the unrepresentable, by a "lessening of the glory of the economy in the flesh of our Lord Jesus Christ," as was said in the sixteenth century. When the so-called "mystical-didactic" icons appeared, the realism of the Gospel was placed side by side with its abstract commentaries. The image conveying a concept, an abstract idea, was seen as having the same witnessing power; it was placed on the same level as the image of the concrete person of the incarnate Word, and thus the latter lost its exclusivity. Such a lowering of the hypostatic principle in the image was a flagrant departure from Orthodox doctrine (as expressed in particular by the Sixth and the Seventh Ecumenical Councils).

The next stage in the change of Orthodox sacred art was the introduction of the "likeness to real life," on the pretext that the iconographic style "did not recognize the truth." This was another consequence of the *filioque*, but in the domain of the divine economy.

The theology of the *filioque* excludes the Orthodox doctrine of the divine energies—the radiance of God outside His essence, the Giver of which is the Holy Spirit. The gifts of the Holy Spirit are identified with their Giver by the transposition of the temporal plane into the extra-temporal being of the Holy Trinity. Since the Holy Spirit is understood as a relationship defined as "the bond of love" between the Father and the Son, there is no room left for grace as deifying gift,[110] and the Holy Spirit appears as the gift which He bestows. Thus the Holy Trinity is, as it were, enclosed in its essence, limited by it; everything outside the Godhead is viewed as belonging to the created world. There is the divine nature, and there are the "supernatural," but always created, results of His action.[111] This is why, in the theology of the *filioque*, there is no deification in the proper sense of the term, and the creature is, in turn, enclosed in its created being. The possibility of acquiring revelation as a road to salva-

110 The monk Hilarion, "Réflexions d'un moine orthodoxe à propos d'un dossier sur la procession du Saint-Esprit publié récemment," *Messager de l'Exarchat du Patriarche russe en Europe occidentale*, nos 81-82 (1973), 25.

111 According to Roman Catholic doctrine, such created grace only enables the human being to perform "meritorious acts." Thanks to such "merits," the human being will after death have the possibility of contemplating the very nature (essence) of God.

tion, the deification of man, the acquisition of the Holy Spirit which, according to the Fathers, constitutes the very essence and aim of the Christian life—all this has no place in this system.[112] The Holy Spirit is no longer the source of man's deification. He is no longer, through His divinity, the "witness of the truth," that is, of the divinity of Christ. Hence the focus on the humanity of the Lord, as much in western theology and spirituality as in art. This "cult of the humanity of Christ that makes abstraction of His Divinity, such devout concentration on His humanity alone, strikes the Orthodox as being 'spiritual' Nestorianism."[113]

The image of Christ was divided. On the one hand, He seems exalted because He overshadows the other Persons of the Trinity. On the other hand, the glory of God, manifested in His deified flesh, is dimmed, hidden by His "aspect of a servant."

Through the abstract system of the *filioque*, theology was transposed from the level of a lived experience of grace to that of philosophic, rationalistic speculations, and this rationalist conception was called "metaphysical triadology."

The Orthodox Church preserves the image of Christ not only in its historical remembrance but also in the charismatic memory of its faith—in the Tradition of the catholic Church, for "it is of the Holy Spirit who dwells in it." Such charismatic remembrance is the testimony which the Spirit brings to the truth—the incarnation of God and man's deification, since the grace that sanctifies both the humanity of Christ and the body of a deified man is the same. This is why in Orthodox art their representations are done in the same manner. The intrusion of Roman Catholic art with its cult of the non-sanctified flesh, flesh which has not overcome decomposition, resulted not in a "discernment of the truth," as the seventeenth-century innovators thought, but in a distortion of the truth, a modification of the Orthodox doctrine of salvation.

112 The examples of holiness in Roman Catholicism, when such sanctity approaches Orthodoxy, are at odds with the theology and are outside the official doctrine of their Church.

113 Archbishop Basil (Krivochéine), "Quelques mots supplémentaires sur la question des stigmates," *Messager de l'Exarchat du Patriarche russe en Europe occidentale*, no 44 (1963), 204. Hence the emotional intensity in the contemplation of the passion of Christ—an emotion which occasionally may lead to a literal imitation in *stigmata*; hence also the series of "anatomical," so to speak, feasts in the Church of Rome: the Sacred Heart of Jesus, His Body, His Blood, and so forth.

The Roman Church has revealed itself incapable of assuming the fullness of Revelation as a path to salvation. It developed the qualities of human nature that were directly tied to the activity of the mind and will. Having placed faith itself under the control of reason, it assured the development of what may be called "humanism." But the road taken by such "humanism" was not only extra-ecclesial but also anti-ecclesial, and led to disintegration. That such "humanism" which emerged from Roman Catholicism is not a true Christian anthropology is clear. The inability to partake fully of the Revelation cut the path which Christ himself had opened up to man for the fulfillment of his destiny. It destroyed the initial meaning of man's existence: to cooperate with God in guiding the created world toward the fulfillment of its history—its transfiguration.

The powerful stream of western art invaded the Church, certainly, but it did not destroy Orthodox art. This art "has lived in Russia for a long time, and still lives since the beginning of the eighteenth century, under the form of artisanry and craftsmanship," N. Kondakov writes.[114] The icon existed alongside the official art and in spite of it, despite the tastes of cultivated society. As before, it was nurtured by the liturgical life and the perpetually living stream of popular devotion. During the period when spiritual life was in decline, ignored or despised, and the icon was forgotten, the role of preserving the proclamation of Orthodox faith and spirituality in the image fell precisely on this artisanry. The manuals of iconography (*podlinniki*) preserved the traditional iconography. Icon artisanry had to protect and transmit the traditions of the ancient techniques to our times. Let us note, moreover, that during the centuries of decadence, the work of iconographers often rose above the level of mere artisanry. The power of the tradition was revealed in such a way that even on the lowest level of artisanry the icon reflected the grandeur and the beauty proper to it. It was not unworthy of the totality of great art in the Orthodox Church.

However, during the second half of the nineteenth century, even this artisanry was overwhelmed by the general trend of industrial development, which was first concentrated in large enterprises. The end of the century witnessed an invasion of printed "icons," as well as their importation from abroad, which was disastrous for artisanry.

114 N. P. Kondakov, *The Russian Icon* (in Russian), Part One (Prague, 1931), 3.

The unending complaints of the iconographers and the discontent among the faithful prompted the creation of a Committee for the Protection of Russian Iconography (1900), which received the approval of the tsar himself. The circumstances under which the activity of this committee evolved are a revealing page in the history of Russian iconography. The committee undertook an energetic, resolute struggle against the mechanical production of "icons." In this struggle, the committee ran into opposition from the Holy Synod and from the Ministry of Finance, as well as against the interests of large monasteries, which were the chief disseminators of such productions. Unfortunately, the committee defended the icon not on the doctrinal level, but as a national artisanry, as a traditional enterprise. In other words, for this committee, the art of the icon did not transcend the boundaries of folklore. The activity of the committee was marked by half-measures, which were characterized by lack of precision and clarity in their ecclesial orientation. A request to prohibit the importation of "icons" printed abroad and to limit their production in Russia—a request presented by the committee and approved by the tsar, after it had been submitted to all the Ministries, including that of National Defense—met with strong opposition when it arrived at the Ministry of Finance and the Synod. The first was worried that the needs of the faithful would not be met and recommended all types of half-measures. The second, in the person of Pobedonostsev, the Procurator General, contested all the points contained in the request. He was of the opinion that the prohibition against importing printed images from abroad to replace the icon "did not depend on the spiritual authorities, who had no ecclesial reason for this, but on the legislative power."[115] According to Pobedonostsev, the whole matter ultimately fell under the jurisdiction of the Ministry of Finance. Despite the emperor's support, the efforts of the committee failed completely. After four years of effort, "the problem of restricting the mechanical production of icons still remained at the same point," as N. P. Kondakov, one of the most active members of the committee, attests.[116]

Nonetheless, in spite of this failure in the domain of mechanical production, the activity of the committee turned out to be useful and of great relevance to

115 Collection *Ikonopisnii Sbornik* I (St Petersburg, 1907), 13.

116 Minutes of the March 20, 1907, Meeting of the Committee (in Russian), Coll. *Ikonopisnii Sbornik* 3 (St Petersburg, 1908), 32.

the age, especially in the realm of published manuals. It caused numerous and varied echoes. In general, at the dawn of the twentieth century, a series of circumstances contributed to a re-evaluation of the attitude toward the icon.

Toward the end of the nineteenth century, intellectuals began returning to the Church. "After the stormy experiences of nihilism, apostasy, and neglect," there occurred "a meeting of the intellectuals with the Church,...a return to the faith."[117] The desire was expressed openly to see the canonical norms, freedom, and conciliarity reestablished in the church, to see the Church freed from the control and protection of the secular power, and from the task imposed upon it by the state. Particularly after 1905, these questions were debated with passion. A pre-conciliar commission was formed; the question of reestablishing the patriarchate was raised.

In the domain of art, a reversal of values could be detected, a true revolution in knowledge. Byzantine art was rehabilitated, first in the West (G. Millet, Ch. Diehl, Dalton, and others), then in Russia (P. Muratov, Shtekotov, Anisimov, *et al*). H. Matisse, who came to Russia in 1911, expressed his opinion about the ancient Russian icons in this way:

> The Russians have no idea of the artistic treasures they possess. Your young students have here, at home, art models that are incomparably better than those from abroad. French painters should come and study in Russia. In this field, Italy offers less.[118]

More and more, the clear superiority of traditional art in the spiritual domain encouraged an understanding of the meaning of the icon; and even when such understanding was still limited and superficial, it nonetheless opened a way for the "discovery" of the icon. In educated circles,

117 G. Florovsky, *Ways*. Having broken with the Church, the intellectuals who returned expected reforms from it: at all times, it is the temptation of reformers to renew the church. "Psychologically, this is where the point of concentration was...In his time, S. N. Bulgakov spoke of this quite correctly. Intellectual heroism, decked out in Christian garb, and sincerely viewing its intellectual emotions and customary impassioned emphasis as true. Christian anger shows itself most easily in an ecclesiastic attitude of revolt; in the contrast between its fresh, new holiness, its new religious awareness and the injustice of the 'historic' church. It is so easy for a christianizing intellectual, often unable to satisfy in a suitable manner what is normally expected of a member of the 'historic' church, to identify with Martin Luther or, rather to view himself as the bringer of a new religious awareness, called not only to renew the life of the Church but also to create new forms for it, one might even say, a new religion" (G. Florovsky, *Ways*).

118 *Catalog of Ancient Russian Painting in the Tretiakov Gallery* (in Russian), *op. cit.* 21.

"official" art gradually lost its support and its dominant role. The taste for authentically traditional Orthodox art and architecture returned. In various places in Russia, some churches were built following the traditional architecture, with canonical wall decoration, and iconostases composed of ancient icons. The conscious movement back to the Church, the growing number of scholarly studies, the opening of old-ritualist churches, the establishment of private collections, the restoration of an ever-growing number of icons—all this led a segment of Russian society to a complete reevaluation of the icon. The icon exposition of 1913 was a true revelation to the larger circles of society. "It is as if a veil had suddenly dropped from the eyes of those who visited this exposition," V. N. Lazarev wrote. They discovered that "this art was one of the most perfect creations of the Russian genius."[119] On the other hand, as P. Muratov attested, with people for whom the icon was something new and who venerated Fra Angelico and Simone Martini, one observed

> a curious, slight disappointment with the icon (but only at first sight). No doubt, these people were sincere, even ardent Orthodox. But during the eighteenth and nineteenth centuries, Russian Orthodoxy had moved away from its initial historical dimension to such an extent that at present it sometimes did not recognize itself from this perspective [of the traditional icon].[120]

For contemporary culture, the art created during the "fallow" period turned out to be of an inaccessible height, even on the artistic level. As for the spiritual plane, what was clear and evident to a religiously cultured person was an enigma for the person of modern culture. Indeed, Anisimov wrote in 1914,

> we will understand it [the icon] only when we will have ceased requesting from the icon what it never requested from itself, have stopped seeking in it what it never sought, evaluating it not according to what it has but in terms of what it does not, and could not, have.[121]

During this epoch, not only art critics but even religious philosophers such as, for example, Florenskii, occasionally saw in the icon a consonance with Platonic ideas and the Aristotelian concept of form, all this mixed with a certain "Christianity." The end of the Synodal period was marked by a living and truly ecclesial approach to the icon, even if it was tainted by a

119 V. N. Lazarev, *The Art of Novgorod* (in Russian) (Moscow-Leningrad, 1947), 20.

120 P. Muratov, "Concerning the Icon" XI (in Russian), *Vozrozhdenie* (Paris, February 1933).

121 A. Anisimov, "Study of the Iconographic Art of Novgorod," (in Russian) *Journal Sofia* 3 (Moscow, March 1914), 12.

certain romanticism, notably in the works of E. Trubetskoi, who was the first to become aware of and to fathom the meaning of the Orthodox icon.

This is a significant phenomenon of the epoch: the culture which had rejected the icon, and in the name of which the icon was rejected, now adopted a diametrically opposed attitude toward it. It moved from a denial of the icon to its veneration, as much on the artistic level as on that of its content, this independently of whatever confessional attitude, or of its absence, independently also of any national attachments. This culture had prompted Orthodoxy away from the icon; this culture of fragmentation and disintegration reached its own decomposition, and, in its art, reached a professed iconoclasm, the image of disincarnation, an abstraction, an insubstantial image.

18

The Icon in the Modern World

One of the greatest discoveries of the twentieth century is the icon, as much from the artistic as from the spiritual point of view. Let us recall that the discovery occurred on the eve of the great historic upheavals: the First World War, and the wars and revolutions that followed it. In 1916, Eugene Trubetskoi wrote that mankind was at the dawn "of a long turbulent period in world history that will bring horrors unseen and unheard of before."[1] It was precisely during this "turbulent period" that the icon appeared as the supreme treasure of human art. For some, it represented the precious inheritance of a distant past. For others, it was an object of aesthetic delight. Still others began dimly to perceive the meaning of the icon, and in its light, the significance of contemporary events. We cannot help but believe that the long process of this progressive discovery had to emerge providentially in our own time. Indeed, if spiritual decline manifested itself in a neglect of the icon, the spiritual renewal prompted by catastrophes and upheavals leads back to and encourages man to learn its language and meaning, and to become truly aware of the icon. It is no longer viewed as something from the past: it is reborn in the present. New expressions are found to describe the icon. A slow appreciation of the spiritual meaning of the icon has arisen; a spirit discovered in the icon that is infinitely more uplifting than ours, the product of our civilization. The icon no longer represents only a cultural or spiritual value: it is a revelation of the Orthodox spiritual experience through artistic means, a "theology in images," demonstrated already in the past, in times of disaster and catastrophe. It is precisely in times of disaster that one glimpses the meaning of modern catastrophes in light of the icon's spiritual power. "The icon, silent for centuries, has begun to speak to us, in the language in which it spoke to our distant fathers."[2]

1 "Two Worlds in Old-Russian Icon Painting," in *Icons: Theology in Color*, trans. G. Vakar (New York: St Vladimir's Seminary Press, 1973), 69.

2 E. Trubetskoi, "A World View in Painting," in *ibid.*, 35.

We notice here how

> Again the fate of the ancient icon coincides with that of the Russian church. In life as in painting, the same thing happens: the darkened face is freed from age-old layers of gold, smoke, and tasteless, unskilled overpainting. The image of the world-embracing church that shines for us in the cleaned icon is miraculously revived in the real life of the church. In life as in painting, we see the undamaged, untouched image of the church-sobor.[3]

Having been freed from the "secular splendor" and from the comfort into which it had sunk, the destiny of the Russian Church is now leading it on the way of the cross and of tribulations.

The arrival of Soviet power imposes a new world-view born of a culture alienated from the Church—a culture which, at present, rejects its mask of Christianity. This new conception of the world is that of the state. In its eyes, all beliefs, including that of the Church, are subsumed into the general concept of "religion." This religion, then, is viewed as "a reactionary ideology," "an illusion," "the opium of the people." This last formula "is the cornerstone of the Marxist attitude toward religion."[4] The Church is viewed as a foreign body within the state, since it embodies a world view that is "hostile" to it. The state takes upon itself to watch over not only the material well being of the people, but also its education, "the formation of the new man." Thus, on the one hand, "Soviet legislation on the freedom of conscience is permeated by the desire to guarantee its citizens the right to confess the religion of their choice or to confess none";[5] yet, on the other hand, "an uncompromising struggle against religious convictions which are incompatible with the materialistic view of the world, with scientific and technical progress, is a crucial, decisive condition for the formation of the new man."[6] Thus the struggle against religion is carried on in the very name of freedom of conscience. And such freedom assumes the form of a whole series of prohibitions, such as the one forbidding all contact with religion outside of church services, a contact which is viewed as religious propaganda. Likewise, "the teaching of the doctrines of the faith to persons under the age of eighteen is forbidden in churches, chapels or private homes."[7]

The Church and the icon are entering a process of purification:

3 E. Trubetskoi, "Russia and her Icons," *ibid.*, 98.

4 A. Sedulin, *The Legislation on Religious Cults* (in Russian) (Moscow, 1974), 6.

5 *Ibid.*, 46.

6 *Ibid.*, 41. See also V. Zots, *Groundless Pretensions* (in Russian) (Moscow, 1976), 135-6.

7 *Su RSSU* 1922, no 49, art. 729, quoted by A. Sedulin, 32.

everything that was linked to the Church by way of ritual obligation is being removed. Likewise, everything that has been superimposed on the icon is disappearing, including its mechanical production, which neither the leaders of the committee nor the tsar himself were able to stop. Businesses for the painting of artisanal icons or for their mechanical reproduction have been liquidated.

Because religion is understood as belonging to a bygone past that has no place in the new society, everything that has been created in this past is accepted only as a cultural inheritance; it is preserved and studied only as such. Everything the churches contained, including the icons, became the property of the state, which has assumed responsibility for it since 1918.[8] The state has created restoration workshops, has nationalized the private collections of icons, and organizes expositions. At the same time, the hostility of the prevalent ideology toward religion extends to everything associated with it, including the icon. If, in the eighteenth and nineteenth centuries, vandalism arose out of indifference and incomprehension, the contemporary massive destruction of churches and icons is the result of ideological causes. From the perspective of the official ideology, the work of the iconographer becomes not only useless, but also harmful to society.

Thus, after centuries of neglect and disdain, nowadays the icon is, on the one hand, being destroyed while, on the other, its discovery extends well beyond the confines of the Orthodox world and reaches a world the culture and heterodoxy of which had driven the icon into oblivion even among the Orthodox. The immense labor done by the restorers who have brought the ancient icon back to life is accompanied in our day by an ever increasing number of illustrated publications in various languages, theological and scientific publications by Orthodox, non-Orthodox and even atheist authors. The icon itself is infiltrating the world of western culture in a massive fashion: icons are exported from Orthodox countries, they are seen in museums; private collections and expositions multiply in numerous cities of the western world. The Orthodox icon attracts believers and unbelievers alike. It generates various types of interest. There is

8 "Decree on the Recording, Inventory, and Protection of Ancient Art Monuments." See V. I. Antonova and N. E. Mneva, *Catalog of Ancient Russian Painting*, (in Russian) the Tretiakov Gallery (Moscow, 1963), vol. 1, 26.

certainly the infatuation for everything that is old, and the passion for collecting in general. But there is above all the attraction on the religious plane, a desire to understand the icon, and through it, Orthodoxy. "For our markedly visual epoch," E. Benz writes, "the appeal to the eye, to the contemplation of images is recommended. To understand the Eastern Orthodox Church such an approach is all the more appropriate as the exposition of the world of the saints through images occupies a central role in it."[9] A little further we read: "The importance of the icon in Orthodox piety and its theological basis open the way to the crucial domain of Orthodox dogmatics. Indeed, the concept of the icon is one that is dogmatically central and is found in all aspects of theology."[10] Most non-Orthodox believers view the icon either consciously as a witness to Orthodoxy or, absent a conscious confessional context, as an expression of authentic Christianity on the level of prayer with the help of art. Contrary to the degradation of this aspect in the image within Roman Catholicism, the icon "invites to prayer." "In icons, everyone will find rest for the soul. They have a great deal to tell us, westerners; and they can arouse in us a holy orientation toward the supernatural."[11] The age of the icon is not that important; people are interested as much in the ancient icon as in the more recent and even contemporary one, which while still remaining within the canons, is frequently of an eclectic character.[12] Indeed, whatever its artistic or even artisanal quality, the Orthodox icon is the only art in the world that discloses the imperishable meaning of life, the need for which is presently felt in the world of contemporary western culture.

It is precisely in this context that the question of the icon has been raised on a more official level by Anglican representatives inquiring about the importance of the Seventh Ecumenical Council. During their meeting with the Orthodox in Rymnik (Romania) in July 1974, the Anglicans put this question in its true theological context. They were hopeful that

9 E. Benz, *The Eastern Orthodox Church: its Thought and Life*, trans. R. Winston (New York, 1963), 1.

10 *Ibid.*, 21.

11 Review of L. Ouspensky and V. Lossky, "Der Sinn der Ikonen," in *La pensée catholique*, nos 75-76 (14 February, 1953).

12 In France, in Paris alone, there are four schools for icon painting, some of which have existed for twelve years, including the Jesuit school. This is all the more significant because it was precisely the Jesuits who formerly made great efforts to destroy traditional icon painting.

the dogma of the veneration of icons would be explained by the Orthodox as it applied to contemporary reality, because "a deeper understanding of the principles of icon painting that reveal the truth and consequences of the Incarnation of the Word of God can in our day help Christians better to understand the Christian doctrine about man and the material world."[13]

This way of posing the question already illustrates how, in "our markedly visual epoch," the need arises for Orthodox and non-Orthodox alike to become aware of the meaning of the dogma of the veneration of icons for contemporary Christianity. In the West, the dogma of the Seventh Ecumenical Council never permeated the consciousness of the Church; as for the Orthodox world, the understanding of the icon became blurred, and the awareness of its crucial importance evaporated, so to speak, during the period of decadence of the icon itself, when the meaning of its theological content was lost. Indeed, were entire generations of Orthodox not raised in the presence of an art which, though it justified itself through the dogma of the veneration of icons, did not correspond to it in reality? Let us recall that, from the seventeenth century, everything related to the confessional content of the image was excluded from the Russian text of the Synodicon of the Triumph of Orthodoxy. In our own time, only rarely does one hear a sermon which addresses the connection between this feast and the icon. Through its dogma on the veneration of icons, the catholic consciousness of the Church condemned iconoclasm as a heresy, and the image thus kept its place in the life of the Church. Nonetheless, the vital significance of the icon is no longer perceived in all its fulness, and this has caused indifference toward its content and role.[14]

13 Report of the Sub-committee on "the Authority of Ecumenical Councils," see *Messager de l'Exarchat du Patriarche russe en Europe occidentale*, nos 85-88 (1974), 40. This question was further discussed by the same subcommittee in 1976, in Moscow.

14 Thus, to the question of a Protestant theologian on the meaning of the veneration of icons, an Orthodox bishop replied, "We are in the habit of doing it." Since the eighteenth century, the painting of icons has become the domain of secular painters who are not bound by the dogmas of the Church. Later, the study of the icon was handed over to a science, which was likewise unattached to dogma. The one thing that was left for the faithful was the pious habit of praying before an icon. But even worse things happen. In a private conversation, an Orthodox bishop said, "To hear you talk, one might think that without icons there could be no Orthodoxy." A Protestant pastor, J. Ph. Ramseyer, wrote that "the image belongs to the very essence of Christianity" (*La Parole et l'Image* [Neuchâtel, 1963], 58). As we can see, the roles

To understand the meaning of the veneration of icons in our time is to understand the icon itself, not merely as a church ornament or as a help in prayer. It is also to understand its message, its significance for modern man, to be aware of its spiritual witness transmitted from the depths of Orthodoxy, the meaning of the Christian revelation.

There is, however, a point of view, not only among non-Orthodox but also in certain Orthodox circles, which falsifies the understanding of the icon, even when it arises from the best of intentions. This viewpoint may be summarized as follows: the Seventh Ecumenical Council, which formulated the dogma of the veneration of icons, did not define the character of the image to be venerated, and "the theology of the defenders of the icon gives no information on its style." In other words, the Church has not canonized any "style" or artistic genre. For someone educated within the modern culture, who often lacks a clear awareness of the Church, this point of view allows him to consider, or even to state, that alongside the canonical icon, supposedly linked to a certain epoch and to a given culture, there can be other genres or artistic styles in the Church, reflecting other periods.

This attitude is largely the result of contemporary science which has decreed that icon painting, a product of the Middle Ages and of its specific view of the world, ended in the seventeenth century. As the medieval culture of the icon disappeared, the icon too was relegated to the past. Such a view defies the evidence; nonetheless, this view prevails in the contemporary scholarly world, as it did in the nineteenth century, and it sees in the icon a certain stage (Byzantine, Russian, and so forth) in the development of culture. It is interesting to note in passing that the "new world view" is considered as being entirely different, a break with the old; while the new art, the product of this conception of the world, is seen (for what inexplicable reason?) as the organic development of ancient art, from which it apparently derived naturally. Scholarship disconnected from dogma has inserted the icon into the general trend of art as such, and defined its creation as belonging to the domain of general culture, thereby separating it from the Church. It must be acknowledged that, since the "Age of Enlightenment," the Church has itself surrendered to this view and has passively accepted the opinion that

are sometimes reversed: what one would expect to hear from the mouth of an Orthodox bishop is expressed by a Protestant pastor, and vice versa. Thus the centuries-old absence of the icon has led a Protestant pastor to an Orthodox conception of it, while the distortion of the image, also centuries-old, led an Orthodox bishop to a Protestant attitude toward it.

artistic creation is not in its domain, thereby surrendering it to secular culture.[15] But if the icon has survived the last three centuries and continues to live in our day, it is certainly not because of any attachment to medieval culture: it has survived as an expression of faith.

For centuries the Church was creative, a bearer of culture. As theology dominated all aspects of life, faith was shared by all; life itself was guided by this faith, and found meaning in it. Art expressed this faith, that is, the revelation carried by the Church, which prompted a corresponding view of the world, thereby producing an ecclesial culture. Revelation, however, has not changed; our faith, likewise, has remained the same. An ecclesial culture also continues to exist. But the content of the icon, the message it bears, does not depend on a culture, even if it is ecclesial. Only the artistic, historical-ecclesiastical aspect of the image depends on culture. It is typical that the *oros* of the Seventh Ecumenical Council puts on the same level "the Gospel book, the image of the cross, painted icons, or sacred relics of the martyrs." But the Gospel, the cross, and the relics of the saints have nothing to do with culture. Thus, the icon is viewed as a sacred inheritance, arising out of the depths of the catholic consciousness of the Church. "The painting of icons...is an approved institution, a tradition of the catholic Church" (*oros*). The issue in the bitter struggles of the iconoclastic period was not merely the right to represent God and His saints; the central issue was precisely the image, bearing and revealing the truth; that is, precisely a certain "style" of art which corresponded to the Gospel. What was at stake was the same truth, translated either in words or through images, for the expression of which the confessors suffered martyrdom. Fashioned progressively by the Church, the artistic language of the icon was from the beginning proper to all Christian peoples, regardless of any national, social or cultural differences, because its unity resulted not from a common culture of administrative rules, but from a common faith. At the time of the Seventh Ecumenical Council, the artistic language of the Church was identical to that of the preceding epochs, even when it was not sufficiently purified, or focused on its goal. For a thousand years, the "style" of the icon was the common heritage of all of Christendom, whether in the East

15 Over the past centuries, it is true, the Orthodox hierarchy was completely freed from the need to know anything at all in the domain of sacred art: all things were decided by the secular authorities and by the Academy of Fine Arts.

or the West. There was no other. The historical course of this artistic language is epitomized by periods of greater precision and purity or, by contrast, of decay and deviation. Indeed, this "style" and its purity depend on Orthodoxy, on an assimilation of revelation that is more or less complete. This language is thus necessarily subject to change, and what we see along the two millennia of its history are changes within this iconic "style," or, more precisely, within the iconographic canon.

It is partly by reason of a conception of the icon as a mere inheritance from the past or as one of the possible art forms in the Church, that for the majority of the faithful, clergy, and bishops, there has been no "discovery" of the icon. One must also say that from the point of view of the Church there was indeed nothing to "discover": icons have remained in the churches (generally repainted, though some were not), and people prayed before them. It is therefore more correct to speak of a "return" to the icon. The veneration of the icon has remained the same; its place in the liturgical life of the Church has not changed. But alongside it, there exists a "religious" art that is venerated in the same way. The doctrinal aspect of the icon, expressed in conciliar decisions, patristic writings or the Liturgy, has disappeared from the general awareness, together with the Orthodox link between the image and revealed doctrine. This is why the doctrine of the Church is applied to any image, provided it has a religious subject. This attitude, proper to the eighteenth and nineteenth centuries, has become congealed in its rigidity, just as another epoch became congealed in ancient ritualism. People have fallen into the habit of not seeing, even of not being interested in, the image itself and its Orthodox aspect. After centuries of decadence, the return to this image is taking place slowly, particularly in ecclesiastical circles, however paradoxical this may seem.[16] The slowness of this process reveals the depth of the gap that exists

16 Christian archeology is taught in seminaries and academies. But the doctrinal content of the image has up to now not been taught. In 1954, a course on iconology as a theological discipline was introduced (for the first time) in the seminary of the Exarchate of the Patriarchate of Moscow in Western Europe, located in Paris. The clergy have to draw their knowledge about the content of the image from scientific works on the history of art, which sometimes contain unexpected "theological" digressions. Far be it from us to deny the importance of scientific works for the knowledge of the icon. On the contrary, we see in them a valuable contribution to the education of the clergy. Nonetheless, they are for them only a secondary source. The dogmatic content of the image must be the foundation of the clergy's knowledge. No one is under the obligation to know art history, but to know one's faith, and to discern whether the image before which one prays expresses this faith or not, is the duty of every believer, and all the more of the clergy.

between us and the icon. A letter received from Russia states:

> Meanwhile, the Orthodox believers who belong to the Church are searching feverishly for psychological and other means that would give them a better approach to Orthodoxy—in El Greco, Chekhov, just about anybody. *Provided that they do not have to concentrate on the fulness of the Church.*

Indeed, this is where the shoe pinches. Such insensitivity toward the icon as the image of an existentially integrated revelation is due to an equally deep insensitivity toward the Church. The Church is misunderstood: for many, it is only one "cultural (or spiritual) value" among others, some type of appendage to culture; and it has to justify its existence by serving as a stimulus to artistic activity, to the advent of social justice, and so forth. In other words, the issue here is the same temptation about the "Kingdom of Israel" (Acts 1:6), to which the apostles gave in.[17]

For the educated person today, the awareness of the Church and of the icon follow the same path. In both cases we see the same stages of trial and error, and finally the revelation (a theology in image). Paraphrasing Alexander Schmemann, we may say that in order to sense in the icon something more than a work of art or an object of personal devotion, "it is necessary to see and sense the Church as something more than a 'society of believers.'"[18] Even when attracted by the icon, the believer sometimes hesitates: he is not sure that it is the icon, and not a naturalistic image, that expresses his faith. He sees icons in museums, and it seems to him that if a church is decorated with nothing but icons, it becomes a

17 If, in the nineteenth century, an intellectual "was ashamed of being a believer," in our time, "the modern intellectual is ashamed to enter the church. There's much that needs to be cleaned up in the church, much to be renewed and reorganized if she is to become accessible to the modern mind" (Dmitri Dudko, *Our Hope*, trans. Paul D. Garrett [New York: St Vladimir's Seminary Press, 1977], 183). An intellectual might be a believer, but for him, the Church should adapt itself to "the modern mind." He does not want to understand the Church but to make it conformable to his own lack of understanding, thereby to save it. It must be said that this desire to "renovate and restructure," to approach the needs of the time, of which we have already spoken (see the preceding chapter, note 118), is far from being unique to our time. Toward the end of the fourth century or the beginning of the fifth, St Vincent of Lérins wrote: "They are not satisfied with a traditional rule of faith, received from antiquity. From day to day, they desire what is new, always what is new. They are dying to add, change, suppress something in religion" (*Comminotorium*, ch. 21, Commentary on 1 Tim [Namur, 1960], 97). Thus, "If there is one thing of which they say, 'Look! This is new,' such a thing already existed in the centuries that have preceded us" (Ec 1:10).

18 Alexander Schmemann, *Introduction to Liturgical Theology*, trans. A. Moorhouse (New York: St Vladimir's Seminary Press, 1986), 13.

museum. (We ourselves have heard this.) Moreover, the difference between an icon and a naturalistic religious image is frequently defined precisely as a difference in "style," whether ancient or new, or rather old-ritualistic or Orthodox.

In addition to the point of view according to which the icon represents one possible "style" among others in sacred art, let us note another, which serves as a basis, as a justification for the first. It is so widespread that it has even been expressed in the discussions of the pre-conciliar Commission.[19] The attitude expressed there is one of pastoral and doctrinal concern. "The icon is an expression of Orthodoxy with its moral and dogmatic teaching...a revelation of the life in Christ and of the mysteries of the divine economy for the salvation of man." It would be difficult to state it better. However, a little further, we read: "The realistic trend in art is spiritual milk for the simple people." This prompts several questions. First, it is strange, even incomprehensible, to classify the people in the Church in cultural categories. Is it not the task of the Church to reveal the mysteries of the divine economy to all its members, educated or not? Does revelation not address itself to man, regardless of his cultural level? It is also independently of the latter that one assimilates this revelation and grows spiritually.[20]

On the other hand, since the icon "reflects Orthodoxy most fully, most exhaustively, and with all possible depth and breadth," this means that the "realistic trend in art" does not do this. The "realistic trend" is therefore not a "revelation of the life in Christ," or at the least it truncates it. Would the mysteries of the divine economy for the salvation of man not be intended for "the simple people"?[21] Has the Church ever diminished or lowered its doctrine in order to tailor it to the mind of any particular layer of society? Does it initiate people into the mysteries of salvation to a greater or lesser extent? The "realistic" trend in painting, the outcome of an autonomous culture, expresses the existence of a visible

19 See *Journal of the Moscow Patriarchate*, no 1 (1961).

20 It is interesting to note that if, in the past, the icon was linked with the lack of culture among "the simple people," at present, by contrast, it is precisely the icon that is intended for the cultivated world, while so-called "realistic" painting is viewed as "milk for the simple people."

21 If, during the course of its history, the Church followed a certain progression in the initiation into the mysteries of the divine economy, this had nothing to do with the concept of "the simple people": it addressed itself to catechumens, people preparing themselves to receive baptism.

world which is independent of the divine world; it evokes life "according to the elements of this world," even if such life is idealized by the painter's personal piety. Thus art, as indeed any art that limits itself only to the humanity of Christ, cannot possibly reveal the life in Christ or show "the way of salvation." This way of salvation for man and the world certainly does not consist in accepting their actual condition as normal and in representing it through art; it consists in showing how the fallen world is removed from the divine plan, where man's salvation lies and through it, that of the world. "For if a saint [as portrayed by the trend of 'realism'] resembles [the believer] in everything, wherein does his power lie? How can he come to the aid of man sunk deep in worries and grief?" The author of these words, an art historian, reasons on the practical level with a logic that informs her correct point of view (even though, in her eyes, the icon is a "legendary image," "an invention").[22] She understands the difference between an icon and a "realistic" image much better than many faithful and members of the clergy. One could argue that logic is one thing and faith another: the icon is made not for God but for the believer, and simple logic does not contradict this. When St Basil, for example, said, "The one who picks up someone who has fallen must necessarily be higher than the latter,"[23] this is nothing but simple logic, and yet it can be applied precisely to the spiritual life. The "realistic" image is the result of a "free" creation not bound by the dogmas of the Church, a creation the seventeenth century innovators demanded so doggedly.

If, on the doctrinal level, the work of a non-Church related painter does not express the teaching of salvation, his creation—based on the concept the painter has of the spiritual life, that is, based on his imagination—runs the risk of being spiritually destructive. Let us listen to someone more competent in this field than I—Bishop Ignatius (Brianchaninov):

> The power of imagination is developed especially in passionate people. It operates in them in accordance with its own rules and transforms everything that is sacred into something passionate. Scenes by famous, but passionate, painters in which sacred events and people are depicted may convince us of this. These painters have tried to imagine and represent holiness and perfection in all their aspects. But permeated by sin, they portray sin—only sin. A refined voluptuous-

22 K. Kornilovich, *Toward a Chronicle of Russian Art* (in Russian) (Moscow-Leningrad, 1960), 89.

23 *Homilia in martyrem Julittam*, PG 31:257B.

> ness radiates from the image through which the brilliant painter wanted to represent a divine love and a chastity unknown to him...The works of such painters enchant passionate viewers, but to people imbued with the spirit of the Gospel, such works of genius inspire sadness and revulsion, marked as they are by blasphemy and the stain of sin (Fig. 50).[24]

P. Florenskii adds that the painter, in the modern understanding of the term, "by presenting a divine love and a chastity unknown to him," can even be motivated by pious intentions and devout feelings. But in depending only on a semi-conscious remembrance of the icon, such painters

> confuse canonical truth with their own free will. They take upon themselves the highly responsible work of the Fathers. But not being Church Fathers themselves, they act as imposters and false witnesses. Such a contemporary icon is nothing but a false witness publicly proclaimed in the Church.[25]

The reference here is not merely to the person of the painter: it is to art itself, borrowed from the West—an art that is alien to the dogmatic teachings and the spiritual experience of Orthodoxy, one that applies its powers of expression in a domain where they are not applicable, to something they cannot transmit.[26] Such art, introduced into Orthodoxy, was the outcome of spiritual decay, not the result of any change in doctrine. As compared to the doctrine, it remained a borrowed element, a foreign body with no link to the Tradition, and thus to the spiritual inheritance of the historic Church. It is this art, the product of a dechristianized culture—an art which not only cannot be justified by the Seventh Ecumenical Council, but which totally disagrees with its conclusion—that one proposes to legitimize by conciliar action in the Church, under the guise of "spiritual milk," on the same basis as the icon.

There is, however, a more serious argument in favor of the "realistic style" alongside the icon. This is the existence of miraculous images:

24 *Works of Bishop Ignatius Brianchaninov*, vol. 3, *Ascetical Essays* (in Russian) (St Petersburg, 1905), 287.

25 P. Florenskii, "The Iconostasis," (in Russian), *Bogoslovskie Trudy*, no 9 (Moscow, 1972), 107. This is how the author characterizes the painting of Vasnetsov, Nesterov, and Vrubel.

26 Let us note an amusing attempt to present the transplantation of Latin art into Orthodoxy as "a progressive transformation of Byzantine art." It claims that baroque and rococo art "were immensely popular among a large part of the Russian population in the eighteenth century," and that by expressing a Christianity of the Franciscan type, the Russians "nevertheless did not go outside the accepted Orthodox tradition." This instructive excursus into art history ends with the advice: "Begin to learn from an age favored by grace" (that of the "Enlightenment"? from Franciscans?). J. P. Besse, "Affinités spirituelles du baroque russe," *Contacts*, no 91 (Paris, 1975), 351-8.

50. *St Barbara.* Russian "icon" of the 18th century.

"Both genres of sacred art are acceptable to express the Christian truths in Orthodoxy by virtue of the miracles that have appeared in these two types of ecclesiastic, iconographic creation."[27] Thus, if the "realistic style" does not express the fulness of the truths of salvation, this is somehow compensated for by the existence of miraculous images.

This argument raises a basic question, one of principle: is it possible to consider miracles as the guiding principle in the life of the Church, whether it be in its entirety or in one of its manifestations (in this case, art)? Are miracles a criterion? As we have seen,[28] this question arose already in the seventeenth century, but in an opposite sense: miracles were rejected as a criterion in canonical iconography, precisely by the advocates of the new, "realistic" trend in art.

In a miracle, "the order of nature is overcome": for the salvation of man, God makes the order He established stand still. The divine mercy sometimes works miracles within the framework of the commandments and canons, sometimes by suspending the divine commandments and the canons of the Church. God can also perform miracles apart from icons, just as He sometimes acts through unworthy people and through the forces of nature. But a miracle, by definition, cannot be a norm: it is a miracle precisely because it is outside the norm.

The entire life of the Church is certainly based on a miracle, the miracle *par excellence* that gives meaning and structure to this life—the Incarnation of God and man's deification. "The amazing miracle in heaven and on earth is that God is on earth and man in heaven."[29] It is precisely this miracle that is the norm of the life of the Church, a norm fixed in its canon, one which the Church places against the actual condition of the world. The entire liturgical cycle of the Church is defined by this: its annual cycle is based on the stages, the aspects of this fundamental, decisive miracle—and not on various specific miracles, even those worked by Christ himself. The Church lives not by what is passing and specific, but by what is immutable. Is this not the reason why, for the Church, miracles have never been a criterion in any domain whatsoever?

27 Documents of the preconciliar discussion, *Journal du Patriarchat de Moscou*, no. 1 (1961).

28 See ch. 15, entitled, "The Art of the Seventeenth Century: an Art Divided. The Tradition Abandoned."

29 St Abbas Thalassios, "To the Priest Paul, on Love, Abstinence and the Spiritual Life" (in Russian), par. 98, *Philokalia*, vol. 3 (Moscow, 1888).

Its life has never been ruled by them.[30] It is significant that the conciliar decisions ordain that icons be painted not based on miraculous models (indeed, the miracles performed by an icon are an external, temporal manifestation, not an enduring display), but in the same manner in which the ancient iconographers painted, that is, according to the iconographic canon. What is at issue, we must emphasize, is the Orthodox, canonical image, that is, the unchanged expression "of the mysteries of the divine economy for the salvation of man."

As for the "realistic style," how can an image that does not express the teaching of the Church and does not bear "the revelation of the life in Christ" become a message of the Church? How can this image, through miracles, become acceptable to express "the Christian truths in Orthodoxy" on the same basis as the image that expresses these? Nonetheless, such an image can sometimes serve as the starting point for a new type of canonical icon and can be introduced into the canon of the Church, if its subject does not contradict Orthodox doctrine, that is, if it is not heretical, and provided the miracle be authentic.

At present, the dogma of the veneration of icons is important not only on the doctrinal level vis-à-vis the non-Orthodox, but also from an extra-religious perspective. Indeed, the encounter with Orthodoxy and the return to the sources of Christianity so typical of our age are, on the one hand, also a true encounter with the icon, and thus with the original fulness of the Christian revelation, expressed by word and image. On the other hand, the message of the Orthodox icon is an answer to the problems of our times precisely because these problems are clearly of an anthropological nature. Man is the central problem of our age, man led to an impasse by secularized humanism.

A civilization in disarray and a whole series of scientific and technical revolutions confront the world with the question: how to preserve the human in man? Further, how can the human race itself be preserved? The goal of scientific and technical progress is the well-being of man especially

30 Let us keep in mind that the qualitative range of miracles is wide. In addition to the authentic miracles, there are "miracles" that result from psychological neuroses, or credulity; some are known to be mere deceptions; finally, there are also miracles of diabolical origin (see Mt 24:24; 2 Th 2:9; Rev 13:13-14; 19:20; cf. 16:14). Lastly, the true, that is, salutary miracles have most often been performed by Christ not upon His disciples but on strangers, just as now they often occur outside the Church.

by freeing his creative energy, and such progress enjoys a success unknown in the past. But in this world where science and technology have undergone dizzying degree of development, in this world where contemporary ideologies are likewise directed toward the good and the progress of man, one notices, paradoxically, an irresistible tendency toward savagery, both outward and inward: the spiritualization of man's animal life is replaced by a bestialization of his spirit.

Man is turning into a means of production; his essential value lies not in the person, but in his function. Our daily life is dominated by what is false, fifth-rate, and also by a fragmentation that leads to decomposition in all areas. The result is a loss of physical and spiritual harmony, a search for "artificial paradises," including drugs.

> The humanity which we observe and which we are seems to be a broken humanity, broken first of all in each of us...Here we are, "ass up in the air," with no center where everything is reconciled. Separated from ourselves, we are also separated from one another.[31]

In our modern world, then, this broken, divided human being is "the measure of all things." As Schmemann has noted, this elevated position of modern humanity coincides paradoxically with a distortion of our vocation, and of God's plan for us. Our epoch is anthropocentric; but man, the center, is insignificant, a dwarf. The autonomous man of our contemporary, humanistic culture denies his resemblance to the Prototype. He has not accepted the image of glory, revealed in the humiliated body of Christ. Our civilization began precisely with the refusal of this ineffable image of glory—it began with what should, by theological analogy, be called "a second fall."[32] By mutilating his nature, man has violated the hierarchy of being. He has thereby adulterated his role in relation to the surrounding world. Instead of submitting to the will of God, he submitted to the world of matter which he was called to dominate. Having refused God the Creator, and declaring himself creator, man has created for himself other gods more eager for human victims than the pagan gods were.

On the spiritual level, this struggle against God, whether open or secret, leads paradoxically to faith. Fragmentation and disintegration lead

31 Olivier Clément, *Questions sur l'homme* (Paris, 1972), 7.

32 Alexander Schmemann, "Can One Be a Believer, Being Civilized?" (in Russian), *Messager de l'ACER*, no 107 (Paris, 1974), 145-52.

to a quest for unity; the false and the artificial, to a taste for what is authentic. Man searches for the meaning of existence when the question arises in this fragmented world of how one can believe, why, in whom, and in what.

Here the destinies of the Orthodox Church and of the icon coincide once again. If during the Synodal period the leading role fell to the Russian Church, linked to a powerful state, none of the local churches presently finds itself in such a situation. The rapid growth of a desacralized culture has limited the means of action the Church once had at its disposal.

It is when Orthodoxy is oppressed by militant atheism and other religions, weakened by schisms and confusion, that it reaches out to the world outside. In our day, the leading role in this mission does not belong to any particular local church, but to Orthodoxy, as a manifestation of the revelation which is the Church. The nature of the mission has also changed: it is no longer only a question of preaching Christianity to unenlightened peoples but, above all, of presenting it as an alternative to the dechristianized world, whose culture is in total disarray. This culture, marked by fragmentation and artificiality, is confronted by Orthodoxy as its antithesis, as truth, unity and authenticity, because the very nature of the Church, its catholicity, represents the opposite of separatism, disunity, discord, and individualism.

Christian revelation brings a momentous reversal to the relationship of fallen man with God on the one hand, and on the other, with the world in its actual condition: it announces that God's design had been re-established. "For my thoughts are not your thoughts, neither are your ways my ways, says the Lord. For as the heavens are higher than the earth, so are my ways higher than your ways" (Is 55:8-9).

Christianity does not address itself to any particular category of people, to any particular class, society, organism, national or social group; it is not an ideological expedient to improve the fallen world, to establish "the Kingdom of God" on earth. It reveals the Kingdom of God not in the external sphere, but within man.[33] In the preaching of John the Baptist, "repent," that is, "change your purpose" (*metanoiete*), in the

33 For the Judaic tradition, the coming into the world of the Messiah proved to be a "scandal" precisely because the promised Kingdom of God turned out to be not a kingdom of this world but a kingdom within man; and because the way that leads to it passes through the cross.

literal sense of the term, requires that one refuse to walk the path followed before, and that one adopt a new path, the opposite of sin. "Therefore, if anyone is in Christ, he is a new creature. The old has passed away. Behold, the new has come" (2 Cor 5:17). The entire preaching of the Gospel (the parables of the Kingdom of God, the Sermon on the Mount, and so forth) points in a direction opposite to the ways of the fallen world. As an expression of the very essence of Christianity, the evangelical perspective gives the lie to the attitude that considers the disunity and disintegration present in the world as natural. As reality, truth, and way of salvation, it represents the opposite of the law of "the prince of this world," that unhealthy condition which is generally called "normal," natural, proper to creation ("such is nature"—is the most current rationalization). But the world as created by God is good and beautiful. Sin, division, decay, disintegration are not natural: they are a condition imposed upon nature by man. Inherent to Christianity is not the denial of this world, but on the contrary, its healing, through the intermediary of man. Man is called to bring himself and the surrounding world into union with and in the Creator. The image of a world transformed in the humanity of Christ (such is the meaning of its existence from the perspective of this ultimate destiny) is contrasted to a world ruled by evil, violence, and bitter discord.

In our day, with the advent of Orthodoxy in this "upside-down" world, two completely different orientations of man and of his creativity confront one another: the anthropocentrism of a secularized, a-religious humanism, and Christian anthropocentrism. In this confrontation, the icon plays a leading role. The essential meaning of its "discovery" in our epoch does not lie in the fact that it is now appreciated and understood to a greater or lesser extent, but in the witness it offers to contemporary man: a witness to the victory gained by man over all discord and disintegration, a witness to another way of life that puts man in a totally different perspective in relation to his Creator and radically reorients his attitude toward the fallen world, gives him a different understanding, another vision of the world.

Returning to the Seventh Ecumenical Council, we should say that it proclaimed nothing essentially new. It merely defined the significance of the Christian image, as it had been from the beginning. Here we will briefly mention only those major themes that are directly related to various aspects of present-day problems.

In its *oros* and in its judgments, the Council linked the icon above all to the Gospel, that is, to theology understood in its elementary sense, made visible, in the words of St Gregory Palamas, "by the Truth itself which is Christ. Being God above the ages, He has become for us also a theologian."[34]

We are here in the presence of the Christian concept of the image and its meaning in theology, and hence in the life of man, created in the image of God.

> If man is *logikos*...if he is "in the image" of the Logos, everything which touches the destiny of man—grace, sin, redemption by the Word made man—must also be related to the theology of the image. And we may say the same of the Church, the sacraments, sanctification, and the end of all things. There is no branch of theological teaching which can be entirely isolated from the problem of the image without danger of severing it from the living stock of Christian tradition. We may say that for a theologian of the catholic tradition in the East and in the West, for one who is true to the mainline of patristic thought, the theme of the image (in its twofold acceptance—the image as the principle of God's self-manifestation and the image as the foundation of a particular relationship of man to God) must belong to the essence of Christianity.[35]

> Through the Incarnation, which is the fundamental dogmatic fact of Christianity, "image" and "theology" are linked so closely together that the expression "theology of the image" might become almost a tautology—which it is, if one chooses to regard theology as a knowledge of God in His Logos, who is the consubstantial Image of the Father.[36]

Thus, since it is the one, divine hypostasis of Jesus Christ who in the Incarnation reveals the Word and the Image of the Father to the world, theology and the icon together express the same revelation—by work and through the image. In other words, theology in word, and theology in image constitute an ontological totality, and thereby one and the same instruction for man: they guide him as he assimilates the revelation. They are the path of his salvation.[37] Being one of the basic truths of revelation,

34 As quoted by Archimandrite Amphilochius (Radovic), *To Mysterion tes Hagias Triados kata ton Gregorion Palaman* (Thessalonika, 1973), 144.

35 V. Lossky, "La Théologie de l'Image," *Messager de l'Exarchat du Patriarche russe en Europe occidentale*, nos 30-31 (1959), 123.

36 *Ibid.*, 129.

37 When the word no longer corresponds to the visible image, a break between them results: two different ways of expressing the same truth become disunited; their ontological fullness which corresponds to the unity of truth itself disintegrates at the expense of the fullness of revelation. Thus the expression "theology in image," which has been traditionally applied to the icon, is acceptable only when it corresponds to theology in the patristic sense, as the concrete

the image is therefore one of the components of the doctrinal fullness of the Church.

By grounding the icon on the Incarnation, that is, on christological dogma, the Council insistently (and repeatedly) referred to the veneration of icons as unbroken since the time of the apostles, that is, to the uninterrupted succession of the apostolic tradition. It is true that modern man (with his faith in the infallibility of science) may be skeptical about this statement, all the more since references to antiquity have often been used as proofs of authenticity without sufficient reason. But in the case before us, the Fathers of the Council based themselves not on data used by contemporary science but, as we have seen, on the very essence of Christianity, on the appearance in the created world of "the image of the invisible God, the first born of all creation" (Col 1:15—pericope read on the feast of the Icon of "Christ not Made by Human Hands," the Holy Face). "When the Word of God became flesh," Irenaeus states, "He showed forth the image truly, since He himself became what was His image; and He reestablished the likeness—by rendering man altogether similar to the invisible Father."[38] It is this image of the invisible God, imprinted in matter as a witness "of the true, non-illusionary Incarnation of God the Word" (*oros* of the Council) which, on the one hand, is contrasted to the absence of any image of God in the Old Testament, and, on the other, to the false image in paganism, the idol. Faced with this false image of God created in the image of man, Christianity raises the image of Christ before the world. Christianity shows the prototype according to which man was created, but which is now hidden because of his sin. This image lives in the Tradition, which is the charismatic or mystical memory of the Church, its inner life. Above all, this Tradition is "the unity of the Spirit, the living and interrupted link with the mystery of Pentecost."[39] Hence the insistence on apostolic tradition in the references of the Council Fathers.[40] Since the Christian revelation was, at the beginning, given to

knowledge of God, leading to direct contact with Him. If not, then the patristic terminology is in danger of being applied to the image by virtue of a mere combination of words; we have seen this happen in the seventeenth century.

38 *Contra Haereses*, V, 16, 2 (Paris, 1969), vol. 2, 217.

39 G. Florovsky, "Theological Fragments" (in Russian), *Put*, no 31 (Paris, 1931), 23.

40 Both the word and the image live only in the Tradition. Outside the latter, the Gospel becomes, as we see today, a historic document from the first centuries of our era; the Old Testament, the history of the Jewish people and the Church fades into the general concept of

the world in a twofold manner, by the word and through the image, "by following the teaching of the Holy Fathers and the tradition of the catholic Church" (*oros*), the Council confirmed that the image has existed from the beginning; not only is the image necessary, but it belongs organically to Christianity, because it derives from the Incarnation of a divine Person. This is why iconoclasm—despite its antiquity that dates to the beginning of Christianity, and even though its opposition to the image is based on the Old Testament prohibition and is nourished by spiritual trends of an Origenistic tendency—came up against an insurmountable obstacle, and only served to clarify and make the revealed truth still more manifest.

For our epoch, the significance of the Seventh Ecumenical Council lies above all in the fact that by its response to an open iconoclasm, it has proclaimed for all time that the icon is an expression of the Christian faith, an inalienable attribute of orthodoxy. Thus the dogma of the veneration of icons is an answer to all heresies—iconoclasm being "the sum of numerous heresies and errors," according to the council—that undermined and continued to undermine, openly or secretly, a certain aspect of the divine humanity and this Divine-Humanity in its totality, and therefore Christian anthropology. Through the dogma of the veneration of icons, the Fathers of the council defended Christian anthropology, that it, the relationship between God and the human being revealed in the Person of Jesus Christ. They saw its center of gravity not in their theological pronouncements but in the concrete experience of holiness, and in the image. Indeed, "if the Incarnation of God the Word, as a realization of the perfect man, is above all an anthropological event, His indwelling in man is also an anthropological event."[41] This is why in the victory over iconoclasm, the catholic consciousness of the Church confirmed the icon as a triumph of Orthodoxy, as a witness by the Church of the revealed truth. Indeed, Christian anthropology found its most direct and clearest expression in the Orthodox icon. Does the icon not show "the truth and consequences of the divine Incarnation"? Does it not illustrate with the

"religion." Indeed, "to refuse the image of the Tradition is essentially to repudiate the Church as the Body of Christ, to belittle it" (G. Florovsky, "The House of the Father" [in Russian], *Put'*, no 27 [Paris, 1927], 78).

41 From a summary in German of the book of Archimandrite Amphilochius (Radovic), *To Mysterion tes Hagias Triados* (Thessalonika, 1973), 231.

utmost fullness and depth the Christian doctrine about the relationship between man and God, and between man and the world? To exclude the image from Christian anthropology is thus not only to exclude the visible image of the Incarnation of God, but also to renounce a witness of the likeness to God acquired by man, a realization of the divine economy. It is to endanger the Orthodox witness of the truth.

Since the icon is above all the representation of a person (be it the divine Person of Christ or a human being) indicated by his proper name, its truth is conditioned by its authenticity: a historic authenticity, because an "image is of like character with its prototype,"[42] and a charismatic authenticity.[43] God, indescribable in His divinity, is joined "without confusion or separation" (dogma of Chalcedon) to describable humanity. Man unites his describable humanity to the indescribable Divinity.

We have already noted that the image of the person of Christ, as a witness of His Incarnation, was for the defenders of the icon also a witness to the reality of the eucharistic sacrament.[44] Thus the authenticity of the image, its content, is seen in its conformity to the sacrament. The faith of the Church is distinguished from all others by its concrete, physical communion with its object. Through such contact, faith becomes vision, knowledge, and community of life with Him. This common life is

42 St John of Damascus, *De imaginibus oratio* I, 9, PG 94(I): 1240C.

43 Let us note here a rather original commentary on the icon and the cross of the *oros* Seventh Ecumenical Council in the book, *The Year of Grace: A Scriptural and Liturgical Commentary on the Calendar of the Orthodox Church* by a Monk of the Eastern Church, trans. Deborah Cowen (New York: St Vladimir's Seminary Press, 1980), 132: "Here, we will touch on the fundamental ideas that concern icons. First of all, an icon is neither a representation nor a resemblance." However, according to patristic teaching, the icon is precisely a portrait reproducing the resemblance of the prototype, from which it is distinguished by nature. If the icon is "neither a representation nor a resemblance," how then, according to the author, can its theme be "the Person of Christ [or] the Mother of God" or other saints? Further down, the author endeavors to convince the reader that the role of the icon in Christian piety ought not to be exaggerated. "The church has never made it obligatory for believers to have icons in their homes or to reserve for them a special place in their prayers or personal devotions" (p. 153). But the Orthodox Church never makes anything "obligatory" (the concept of "obligation" belongs to Roman Catholicism, not Orthodoxy). For the good of its members, the church makes decisions. This is precisely how this is said in the oros of the council: "We decide...that in the holy Church of God, on vessels and sacred vestments, on walls and boards, in houses and on the roads, precious holy icons be placed...; they should be honored with a kiss and a bow of veneration."

44 See the chapter, "The Great Council of Moscow and the Image of God the Father," and J. Meyendorff, *Christ in Eastern Christian Thought*, trans. Y. Dubois (New York: St Vladimir's Seminary Press, 1987), 190.

realized in the Eucharist. The prayer before communion is addressed to a concrete person because it is only by addressing a person in a relationship, that it is possible to partake of what the person carries within, of what subsists in Him. But this contact requires an image, because man does not address himself to an imaginary Christ or an abstract divinity, but to a person: "In truth, *You* are the Christ...; this is *Your* Body..." (the image on the chalice). In the Eucharist, through the action of the Holy Spirit, the bread and wine become the divine Body and Blood of the risen and glorified Christ (Christianity does not know a "spiritual resurrection" outside the body): salvation has been and is still being accomplished through the body.[45] "The Eucharist itself represents for us salvation precisely because it is 'Body' and 'humanity'"[46] The image of the person of Christ only corresponds to the sacrament if it represents a body over which death no longer has dominion (Rom 5:8-9), that is, the Body of Christ in glory. Thus the reality of the glorified Body of Christ in the sacrament of the Eucharist is of necessity linked to the authenticity of His personal image, for the Body of Christ depicted on the icon is this same "Body of God resplendent in divine glory, incorruptible, holy, life-giving."[47] As a witness to the Incarnation, the image is linked here to eschatology, because the glorious Body of Christ is His Body of the Second Coming and of the Judgment (see the prayer before communion). Hence the warning in the third canon of the Council of 869-870: "If someone does not venerate the icon of Christ the Savior, let him not see His face at the Second Coming."[48]

In other words, only the twofold realism of the image—a realism that unites the representable with the non-representable—can correspond to the sacrament of the Eucharist. This link between image and sacrament excludes any image that merely shows "an aspect of the servant," or even an abstract concept.

45 Not only does Christianity not dematerialize matter, but on the contrary, it is resolutely "materialistic." From its inception, it did not content itself with the rehabilitation of the body: it affirmed that it is salutary. It professes the transfiguration of human nature and its resurrection in the body, in matter. "I do not worship matter; I worship the Creator of matter who became matter for my sake...who worked out my salvation through matter. Never will I cease honoring the matter which wrought my salvation!" (St John of Damascus, *On the Divine Images, First Apology*, 16, trans. D. Anderson [New York: St Vladimir's Seminary Press, 1980], 23; see also, *Second Apology*, 14, *ibid.*).

46 J. Meyendorff, *Christ in Eastern Christian Thought*, *op. cit.*

47 Seventh Ecumenical Council, *Acts*, Sixth Session, Mansi XIII.

48 See ch. 11, "The Post-Iconoclastic Period."

Just as for the icon of Christ, the authenticity of the icon of a saint consists of its correspondence to its prototype. The personal experience of deification, then, is the union of representable humanity with the unrepresentable divinity when, in the words of St Ephrem the Syrian, man "having purified the eyes of his heart, always discerns the Lord in himself, as in a mirror,"[49] and "transforms himself into the same image" (cf 2 Cor 3:18). A saint is thus represented not according to the appearance of his corruptible flesh but according to that of the glorified body of Christ.

Here we must make a proviso. Unlike philosophy, theology does not deal with abstract concepts. It has to do with concrete facts, the data of revelation, facts that transcend human means of expression. Iconography is in the same situation, faced with the same facts. As the Christian revelation is beyond words as much as images, no verbal or artistic expression is in itself able to express God, or give an adequate and direct knowledge of Him. In this sense, the one and the other are always "failures," since they must transmit the inconceivable by the conceivable, the unrepresentable by the representable, express in the created what is beyond it and of a different nature. But their value consists precisely in that both theology and the icon reach the height of human possibilities, while realizing their inadequacy. But does God not show by the cross that He himself is the supreme "failure"? It is precisely through this "failure" which is proper to them that theology and the icon are called to witness to God, to make the divine presence perceivable—this presence which, in its reality, is accessible in the experience of holiness.

In this area there are, in both theology and sacred art, two heresies that may be contrasted to one another, as V. Lossky indicated in his courses. The first heresy is "humanization" ("making immanent"), the lowering of the divine transcendence to our human conceptions. The period of the Renaissance may serve as an example for art; for theology, it is rationalism which lowers the divine truths to the level of human philosophy. We have then a theology without "failure," and an art without "failure." Such art is beautiful, but it limits the humanity of Christ and does not in the least point to the God-Man. The other heresy is to surrender to failure from the start, a rejection of the image. In art, it is iconoclasm, the denial of the immanence of the divinity, that is, of the Incarnation itself. In theology,

49 *The Psalter or The Reflections on the Divine* (in Russian) (Moscow, 1904), ch. 51, 107.

it is fideism. The first heresy results in an irreverent art, in impious thought; in the second, impiety is concealed behind an apparent piety.

These two positions, opposite in their manifestations, are based on the same anthropological presuppositions. "In the eastern patristic view, participation in divine life is what makes man to be a man, not only in the ultimate fulfillment, but, since his creation, at any moment of his life." By contrast,

> western theology will traditionally take for granted that the very art of creation supposes that man is not only of a *different* nature, but that he has been given an existence which is, as such, autonomous: the vision of God is perhaps the "goal," or the individual experience of a few "mystics," but it is not a condition of man's being truly man.[50]

Here we find two radically different views of man's destiny, of his life and creation. On the one hand is Orthodox anthropology, understood as the acquisition by man of his resemblance to God—a resemblance that is made manifest existentially, in a creative and living manner, and which therefore determines the content of the Orthodox image. On the other hand is the anthropology of the western confessions that assert man's autonomy in relation to God: certainly, man is created in the image of God, but since he is autonomous he is not really correlated to his prototype. Hence the development of humanism with its anthropology that is independent of the Church and dechristianized, where man is distinguished from other creatures only according to natural categories: he is a "rational animal," a "social being," and so forth.

As we have noted in the preceding chapter, the introduction of the *filioque* and the resulting diminution of the principle, together with the introduction of the doctrine of created grace, led to a non-Orthodox view of the relationships between God and man, and between man and the world. Man's autonomy in relation to God implies the autonomy of his reason and of his other faculties. Thomas Aquinas already acknowledged the total independence of natural reason from faith.

> It is precisely to Thomas Aquinas that dates back the break between Christianity and culture...a break that turned out to be fatal for all Christian culture in the West...the tragic sense of which is presently made clear in all its magnitude.[51]

50 J. Meyendorff, "Philosophy, Theology, Palamism and Secular Christianity," *St Vladimir's Seminary Quarterly*, no 4 (1966), 205.

51 B. Zenkovskii, *The Foundations of Christian Philosophy* (in Russian) (Frankfurt-am-Main, 1960), vol. 1, 9, 11.

Contradicting the Seventh Ecumenical Council, the *Libri Carolini* dissociated artistic creation from the catholic experience of the Church; they considered art to be autonomous and thereby determined its future. To see the icon as a path to salvation equivalent to the word of the Gospel (as the Council Fathers had done) was utterly inconceivable and therefore unacceptable to Charlemagne's theologians. Theoretically, the Roman Catholic Church recognizes the Seventh Ecumenical Council and confesses the veneration of icons. But in practice the position expressed in the *Libri Carolini* remains the official position until today.

If, in the twelfth century and partly in the thirteenth, the image in the West was still linked in some way to Christian anthropology, a slow disintegration gradually led art to a definite break with it. Being autonomous, such art limits itself to an expression of what does not transcend man's natural faculties. Since the creature is no longer permeated by the uncreated, grace, as a created reality, can only improve man's natural powers. What Christianity had rejected from its art since the beginning, the illusionary portrayal of the visible word, became a goal in itself. The moment the unrepresentable was conceived in the same categories as the representable, the language of symbolic realism disappeared, and the divine transcendence was lowered to the level of everyday concepts. The message of Christianity was truncated, adapted to human thought. Yielding to the temptation of "success" (the opposite of "failure"), the "*mimesis* (imitation) of life" invaded art in the period of the Renaissance. Together with an infatuation with antiquity, the cult of the flesh replaced the transfiguration of the human body. The Christian doctrine concerning the relationships between God and man moved in the wrong direction, and Christian anthropology was undermined; the eschatological perspective of the synergism between God and man was thereby suppressed.

> To the degree that the human takes over in art, God is removed from it. Everything is lowered and becomes secular. What was a means of adoration has become an object of idolatry; what was revelation is now content to be illusion. The mark of the sacred has been erased. Art has become nothing but a means of enjoyment and comfort. Man has met himself and worships himself in his art.[52]

"The image of this passing world" has replaced the image of revelation. The falsehood of any "imitation of nature" does not merely consist of the

52 J. Onimus, *Réflexions sur l'art actuel* (Paris, 1964), 80.

substitution of the traditional image by a fiction, but also in the preservation of religious subjects while blurring the limits that separate the visible from the invisible. The distinction between them disappeared, and this led to a denial of the very existence of the spiritual world. The image lost its Christian meaning, which eventually led to its rejection, to open iconoclasm. "This is how the iconoclasm of the Reformation was justified. Justified and relativized, because the issue was not sacred art, but its degeneration in the medieval West."[53]

In this art, which confirms the existing cosmic order, the laws of optical or linear perspective were worked out. These laws came to be viewed not only as the normal, but as the only scientifically correct way to depict space, just as the visible condition of the world was in itself considered to be normal. As P. Florenskii has indicated, this perspective appeared.

> when the religious, stable view of the world disintegrated, when the sacred metaphysic of the *common* awareness of the people was eroded by the individual judgment of the *particular*, isolated person with his individual point of view...This is when the perspective so typical of the isolated awareness appeared.[54]

This is what happened in the West at the time of the Renaissance, and in the Orthodox world during the seventeenth century. This perspective, in turn, disappeared when in our time the humanistic world view that had emerged from it disintegrated, and together with it its art and culture.

In Roman Catholicism, sacred art is viewed as depending on the artist who, in turn, is subordinated to periods and trends.

> The [Roman Catholic] Church has not adopted any particular style of art as her very own; she has admitted fashions from every period according to the natural talents and circumstances of peoples, and the needs of the various rites.[55]

"There is no 'religious,' no 'church' style."[56] In relation to art, the Church is only a patron, just as in other cultural domains. The result of this is that

53 Olivier Clément, "Un ouvrage important sur l'art sacré," *Contacts*, no 44 (1963), 278.

54 P. A. Florenskii, "Reverse Perspective" (in Russian), *Trudy po znakovym sistemam* III (Tartu, 1967), 385.

55 *Constitution on the Sacred Liturgy, General Principles for the Restoration and Promotion of the Sacred Liturgy*, ch. VII, par. 123, "Sacred Art and Sacred Furnishings," trans. *The Documents of Vatican II* (New York: Guild Press, 1966), 175.

56 "Commentaire de la Constitution sur la Liturgie," *La Maison-Dieu*, no. 77 (Paris, 1964), 214. When western art was adopted in Orthodoxy, this attitude, as we have seen, was likewise adopted.

the meaning of the image as an expression, by the catholic experience of the Church, of the Christian revelation has remained foreign to the western confessions. The Seventh Ecumenical Council, as we know, attributed the institution of the painting of icons to the holy Fathers, guided by the Holy Spirit. "The Saints...have left the description of their life for our own well-being and salvation, and have transmitted their works to the catholic Church by means of artistic representation."[57] These "works transmitted for our salvation" are an existential expression of the equivalence of the icon to the preaching of the Gospel. It is this testimony of the holy Fathers, "the authority and the right to express or formulate the experience of the faith of the Church,"[58] that gives the icon the power to teach. During a reception for American painters, Pope Paul VI said, "You, artists are able to read the message of God and translate it for the people."[59] Thus it is in fact sufficient for man to develop his natural talents (in this case, that of painting) to become a bearer of "the message of God." Here we are confronted with the same situation as in the orientation of present-day theological thought. For in the West,

> modern theology is essentially concerned with discovering God's presence in the human experience as such. And this concern leads it to "humanize" God, and it then immediately finds itself at odds with the patristic intuition.[60]

In our day, Roman Catholicism welcomes modern art as a result of this basic attitude. It adapts itself to the fashions of an autonomous culture, just as during the Renaissance it had accepted the "*mimesis* of nature." Having repudiated the ancient universe of forms and concepts, this art has arrived at a fragmentation that results in disintegration, sometimes blasphemy.

> Modern art conveys to us the image of a world swept along toward a new destiny, a world as if consumed by a longing to deny in order to speed up its movement toward the future... [It is] the enticement of the void and the fear of such nothingness which, to our minds, is the absurd; these two thus echo themes found in modern philosophy, especially that of existentialism, in particular Jean Paul Sartre's.[61]

57 *Acts*, Sixth Session.

58 G. Florovsky, "Theological Fragments" (in Russian), *Put*, no 31 (Paris, 1931), 25.

59 *L'Aurore* (Paris: 27 July, 1975).

60 J. Meyendorff, "Philosophy, Theology, Palamism," 206.

61 R. Huyghe, "Nous vivons l'époque du point zéro de l'art," *Arts*, no 848 (20-26 December, 1961). The result of this is that, in order to return to the so-called "simplicity of the first centuries" and to obligatory "poverty," one reaches extreme manifestations of it: the churches have become totally empty and perfectly resemble Protestant temples. "A regrettable confu-

At the moment when such art and the environment from which it sprang are irrevocably shipwrecked, the icon enters this world of fragmentation and decay, like a banner of Orthodoxy, a message that is addressed to the free will of man created in the image of God. By pointing to the Incarnation, the icon pits the authentic, Christian anthropology against the distorted anthropology of the western confessions and against that of the contemporary, dechristianized culture.

Instead of expressing the faculties, even the highest, of the spiritual, psychic and bodily composite of autonomous man, the icon, like the word of the Gospel, fulfills a constant task, which has been that of Christian art from the beginning: to reveal the true relationships between God and man. Just as in the beginning the upheaval ushered into the world by the coming of Christ in the flesh had been a "stumbling-block" and "folly" (1 Cor 1:23), so in our day the icon enters the world which "did not know God through wisdom," a world of illusion and deceit, by the "folly of what we preach" (1 Cor 1:21). To this disoriented world the icon brings a testimony of the authenticity, of the reality of another way of life, of other norms of existential relationships brought about in the world by the Incarnation of God and unknown to man enslaved by biological laws. The icon conveys a new message about God, man and creation, a new attitude toward the world. It specifies the calling of man and what he must become; it places him in a different perspective. In other words, the icon decries the paths followed by man and the world, but at the same time it appeals to man: it suggests other paths for him to follow. In the icon, the perspective of this visible world stands opposed to the perspective of the Gospel; the world lying in sin, *versus* the world transfigured. The entire structure of the icon is directed to bring man in communion with the revelation Christianity gave to the world, to show him, by means of visible forms, the very essence of the reversal introduced by Christianity. To express this reversal, the image must have a very special structure, particular means of expression, a distinct "style."

In this structure of the icon with its so-called reverse perspective, "what

sion," D. von Hildebrand writes, "which suppresses the basic distinction between things, is apparent also in the American and French practice of replacing the painted images of saints and of Christ Himself with photographs of women, children, victims of wars, of misery and social injustice" (*La Vigne ravagée* [Paris, 1974], 109, note). Eventually, the church itself is remodeled for various uses: conferences, dances, theatrical presentations.

strikes one above all is an entire series of particularities of forms that sometimes have the appearance of an insoluble enigma"[62] to man of contemporary European culture. This is why such forms are usually understood as so many distortions. But this "distortion" is such only in relation to the eye accustomed to linear perspective, and to a view of the world presently considered as normal, that is, in comparison to the forms that express the vision of the world proper to our time. In reality, however, we are dealing here not with a "distortion," but with a different artistic language, that of the Church.[63] This "distortion" is natural, or rather indispensable to express the content of the icon. For the traditional iconographer, both in the past and in our day, this structure of the icon is the only one that is possible: it is indispensable. Deriving from the liturgical experience of the Church, along with other art forms, it puts the catholic experience of the Church in opposition to "the individual point of view" of autonomous man, to the painter's personal experience and his "solitary awareness."

Neither the linear perspective nor light and shadow (*clair-obscur, chiaroscuro*) are excluded from the icon, but here they no longer serve to create an illusion of the visible world;[64] they are inserted into the general structure in which the "inverted perspective" dominates (Fig. 51). We should first point out that in this widely accepted technical term, the word "inverted" is not completely accurate, since there is no inversion pure and simple; it is not a type of inverse reflection, as in a mirror. There is no system of inverted perspective that corresponds to the system of linear perspective. Against the latter's rigid law is set another law, another

62 L. F. Genin, *The Language of Painted Work* (in Russian) (Moscow, 1970), 36.

63 Hence the difficulty of a scientific analysis of this language. An explanation of the icon which would be only aesthetic or rational is impossible because the Christian revelation which constitutes its content, the experience of the divine life given to man, is not open to scientific analysis. Only the domain which is peripheral, so to speak, is accessible to science and is in its competence. This is limited, as we have seen, to the artistic aspect of the work, its social and historic context, the structure of the image, influences, borrowings, and so forth. This is why science limits itself to bringing out the parallels between the icon and folklore, saints' lives and secular literature. But when science tries to explain the very essence of the art of the Church, while remaining within its own appropriate boundaries, this results in inept comments about "the painter's devout imagination," "the dematerialization of the visible world and of the human body," and so forth.

64 The Greek word *skiagraphia* refers both to an image in optical perspective, a representation in *chiaroscuro*, and to an illusion.

principle of composing an image, one that derives from its content. This different principle entails a whole series of procedures that create a representation that is either opposite (inverted) in comparison with illusion or entirely different from it (according to the meaning of what is represented). This extremely varied and flexible system secures the painter's complete freedom; it is nonetheless applied in a consistent and uniform manner, in conformity with its proper orientation.[65]

According to contemporary scholarship, "it turns out that we do not see nearby objects as Raphael represented them...We see everything that is nearby as Rublev and the ancient Russian painters depicted it."[66] Let us clarify this statement somewhat. Certainly, Raphael drew differently than Rublev, but he saw in the same way as the latter did, since both are subject to the same natural law of visual perception. The difference lies in the fact that Raphael submitted the natural vision of the human eye to the control of his autonomous reason, and thereby distanced himself from this vision. The iconographers, by contrast, did not move away from this vision,

65 A most interesting result of modern scientific studies on the way of dealing with space in the icon may be noted here (P. Florenskii, "Reverse Perspective" [in Russian], *Trudy po znakovym sistemam* III; E. Panofski, "Die Perspektive als symbolische Form," *Vorträge der Bibliothek Warburg* [1924-1925]; *Aufsätze zur Grundlagen der Kunstwissenschaft* [Berlin, 1964]; L. F. Gegin, "The Language of Painted Work"; and above all, B. V. Rauschenbach, *Spatial Structures in Ancient Russian Painting* [in Russian] [Moscow, 1975]). These studies note if not the superiority of the structural principles of the icon to those of modern art, then at least their equality. It turns out that the richness and the diversity of the procedures of representation in the icon are clearly superior to those used in modern art. Such studies also maintain that the structure of the image, in an art which was viewed as "barbarian" not so long ago, needs, in order to be deciphered, a mathematical apparatus even more complex than the deciphering of a Renaissance painting, which is allegedly equipped with "the only scientifically valid method of representing the visible world." It is significant—and scientific works often note this—that no system of reverse perspective has ever been taught, and that no handbook speaks of it. One may suppose that it was transmitted by tradition. But tradition can only transmit the structure of the icon in its general aspect, otherwise one would find a mechanical repetition of one identical form of perspective, which is not the case. It is always applied in a different manner and to varying degrees, even in identical subjects, and is also combined with optical perspective. Certain elements of reverse perspective which are found in other art forms are sometimes viewed as a proof that this system is not connected to the Christian content of the image. This, it seems to us, proves nothing. Indeed, the halo, for example, as an expression of light, appears in various contexts. The revelation of light was partially known in non-Christian religions. One could therefore conjecture that non-Christians likewise had a partial awareness of structures analogous to that of the icon. What is important, however, is that this principle of spatial structures became a consistent and well attuned system only and precisely in Christian art.

66 *Questions of Literature* (in Russian), no 9 (1976), 40.

51. *St Luke the Evangelist*
16th century Russian, Novgorod.
Icon Museum, Recklinghausen

because the meaning of what they were representing not only did not demand it, but did not even allow them to go beyond the natural perception of the foreground to which the structure of the icon is limited.

Let us try to illustrate the correspondence between the structure of the icon and its content by some examples.

What is particular about the representation of space in the icon is that, even though it is three-dimensional (iconography is not a two-dimensional art), the third dimension is limited by the surface of the panel, and the representation is oriented toward the real space in front of the image. In other words, compared to the illusory representation of space in depth, that of the icon shows the reverse. If a painting, composed in compliance with the laws of linear perspective, represents another space that has no relationship with the real space where it is located, in the icon we see the opposite: the represented space is included in the real space—there is no break between them. The representation is limited to the foreground. The persons depicted on the icon and those before it are united in the same space.

Since the revelation is addressed to man, the image is likewise addressed to him.

The configuration of depth is cut, as it were, by a flat background, "the light," in the language of iconographers. There is no focus of light: the light suffuses everything. Light is a symbol of the divine. God is light, and His Incarnation is the advent of the light into the world: "You have come and revealed Yourself, O Light unapproachable" (kontakion of Epiphany). According to St Gregory Palamas, then, "God is called light not according to His essence, but according to His energy."[67] The light is this divine energy; consequently, we can say that it is essential to the content of the icon. Indeed, it is this light that is the basis of its symbolic language. Here we have to be precise: the background of the icon symbolizes light independent of its color, though its most suitable expression is gold. By its very nature, gold is unrelated to colors, and does not harmonize with them; but the use of other colors for the background-light does not contradict its meaning, though it reduces its meaningful range. Gold is a type of key for discerning background as light.

67 *Contra Acyndinum*, PG 150: 823, quoted by V. Lossky, *The Vision of God*, trans. A. Moorhouse (New York: St Vladimir's Seminary Press, 1983), 160.

The radiance of gold symbolizes the divine glory. This is neither allegorism nor an unfounded imagery, but an expression that is quite adequate. Indeed, gold radiates light, but at the same time it is also opaque.[68] These properties correspond to the spiritual domain gold is expected to express, to the meaning of what is should translate symbolically—the attributes of the Divinity. "God is not called light according to His essence," for His essence is unknowable. "We say," St Basil the Great writes, "that from His activities we know our God, but His substance itself we do not profess to approach. For His activities descend to us, but His substance remains inaccessible."[69] The inaccessibility of the Divinity is called "darkness." "The divine darkness is this 'inaccessible light' (1 Tim 6:16) God inhabits, as it is said."[70]

Thus, "the inaccessible light" is "the light that is more luminous than light,"[71] blinding and therefore impenetrable. Gold, which combines a radiating luminosity with opacity, adequately expresses the divine light—an impenetrable light, that is, something essentially different from natural light, the opposite of darkness.

This light is God's activity, His manifestation to the outside, the energy of His essence by which the represented object is surrounded. "He who participates in divine energy becomes in some way light in himself,"[72] because "the energies bestowed upon Christians by the Holy Spirit no longer appear as exterior causes, but as grace, an interior light, which transforms nature in deifying it."[73] According to St Symeon the New Theologian, when such light illumines the whole person, "Man is united to God spiritually and physically, since the soul is not separated from the mind, neither the body from the soul. By being united in essence, God is united with the whole man."[74] In turn, man becomes a bearer of light to the world outside.

68 See S. S. Averintsev, "Gold in the Symbolic System of Byzantine Culture" (in Russian), Collection in Honor of V. N. Lazarev, *Vizantiia, Iuzhnye Slaviane i drevniaia Rus. Zapadnaia Evropa. Iskusstvo i Kultura* (Moscow, 1973), 43-52.

69 St Basil the Great, *Epistola 234, ad Amphilochium,* PG 32: 868AB, *The Letters.*, vol 3, trans. R. Deferrari (Cambridge: Harvard University Press, 1953), 373.

70 Dionysius the Areopagite, *Epistola* 5, PG 3: 1073A.

71 Dionysius the Areopagite, *De mystica theologia,* ch. 2, PG 3: 1025A.

72 St Gregory Palamas, quoted by V. Lossky, *The Vision of God,* 164.

73 V. Lossky, *The Mystical Theology of the Eastern Church* (New York: St Vladimir's Seminary Press, 1976), 220.

74 St Symeon the New Theologian, *The Discourses,* "Discourse XV," par. 3, trans. C. J. DeCatanzaro (New York: Paulist Press, 1980), 195.

Thus light and its action are knowable and can therefore be represented; what remains unutterable and inaccessible is the source itself, concealed by the impenetrable light-darkness. Starting from the meaning and content of the icon, we may state that this particular feature of the background-light must be understood as a symbolic transposition of the very principle of apophatic theology—the ultimate impossibility of knowing the divine Essence, which remains utterly inaccessible. This background is the boundary beyond which a creature cannot venture into the knowledge of God. The divine Essence always surpasses human ways of knowing. The understanding of such a limit does not arise from dialectical speculations, but from a lived experience of the revelation, an existential sharing in the uncreated light.

According to the teaching of the holy Fathers, man's greatness does not consist in being a microcosm, a little world inside the large one; it is inherent in his destiny because it is his calling to become a great world in the little one, a created god. This is why everything in the icon focuses on the image of man. Faced with man who would be autonomous in relation to God, with man closed in upon himself, the integrity of whose nature is lost, the icon presents man who has achieved his divine likeness, who has overcome fragmentation (in himself, in humanity, in all of visible creation).[75] In contrast to the small human being lost in an immense and hostile world, to the man who has lost a sense of unity with the rest of creation, the icon sets a great human being surrounded by a world that is small in relation to him, one who has re-established his sovereign position in the world and has transformed his dependence upon the world into a submission of the world to the Spirit who dwells in him. In place of the terror man arouses in creation, the icon shows that its hope of being set free from "its slavery to decay" (Rom 8:21) has been fulfilled.

The divine energy, this light that gives form and unity to everything, triumphs over the lack of unity between the spiritual and the corporeal,

75 If people who are not saints are represented in the same manner as saints, there is no contradiction here: the human being is created in the image of God and, for the Church, there does not exist, potentially, a sinner who cannot not repent. According to St Maximus the Confessor, even someone who has become the devil's dwelling place retains the potentiality of conversion, by virtue of his freedom (*Philokalia*, [In Russian], vol. 1 [St Petersburg, 1877], 149). Moreover, the sinner in the icon is not alone: like everything else in the icon, he is linked to the represented saint, that is, in the radiance of his holiness.

even between the created world (both visible and invisible) and the divine world. The world represented in the icon is permeated by the power of this uncreated light. Creation is no longer closed in upon itself, but there is no confusion between the created and the uncreated world. The distinction between these worlds is not abolished (as it is in the art of optical illusion); on the contrary, it is clearly emphasized. By means of various procedures, forms and colors, the visible, depictable world is demarcated in relation to the divine world, which can be conceived only by the mind but cannot be represented. The nature of the uncreated light differs from that of the created light; when it permeates the latter, temporal and spatial categories are transcended. Unified by this uncreated light, what the icon represents is included in another existence, different from the one ruled by the conditions of the fallen world. It is "the Kingdom of God come with power" (Mk 9:11), a world that communes with eternity. It is neither an extra-terrestrial nor an imaginary world; what is depicted is our terrestrial world, but reestablished in its hierarchical order, renewed in God because it is permeated, let us repeat, by the uncreated, divine light. This is why the procedures according to which an icon is composed, both in their totality and in the details, exclude all that is illusory, whether it be the illusion of space, that of the natural light, or that of human flesh.[76] From the believer's point of view, there is neither distortion of space nor a distortion of the perspective; on the contrary, the perspective is restored because the world is seen here not according to the perspective of an "isolated awareness" or from the multiple viewpoints of the autonomous painter, but according to the one point of view of the Creator, that is, as an execution of the divine plan.

What is shown in the icon becomes reality, as first-fruits, in the eucharistic essence of the Church. "Blessed is the Kingdom of the Father, and of the Son, and of the Holy Spirit" is the exclamation with which the eucharistic Liturgy opens. This Kingdom *differs* from that of Caesar: it is the *opposite, the reverse* of the kingdom of "the prince of this world." In its Liturgy, the Church enters a new time, becomes a new creation, where time is no longer broken up into past, present, and future; spatial and temporal categories give way to another dimension. As the space repre-

76 In the image, illusion is as intolerable as in the spiritual life, asceticism, and prayer. It is called "the preeminent trap," and represents not only an obstacle to prayer, but its very opposite.

sented in the icon is united to the real space in front of it, so the depicted event which took place in a time past is united to the present moment. The action represented by the icon and the one accomplished in the Liturgy are united in time ("*Today* the Virgin gives birth to the Super-Essential," "*Today* the Lord of creation and the King of Glory is nailed to the cross"). The present is linked here to eschatological reality: "Of Thy mystical supper...accept me *today* as a communicant." There is no discontinuity either in time or in space between the depicted communion of the apostles and the communicants in the church. By communion with the Body of the risen and glorified Christ, that of His Second Coming, the Body shown by the icon, the visible and the invisible Church are united; in a multitude of persons, living and dead, the unity of their nature transformed by grace is actualized, a unity in the image of the Trinity.

The content of the icon determines not only its structure but also its techniques and the materials used. As P. Florenskii has noted,

> Neither the technique of icon painting nor the materials used can be accidental in relation to worship...It is difficult to imagine, even in formal aesthetic analysis, that an icon could be painted with anything, on just any surface, and by just any methods.[77]

Indeed, just as the authenticity of the image is linked to the Eucharist, so is every material that becomes part of the worship. "Thine own of thine own, we offer unto Thee..." These words are taken from the prayer of David over the materials presented for building the temple: "For all things come from You, and we have given You what has come from Your hand" (1 Chr 29:14). The Church has retained this Old Testament principle which acquires its fullest meaning in the Eucharist, as we have seen. Matter redeemed by the Incarnation participates in the worship of God. This is why in the icon, what is important with regard to its material is not only substance and quality, but above all authenticity. The icon enters into the totality of what man offers to God, into all that the Church uses to accomplish its work, that of sanctifying and transfiguring the world through man, of healing matter sick with sin, making it a path to God, a means of communion with Him.[78]

77 P. Florenskii, "The Iconostasis" (in Russian), *Bogoslovskie Trudy*, no 9 (Moscow, 1972), 115.

78 The traditional technique, developed over the centuries and used in the painting of icons, includes a selection of materials that represent the most complete participation of the visible world in the creation of an icon. In it, we see "representatives" of the vegetable world (wood),

We have attempted to show with the help of some examples that it is the meaning of the icon which, on the one hand, explains its vitality and, on the other, defines its structure in perfect conformity to its goal, and also determines the materials to be used.

> Icon painting is at the same time an effort of artistic creation and a religious effort full of prayerful fervor (this is why the Church recognizes a special order of holiness, that of the iconographers; art as a means of salvation is thereby canonized in them).[79]

Since this means of salvation is an existential participation in the depicted reality, we can affirm that it is precisely this participation that assures the superiority of the icon over modern art in the richness of its means of expression and in its method of composition, even though it is elaborated by painters who knew nothing of the laws of visual perception or of the geometry of multi-dimensional spaces.

Only the Orthodox icon fully reveals the trinitarian economy, because knowledge of God in the incarnate Word who is the Image of the Father, that is, the economy of the second person, is only achieved in the economy of the third hypostasis of the Holy Trinity, in the light of the mystery of Pentecost. It is toward this witness that the entire artistic creation of the Church is directed, a testimony that reached its culmination in hesychasm.

Even until today, the artistic creation of the Church has been viewed by art historians as "fettered" by the dogmas of the Church, subject to an inflexible canon. This canon is understood as the sum total of the external rules imposed by the church hierarchy, of conciliar rulings, manuals and so forth, that subjugate the painter's creation and demand of him a

of the animal (glue, egg), and mineral worlds (chalk, colors). All this is gathered in its natural state, purified, and brought to partake of worship through the work of man. When matter brought by man as an offering to God loses its organic link to the totality of matter created by God, because of modern technical developments, it becomes an obstacle. Thus the use of man-made materials, for example plastic, which is lifeless and has no character of its own, is a perversion. "Plastic matter is a manifestation of the human being's emancipation from nature, from God's creation, from all His works destined to glorify Him" (Cornelia Schubarth, "Über den Glauben der Väter—und seinen Verrat: Neo-Häresie," in *Orthodoxie Heute*, nos 34/35 [1971], 12). The limit between what is acceptable and unacceptable in the domain of matter is crossed when matter loses its authenticity and character, when it gives the appearance of being other than it is, when it too creates a deception. "Everything that is consecrated to God," writes Gregory the Theologian, "must be natural, and not artificial" (*Homilia* 35, PG 35:996C).

79 S. Bulgakov, *The Icon and Its Veneration* (in Russian) (Paris, 1931), 107-8.

passive obedience to existing models.[80] In short, the free art of painting is set against an iconography "tied to canons." However, if we speak of rules and ordinances, the opposite is rather true; it is until recently in "realistic" painting that a whole set of rules has had to be strictly obeyed. These rules were taught in academies, and painting had to comply with them (perspective, anatomy, treatment of the light and shadow, composition, and so forth). It is interesting to note that this system of rules was not in the least resented by painters, or considered as a constraint or a submission: they adhered to these rules in their "free" creation, through which they attempted to serve the Church.[81] But the iconographic canon knows no such rules, or even any analogous concepts. Nonetheless, it was precisely from this canon that painters sought to be "freed." Mesmerized by the West, the progressive painters viewed the canon as a hindrance to their creative freedom, even as a yoke. We have seen in the preceding chapter that they in fact tried to free themselves from the Church and its dogmas: it was from catholic, that is, universal, creation that they wanted to be excluded at all cost. They sought to break away not so much from the faith as from the "ascendency" of the Church. For the autonomous

80 What is more, the anti-Christian ideologies try hard to impose their own views, their specific value system into the domain of ecclesiastical creation. They take pains to prove that art and religion are incompatible: "Christian mythology, with its denial of the world, its devaluation of the human being, its hostility toward culture, its depressing ideas about the punishment to come, about sin being inherent to existence, did certainly not offer a suitable terrain for artistic activity properly speaking" (B. Mikhailovskii and B. Purichev, *Essays on the History of Ancient Russian Monumental Painting* [in Russian] [Moscow-Leningrad, 1941], 7).

See also A. Zotov, *The National Foundations of Russian Art* (in Russian) (Moscow, 1961), vol. 1, 53. In the foreword by I. Volkov to the work of L. Lubimov, *The Art of Ancient Russia* (in Russian) (Moscow, 1974), we read: "The essential function of religion is the spiritual and physical repression of human freedom" (pp. 6-7). Indeed, this view of creation in the Church and of Christianity in general is hardly inspiring. But where is the connection to Christianity? All this could equally be applied, for example, to socialism, and would be equally false. And yet, until recently, one could hardly find a scientific work on sacred art that did not contain such statements: these works are, in fact, only one of the forms of the attack on religion, doing their share in distorting the concept of icon in believers and giving unbelievers a caricature of Christianity.

81 It is true that modern culture, in its artistic expression, has swept all this away in the name of the painter's right to self-expression, thus sinking to an extreme individualism. "Freedom" has turned into what is arbitrary, not the anarchy seen in the various "isms," in "op art," "pop art," and so forth. Such art visibly reflects the lawlessness which has taken over in a society that had been governed by principles and all kinds of moral regulations. In other words, we are faced either with a system of rules or with their total absence and disavowal, always in the name of the same freedom of creation.

painter it was the Church, its canon (unwritten, let us note), and its view of freedom that had become a yoke imposed from the outside. The painters' creation became individualized and thereby isolated. And since they had begun to represent the beyond in categories of the visible, the content of the canonical icon became incomprehensible: its symbolic language and creation had become unintelligible, alien.

In our day, in contrast to the chaotic innovations of modern art trends with their culture of incoherent novelties, the icon offers the traditional form of Orthodox art. Against the isolated creation of the autonomous painter it sets down another principle of artistic creation; against the individual, it sets the universal. In the Church, everything is defined not by "style," but by the canon: every creation, to be ecclesial, inevitably includes itself in the canon. "What is canonical is ecclesial, and what is ecclesial is catholic," Florenskii states.[82] In other words, revelation is not a unilateral action of God performed on man. Revelation necessarily presupposes man's cooperation; it makes an appeal not to passivity, but to an active effort of knowing and of assimilation. In what he creates as a co-worker with God, created in the image of God, man is esteemed only if he conveys and fulfills the divine plan. The creation of man is accomplished in the union of his will with the divine, in the synergism of the two activities: the divine and the human. From this perspective, the character of the artistic language of the Church, as an expression of the Christian faith, is determined by a norm created by the catholic wisdom of the Church—the iconographic canon, in the proper sense of the term.

This norm is the most adequate form found to express the revelation, the very form which the creative relation between God and man takes on. The canon presupposes not isolation, but precisely incorporation into the catholic creation of the Church. The painter's personality is actualized in this catholicity not when he affirms his individuality, but when he surrenders the self; its highest manifestation consists in moving beyond what separates him in relation to others.

The concept of freedom, too, is included in the same evangelical perspective. The Church does not know freedom as an abstract concept; in general, abstraction is alien to it. There is no such thing as freedom as such, freedom in general, only a deliverance from something concrete. For the Church liberation consists of freeing itself from being dominated

82 P. Florenskii, "The Iconostasis" (in Russian), 109.

by the wounds the fall has brought to human nature. Instead of being enslaved to nature, the human being rules over it, "master of one's actions, and free."[83] From this perspective, canonical creation is understood by the painter not as an expression of the personal view he holds of the world and of the faith, but as a transmission of the faith and life of the Church, as a ministry of service (*diakonia*).[84] He expresses the life in which he shares, which means that he includes his life and creation in all the other aspects of the life of the Church guided by the canon. To be authentic, his creation must be attuned, become organically linked to them.[85] "The Church speaks many languages. However, each of them is 'the language of the Church' only inasmuch as it is consistent with the other true expressions of the Christian faith."[86] In the various aspects of church life and artistic creation, the canon is the map with which the Church directs the path of man's salvation. It is in the canon that the iconographic tradition fulfills its function as the artistic language of the Church.

Thus, the iconographic canon is not an unbending law, nor is it an external prescription or a rule: it is an inner norm. It is this norm which places man before the requirement to partake of what the represented carries within.[87] This participation is fulfilled in the eucharistic life of the Church. The unity of the revealed truth is closely linked to the multiplicity of personal experiences one has of this truth. Hence the impossibility of circumscribing the canon by means of a definition. Thus the Hundred-Chapters Council limited itself to ordering that the iconographers follow the example

83 St John of Damascus, *De fide orthodoxa*, Bk. 2, ch. 27, PG 94: 961.

84 In this service (*diakonia*), the creative thinking of the painters has never wilted. They have never felt, nor do they feel in our age, that the iconographic canon is a burden, a restriction imposed upon them from the outside. On the contrary, this is made apparent by the very art of the icon throughout its history.

85 Hence the need for faithful participation in the sacramental life of the Church. Hence also, in times of decadence, the moral demands made upon the iconographers.

86 J. Meyendorff, "Philosophy, Theology, Palamism and 'Secular Christianity,'" 207.

87 This is how the conciliar decisions concerning sacred art guide the iconographer toward a more faithful expression of Orthodox teaching, and how they correct errors that enter iconography, which is always a possibility, if only because of ignorance. As for artistic creation as such, not only do such decisions not restrain it; they do not even deal with the questions that bear upon it. If the iconographic canon curbs anything, it certainly is not creation; but as any canon generally does in all areas of Church life, it harnesses the subjective whim, the free will of individuals, at whatever hierarchical level they are found. The conciliar decisions of the Church are valid for the hierarchy as much as they are for the other members of the Church; both conform to them, regardless of their situation and function in the Church.

of the ancient painters and the rules of morality. This canonical norm assures the faithful transmission of truth, whatever the artist's degree of participation, even if such participation remains formal. This norm is followed by the creative painter as well as by the artisan, both in times past and in our day. This is why the canonical icon witnesses to Orthodoxy, independently of the frailty of those who bring the truth, the Orthodox themselves. Let us repeat: it is precisely the canon that protects the icon from such imperfection. Whatever the painter's spiritual and artistic level, even if he is a third-class artisan, the canonical icon, ancient as well as new, witnesses to the same truth. By contrast, regardless of the painter's talent, the segment of the art that "freed" itself from the canon has not only never reached a high artistic level, not to speak of the spiritual level of the icon, but completely ceased being a witness to Orthodoxy.

We have already noted that the seventeenth century proclaimed nothing new; in the dogma of the veneration of the icon, it merely clarified the faith of preceding councils. Indeed, at the heart of the christological and trinitarian dogmatic discussions of the past always lay the essential question of the relationship between God and man, and thus of Christian anthropology. For Orthodoxy, the dogma of the veneration of icons represents an enduring truth of the Christian faith and teaching, a truth promulgated by an ecumenical council. We should see in the icon what the Fathers and the councils saw: the triumph of Orthodoxy, a testimony of the Church about the truth of the Incarnation. But we should also see in iconoclasm what the defenders of the icon saw: not a mere denial of the image or its destruction, but a war against Christianity, a "Christomachia," to use the expression of St Photius the Patriarch. Indeed, if ancient iconoclasm was rooted in a hellenization that had not been entirely overcome, as Florovsky has indicated, its very essence did not simply lie in the particular issue of the struggle against images. "Not only the destiny of Christian art was at stake, but Orthodoxy itself," that is, the Church.[88] Open iconoclasm, which was the outcome of the heresies of the christological period, had an opposite effect: the canonical conscience of the Church condemned it as a heresy of "disincarnation" and ratified the veneration of icons.[89] After the Triumph of Orthodoxy, this appar-

88 G. Florovsky, "Origen, Eusebius, and the Iconoclastic Controversy," *Church History* 19, no 2 (1950), 96.

89 As is known, the iconoclasm of the eighth-ninth centuries made war not against art in the Church but against the image of the revelation as a witness to the Incarnation of God. However, having

ently extinct heresy continued to fester during the following centuries, sometimes breaking out violently; it also took on other forms and changed masks. Indeed, iconoclasm does not have to be open and premeditated; through incomprehension and indifference it can also be unconscious, even pious.[90] Moreover, did not the ancient, open iconoclasm supposedly fight for the purity of the Christian faith, as Protestantism did later? As we have seen, the distorted Roman Catholic image has led Protestants to a "devout" refusal of the image, to the "image without substance,"[91] that is, to a refusal of the visible, material witness of the Incarnation. In its own way, this "insubstantial image" has contributed to the present-day evacuation of God even in Christianity itself. In our time, "...in the 'liberal' camp of Protestantism, many hold as indifferent for the essential Christian *kerygma* whether Christ was God or not, whether his Resurrection was or was not a historical fact."[92] Such a situation led quite naturally to a "God is dead" theology, that is, to evident non-sense, as much for the believer as for the artist.

begun with the destruction of icons, iconoclasm led to the disincarnation, the desacralization and denial of the Church.

90 Such pious iconoclasm is apparent, among other things, in the fact that some see in the icon an obstacle to prayer; they invoke the ascetic rule which, during prayer, forbids access to the mind of any image whatsoever. A rather widely accepted opinion maintains that this rule also applies to the icon. This is a misunderstanding indeed, because the ascetic rule deals with images created in the mind by the imagination—images which on no account could be identified with the icon, the image of reality, "of the true, non-fictional Incarnation of God the Word." As such, the icon is not only incompatible with an image created by the human imagination, but is in direct contradiction to it. If it were otherwise, it would be inconceivable that the Church, gathered in an ecumenical council, could have confirmed and dogmatized the veneration of something that was in danger of becoming an obstacle to prayer or of leading it in the wrong direction. Moreover, it is typical that the most tenacious defenders of icons were monks, that is, people who had devoted their entire life to prayer. We have the testimony of one of the greatest mystics of the church, St Symeon the New Theologian: "[One day] I went to reverence the spotless icon of her who bore You. As I fell before it, before I rose up, You yourself didst appear to me within my poor heart, as though You had transformed it into light; and then I knew that I had You consciously within me" (*The Discourses*, "Discourse xxvi," par. 11, trans. C. J. deCatanzaro [New York: Paulist Press, 1980], 376).

This is because the icon is "a beneficial help for the one who prays, so that in its search for the presence of God, the mind would not fall into imaginary representations, so that thoughts may be concentrated and preserved from distraction. The holy image of God which makes Him visible in His flesh is presented at the same time to the bodily eye and to spiritual contemplation. The icon collects the thoughts and the outer and inner feelings in the same, one contemplation of God" (*Choix de sermons et discours de S. Em. Mgr. Philarète*, vol. 3 [Paris, 1866], 230).

91 J. Ph. Ramseyer, *La Parole et l'Image*, 78.

92 J. Meyendorff, *Orthodoxy and Catholicity* (New York, 1966), 138.

52. *St Silouan*
Icon painted by Leonid Ouspensky
Photo: Andrew Tregubov.

53. *St Spyridon*
Icon painted by Monk Gregory Kroug
Photo: Andrew Tregubov.

In Orthodoxy's past relationship with heterodoxy, it was the image that proved most valuable. The lack of understanding and the indifference to its content were such that during the Synodal period, the Orthodox icon came to be removed from churches and destroyed as "barbarian," only to be replaced, it is true, by imitations of a non-Orthodox, "enlightened," western art. The so-called "realistic trend," made Orthodox, so to speak, by a "half-conscious remembrance of the icon," introduced "the false testimony" of which Florenskii speaks—a lie about Orthodoxy. This false witness could only confirm the unbelievers in their unbelief. Among believers, it falsified the understanding of Orthodoxy and helped to deform their ecclesial consciousness. Let us recall that during the same period and for the same reason, the spiritual praxis that had nourished icon painting in its heyday was persecuted, branded as heretical, and "exterminated like an infection, a plague," as Metropolitan Philaret wrote.

Thus all iconoclasm in any form, open or secret, even pious, contributes to "disincarnate" the Incarnation, to undermine the economy of the Holy Spirit in the world, to destroy the Church. It is therefore a question of Orthodoxy itself. The struggle for the image has never ceased: it has become more acute in our day because iconoclasm no longer shows itself only in the deliberate destruction of icons, or in their rejection by heresies of a protestantizing type. Encouraged by various economic, social or philosophical ideologies, it manifests itself in a tendency to destroy the image of God in man.

The present situation of Christianity in the world is often compared to that of the first centuries of its existence. "Is the atheistic, unbelieving world of our day in a sense not precisely this pre-Christian world emerging once more in this amalgam of pseudo-religious, skeptical, and atheistic trends—all strongly opposed to God?"[93] But if, in the first centuries, Christianity stood before a pagan world, the world it faces today is a dechristianized world, the outcome of apostasy. It is before this world that Orthodoxy is "called to bear witness," to give evidence of the truth. It does so by its Liturgy and its icon. Hence the need to regain awareness of the dogma of the veneration of icons and to express it in conformity to the needs of our present life, to the problems and questions of modern man. This is why an awareness of this dogma and an understanding of the image as an expression of our faith are above all an awareness of Ortho-

93 G. Florovsky, *Ways.*

doxy itself, that of the ecclesial unity given in Christ. As an expression of the faith and communal life of the Church, the icon transcends the divisions which empirically exist in the life and activities of the Orthodox. A visual testimony of this unity is important, not only towards the non-Christian world but also towards the heterodox, because a merely verbal expression of Orthodoxy proves to be insufficient to answer the problems of our time. "Now more than ever, the Christian West has widened its perspective: it stands as a living question mark before Orthodoxy."[94] This question, then, is above all the search for a way out of the impasse in which the Christian West, especially Roman Catholicism, finds itself. In the words of the prelate Dr. K. Gamber,

> The Roman Catholic Church will eradicate its present errors and will arrive at a new renaissance only when it is able to incorporate the fundamental strengths of the Eastern Church: its mystical theology based on the great Fathers of the Church, and its liturgical piety...One thing seems beyond doubt: the future does not lie in a reconciliation with Protestantism, but in an inward union with the Eastern Church, that is, in a steadfast spiritual contact with it, with its theology and piety.[95]

On our part, we are deeply convinced that the dogma of the veneration of icons, as well as the introduction of the icon into the heterodox confessions, would help overcome the basic flaws of the western confessions and their essential divergence and disagreements with the Orthodox Church: the doctrines of created grace and of the filioque. Indeed, the icon presupposes both the Orthodox understanding of the person and the Orthodox confession of the economy of the Holy Spirit, and therefore Orthodox ecclesiology. It is certainly not by chance that in our day the icon is entering the non-Orthodox world. It has begun to affect the awareness of western man, and if western art in its Roman Catholic form had formerly influenced Orthodoxy, at present, by contrast, the icon—witness of Orthodox dogma, expression of the Christian faith, and way of salvation—is penetrating Roman Catholicism and Protestantism. "The Christian," G. Wunderle writes,

> must be deeply engaged with the realism the icon offers him; if not, he will never approach its mystery and it will for him only be a design without a soul. And for him to whom it is given to contemplate God in the holy icon, it becomes an unerring path toward a transfiguration in Christ.[96]

94 *Ibid.*,

95 Bishop K. Gamber, "Zum Streit zwischen dem Papst und dem Erzbishof Lefèvre aus ekumenischer Sicht," *Orthodoxie Heute*, no. 57 (1976), 21-4.

96 Georg Wunderle, *Um die Seele der heiligen Ikone* (Würzburg, 1947), 78.

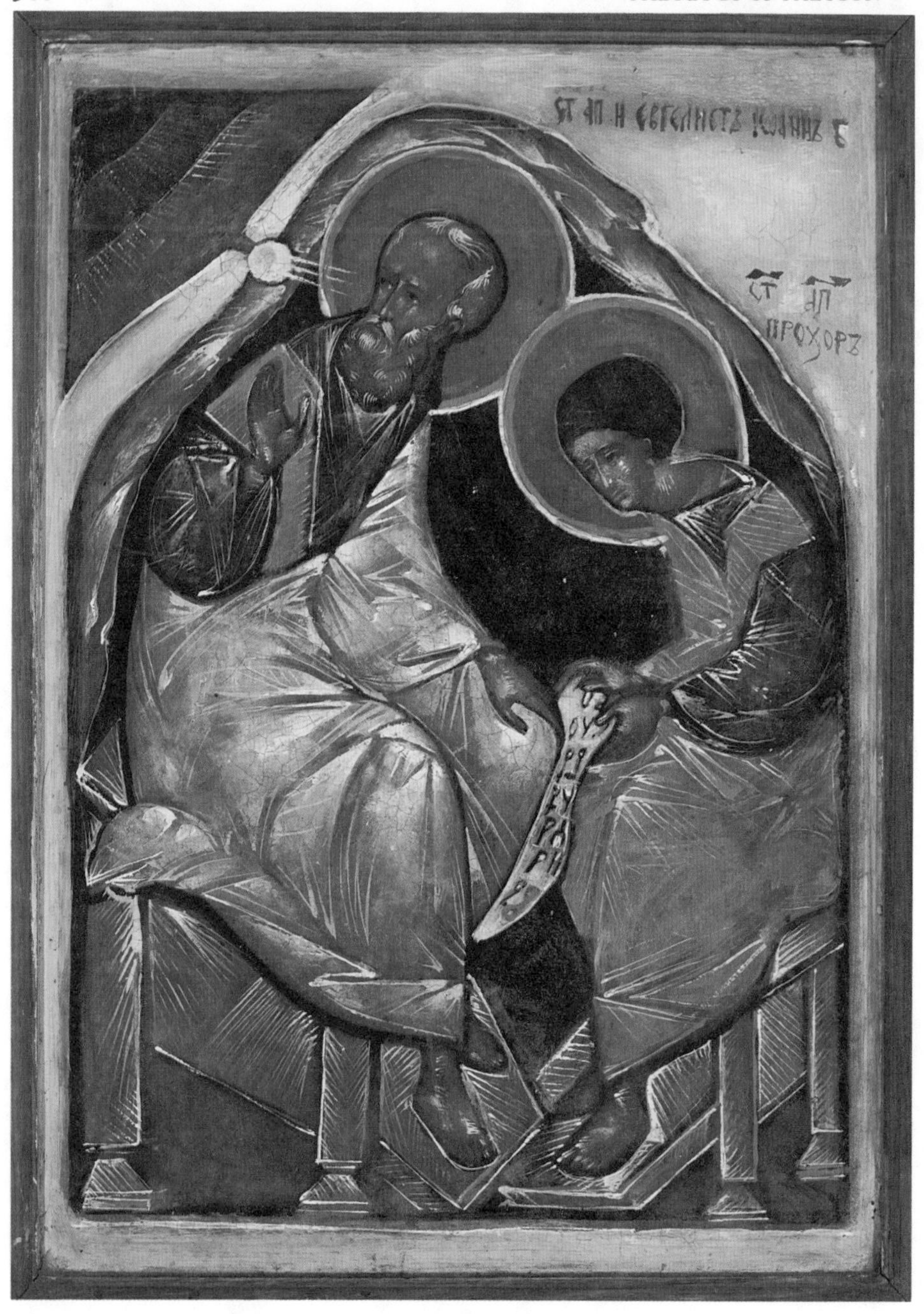

54. *St John the Evangelist*
Icon painted by Monk Gregory Kroug
Photo: Andrew Tregubov.

55. *St Nicholas and St Genevieve*
Icon painted by Monk Gregory Kroug
Photo: Andrew Tregubov.

In the Christian believer, independent of his confessional allegiance, the icon prompts a direct reaction on the level of prayer. Because of its clarity, it does not, like a sacred text, need to be translated into another language.

But what is of crucial importance is a renaissance of the icon within Orthodoxy. Such a renaissance is a vital need for our time. However, as was true for the "discovery" of the icon, it is presently taking place without connection to theological thought[97] and liturgical piety, and thus outside its immediate context. If theology is experiencing a slow emancipation from scholasticism, the attitude toward the image is, by contrast, still dominated by the inheritance of past centuries. As for liturgical piety, this heritage from the past seems particularly insurmountable. Indeed, is the tradition of the Church not associated by many faithful with mere conservatism?[98]

Let it be said again that the renaissance of the icon is a vital necessity for our time. However important the works that led to the discovery of the icon, what is revealed in the icon only takes on life in its practical application. In the Church, everything rejuvenates itself, including the icon.

> Always alive and creative, the Church does not in the least seek to defend ancient forms as such, nor does it set them against new forms as such. For the Church, art, whether now, in the past, or in the future, means the same thing: realism. What this means is that the Church, pillar and herald of truth, demands only one thing, the *truth*.[99]

Not only can the icon be new; it must be new (when we differentiate between icons of various epochs, this means that they were new in relation

97 Since the time of decadence, one no longer sees in the image a witness of Orthodoxy equivalent to the word. The concordance between the icon and theology is no longer seen or understood; the link between them is on occasion even denied. In other words, the image has lost its significance as a means proper to Orthodoxy for the expression of revelation. Many of the faithful no longer see any connection between the image and the truth of Orthodoxy.

98 In our time, such conservatism is aggravated by the pressure of atheism. People are beginning naively to view any object as "sacred," provided it stems from the pre-atheistic period. Such origin is sufficient to have the object not only preserved and venerated but also imitated. A typical example of such pious conservatism is the work edited by the so-called "Synodal" or "Karlovtsy" group in New York, entitled *The Miraculous Icons of the Mother of God in Russian History* (in Russian) (1976). We learn from it that "the reason for the origin of the veneration of icons" is neither revelation nor the need to bear witness to the divine Incarnation and the deification of man, but "the aptness of human souls to ascend by thought and heart toward beloved beings by looking at their representations" (p. 60). In conformity with such a concept, the work reproduces, in the same way as Orthodox icons of the Virgin, an entire series of representations that imitate western images with the sentimentality so typical of them. In a word, the same conservative attachment of this group to the synodal period of the Russian Church, which expresses itself in its anti-canonical situation, is conveyed by a predilection for the past and for miracles, which replaces the Orthodoxy of the image.

99 P. Florenskii, "The Iconostasis" (in Russian), *Bogoslovskie Trudy*, no. 9 (Moscow, 1972), 106.

to the preceding periods). But the new icon must express the same truth. The contemporary renaissance of the icon is neither an anachronism, nor an attachment to the past or to folklore, nor an attempt to make the sacred image be "born again" in a painter's studio. It is a more intense awareness of the Church, of Orthodoxy, a return to the authentic transmission in art of the patristic experience, of a true knowledge of the Christian revelation.[100]

As in theology, such a renaissance is contingent upon a return to the tradition of the Fathers, and "fidelity to the tradition is not fidelity to everything that is ancient, but a living link with the fullness of life in the Church" (Figs. 52, 53, 54, 55, 56, 57),[101] with the spiritual experience of the Fathers. This renaissance is an indication of a return to wholeness, to the consonance of doctrine, life and creation, that is, to an integrity so indispensable today. As an expression of the unchanging, revealed truth, the icon, whether modern or old, witnesses to the salvation "prepared before the face of all people." It bears witness to the existential actualization of the sudden change brought about by the creation in the world of the Church, "a light to lighten the nation and the glory of thy people," the new Israel. Addressed to mankind, this revelation is given to the Church and is realized by it. Indeed, it is the Church that is the revelation "before the face of the world." The image of the revelation the Church brings to the world is that of the glorified Body of Christ, itself an image of the Church, the authentication of its faith and holiness, the witness of the Church about itself. This is why the specific character of the Orthodox icon, and the entire structure proper to it, designate the possibilities, the means, as well as the limits of Christian knowledge, so as to reveal to man the significance of his life in history, his destiny, and the paths that lead him to the ultimate goal. The icon opens an immense vision that embraces the past and the future in an enduring present. Human creation, however impoverished its means, serves the Church as a language to reveal to the world the mystery of the age to come.

100 This renaissance is taking place within the structure of the iconographic canon. It is not a question of eclecticism, but of an authentic creation of the icon in conformity with our time, for it is the canon that ensures the freedom of artistic expression. An example of this is the art of the monk Gregory (Kroug).

101 G. Florovsky, "Theological Fragments" (in Russian), *Put*, no. 31 (Paris, 1931), 23.

56. *St Photius the Great*
Icon painted by Monk Gregory Kroug
Photo: Andrew Tregubov.

57. *St Seraphim of Sarov*
Icon painted by Monk Gregory Kroug
Photo: Andrew Tregubov.

Index

D

E

F

G

J

K

T

List of Plates*

* Asterisks indicate color plates.